GUINNESS WORLD RECORDS 2019

This year's book takes its inspiration from the "Maker Movement" (see our featured chapter on pp.126–47). Thomas is a prime example of a "Maker": he designs, builds and wears amazing cosplay outfits. His autobot, pictured here, had its first outing at New York Comic Con in Oct 2017.

Meet the Makers…

Introducing this year's book is cosplay designer Thomas DePetrillo (USA) of Extreme Costumes. He's joined by one of his latest record-breaking creations: the autobot Bumblebee from the Transformers franchise. At 9 ft 6 in (2.89 m) tall to the top of its "wings" and 8 ft 9 in (2.66 m) tall to the top of its antennae, it's the **tallest mobile cosplay costume (single person)**. Bumblebee is just one of the awe-inspiring projects you'll find inside the "Maker"-themed *Guinness World Records 2019*…

CONTENTS

Our 10 fact-packed chapters include a **Meet the Makers** section, detailing the stories behind 10 record-breaking structures. Watch out too for our **Making History** features, which celebrate eight iconic constructions by means of stunning LEGO® models.

Each section of the book is colour-coded by chapter.

Infographics at the top of the page provide you with snappy, bite-sized chunks of information.

Hungry for more detail? These In Focus pages offer an extended study of one subject. They're illustrated with full-colour photographs and sumptuous artwork.

Meet the Makers! On these pages, you'll get behind-the-scenes insights into some of our most inventive records. There are also Q&As with the record holders, who explain how they planned their attempt and reveal what inspired them to try for a GWR title.

Look out for these strips at the bottom of pages. They feature records that are related in some way.

You'll find 1,000-plus photographs in this edition of GWR!

The 100% icon means you're seeing a record holder at actual size.

100%

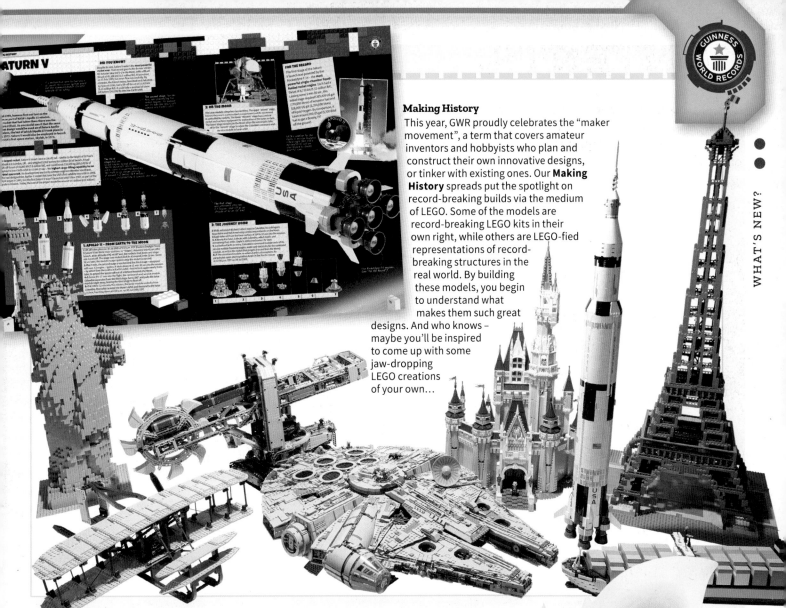

Making History

This year, GWR proudly celebrates the "maker movement", a term that covers amateur inventors and hobbyists who plan and construct their own innovative designs, or tinker with existing ones. Our **Making History** spreads put the spotlight on record-breaking builds via the medium of LEGO. Some of the models are record-breaking LEGO kits in their own right, while others are LEGO-fied representations of record-breaking structures in the real world. By building these models, you begin to understand what makes them such great designs. And who knows – maybe you'll be inspired to come up with some jaw-dropping LEGO creations of your own…

Meet Ally Zing!

Get ready to welcome a new member to the Guinness World Records team: Ally Zing! You can follow Ally's adventures on our kids' website (**guinnessworldrecords.com/kids**) and over at our PopJam channel – and you might even meet him in person at one of our GWR LIVE! events. It's Ally's job to collect the world's most amazing superlatives, so don't be surprised if he turns up at a record attempt near you. It's time to "Bring the Zing!"

EDITOR'S LETTER

Welcome to the latest edition of *Guinness World Records*! This new volume has been fully updated and represents the very best of the most recent records – whittled down from nearly 40,000 applications! – alongside some classic favourites...

In the past 12 months, our Records Management Team has logged an incredible 38,205 applications from wannabe record-breakers – that's more than 100 every day! In total, 3,178 records were approved during this same period – a success rate of 8%. The idea that Guinness World Records "will accept records for anything these days" is simply not true!

If you're one of the lucky few, congratulations! You've joined an elite group – only 0.0054% of the world's population has the right to display a Guinness World Records certificate on their wall. Out of this happy few, an even smaller group has been included in the pages of this book. With only room for about 3,500 records, we have to make an editorial decision about what to include.

Largest touch-screen display
On 7 Apr 2017, two 525-sq-ft (48.77-m²) screens were unveiled for the *Candy Crush* TV game show in Los Angeles, California. The touch screens are used to play a supersized version of the King-developed mobile game. Host Mario Lopez was on hand to receive an official certificate from GWR adjudicator Kimberly Partrick.

To help with the records selection, we've been inspired this year by the "Maker Movement". This exciting cultural trend encourages everyone to channel their inner creative and have a go at building or crafting something awesome from scratch, or modding something to recycle it or extend its usefulness.

To help us honour the most inventive of our Maker-inspired record holders, we've joined forces with TV star Edd China – the mad inventor behind records such as the **fastest toilet**, **garden shed** and **sofa**. On pp.126–47, Edd introduces us to 10 of his favourite Makers in his "Meet the Makers" chapter.

The Maker theme continues in another new feature: "Making History". These poster-style pages explore eight technological wonders from history, including the Statue of Liberty (**heaviest statue**, pp.10–11), the *Wright Flyer* (**first powered flight**, pp.48–49) and the Saturn V rocket (**largest rocket**, pp.78–79). Our unique spin on these features is that we've built them all from LEGO® bricks, which means that you can build the same models at home and learn first-hand what goes into designing these pioneering vehicles and structures.

One final nod to the Maker Movement comes in our "Do Try This At Home" feature at the back of the book. Turn to pp.242–47 and you'll find our guide to becoming a record holder, plus five newly minted GWR challenges with a make-at-home theme. Whether you have a go at the records, or just attempt the projects for

Tyler will have to return to the bricks if he wants the LEGO record back – YouTube show *REBRICKULOUS* has since beaten his mark with a sole-crushing 385.4-m (1,264-ft 5-in) walk!

Farthest distance walking barefoot on LEGO® bricks
On the "Absurd Recurds" segment of Dude Perfect's new *Overtime* show, Tyler Toney walked barefoot on LEGO® bricks for 44.78 m (146 ft 10.9 in) on 13 Feb 2018. That same day, fellow Dude Cody Jones set the **fastest time to find and alphabetize the letters in a can of alphabet soup** – 3 min 21 sec – while Coby Cotton (all USA) achieved the **farthest distance to blow a pea** – 8.8 m (28 ft 10.45 in).

Fastest half marathon dressed as a chef (male)
On 22 Oct 2017, Daniel Janetos (CAN, above right) ran the Scotiabank Toronto Waterfront Marathon in Ontario in 1 hr 34 min 53.5 sec. He recorded the **fastest marathon dressed as a chef (male)** at the 2016 edition of the race, although his time has since been broken.

Daniel's fellow record-breaker Petro Czupiel (CAN, above left) ran the **fastest half marathon dressed as a clown (male)** – 1 hr 30 min 32 sec. For more officially amazing runs in Toronto on 22 Oct 2017, see below.

FASTEST HALF MARATHONS

Dressed as...	Time	Holder
A cowboy	1 hr 51 min 56 sec	Robert Winckler (CAN)
An awareness ribbon (female)	2 hr 11 min 10 sec	Shelby Jones (USA)

Longest career as a game-show announcer (same show)
As of 28 Jul 2017, Johnny Gilbert (USA) had opened game show *Jeopardy!* with the famous lines "This is....*Jeopardy!*" for 32 years 321 days.

Longest sheet of pasta rolled in one minute
Chef Gordon Ramsay (UK) rolled a 1.45-m (4-ft 9-in) sheet of pasta in 60 sec on FOX's *The F Word with Gordon Ramsay* on 16 Aug 2017. He also achieved the **fastest time to fillet a 10-lb fish** – 1 min 5 sec – on 12 Jun 2017. Below are more GWR titles cooked up on the show.

FAST FOOD

Most juice extracted from grapes by treading in 1 min	12.76 litres (3.37 US gal)	Martina Servaty (DEU)
Fastest time to dice a watermelon	18.19 sec	Matt Jones (USA)
Most oysters opened in 1 min	39	Patrick McMurray (CAN)
Largest pizza base spun in 1 min	72 cm (28.35 in)	Joe Carlucci (USA)
Most slices of carrots sliced blindfolded in 30 sec	88	Hiroyuki Terada (JPN)

fun, you can become a Maker in your own right.

These Maker features attest to the fact that GWR is constantly monitoring the latest trends, fashions and technologies. That's why you'll also find records involving fidget spinners (p.176), slime (p.152), VR (pp.156–57), quantum computing (p.155) and cosplay (p.180). Some of these topics didn't even exist 10 years ago! The same goes for Instagram and Twitter (pp.194–97), social-media phenomena such as unboxing (p.152)

and streaming TV shows such as *Stranger Things* (p.191).

Finally, if you're not one of the 0.0054% but want to join the club, then pay us a visit at **www.guinnessworldrecords.com**. It's easy to apply and we're keen to hear your ideas. There's no guarantee you'll make it as a record holder, but it's all about making the effort and having a go.

Craig Glenday
Editor-in-Chief

Most hugs given by an individual in one minute
Kevin (Probably) Saves the World star Jason Ritter (USA) hugged 86 people in 60 sec during a live filming of ABC's *The View* in New York City on 9 Oct 2017. The audience were only too happy to lend a hand, helping the actor beat the previous record of 79 hugs – which had itself earned 5.7 million views on GWR's Facebook page.

Break it TODAY
NBC's national morning show *TODAY* celebrated the launch of *GWR 2018* with a week-long segment featuring six record attempts. On 5 Sep 2017, Ron Sarchian (USA, top) achieved the **most watermelons split by karate chop in one minute** – 42. On 4 Sep, Annie Thorisdottir (ISL, right) crushed the record for the **most weight lifted in one minute by barbell thruster (female)**. She hoisted 2,805 lb (1,272.32 kg) in 60 sec.

On 6 Sep, Michael Kettman (left) set the **longest time to spin a basketball on a toe** – 35.03 sec, live on *TODAY*. And his son Carson (right) set the **longest time to spin a basketball on a finger while pogo-stick jumping** – 40.31 sec.

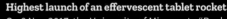

Highest launch of an effervescent tablet rocket
On 8 Nov 2017, the University of Minnesota "Rocket Team" (USA) won the Big 10 Alka-Rocket Challenge at Space Center Houston in Texas by launching their craft 131 m (429 ft 9 in) into the air. The competition, organized by Bayer (DEU), was hosted by astronaut Mae Jemison (second from right).

Alex Rodriguez
In Oct 2017, GWR caught up with retired baseball star Alex Rodriguez (USA) in Los Angeles, California, to present him with three official certificates, including **most grand-slam home runs in an MLB career** – 25.

Most contributions to a collection of Mad Libs
Visitors to the Guinness World Records Adventure in Gatlinburg, Tennessee, were given an opportunity to be part of a world record of their own, thanks to its interactive word-game machine. As of 15 Mar 2018, a total of 17,294 wacky and wonderful Mad Libs had been entered by the attraction's guests.

INTRODUCTION

KENNEDY SPACE CENTER

Do you have what it takes to train like an astronaut? Read on for a chance to hone your docking skills, navigate the terrain of Mars, and experience the sensation of spacewalking in a microgravity environment during an Astronaut Training Experience at Kennedy Space Center Visitor Complex℠...

Kennedy Space Center℠
VISITOR COMPLEX

Kennedy Space Center (KSC) is the birthplace of American space travel. During the early years of the "Space Race", the NASA scientists and engineers behind projects Mercury and Gemini gathered at KSC to strive to make their dreams of spaceflight a reality. The United States Astronaut Hall of Fame, located at the Visitor Complex, pays tribute to the courageous men and women who took a trip into the unknown, such as Alan Shepard – who, on May 5, 1961, became the first American in space – and John Glenn, the first American to orbit the Earth, on Feb 20, 1962. On Jul 16, 1969, the crew of Apollo 11 launched from KSC on their iconic flight to the Moon (see below). The program was indebted to Saturn V, the **largest rocket** (pictured), which launched 13 times from nearby Cape Canaveral.

Now, NASA's attention is fixed firmly on the next great leap: a crewed mission to Mars. Someone reading this book could well be the first human to set foot on the Red Planet! So to give you a head start, we've teamed up with KSC to offer readers the chance to win an incredible trip to Florida to participate in its Astronaut Training Experience and Mars Base 1 program. Have you got what it takes to make humankind's next big leap…?

Win an Astronaut Training Experience!

You could win the chance to enjoy an out-of-this-world vacation for four guests at Kennedy Space Center. The **three-night stay** includes **round-trip airfare** and **admission**, entry into the **Astronaut Training Experience** (below left and right), **Lunch With An Astronaut**, and the chance to **break an official GWR title**! Visit **www.GWRSpace.com** to enter.*

GATEWAY TO THE STARS

Kennedy Space Center, located near Orlando, Florida, has been NASA's primary launch site for human spaceflight since 1968. It's connected to Cape Canaveral Air Force Station, which has launched US spacecraft from *Explorer 1* in 1958 to SpaceX's Falcon Heavy on Feb 6, 2018. Kennedy Space Center Visitor Complex, home to the Astronaut Training Experience, provides a fully immersive program to help you train like the next generation of space explorers (see right).

COMMAND MODULE

SERVICE MODULE

Kennedy Space Center Visitor Complex is home to a Saturn V rocket – the **largest rocket**, stretching 363 ft (110.6 m) tall and weighing up to 3,268 US tons (2,965 tonnes).

ATTRACTIONS AT THE VISITOR COMPLEX

◀ **Apollo 14 *Kitty Hawk* Command Module**
On display at the Apollo/Saturn V Center, *Kitty Hawk* took the astronauts of the Apollo 14 mission (launched on Jan 31, 1971) into lunar orbit and back to Earth. On Feb 5, 1971, Apollo 14 astronaut Alan Shepard (USA, b. Nov 18, 1923) became the **oldest person to walk on the Moon**, aged 47 years 79 days.

◀ **Space Shuttle *Atlantis*℠**
On Jun 29, 1995, *Atlantis* completed the **first shuttle docking** with the Russian Mir space station, beginning the Shuttle-Mir Program. The shuttle is now located at Kennedy Space Center Visitor Complex, with its payload bay doors open and angled as if just undocked from the *International Space Station*.

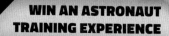

Astronaut Training Experience

n 2018, Kennedy Space Center unveiled its new Astronaut Training Experience, which, together with the companion program Mars Base 1, brings guests as close to the Red Planet as possible without leaving Earth.

Inside Mars Base 1, budding astronauts are given scientific and engineering challenges (**1**), and learn how to grow and harvest plants in the Botany Lab (**2**). There is extensive astronaut training (**3**), with a Robotics Lab where robots are programmed to clear debris from solar panels (**4**). A walking-on-Mars virtual-reality simulation also offers guests the chance to perform a spacewalk through exciting and immersive microgravity simulation technology (**5**).

◄ *Eagle* Lunar Module

The Lunar Theater recreates the dramatic events of Jul 21, 1969, when the world stood still to watch Apollo 11 astronauts Neil Armstrong and Buzz Aldrin (both USA) become the **first people on the Moon**. The theatrical presentation includes NASA film footage, mission control recordings, and a model of the *Eagle* lunar module.

◄ Mars Rover Vehicle Navigator®

Commissioned by Kennedy Space Center Visitor Complex, the concept vehicle Mars Rover is a mobile laboratory whose 4-ft 2-in-high (1.27-m) wheels are designed to cope with the extremes of Martian terrain. It runs on an electric motor powered by solar panels and a 700-volt battery.

GWR DAY

Every year in November, would-be record holders worldwide take on a huge variety of challenges to mark Guinness World Records Day. Some are genuinely awe-inspiring; others are magnificently eccentric. You'll find a selection of highlights from recent events on these pages, ranging from the **longest videogame marathon on a hack-and-slash game** (24 hr 25 min, by Germany's Peer Bresser and Jimmie Smets in 2017) to the **most Queen songs recognized by their lyrics in one minute** (17, by the UK's Bernie Keith in 2017).

Have you got an idea for a record that you think you could achieve? If you'd like to try for a place in the *Guinness World Records* book, start by visiting our website **guinnessworldrecords.com**. And turn to p.242 for more information on how to be a record-breaker.

▲ **Largest vegan cake**
Therese Lindgren (SWE) created a vegan cake weighing in at 462.4 kg (1,019 lb 6 oz) – about the same weight as a concert grand piano – that was presented and measured in Stockholm, Sweden, on 3 Nov 2017. The cake was made to create awareness about veganism (a diet that includes no animal products) and the importance of healthy eating.

▼ **Largest hula hoop spun**
Japan's Yuya Yamada rotated a hula hoop with a diameter of 5.14 m (16 ft 10 in) six consecutive times in Yokohama, Kanagawa, Japan, on 9 Nov 2017. The outer circumference of the hoop measured 16.17 m (53 ft 0.6 in). Yuya's shown here celebrating – while GWR adjudicator Kaoru Ishikawa (right) helps hold up the hoop – and in action.

▼ **Fastest time to build a 171-cup pyramid**
Nimble-fingered James Acraman (UK) assembled a pyramid comprising 171 cups in just 59.10 sec in London, UK, on 9 Nov 2017. In doing so, he comfortably broke his own record of 1 min 26.9 sec, set on 3 Jan earlier the same year. His successful attempt was broadcast on Facebook Live.

▲ **Fastest speed in a body-controlled jet-engine-powered suit**
Taking inspiration from Iron Man's famous armour, the UK's Richard Browning flew in his own levitating outfit on GWR Day 2017. For further details about his record-breaking invention, take off for p.96.

◀ **Fastest time to travel 20 m in a contortion roll**
Liu Teng (CHN) covered a distance of 20 m (65 ft 7 in) in a contortion roll in 15.54 sec at the NUO Hotel Beijing in China's capital city on 6 Nov 2017. A contortion roll requires the performer to start with her feet on the ground before arching backwards and propelling herself forward in a chest-down roll.

The **most people sport stacking across multiple venues** is 622,809, by the World Sport Stacking Association (USA) during their 11th annual WSSA STACK UP! event on 17 Nov 2016.

◄ **Most Star Wars characters identified from quotes in one minute**

On 9 Nov 2017, the UK's Nathan Tansley identified 16 Star Wars characters from quotes in 60 sec in London, UK. Nathan had a high hit rate, missing just four of the 20 quotes read out by *GWR*'s Editor-in-Chief, Craig Glenday.

▲ **Heaviest aircraft pulled for 100 m by a team**

A team selected from the Dubai Police Force (UAE) tugged a 302.68-tonne (667,295-lb) Boeing 747 a distance of 100 m (328 ft) at Dubai International Airport, UAE, on 9 Nov 2017. The attempt lasted 2 min 38 sec and was part of Dubai Fitness Challenge, a communal 30-day health drive in the city.

▲ **Loudest crunch of an apple**

Felix Michels (DEU) registered a volume of 84.6 dBc when biting into an apple on the set of *So Geht Das* in Cologne, Germany, on 7 Nov 2017. Felix achieved the feat during a contest with his co-host Kim Unger. The microphone recording his crunch was placed 2.5 m (8 ft 2 in) away and 1.5 m (4 ft 11 in) above the ground.

▶ **Most full-twist fire-breathing backflips in one minute**

On 9 Nov 2017, Australia's Aiden Malacaria achieved the double challenge of 10 full-twist backflips while fire-breathing at the same time – and all in 60 sec. The record took place at Studio 10 in Sydney, New South Wales, Australia. Aiden achieved the record on his first attempt.

◄ **Most hula hoops spun while suspended from the wrists**

Marawa Ibrahim (AUS) kept 50 hula hoops circling around her waist while hanging from her wrists at Hollywood Aerial Arts in Los Angeles, California, USA, on 17 Nov 2016. Her feat was streamed live on Facebook. GWR requires that at least three 360° rotations must be made during any attempt.

▲ **Highest upwards basketball shot**

Corey "Thunder" Law (USA) of the Harlem Globetrotters launched a basketball 15.26 m (50 ft 1 in) up through the air and into a hoop outside the Capitol Building in Salt Lake City, Utah, USA, on 5 Nov 2017. This head-turning trick shot is the talented player's fourth solo Guinness World Records title, all of which have been attempted for GWR Day.

▼ **Most football (soccer ball) rolls from eye to eye in one minute**

On 6 Nov 2017, Japan's Yuuki Yoshinaga managed to roll a football between his eyes an astonishing 189 times in just 60 sec in Nerima, Tokyo, Japan.

The previous month, on 9 Oct, Yuuki had achieved a new world record for the **most football touches with the shoulders in one minute (male)**: 230.

▲ **Most Risley flips in 30 seconds**

Giuliano and Fabio Anastasini (both USA) performed 32 Risley flips in 30 sec in the Big Apple Circus tent at Lincoln Center in New York City, USA, on 31 Oct 2017. In this manoeuvre, one acrobat lies on a surface as the base, flipping the other acrobat (or "flyer") with the feet. Circus tricks are very much in this family's blood: the brothers' father, Giovanni, performed a Risley act with his own brother, Luciano, for more than 25 years.

STATUE OF LIBERTY

Since its dedication on 28 Oct 1886, the Statue of Liberty has stood watch over the harbour of New York City, USA. It was a powerful symbol of freedom and democracy to the scores of immigrants who came to the USA in the 20th century to start a new life in the New World. Yet this feat of monumental engineering was conceived, designed and constructed thousands of miles away, on the other side of the Atlantic Ocean.

Originally entitled *Liberty Enlightening the World*, the statue was the brainchild of sculptor Frédéric Auguste Bartholdi, who was inspired to celebrate the USA's independence. On a visit to the country in 1871, he selected Bedloe's (now Liberty) Island in the harbour of New York City – which he viewed as the "gateway to America" – as the location for his creation. With the aid of construction visionary Gustave Eiffel, Bartholdi spent the next 15 years building the Statue of Liberty in France before shipping it over to the USA. The completed statue's total weight was 27,156 tons (24,635.5 tonnes) – making it the **heaviest statue.**

VIEWING PLATFORM

The Statue of Liberty's crown has a viewing platform with 25 windows, representing the 25 different types of gemstones found on Earth. Sightseers must climb 377 steps from the main lobby to the observation platform. Only 365 tickets are available each day, and must be purchased in advance. Originally there was also public access to the torch, but this was closed in 1916 in the wake of the "Black Tom" explosion, an act of wartime sabotage that damaged the statue.

CRATE EXPECTATIONS

Construction of the statue was completed in Paris, France, in 1884. She was then disassembled into 350 individual pieces and delivered to New York by the French frigate *Isère*, arriving on 17 Jun 1885. Liberty remained in crates for 11 months while the concrete base upon which she would stand was being finished. When she was finally uncrated on Bedloe's Island in New York City harbour (above), Liberty's face was revealed in all its glory, roughly 17 ft (5.18 m) in length, with a 4.6-ft (1.37-m) nose.

In 1986, the copper torch was replaced by one overlaid with 24-carat gold

The crown has seven rays to represent the world's seven seas and continents

The torch-bearing arm measures 42 ft (12.8 m) in length

The statue carries a tablet inscribed with the date of the US Declaration of Independence – 4 Jul 1776 – in Roman numerals

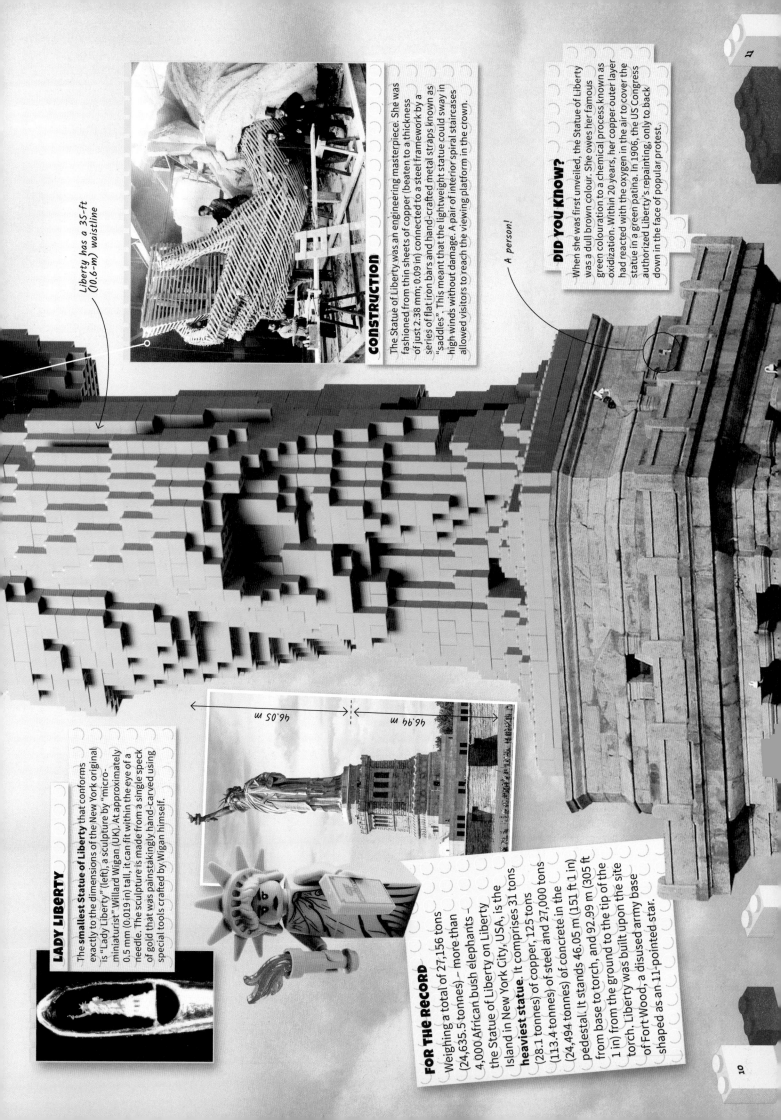

Liberty has a 35-ft (10.6-m) waistline

CONSTRUCTION

The Statue of Liberty was an engineering masterpiece. She was fashioned from thin sheets of copper (beaten to a thickness of just 2.38 mm; 0.09 in) connected to a steel framework by a series of flat iron bars and hand-crafted metal straps known as "saddles". This meant that the lightweight statue could sway in high winds without damage. A pair of interior spiral staircases allowed visitors to reach the viewing platform in the crown.

A person!

DID YOU KNOW?

When she was first unveiled, the Statue of Liberty was a dull brown colour. She owes her famous green colouration to a chemical process known as oxidization. Within 20 years, her copper outer layer had reacted with the oxygen in the air to cover the statue in a green patina. In 1906, the US Congress authorized Liberty's repainting, only to back down in the face of popular protest.

LADY LIBERTY

The **smallest Statue of Liberty** that conforms exactly to the dimensions of the New York original is "Lady Liberty" (left), a sculpture by "micro-miniaturist" Willard Wigan (UK). At approximately 0.5 mm (0.019 in) tall, it can fit within the eye of a needle. The sculpture is made from a single speck of gold that was painstakingly hand-carved using special tools crafted by Wigan himself.

46.05 m

46.94 m

FOR THE RECORD

Weighing a total of 27,156 tons (24,635.5 tonnes) – more than 4,000 African bush elephants – the Statue of Liberty on Liberty Island in New York City, USA, is the **heaviest statue**. It comprises 31 tons (28.1 tonnes) of copper, 125 tons (113.4 tonnes) of steel and 27,000 tons (24,494 tonnes) of concrete in the pedestal. It stands 46.05 m (151 ft 1 in) from base to torch, and 92.99 m (305 ft 1 in) from the ground to the tip of the torch. Liberty was built upon the site of Fort Wood, a disused army base of Fort Wood, shaped as an 11-pointed star.

UNIVERSE

Largest anticyclone in the Solar System

The Great Red Spot on Jupiter – the **largest planet in the Solar System** – varies in size but can be 40,000 km (24,800 mi) long and 14,000 km (8,700 mi) wide. The clouds in this raging high-pressure storm rise some 8 km (5 mi) above the surrounding cloudscape, and the entire anti-clockwise cyclone can grow to three times the size of Earth.

The dark spot on the right is the shadow of Jupiter's third-largest moon, Io. Although not visible here, enormous volcanic plumes erupt from the moon's surface, making it the **most volcanically active body in the Solar System**. Io's intense geological activity is the result of the interaction between Jupiter, Io and another moon, Europa (Jupiter's fourth-largest satellite), which can be seen below.

This image was pieced together from 16 frames captured by the *Voyager 1* probe during a flyby on 3 Mar 1979. *Voyager 1* is the **most remote man-made object**, 21.15 billion km (13.14 billion mi) from Earth, and counting, as of May 2018.

DEEP SPACE

Largest structure in the universe
The Hercules-Corona Borealis Great Wall is a massive superstructure of galaxies measuring around 10 billion light years across. Its existence was announced on 5 Nov 2013, in the wake of its discovery by astronomers charting the locations of gamma-ray bursts that had been detected by the *Swift* Gamma-Ray Burst mission.

The **largest galaxy** is IC 1101. Located at the centre of the Abell 2029 galaxy cluster, it has a major diameter of 5,600,000 light years – around 50 times larger than our own Milky Way. Its light output is equivalent to 2 trillion Suns.

Largest void
AR-Lp 36 – also known as the Giant Void – is a huge area of space with an abnormally low density of galaxies and other matter within the constellation Canes Venatici. Described in 1988 by the Special Astrophysical Observatory in Nizhny Arkhyz, Russia, it has an estimated diameter of 1–1.3 billion light years. Our galaxy may be part of an even larger void, first suggested in 2013. Known as the KBC Void, it could be 2 billion light years across.

Farthest object visible to the naked eye ever
At 06:12 Coordinated Universal Time on 19 Mar 2008, NASA's *Swift* satellite detected a gamma-ray burst from a galaxy some 7.5 billion light years away. Known as GRB 080319B, it reached a peak apparent magnitude of 5.8 and was visible to the naked eye for around 30 sec. Apparent magnitude is a measurement of the brightness of an object as seen from Earth.

Fastest-approaching galaxy
M86, a lenticular (lens-shaped) galaxy some 52 million light years away in the Virgo cluster, is nearing the Milky Way at 419 km/s (260 mi/s). It is one of a small number of galaxies approaching our own, moving counter to the overall expansion of the universe.

Longest galactic jet
In Dec 2007, astronomers announced the discovery of an energetic jet of matter issuing from a supermassive black hole in the centre of the active galaxy CGCG 049-033. Measuring some 1.5 million light years long, the high-energy jet happens to be aimed at a nearby galaxy. Any planets caught in its line of fire would have their atmospheres ionized, and all life would be extinguished.

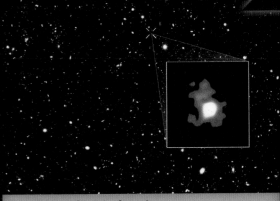

Most distant object in the universe
Light detected by the *Hubble* space telescope from the galaxy GN-z11 (inset) dates back 13.4 billion years. Given the expansion of the universe, it is estimated that GN-z11 is now around 32 billion light years from Earth. The galaxy possesses a redshift (a measure of how light stretches as it travels through the cosmos) of 11.1.

Coldest place in the Milky Way
A cloud of dust and gases 5,000 light years from Earth, the Boomerang Nebula has a temperature of -272°C (-457.6°F) – only just warmer than absolute zero: -273.15°C (-459.67°F).

Deepest note in the universe
Acoustic waves generated by a supermassive black hole in the centre of the Perseus cluster of galaxies sound a B flat that is 57 octaves below middle C. This is more than a million billion times lower than a human ear can detect.

Most remote object visible to the naked eye
Located in our galaxy cluster (the "Local Group"), the Andromeda spiral galaxy M31 lies some 2.5 million light years from Earth. Results announced in Jan 2007 suggest Andromeda is five times larger than previously thought, with the discovery of stars orbiting its centre at a distance of at least 500,000 light years.

Heaviest black hole
The supermassive black hole at the centre of the quasar S5 0014+81 has a mass of around 40 billion solar masses. This makes it about 10,000 times more massive than the supermassive black hole at the centre of the Milky Way galaxy. It was measured in 2009 by astronomers utilizing NASA's *Swift* gamma-ray space telescope, based on the quasar's luminosity output.

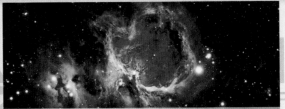

BRIGHT LIGHTS

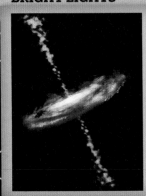

◄ Brightest active galaxies
Active galaxies have a bright centre and emit energy over the electromagnetic spectrum. Their cores are believed to house supermassive black holes, which suck in matter around them and eject jets of ionized gas at near the speed of light. When a jet is pointing towards Earth, these galaxies appear more luminous and are known as "blazars".

▲ Brightest nebula
The Orion Nebula – a vast, diffuse cloud of gas and dust – has an apparent magnitude of 4. Located in the "sword" of the constellation of Orion, it is the nearest star-formation region to Earth, and is visible to the naked eye as a fuzzy patch of light.

Brightest quasar in the sky
Quasars are bright discs of matter that swirl around supermassive black holes at the centres of distant galaxies. The quasar 3C 273 has an apparent magnitude of 12.9 – bright enough to be seen with relatively modest telescopes. This is despite its location in the Virgo constellation, 2.5 billion light years away. It was the first quasar ever identified.

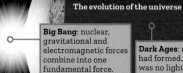

The evolution of the universe

Big Bang: nuclear, gravitational and electromagnetic forces combine into one fundamental force.

Dark Ages: no stars had formed. There was no light.

Formation of the first astronomical objects: first stars begin to form from hydrogen, helium and lithium.

At **4 billion years old**, the universe contains stars and galaxies.

Present day: many of the earliest stars are dead, having created heavier elements.

Nearest bright planetary nebula

The Helix Nebula (also known as NGC 7293) lies around 700 light years from Earth. It formed when a dying star threw off its outer layers, which are gradually expanding into space. Planetary nebulae are so-called because they were originally believed to be new planets, owing to their often spherical shapes. The Helix Nebula remains around 100 times more distant than the nearest stars (excluding the Sun).

If the Helix Nebula was bright enough to be easily visible to the naked eye, it would cover an area of sky around half the size of the full Moon.

Nearest active galaxy

The enormous elliptical galaxy Centaurus A is "just" 11 million light years from Earth. Active galaxies contain a compact, highly luminous core that emits intense radiation. The source of this is thought to be a vast disc of shredded stars and other matter being swallowed by a supermassive black hole.

▶ **Brightest open star cluster**

Even from within a major light-polluted city, around six of the Pleiades (M45) – also known as the Seven Sisters – can be seen with the naked eye. Located in the constellation of Taurus ("The Bull"), this cluster contains around 500 individual stars. Many of the brighter ones are still surrounded by dusty nebulae – the leftover material from which they formed.

Brightest supernova

Noted in Apr 1006 CE near the star Beta Lupi, the supernova SN 1006 flared for two years and reached a magnitude of -7.5. This titanic cosmic explosion was brilliant enough to be seen with the naked eye and, at its most luminous, was 1,500 times brighter than Sirius, the **brightest star viewed from Earth**. The supernova took place around 7,000 light years away.

◀ **Brightest supernova remnant**

The Crab Nebula (M1), situated in the constellation of Taurus, has a magnitude of 8.4. The massive star that formed it was seen to explode in a supernova by Chinese astronomers in 1054 CE. The explosion was sufficiently bright to be seen with the naked eye in broad daylight for 23 days.

STARS

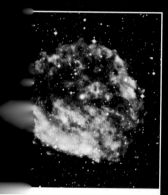

Smallest stars

Neutron stars, which may have a mass three times that of the Sun, only have a diameter of 10–30 km (6–19 mi). By contrast, the Sun's average diameter is 864,000 mi (1,390,473 km). Neutron stars are also the **densest stars** in the universe. A sand-grain size of neutron star material would have the mass of a skyscraper.

Largest star

UY Scuti has an estimated radius 1,708 times that of our Sun. This corresponds to a diameter of 2,276,511,200 km (1,414,558,478 mi), but owing to the difficulty in measuring the sizes of stars accurately, the margin of error could be as high as +/- 192 solar radii. The inset above shows the Sun in relation to UY Scuti.

Most common type of star

By far the most numerous class of star is the red dwarf, which accounts for around 80% of all stars in our local neighbourhood. These are weak, dim stars with no more than 40% of the mass of the Sun, and the brightest of them shine at only 10% of the Sun's luminosity. Because they burn their fuel so slowly, they have lifespans of at least 10 billion years.

Largest star with a planet

Astronomers using the Hobby-Eberly Telescope at the McDonald Observatory in Texas, USA, announced in Oct 2011 that they had discovered a planet orbiting HD 96127, a star around 540 parsecs from Earth in the constellation Ursa Major. It is a K2-type red giant, whose radius is around 35 times that of the Sun. The orbiting planet is believed to possess a mass four times that of Jupiter, and 1,271 times that of Earth.

Oldest star in the galaxy

HD 140283, some 190 light years from Earth, is believed to have formed soon after the Big Bang, 13.8 billion years ago. When the universe formed, it consisted of hydrogen with some helium. As it evolved, the other chemical elements appeared, formed by nuclear synthesis in stars. HD 140283 has almost no metal content, so must have formed from clouds of gas comprising almost pure hydrogen and helium, when the universe was still in its infancy.

The **oldest stars to form planets** are BP Piscium and TYCHO 4144 329 2, both c. 400 million years old. In Jan 2008, astronomers announced their discovery of what seem to be dusty discs around these stars. Such discs formed the planets orbiting the Sun, but are usually seen around recently formed stars. These two stars probably threw out stellar material to form the discs after swallowing another star or an earlier system of planets.

Fastest star in the galaxy

On 8 Feb 2005, a team from the Harvard-Smithsonian Center for Astrophysics in Cambridge, Massachusetts, USA, announced their discovery of a star travelling at more than 2.4 million km/h (1.5 million mph). Named SDSS J090745.0+24507, it was probably accelerated by an encounter with the supermassive black hole at the centre of our Milky Way galaxy slightly less than 80 million years ago.

The **fastest-moving star in the sky** is Barnard's star, which moves at 10,357.704 mas/yr (milliarcseconds/year). To put that in perspective, an arcminute is just one-sixtieth of an angle of one degree. In 170 years, Barnard's star moves a distance in the sky equivalent to the size of a full Moon. This shift in the apparent positions of stars in the sky is termed "proper motion".

Most stars in a star system

The greatest number of stars in a single star system is six. There are several known examples, but the best known is Castor, the second-brightest star in the constellation of Gemini. From a distance, Castor appears as a single entity, but it actually consists of three pairs of stars.

Flattest star

The least spherical known star in our galaxy is the southern star Achernar (Alpha Eridani). Observations made using the VLT Interferometer at the European Southern Observatory's Paranal Observatory in Atacama, Chile, have revealed that Achernar is spinning so rapidly that its equatorial diameter is more than 50% greater than its polar diameter.

Most luminous star in the galaxy

A "Wolf-Rayet star" is a very hot and bright star in its early stages. WR 25 (seen near the centre of the image above) is a Wolf-Rayet star in the Trumpler 16 cluster within the Carina Nebula, some 7,500 light years from Earth. The presence of a companion star makes it difficult to ascertain the absolute luminosity of WR 25, but it is believed to be around 6,300,000 times more luminous than the Sun.

MOST COMMON TYPES OF STAR

Astronomers classify stars according to the Morgan-Keenan system, which categorizes them by surface temperature, from hottest (O) to coolest (M). They may be further subdivided by temperature and brightness. The hottest stars are also the most luminous and the largest, but are far less abundant than the coolest stars. Hot stars also have shorter lives: Class M stars, or red dwarfs, can theoretically last for some 200 billion years, but those of Class O have a lifetime of "just" 10 million years.

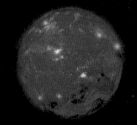

▲ **Class O**
Rare, hot stars (30,000 kelvin) around 100,000 times brighter than our Sun.

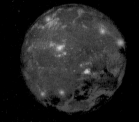

▲ **Class B**
A lifetime of c. 100 million years. Surface temperatures reach c. 15,000 kelvin.

▲ **Class A**
Temperatures reach 10,000 kelvin, with a mass around twice that of our Sun.

What is our Sun?

Gas: like all stars, the Sun is a large ball of gas. Hydrogen accounts for more than 70% of its mass and helium 27%.

Diameter: at 864,000 mi (1,390,473 km) across, the Sun is around 109 times larger than Earth.

Temperature: the heat at the Sun's core is c. 27,000,000°F (15,000,000°C). At its surface, it is "just" 10,000°F (5,537°C).

Rotation: the Sun rotates faster at the equator (about 27 days) than it does at the poles (about 36 days).

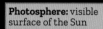

Photosphere: visible surface of the Sun

Radiative zone: energy from the core moves outwards as electromagnetic radiation

Core: hottest part of the Sun (c. 27,000,000°F; 15,000,000°C) – where nuclear fusion occurs

Prominence: a large eruption from the Sun's surface that extends into space

Sunspots: cooler spots on the surface, where temperatures are around 10,000°F (5,537°C)

Nearest star

At "just" 149,600,000 km (93,000,000 mi) from Earth, the Sun is considered astronomically close. The next nearest star, Proxima Centauri, is 4.2 light years away, or 40,000,000,000,000 km (24,000,000,000,000 mi).

The pioneering work carried out by Father Angelo Secchi (ITA, 1818–78) in spectroscopy led to his classification scheme for stars, and to his conclusion that our own Sun was a star and not a phenomenon unique to the Solar System.

The Sun has a mass around 333,000 times greater than that of Earth. This represents more than 99% of the mass of the entire Solar System, which is held together and kept in orbit around the Sun by our star's immense gravity.

▲ Class F
Surface temperatures of up to 7,400 kelvin. Live for c. 3 billion years.

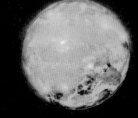

▲ Class G
Includes our Sun. Temperatures may reach 6,000 kelvin.

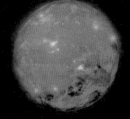

▲ Class K
Surface temperature of c. 5,000 kelvin. May live for more than 20 billion years.

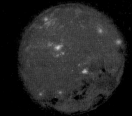

▲ Class M
Most common and, at c. 3,000 kelvin, coolest of the main star types.

PLANETS

First discovered
On 13 Mar 1781, from his garden in Bath, UK, British astronomer William Herschel observed a "star" that would eventually be named the planet Uranus. Venus, Mars, Jupiter and Saturn were all bright enough in the sky to be known to ancient civilizations. Uranus had been seen before, but never actually recognized as a planet.

Hottest
Venus has an average temperature of 462–480°C (863–896°F), with a surface hot enough to melt lead. Its toxic atmosphere contains the **most acidic rain in the Solar System**, with showers of almost pure sulphuric acid falling from clouds around 48–58 km (30–36 mi) above the surface. This extreme environment would make exploration of the Venusian surface very difficult.

Fastest
Mercury has an average speed in orbit of 172,248 km/h (107,030 mph). This is almost twice as fast as Earth. Mercury orbits the Sun at an average distance of 57.9 million km (35.9 million mi) – making it the **closest planet to the Sun** – and has an orbital period of 87.9686 days.

Lowest density
Saturn's average density is only 0.71 that of water. The planet is composed mostly of hydrogen and helium, the two lightest elements in the universe.

The **densest planet** is Earth, which has an average density 5.517 times that of water.

Largest tilt
The axis of spin of Uranus is tilted 97.86° from its plane of orbit – compared to 23.45° on Earth. One possible theory suggests that Uranus was struck by another planet during the formation of the Solar System, knocking it over on its side.

Owing to this axial tilt, Uranus's polar regions take turns to point directly at the Sun. Over the course of the planet's 84-year-long orbit of the Sun, each pole receives 42 years of sunlight followed by 42 years of darkness – the **longest period of darkness/daylight on a planet in the Solar System**.

Strongest magnetic field
Generated by the liquid metallic hydrogen in its interior, Jupiter's magnetic field is 19,000 times stronger than Earth's and extends several millions of kilometres into space from the planet's cloud tops. Were it visible to the naked eye from Earth, it would appear twice as large as the full Moon, despite being almost 1,700 times further away.

Longest day
While Earth has a rotation period or day lasting 23 hr 56 min 4 sec, Venus takes 243.16 "Earth days" to spin on its axis. Its proximity to the Sun means that a Venusian year is shorter than a Venusian day, lasting just 224.7 "Earth days".

Brightest planet from Earth
In astronomy, "magnitude" describes the brightness of an object seen from Earth; the lower the number, the higher the brightness. Venus, has a maximum magnitude of -4.4. This is due in part to the highly reflective clouds in its atmosphere, which contain droplets of sulphuric acid (see right).

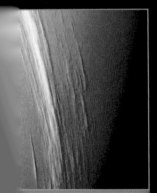

Fastest winds in the Solar System
The winds on the planet Neptune blow at around 2,400 km/h (1,500 mph), as measured by NASA's *Voyager 2* in 1989. The probe also captured images of white clouds of frozen methane crystals (pictured) and a fast-moving anticyclonic storm.

Largest core
The metallic core of the planet Mercury has a radius of approximately 1,800 km (1,118 mi) and accounts for around 42% of its volume and 85% of its radius, making it the largest core relative to planet size. The combination of large core and comparatively thin outer shell has led to speculation that Mercury suffered a violent impact early in its formation that stripped away part of its crust.

Tallest volcano in the Solar System
The peak of Olympus Mons on Mars is 25 km (15 mi) above its base – nearly three times the height of Everest on Earth. Termed a shield volcano owing to its shape – it's more than 20 times wider than it is high – it is the result of the build-up of many thousands of lava flows from eruptions. Olympus Mons is also the **tallest mountain in the Solar System**.

HEAVENLY BODIES

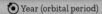 Year (orbital period)   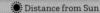 Distance from Sun   Mass (x10²⁴ kg)   Diameter   Temperature

▲ **Mercury**
◉ 87.9 days
☀ 57.9 million km
⚖ 0.330
⊖ 4,879 km
🌡 167°C

▲ **Venus**
◉ 224.7 days
☀ 108.2 million km
⚖ 4.87
⊖ 12,104 km
🌡 480°C

▲ **Earth**
◉ 365.2 days
☀ 149.6 million km
⚖ 5.97
⊖ 12,756 km
🌡 15°C

▲ **Mars**
◉ 687 days
☀ 227.9 million km
⚖ 0.642
⊖ 6,792 km
🌡 -65°C

Largest ring system in the Solar System

The intricate system of rings around the gas giant Saturn have a combined mass of around 4 x 10^{19} kg (9 x 10^{19} lb) – the equivalent of 30 million Everests on Earth. Saturn's rings are made up of millions of independently orbiting particles of ice and dust. It is likely that they were formed from the debris of a small moon following its destruction by a comet. The other gas giants in the Solar System – Jupiter, Uranus and Neptune – also have rings, but none on Saturn's scale.

Saturn's rings are being slowly eroded as particles spiral downwards on to the planet itself. Some scientists estimate that the rings will have disappeared completely in around 100 million years.

*Seen here is the dark-red eye of a hurricane at Saturn's north pole bordered by a jet stream and clouds, representing the **largest hexagon in the Solar System**.*
*In 2009, the **longest-lasting lightning storm** raged for more than eight months in Saturn's upper atmosphere. With a diameter of several thousand kilometres, it saw lightning flashes 10,000 times the intensity of Earth's.*

▲ **Jupiter**
⊙ 4,331 days (11.8 yr)
☀ 778.6 million km
⚖ KG 1,898
⊖ 142,984 km
🌡 -110°C

▲ **Saturn**
⊙ 10,747 days (29.4 yr)
☀ 1,433.5 million km
⚖ 568
⊖ 120,536 km
🌡 -140°C

▲ **Uranus**
⊙ 30,589 days (84 yr)
☀ 2,872.5 million km
⚖ 86.8
⊖ 51,118 km
🌡 -195°C

▲ **Neptune**
⊙ 59,800 days (164.8 yr)
☀ 4,495.1 million km
⚖ 102
⊖ 49,528 km
🌡 -200°C

MOONS

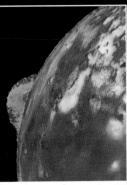

Most powerful volcano in the Solar System
Loki Patera on Jupiter's moon Io emits more heat than all of Earth's active volcanoes combined. It is seen here erupting above Io's surface. The volcano's caldera (crater) – more than 10,000 km² (4,000 sq mi) in size – often floods with molten lava.

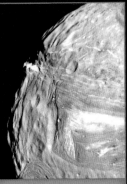

Highest cliffs in the Solar System
In 1986, NASA's *Voyager 2* probe encountered Uranus and its moons. Miranda, a small moon with a 472-km (293-mi) diameter, has a cliff with a vertical relief of about 20 km (12 mi). Named Verona Rupes, it is more than 10 times higher than the walls of Arizona's Grand Canyon. The white material in the cliff face is probably mostly water ice.

Earth
The **youngest Moon rocks** date back some 3.2 billion years. They are a type of volcanic basalt, originating from the dark lunar maria (seas), and are not dissimilar in age to the oldest dateable rocks on Earth.

Mars
Of the Solar System's inner rocky planets, only Earth and Mars have moons. Mars has two – Phobos (see right) and Deimos – the **most moons for a rocky planet**.

Jupiter
One of the four largest moons of Jupiter, Io (see left) has an average density of 3.53 g/cm³ (2.04 oz/cu in), making it the **densest moon**. Earth's own Moon is the second-densest, at 3.346 g/cm³ (1.934 oz/cu in).

On 6 Aug 2001, NASA's *Galileo* spacecraft performed a close flyby of Io. Over the following months, mission scientists realised that the spacecraft had passed through the top of a 500-km-high (310-mi) volcanic plume. This is the **highest volcanic eruption** ever witnessed in the Solar System.

Jupiter's icy moon Europa has the **smoothest surface of any solid body in the Solar System**. The only prominent relief on its surface are ridges a few hundred metres tall. The tidal forces that cause Io's intense volcanic activity (see above left) also affect Europa. There are very few impact craters, meaning that the surface is geologically young.

By contrast, Callisto – the outermost of the Galilean moons (see below) – is the **most heavily cratered moon**. This ancient relic is 100% covered with impact craters.

Saturn
With orbital paths 50 km (31 mi) apart, Saturn's moons Janus and Epimetheus are the **closest moons to each other**. Every four years, the two satellites come within 10,000 km (6,200 mi) of each other and swap orbits.

Kraken Mare, on Saturn's moon Titan, is the **largest methane sea**. It is 1,170 km (727 mi) across and has an area of 400,000 km² (154,000 sq mi) – larger than Earth's Caspian Sea.

Observations of Saturn's moon Iapetus by the NASA/ESA spacecraft *Cassini-Huygens* on 31 Dec 2004 revealed a huge ridge at least 1,300 km (800 mi) long. Reaching an altitude of 20 km (12 mi) above the surface, it is the **tallest ridge in the Solar System**. Iapetus is 1,400 km (870 mi) in diameter.

Neptune
When *Voyager 2* passed by Neptune and its moon Triton in 1989, its cameras recorded active cryovolcanism in the form of eruptions of nitrogen gas and snow. The **tallest nitrogen geysers**, these reach heights of 8 km (5 mi) and are thought to be caused by weak sunlight heating nitrogen ice just below the moon's surface.

With a diameter of 2,706 km (1,681 mi), Triton is the **largest retrograde moon** (i.e., it orbits Neptune in the opposite direction to Neptune's orbit around the Sun). It is also the seventh-largest moon in the Solar System.

Closest moon to a planet
The tiny Martian satellite Phobos is 9,378 km (5,827 mi) from the centre of Mars, or 5,981 km (3,716 mi) above the Martian surface. This small, potato-shaped irregular moon measures 27 x 22 x 18 km (17 x 14 x 11 mi). Dark and covered with dusty craters, it is almost certainly an asteroid captured by Mars's gravity millions of years ago.

Largest object chaotically rotating
Saturn's highly irregularly shaped moon Hyperion measures 410 x 260 x 220 km (254 x 161 x 136 mi). It is notable for its completely chaotic rotation – that is to say, it is randomly tumbling in its orbit around the planet Saturn. The asteroid 4179 Toutatis, as well as Pluto's moons Nix, Hydra, Kerberos and Styx, are also believed to rotate chaotically.

MOONS WITHIN THE SOLAR SYSTEM

Moons are natural satellites that orbit a planet. Only two planets in our Solar System have no moons – Mercury and Venus. The **planet with the most moons** is Jupiter, with 69, but new moons are still being discovered. In Apr 2016, NASA revealed that Earth has a "mini moon", named 2016 HO3, that follows a similar orbital path around the Sun – at a distance of some 9 million mi (14.5 million km). "Since 2016 HO3 loops around our planet, but never ventures very far away as we both go around the Sun, we refer to it as a quasi-satellite of Earth," says Paul Chodas, of NASA's Center for Near-Earth Object (NEO) Studies. For more about moons, read on...

▼ **Earth (1)**
The Moon takes 27 days to orbit Earth, and the same time to rotate once. So the same side of the Moon always faces Earth and the other side (the "dark side") always faces away. This is termed "tidal locking".
In reality, of course, both sides of the Moon see sunlight as it turns.

▼ **Mars (2)**
The two Martian moons, Phobos and Deimos, are named after the sons of the god of war, Ares, in Greek myth (known as Mars in Roman myth). Both were discovered in 1877 by US astronomer Asaph Hall.

▼ **Mercury (0)**

▼ **Venus (0)**

The make-up of a moon

Rock: moons are generally solid and usually rocky. It's likely that most were formed from discs of dust and gas.

Atmosphere: there are thin atmospheric layers around several moons, including some Jovian and Saturnian satellites.

Volcanic activity: ancient lava flows scar our Moon's surface, while Jupiter's moon Io is volcanically very much alive (see p.20).

Rings: the *Cassini–Huygens* probe found evidence suggesting that Rhea, Saturn's second-largest moon, may have its own rings.

GUINNESS WORLD RECORDS

The Moon has a negligible atmosphere, so as it rotates in and out of sunlight its surface heats up and cools down dramatically. The lunar temperature ranges from -250°F (-156°C) to 250°F (121°C).

Largest moon compared with its planet

At 3,474 km (2,158 mi) across, our Moon is 0.27 times the diameter of Earth. This natural satellite is the largest of the three moons in the inner Solar System and the only other world to have been visited by humans. According to the prevailing scientific theory, it was formed around 4.6 billion years ago from the debris created when a Mars-sized planet struck Earth. Gravity brought the lumps of material together, creating the Moon.

Largest moon in the Solar System

Jupiter's Ganymede has a diameter of some 5,262.4 km (3,269.9 mi) and is more than twice as heavy as our Moon. It is also the **largest body in the Solar System without a substantial atmosphere**.

▼ Jupiter (69)

The four largest Jovian moons – Io, Callisto, Ganymede and Europa – are called the "Galilean" satellites, as they were discovered by Galileo Galilei in 1610.

▼ Saturn (62)

The characteristic rings encircling Saturn are partly the result of the gravitational effect of some of its moons – known as "shepherd moons".

▼ Uranus (27)

Most Uranian moons are named after characters in Shakespeare's works. Oberon and Titania, the largest, were the first to be discovered, in 1787.

▼ Neptune (14)

Astronomer Gerard Kuiper discovered Nereid, Neptune's third-largest moon, in 1949. But he missed the second-largest, Proteus. It was too close to Neptune, and too dark, to be seen with his telescope.

60 YEARS OF NASA

The year 2018 sees NASA celebrate its 60th anniversary, while 2019 marks 50 years since the first manned mission landed on the Moon. Here, we commemorate these two milestones with an overview of the space agency's key record achievements.

NASA insignia
Affectionately known as the "meatball", the NASA emblem was designed by James Modarelli in 1959 and visually references the organization's aims. Within the round blue planet is a starscape. The red arrow signifies aeronautics, while the orbital ellipsis around the name denotes space travel.

In the 1950s, the "Space Race" between the US and Soviet Union space agencies accelerated research and development on both sides. On 4 Oct 1957, the Soviet Union launched the **first artificial satellite**, *Sputnik 1*. In response, the President of the USA and the US Congress initiated the National Aeronautics and Space Administration (NASA) on 1 Oct 1958 with "An Act to provide for research into the problems of flight within and outside the Earth's atmosphere, and for other purposes."

Another Soviet coup came with the **first manned space flight** (by cosmonaut Yuri Alekseyevich Gagarin in *Vostok 1* on 12 Apr 1961). The following month, however, Alan B Shepard became the first American in space and completed the **shortest manned space flight** (15 min 28 sec). President John F Kennedy gave NASA renewed impetus on 25 May 1961, declaring: "I believe that this nation should commit itself to achieving the goal, before this decade is out, of landing a man on the Moon and returning him safely to Earth." In 1962, John H Glenn Jr became the first US astronaut to orbit Earth; on 3 Jun 1965, Edward H White Jr took the first spacewalk by an US astronaut. NASA finally delivered on Kennedy's challenge in Jul 1969, when Armstrong and Aldrin set foot on the Moon.

The programme had cost $25.4 billion (£10.8 billion) by the time of the sixth and final Apollo lunar landing in 1972. But the work was far from over. NASA launched the *Pioneer 10* and *11* probes in 1972 and 1973 respectively, on a fact-finding journey to Jupiter and Saturn. In 1977, the two *Voyager* probes set off for

Mission Control
Located in the Lyndon B Johnson Space Center in Houston, Texas, USA, this famous room is the coordination and communication hub for NASA's space flights. Also known as FCR-1, it became operational in 1965.

Skylab
Launched on 14 May 1973, NASA's space station *Skylab* (below) housed the **largest room in space**. The workshop in this cylindrical construction had a pressurised volume of 238.3 m³ (8,419 cu ft), of which 173 m³ (6,112 cu ft) was accessible to crew members.

the four giant outer planets Jupiter, Saturn, Uranus and Neptune. Both are still in touch with NASA, making them the **most durable nuclear-powered interplanetary spacecraft**. On 12 Apr 1981, the first Space Shuttle mission (STS-1) took off; the seventh mission, which launched on 18 Jun 1983, saw Sally K Ride become the first female US astronaut in space.

Today, human space flight is firmly back on the agenda. NASA plans to use its *Orion* spacecraft to return to the Moon, where astronauts will test technologies that will enable us to journey farther into the Solar System, and for longer. NASA's *Sojourner* (the **first Mars rover**) explored the Martian surface way back in 1997, but now the agency hopes to send manned missions to Mars by the 2030s.
Watch this space.

NASA's latest recruits line up for a selfie
The recruitment process for Astronaut Group 22 began in Dec 2015 and saw NASA receive the **most applications for an astronaut selection process**: 18,300. These were rigorously whittled down to 12 people (seen here), whose names were announced on 7 Jun 2017.

NASA TIMELINE

◀ **1969: Fastest speed achieved by humans**
The command module of Apollo 10, carrying Thomas Patten Stafford, Eugene Andrew Cernan and John Watts Young (all USA), reached a speed of 39,937 km/h (24,816 mph) on 26 May 1969. The record was achieved during the module's trans-Earth return flight.

▲ **1976: First successful Mars lander**
Viking 1 touched down on the "Red Planet" at 11:53 a.m. UTC (Coordinated Universal Time) on 20 Jul 1976. This stationary lander was fitted with a suite of cameras, scientific instruments and a robot arm. The Soviet Union's *Mars 3* lander had touched down five years earlier, on 2 Dec 1971, but failed soon afterwards.

1977: launch of the **first probe to leave our Solar System**
Voyager 1 and *Voyager 2* were launched on 5 Sep and 20 Aug 1977 respectively. On or around 25 Aug 2012, *Voyager 1* entered interstellar space.

En route, *Voyager 1* made the **first observations of Jupiter's ring system** (on 5 Mar 1979), while *Voyager 2* recorded the **first flyby of Uranus** (on 24 Jan 1986) and **Neptune** (on 25 Aug 1989).

The pioneering astronauts of the Apollo 11 mission. From left to right: commander Neil Alden Armstrong, command module pilot Michael Collins and lunar module pilot Buzz Aldrin (b. Edwin Eugene Aldrin Jr).

First manned mission to land on the Moon

At 22:56 and 15 sec EDT (Eastern Daylight Time) on 20 Jul 1969, NASA astronauts Neil Armstrong and Buzz Aldrin (both USA) became the first people ever to set foot on the Moon. They spent some two-and-a-half hours on the surface, while their colleague, Michael Collins (USA), orbited in the Command Module. This photograph of Aldrin standing near the *Eagle* lunar module was taken by Armstrong, who is visible in Aldrin's visor.

The Saturn V rocket took Aldrin, Armstrong and Collins on their historic flight to the Moon in 1969. Altogether, 13 Saturn Vs were launched between 1967 and 1973. For more about this remarkable spacecraft, see pp.78–79.

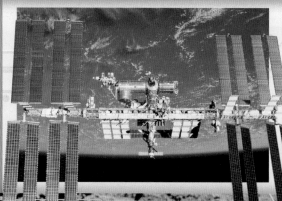

◀ 1981: First reusable spacecraft

The *Columbia* Space Shuttle made its maiden flight on 12 Apr 1981. Over a series of 135 missions, running up to 2011, the five Space Shuttles carried out many roles, including astronaut transit and supply carrying. They were also pivotal in the 10-year project to build the **largest artificial satellite**, the *International Space Station* (ISS).

◀ 1998: Largest space station

The *International Space Station* has been under construction since its first component, the *Zarya* module, was launched in Nov 1998. It is some 357 ft (109 m) long and weighs 924,739 lb (419,455 kg). The internal pressurized volume is 32,333 cu ft (916 m^3), similar to that of a Boeing 747, but less than half of this is habitable.

NEAR-EARTH OBJECTS

Greatest impact on Earth

Most astronomers now believe that, 4.5 billion years ago, a planet the size of Mars collided with the young Earth. Some of the debris from this cataclysm went into orbit around the Earth and collected under its own gravity to form the Moon.
The **largest impact crater on Earth** is the Vredefort crater near Johannesburg in South Africa, which has a diameter of 300 km (186 mi). The now largely eroded crater was formed around 2 billion years ago, when an asteroid or comet collided with Earth.

Shortest period comet

Encke's Comet has an orbital period of 1,198 days (3.28 years). The first periodic comet discovered after Halley's Comet, it was initially recorded in 1786, and its orbit calculated by Johann Franz Encke in 1819.

Largest recorded impact in the Solar System

On 16–22 Jul 1994, more than 20 fragments of comet Shoemaker-Levy 9 collided with Jupiter. The greatest impact was made by the "G" fragment, which exploded with the energy of roughly 6 million megatons of TNT – around 1,000 times Earth's combined nuclear arsenal. The comet was discovered in Mar 1993 by David Levy and Carolyn and Eugene Shoemaker (below).

Largest observed coma

The coma – the cloud around the nucleus in the head of a comet – that encircled the Great Comet of 1811 was about 2 million km (1.2 million mi) in diameter.

Largest comet

Discovered on 1 Nov 1977 – and initially reported in some quarters to be the 10th planet of the Solar System – Centaur 2060 Chiron possesses a diameter of 182 km (113 mi). Also classified as a minor planet, the giant comet get no closer than 1,273 million km (791 million mi) to the Sun.

Closest approach to Earth by a comet

On 12 Jun 1999, the tiny comet P/1999 J6 passed within 0.12 astronomical units (1,795,169 km; 1,115,466 mi) of Earth. This is only 4.7 times farther away than the Moon.

Darkest object in the Solar System

The least reflective body in the Solar System is Comet Borrelly, a comet nucleus imaged by the *Deep Space 1* unmanned spacecraft on 22 Sep 2001. Owing to its coating of dark dust, Borrelly reflects less than 3% of the sunlight it receives.

Longest measured comet tail

The tail of the comet Hyakutake measured 570 million km (350 million mi) – more than three times the distance from the Earth to the Sun. It was discovered by Geraint Jones of Imperial College London, UK, on 13 Sep 1999, using data gathered by the ESA/NASA spacecraft *Ulysses*.

Planet with the most Trojan asteroids

Trojan asteroids circle the Sun in the same orbit as a planet. As of 9 Nov 2017, some 6,703 Trojan asteroids had been discovered sharing Jupiter's orbit, with Neptune having 17, Mars nine, and Earth and Uranus one apiece.

Most recent Great Comet

First discovered by Robert McNaught (AUS, b. UK) in 2006, Comet McNaught (also known as C/2006 P1) achieved peak brightness on 12 Jan 2007, its tail measuring a maximum of 35° long in the sky. Great Comets are spectacularly bright in the night sky: notable examples include the Great Comets of 1577, 1811 (see left) and Halley's Comet.

Most distant observations of a comet

On 3 Sep 2003, astronomers at the European Southern Observatory in Paranal, Chile, released an image showing Halley's Comet at 4,200 million km (2,609 million mi) from the Sun. The image shows Halley as a fuzzy dot with a brightness of magnitude 28.2, nearly a billion times fainter than the faintest objects visible with the naked eye. It was the **first comet discovered to be periodic**, by Edmond Halley in 1705.

Largest meteorite

A block measuring 9 ft (2.7 m) long and 8 ft (2.4 m) wide and with an estimated weight of 130,000 lb (59 tonnes) was found in 1920 at Hoba West, near Grootfontein in Namibia. The meteorite, which is largely composed of iron and is notable for the flatness of its major sides, was declared a national monument in 1955 in an effort to protect it from trophy hunters removing pieces (see inset).

AMAZING ASTEROIDS

◀ Brightest asteroid

Discovered on 29 Mar 1807, 4Vesta is the only asteroid visible to the naked eye. This is owing to a combination of the brightness of its surface, its size (576 km; 357.9 mi across), and the fact that it can approach Earth as close as 177 million km (110 million mi).

First near-Earth asteroid discovered

In 1898, astronomers Carl Gustav Witt (DEU) and Auguste Charlois (FRA) independently discovered the asteroid 433 Eros. Its curious orbit brought it closer to Earth than any other asteroid or any major planet, leading to its near-Earth asteroid designation.

◀ Largest metal asteroid

Located in the main asteroid belt orbiting the Sun, 16 Psyche measures around 279 x 232 x 189 km (173 x 144 x 117 mi). Radar observations indicate that it is probably 90% iron. In Jan 2017, NASA approved a mission to this body, which may be a suitable candidate for future asteroid mining.

Four types of asteroid orbits

Amors
Earth-approaching NEAs* with orbits exterior to Earth's but interior to Mars'. Named after asteroid 1221 Amor.

*Near-Earth Asteroids

Apollos
Earth-crossing NEAs with semi-major axes larger than Earth's. Named after asteroid 1862 Apollo.

Atens
Earth-crossing NEAs with semi-major axes smaller than Earth's. Named after asteroid 2062 Aten.

Atiras
NEAs whose orbits are contained entirely within the orbit of the Earth. Named after asteroid 163693 Atira.

Fastest meteor shower

Typically occurring between 15 and 20 Nov each year, the Leonids meteor shower enters Earth's atmosphere at around 71 km (44 mi) per second and begins to glow at an altitude of around 155 km (96 mi). The high speed of the Leonids is due to the fact that the motion of the parent meteoroid stream – from comet 55P/Tempel–Tuttle – is almost directly opposite to the orbital motion of Earth around the Sun. This results in an almost head-on collision between the tiny particles and the Earth.

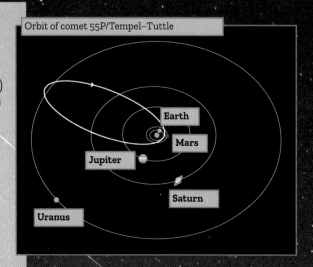

Orbit of comet 55P/Tempel–Tuttle

Earth
Mars
Jupiter
Saturn
Uranus

The Leonids were named in the aftermath of a spectacular shower over the Western Hemisphere on 12 Nov 1833. Contemporary estimates suggest that as many as 240,000 meteors fell over the course of 9 hr.

Largest concentration of asteroids

The main asteroid belt lies between the orbits of Mars and Jupiter and contains between 700,000 and 1.7 million asteroids that are at least 1 km (0.6 mi) across. The total mass of the belt is equivalent to just 4% of the Moon, with around half of this accounted for by the four largest asteroids.

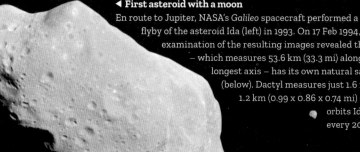

◄ First asteroid with a moon

En route to Jupiter, NASA's *Galileo* spacecraft performed a flyby of the asteroid Ida (left) in 1993. On 17 Feb 1994, examination of the resulting images revealed that Ida – which measures 53.6 km (33.3 mi) along its longest axis – has its own natural satellite (below). Dactyl measures just 1.6 x 1.4 x 1.2 km (0.99 x 0.86 x 0.74 mi) and orbits Ida once every 20 hr.

Most tails for an asteroid

On 10 Sep 2013, the Hubble Space Telescope spotted a bizarre asteroid with six distinct tails like a comet. Asteroid P/2013 P5 is a rocky body around 480 m (1,574 ft) across and it is likely that the tails are due to the pressure of solar radiation, which has increased the asteroid's spin to the extent that it loses mass owing to its own rotation.

ROUND-UP

First interstellar asteroid

On 19 Oct 2017, astronomer Robert Weryk (CAN) spotted an unusual object through the Pan-STARRS telescope at Haleakala Observatory in Hawaii, USA. Along its longest axis, it measures some 400 m (1,312 ft), but it is only about one-tenth as wide. Named 'Oumuamua, it is now thought to be an elongated asteroid. It originated outside the Solar System and will leave it again in around 20,000 years.

Most magnetic objects in the universe

Magnetars are neutron stars that possess stupendously powerful magnetic fields of up to 100 billion teslas. By way of comparison, Earth has a magnetic field of around 50 microteslas. Measuring around 20 km (12 mi) across, a magnetar should theoretically be able to strip the data from a credit card at a distance equivalent to halfway to the Moon.

Closest black hole to Earth

The nearest black hole to our home planet is A0620-00, a binary system containing a low-mass K-type star (aka an orange dwarf) and a stellar black hole. The system is some 3,000 light years away, in the constellation Monoceros.

First white dwarf pulsar

On 23 Jan 2017, a team at the University of Warwick, UK, published research on AR Scorpii, 380 light years from Earth. This binary star system comprises a white dwarf stellar remnant (the pulsar) and a cool star in close orbit. The white dwarf rotates once every 2 min, blasting its star with a bright radiation beam as it turns – rather like a lighthouse lamp.

Oldest recorded sound from a star

In Jun 2016, scientists at the University of Birmingham, UK, announced that they had measured the 13-billion-year-old acoustic oscillations of stars in star cluster M4 in our Milky Way. By applying a technique called "asteroseismology" on data from NASA's Kepler/K2 mission, they could measure the oscillations and record the low frequencies of sound inside the star that cause them. The scientists were hearing the sound stars had made in their nuclear furnaces "just" 0.8 billion years after the Big Bang.

At the instant of the Big Bang, the universe is thought to have been infinitely hot – the **highest temperature ever** – as well as infinitely small and infinitely dense.

Longest-lasting supernova

In Sep 2014, astronomers noticed an exploding star, or supernova, in a dwarf galaxy 509 million light years away. The supernova, which was given the name iPTF14hls, was expected to fade after around 100 days. Several months later, however, it became brighter again. After studying archive data, astronomers discovered that iPTF14hls had exploded in 1954 too, but somehow survived. As of Dec 2017, the supernova is still ongoing after more than three years. This unique event may represent the first time a theoretical "pulsational pair instability supernova"

(in which a star's outer layers blast off but the core remains) has been observed.

Largest planetary system (number of planets)

On 14 Dec 2017, NASA and Google announced that the *Kepler* spacecraft had discovered the planet Kepler-90i orbiting the star Kepler-90, some 2,545 light years away. This new planet joins seven other worlds known to orbit this star. Kepler-90 now ties with our own Solar System in having eight known planets, more than any other planetary system.

Of the 3,700 known planets orbiting other stars, none lies in a planetary system as large as our Solar System. Some 100,000 AU (9.3 trillion mi; 15 trillion km) across, it is the **largest planetary system by diameter**.

Most distant supermassive black hole

On 6 Dec 2017, a team of astronomers revealed their discovery of a black hole some 800 million times larger than the Sun, in the centre of a galaxy with a redshift of 7.5. This redshift value means that the light we see from this quasar was emitted "only" 690 million years after the Big Bang. It is not yet clear how something so large could have formed so soon after the birth of the universe.

Closest galaxy to the Milky Way

The Canis Major dwarf galaxy was discovered in 2003 and lies an average of "just" 42,000 light years from the centre of our galaxy. It was hard to detect as it is behind the plane of our spiral galaxy, as seen

First observations of merging neutron stars

On 17 Aug 2017, scientists at the US-based Laser Interferometer Gravitational-Wave Observatory (LIGO) and the Europe-based Virgo interferometer detected gravitational waves from around 130 million light years away. These ripples in space-time were followed by a gamma-ray burst. The ripples are thought to have been caused by two neutron stars spiralling together and colliding, creating the gamma-ray burst. The event has been given the designation GW170817.

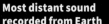

Most distant sound recorded from Earth

In May 2013, the NASA space probe *Voyager 1* – the **most remote man-made object** – recorded sounds in denser regions of ionized gas and plasma in interstellar space. Although there is no oxygen atmosphere in space, gas and plasma are present, and these can vibrate at audible frequencies. When *Voyager 1* recorded and played these vibrations back to Mission Control, they took the form of a rising tone as the density of the plasma increased. Mission Control heard these sounds twice: once from Oct to Nov 2012 and then again from Apr to May 2013, when the probe was 12 billion mi (19 billion km) from the Sun.

Largest planet compared with its parent star

On 31 Oct 2017, an international team of astronomers located a planet orbiting the star NGTS-1, some 600 light years away. The star is a red dwarf around half the radius of the Sun. But the planet, NGTS-1b, is a type of extrasolar planet known as a "hot Jupiter". Approximately one-and-a-third times the radius of Jupiter, this gas giant orbits its star in just 2.6 days, owing to its proximity.

Most planets devoured by their parent star

On 12 Oct 2017, astronomers at Princeton University, USA, announced their discovery of the strange properties of the binary stars HD 240430 and HD 240429. One, dubbed Kronos, contains high amounts of silicon, magnesium, iron, aluminium and other metals. They are concentrated in the star's outer atmosphere, suggesting that Kronos has devoured around 15 Earth-sized rocky planets orbiting it.

rom Earth. Its shape indicates hat it is in the process of being ipped apart and absorbed by he gravity of the Milky Way.

Smallest orbital rocket

SS-520-5 is just 9.54 m (31 ft 3.5 in) tall by 52 cm (1 ft 8 in) n diameter and has a mass of only 2,600 kg (5,732 lb). This tiny rocket was launched at 2:03 p.m. (Japan Standard Time) on 3 Feb 2018 from the Japanese space agency's Uchinoura Space Center n Kagoshima Prefecture, Japan. It carried a 3-kg (6-lb 9-oz) CubeSat satellite called TRICOM-1R, which was renamed "Tasuki" once n low-Earth orbit. SS-520-5 reportedly reached orbit less than 4 min 30 sec after lift-off.

Most powerful ion thruster

In Jul and Aug 2017, scientists at the NASA Glenn Research Center in Cleveland, Ohio, and The University of Michigan (both USA) tested the X3 Hall thruster. This system accelerates a stream of ionized (electrically charged) atoms from an engine, creating thrust. In the tests, the X3 operated at 102 kW of power, producing 5.4 N (1.2 lbf) of thrust. Ion thrusters have a much higher fuel efficiency than chemical rockets, which gives them added potential for long-distance space travel.

First trans-Neptunian object with a ring

On 11 Oct 2017, an international team of astronomers revealed the discovery of a ring surrounding the dwarf planet Haumea. They had predicted that Haumea would occult (pass in front of) a star on 21 Jan 2017. An array of a dozen telescopes from 10 European observatories focused on the event, to refine knowledge of the dwarf planet's size and shape. In the process, a ring was observed around this small, distant object. Haumea is some 50 times farther from the Sun than Earth, and takes 284 years to complete an orbit. It has a "rugby ball" shape, with a long axis of some 2,320 km (1,441 mi).

Largest cloud of primordial hydrogen

Discovered in 2000, LAB-1 is a type of astronomical object known as a lyman-alpha blob. Measuring around 300,000 light years across and some 11.5 billion light years from Earth, LAB-1 is a cloud of hydrogen gas that has yet to coalesce into galaxies. The blob is glowing – possibly due to the light from galaxies within, which have already formed. Owing to its distance we see LAB-1 as it was when the universe was only around 15% of its current age.

Largest lunar cave

On 18 Oct 2017, Japan's space agency JAXA reported that its lunar orbiter probe SELENE (or "Kaguya") had discovered a large cave below the Moon's surface in the Marius Hills region. With an opening (right) of around 50 m (164 ft) across, the cave descends some 50 m below the surface. SELENE's lunar radar sounder revealed that the opening leads to a larger cavity around 50 km (31 mi) long and 100 m (328 ft) wide. This could be a spot for a future manned lunar base.

Largest eruptive ice plumes

In 2005, the NASA/ESA *Cassini* spacecraft recorded eruptions of water ice from Saturn's moon Enceladus rising at least 505 km (313 mi) into space. In Feb 2017, Ted Stryk (USA) announced that he had processed an image taken by *Voyager 1* as it passed Saturn on 13 Nov 1980 that appeared to show even earlier evidence of this phenomenon.

EIFFEL TOWER

One of the most iconic landmarks on Earth, the Eiffel Tower pierces the skyline of the French capital, Paris. Built by Gustave Eiffel's company for the 1889 World Fair, its wrought-iron lattice design and unprecedented height made it an engineering marvel. At the time of its unveiling in Mar 1889, the tower was the tallest man-made structure in history, a record it would hold for more than 40 years.

Digging for the tower began on 28 Jan 1887. Each one of its 18,038 metallic parts was manufactured and measured at Gustave Eiffel's factory on the outskirts of Paris, before transportation to the construction site on the Champ de Mars. The Eiffel Tower was completed in a little over two years, with work finishing in Mar 1889.

There had been angry protests by prominent writers and artists that such a giant construction – at 300 m (984 ft 3 in), it is the **tallest iron structure** – would ruin the city. Yet today the Eiffel Tower attracts as many as 7 million annual visitors, with around 300 million people thought to have visited it over the years.

EXPOSITION UNIVERSELLE

The design for the "Iron Lady" was selected from more than 100 submissions for a competition to build an entrance arch for the 1889 Exposition Universelle (World Fair) held in Paris. The fair marked the 100th anniversary of the storming of the Bastille prison, and the beginning of the French Revolution.

ROOM AT THE TOP

Near the summit of the tower is a 276-m-high (905-ft) viewing platform offering panoramic views of Paris. Gustave Eiffel had his office here, where he entertained guests such as the American inventor Thomas Edison.

ORIGINAL DRAWINGS

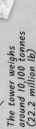

It may have borne his name, but the Eiffel Tower was not actually designed by Gustave Eiffel (above left). It was Maurice Koechlin (above right), a structural engineer who worked for Eiffel's company, who together with Émile Nouguier came up with the idea for a tall, pylon-like tower built on four columns of latticed work girders. Koechlin's original drawings can be seen left: to the right of the tower are size comparisons with other famous buildings such as the Notre-Dame cathedral and the Statue of Liberty (see pp.10–11). Eiffel and Koechlin had also worked together on the iconic American monument, which was unveiled three years before the Eiffel Tower.

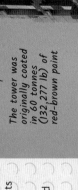

The tower weighs around 10,100 tonnes (22.2 million lb)

An antenna enables the tower to make radio transmissions

The tower was originally coated in 60 tonnes (132,277 lb) of red-brown paint

There are 1,665 steps from the base to the top

FOR THE RECORD

Upon completion on 31 Mar 1889, the Eiffel Tower in Paris, France, was the world's **tallest man-made structure.** It stood 300 m (984 ft) tall – a 24-m (78-ft 8-in) television antenna was added in the 1950s, but this is not usually counted as part of the structural height. The tower remained the tallest until 1930, when the 319-m (1,046-ft) Chrysler Building in New York City, USA, was completed.

Base pillars are aligned to the four cardinal points of the compass

ELEVATORS

Glass-cage hydraulic lifts became operational on 26 May 1889, only days after the Eiffel Tower had opened to the public. They were powered from below, rather than being pulled from above. Two of the original elevators are still in operation today, a testament to the durability of their design. In total, the lifts travel more than 103,000 km (64,000 mi) a year – or two-and-a-half times around the world.

DID YOU KNOW?

Restaurants, booths and boutiques were set up inside the tower to take advantage of the large numbers of visitors. *Le Figaro* newspaper installed a printing press on the second floor, where it printed a daily edition entitled *Le Figaro de la Tour*. Visitors could have their names inserted into the paper to prove that they had been there.

This image was produced by NASA's satellite *Terra*, which launched on 18 Dec 1999. Its sensors monitor Earth, providing data that enables scientists to track our planet's changing climate. There are a series of satellites involved in this mission, collectively known as the Earth Observing System. *Terra* is the mission's flagship satellite.

PLANET EARTH

Largest terrestrial planet

Of all the known planetary bodies in our Solar System comprising mostly silicate metals or rocks, Earth is the largest. It has a diameter of 12,742 km (7,917.5 mi), a mass of around 5.9722×10^{21} tonnes (6.5832×10^{21} US tons) and is home to the only confirmed life in the universe. The name "Earth" is around 1,000 years old and has its roots in Old English and Proto-Germanic nouns. All of the other planets in the Solar System bear Greek or Roman titles.

CONTINENTS

Earliest continent
Geological evidence suggests that there was a single continental land mass on Earth from around 3.6 billion to 2.8 billion years ago. Referred to as Vaalbara, this continent was smaller than any of today's continents. The Kaapvaal and Pilbara cratons in southern Africa and north-west Australia are surviving remnants of Vaalbara.

Longest-inhabited continent
For many years it was thought that modern humans, *Homo sapiens*, first appeared in East Africa around 200,000 years ago. However, in 2017, remains of human face and jaw bones dating to approximately 315,000 years ago were found at Jebel Irhoud in Morocco. This means that *Homo sapiens* was living in Africa some 100,000 years earlier than had previously been assumed.

Most countries in a continent
There are 54 internationally recognized sovereign states on the continent of Africa. The most recent, South Sudan, gained independence on 9 Jul 2011. The disputed territory of Western Sahara is a member of the African Union, but as of 2018 had not been recognized by the United Nations.

Antarctica has the **fewest countries in a continent**, with no native population and no countries recognized below the latitude of 60°S. Although various countries have claimed parts of the territory, the Antarctic Treaty of 1959 pledges to keep the continent open for peaceful scientific investigation and precludes any military activity.

Smallest continent
Australia has a west-to-east width of some 4,042 km (2,511 mi) and an area of 7,617,930 km² (2,941,299 sq mi), including offshore territories and islands. It is simultaneously the smallest continent and the sixth-largest country, behind Russia, Canada, China, the USA and Brazil.

Flattest continental land mass
Australia's mean elevation is just over 330 m (1,082 ft) above sea level, not including its outlying islands. It is the only major land mass on Earth to lack a major mountain range. The highest point on its mainland is the summit of Mount Kosciuszko, at 2,228 m (7,310 ft) above sea level.

Highest seasonal population difference
Over the course of a year, the population of Antarctica swells by a factor of five, from around 1,000 in the winter to around 5,000 in the summer. The vast majority of scientists who work in the continent's research stations only live there during the summer, in order to avoid the harsh Antarctic winters.

Thickest crust
The Earth's crust is the cold, solid, outermost layer of its lithosphere. In the Himalayan mountains in China, this crust has a variable thickness of 40–75 km (24.85–46.6 mi).

The **thinnest crust** is just 6 km (3.7 mi) thick, and can be found in parts of the Pacific Ocean.

Highest continent
According to the British Antarctic Survey, excluding its ice shelves Antarctica has an average elevation of 2,194 m (7,198 ft) above the OSU91A Geoid, a geopotential model similar to sea level. Its highest point is the summit of Vinson Massif, at 4,897 m (16,066 ft) above sea level.

Largest continent
Asia covers an area of 44,579,000 km² (17,212,000 sq mi), ahead of Africa with 30,221,532 km² (11,668,600 sq mi). It is home to 49 internationally recognized sovereign states and more than 4.4 billion people, making it also the **most populous continent** (see top right).

Largest submerged continent
New Zealand represents just the highest part of the continent of Zealandia. With a total area of some 4,900,000 km² (1,891,900 sq mi), Zealandia is around 94% under water and forms a shallow sea around the coast of New Zealand. In 2017, geologists argued that Zealandia fulfilled the criteria to be considered a continent proper.

Largest discrete land mass
The combined continents of Africa and Eurasia form a continuous land mass covering 84,980,532 km² (32,811,166 sq mi). It is referred to as Afro-Eurasia, and sometimes as The World Island. It is home to approximately 85% of the world's human population.

WORLD IN MOTION

It's easy to think of continents as vast, static land masses, but in fact the world is continually shifting beneath our feet.

The rigid outer shell of Earth, known as the lithosphere, is divided into vast tectonic plates that have been slowly moving for millions of years. In the process, they are shaping and re-shaping the world as we know it.

LARGEST TECTONIC PLATES	
Name	Area
Pacific Plate (see right)	103,300,000 km²
North American Plate	75,900,000 km²
Eurasian Plate	67,800,000 km²
African Plate	61,300,000 km²
Antarctic Plate	60,900,000 km²

Source: WorldAtlas.com, retrieved 9 Nov 2017

▶ **Fastest land mass on Earth**
Owing to convection currents in the Earth's mantle, all of the continental plates are in constant motion. Where the boundaries of these plates meet others, one will slide under the other to create a subduction zone. The Tonga microplate, centred near Samoa, is currently moving under the Pacific Plate at a rate of 24 cm (9.4 in) each year.

The **largest** and **most populous continent** on Earth is Asia (see opposite page). It is home to nearly two-thirds of the world's population.

Largest continent ever

By 299–273 million years ago, all of today's continents were joined together in one "supercontinent", Pangea (which means "all lands" in Greek). Pangea began to slowly break apart around 200 million years ago due to plate tectonics, leading eventually to the land masses of today. Evidence of Pangea is apparent when you see how the coastlines of Africa and South America fit together.

A computer projection shows Earth 250 million years into the future. A new supercontinent, Pangea Ultima, has formed, with the Indian Ocean at its heart.

The **first suggestion of continental drift** was believed to have been made by Flemish mapmaker Abraham Ortelius (1527–98), who argued that Africa and South America had once been joined. The theory of continental drift would only gain acceptance by mainstream academia in the latter half of the 20th century.

Pangea's break-up began in the Early Jurassic period, around 200 million years ago. Rifts between continents created the North Atlantic Ocean, gradually leading to the globe we recognize today.

PLANET EARTH

Slowest continental plate

The Eurasian Plate contains most of the Eurasian continent and extends west to the Mid-Atlantic Ridge. In contrast to subduction zones (see left), ridge zones move the most slowly of all continental boundaries. The Eurasian Plate is moving at c. 2.1 cm (0.8 in) a year. Its divergence with the North American Plate has led to volcanic activity on Iceland.

▶ Largest continental collision zone

Around 40–50 million years ago, the Indian subcontinent began colliding with the Eurasian continent. The collision, which is still ongoing along a zone about 2,900 km (1,800 mi) long, created the Himalayan mountains. In the aftermath of the break-up of Pangea (see above), the Indian subcontinent had been part of the southern supercontinent of Gondwana, before becoming separated from the eastern coast of modern Africa and drifting north across the Tethys Sea. It collided with the supercontinent of Laurasia, causing extensive surface uplift in the shape of the Himalayas.

Largest tectonic plate

The Pacific Plate has an approximate area of 103,300,000 km² (39.8 million sq mi). It is moving gradually north-west with respect to North America at a speed of approximately 7 cm (2.7 in) per year, as measured around the Hawaiian Islands. This is more than three times the speed of the Eurasian Plate, the **slowest continental plate** (see left).

MOUNTAINS

Rising majestically up towards the clouds, mountains provide some of the most breathtaking sights of the natural world. Measuring Earth's loftiest mountains is far from easy, and there are more challengers to Everest's crown than might be imagined...

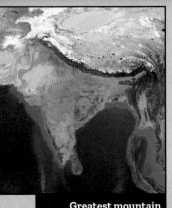

Greatest mountain range on Earth

Separating the Indian subcontinent from the Tibetan Plateau, the Himalayas contain 96 of the world's 109 (as per 1969 figures) peaks of over 24,000 ft (7,315 m) and 10 of the 14 peaks above 8,000 m (26,246 ft). The range takes its name from the Sanskrit *himālaya* – literally, "abode of snow".

A common misconception is that Everest is the tallest mountain in the world. At 8,848 m (29,029 ft), it's actually the *highest* mountain (see right), meaning that its summit lies at the highest altitude above sea level. This is typically how mountain heights are described – from sea level to summit. If you started your climb of Everest at sea level, you would ultimately need to travel a vertical distance of nearly 5.5 mi (8.8 km). (Incidentally, the **first person to climb Everest from sea level** was Tim Macartney-Snape (AUS), whose three-month climb set off from the Bay of Bengal in 1990.)

Everest, however, sits atop the Himalayan Plateau. (The latter – along with the region's famous mountain ranges – was created by the action of the Indian tectonic plate colliding with the Eurasian tectonic plate, a process that began some 50 million years ago.) This means that the climb to the top, which typically begins at base camp, *starts* at an altitude of 5,364 m (17,598 ft), if you take the most popular south route. You "only" need to climb the last 3,484 m (11,430 ft). Still no mean feat, of course, as our adventurers on pp.122–23 attest.

Mauna Kea, located in Hawaii, USA, may peak just 4,205 m (13,796 ft) above sea level, but its base actually lies *below* sea level (Figure 1). If you measure from the submarine base of the mountain to the top, it's a majestic 10,205 m (33,480 ft).

Highest glacier

The Khumbu Glacier in Nepal begins at, and is fed by, the glacial bed of the Western Cwm – a valley of ice between the peaks of Everest and the Lhotse-Nuptse Ridge. The glacier head is situated at an altitude of around 7,600 m (24,934 ft) above sea level, and runs for 17 km (10.5 mi) to the west and south before terminating.

Figure 1:
Tallest vs highest

Everest (4,148 m)

Everest base elevation
4,700 m

8,848 m

Denali (5,500 m)

6,190 m

Denali base elevation
594 m

Sea level
0 m

4,205 m

Mauna Kea (10,205 m)

Mauna Kea (submarine) base
-6,000 m

Figure 2:
Geocentric height

Chimborazo

Everest

6,382.3 km

6,384.4 km

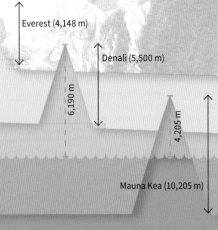

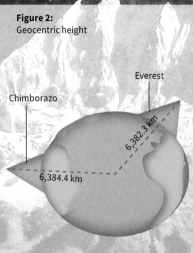

PEAKS OF PLENTY

Highest Arctic mountain

Gunnbjørn Fjeld in Greenland's Watkins Range is the highest mountain north of the Arctic Circle, with its summit reaching 3,694 m (12,119 ft) above sea level. It is a type of mountain known as a nunatak: an exposed rocky peak that protrudes through a glacier or ice field. The summit was first climbed on 16 Aug 1935.

◀ Tallest mountain

Mauna Kea ("White Mountain") on the islands of Hawaii, USA, measures 10,205 m (33,480 ft) from its submarine base in the Hawaiian Trough to its summit. Of this total height, only 4,205 m (13,796 ft) is above sea level, making Mauna Kea the *tallest* mountain in the world, but not the highest (see above).

Highest mountain tabletop

Monte Roraima, on the border of Brazil and Venezuela, is a sandstone plateau measuring 2,810 m (9,219 ft) in height. Its harsh environment has resulted in around one-third of its plant species being unique to the mountain. Monte Roraima is believed to have been the inspiration for Sir Arthur Conan Doyle's *The Lost World*.

Everest, by comparison, has a "height" of 4,148 m (13,608 ft) when measured from the average base elevation (4,200 m on the Nepal side to 5,200 m in Tibet). This makes Mauna Kea the world's **tallest** mountain.

Denali, aka Mount McKinley, in Alaska also beats Everest when measured from its base. It rises 6,190 m (20,310 ft) above sea level but sits on a sloping plain that gives it an average base-to-summit height of about 5,500 m (18,044 ft).

Finally, to complicate matters further, what happens when you take Earth's shape into account? The snow-covered summit of Chimborazo, just one degree south of the equator in Ecuador, rises 6,268 m (20,564 ft) above sea level. This isn't particularly tall – it's not even the tallest peak in the Andes. But the planet is not perfectly spherical, and Earth's radius in Ecuador is longer than the radius at the latitude of Everest (Figure 2). This means that Chimborazo is the **farthest mountain peak from Earth's centre**. Specifically, its summit is 6,384.4 km (3,967.1 mi) from Earth's centre – 2,168 m (7,113 ft) farther away than the summit of Everest, at 6,382.3 km (3,965.8 mi).

Identifying record holders can be a challenge, even when dealing with millennia-old claimants such as mountains. Despite the semantics, though, Everest rightly stands proud as the *highest* point on Earth.

Fastest-rising mountain
Nanga Parbat in Pakistan is growing taller at a rate of 7 mm (0.27 in) per year. The mountain is part of the Himalayan Plateau, which was formed when India began colliding with the Eurasian continental plate between 40 and 50 million years ago (see p.33). Although the Himalayas are still being uplifted fractionally every year (see left), this is often counterbalanced by erosion caused by freeze-thaw, seismic shocks and avalanches.

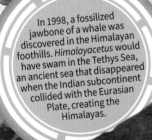

In 1998, a fossilized jawbone of a whale was discovered in the Himalayan foothills. *Himalayacetus* would have swam in the Tethys Sea, an ancient sea that disappeared when the Indian subcontinent collided with the Eurasian Plate, creating the Himalayas.

Highest mountain
The summit of Everest, on the Tibet-Nepal border, rises to a height of 8,848 m (29,029 ft) – the highest point in the world. Originally known as Peak XV, the mountain was given its present name in 1865 in honour of Sir George Everest (1790–1866), formerly the British Surveyor General of India. Everest's official height was obtained in 1955; in 2017, the Nepalese government announced new plans to measure the mountain using GPS receivers.

◄ Highest unclimbed mountain
At 7,570 m (24,835 ft), Kangkar Pünzum in Bhutan is the world's 40th highest mountain. Unsuccessful attempts were made to summit it in the 1980s before a partial ban of mountaineering was declared in the country in 1994. Since 2003, all climbing in Bhutan has been outlawed for religious reasons.

▲ Greatest vertical drop
The granite peak of Mount Thor, located on Baffin Island in the Canadian territory of Nunavut, has a west face that consists of a vertical drop of 1,250 m (4,101 ft). The face has an average angle of 105° and, unsurprisingly, is popular with rock climbers.

Highest mountain face underwater
Monte Pico in the Azores (Portugal) extends 20,000 ft (6,096 m) below the waves to the ocean floor. Above the water, the mountain has a height of 7,711 ft (2,350 m), giving it a total base-to-height summit of 27,711 ft (8,446 m) – just fractionally shorter than Everest (see above).

BODIES OF WATER

Deepest point in the sea
The Challenger Deep, located beneath the Pacific Ocean 300 km (186 mi) south-west of Guam, is the deepest point in the world's oceans. Recent surveys have found that the bottom of the Challenger Deep lies 10,994 m (36,070 ft) below sea level.

The Challenger Deep was the location for the **deepest manned ocean descent**, carried out in the bathyscaphe *Trieste* by Swiss oceanographer Jacques Piccard and US Navy officer Lt Don Walsh on 23 Jan 1960. The two explorers descended to the ocean floor in a section of the Challenger Deep that was 10,911 m (35,797 ft; 6.78 mi) below sea level.

Longest fjord
The Nordvest Fjord in eastern Greenland extends inland 313 km (195 mi) from the sea. Fjords are narrow, steep-sided inlets created by glacial erosion.

Deepest lake
Lake Baikal is a freshwater lake located in a geological rift valley in south-eastern Siberia. It is 395 mi (636 km) long, with an average width of only 30 mi (48 km). In 1974, the lake's Olkhon Crevice was measured by the Hydrographic Service of the Soviet Pacific Navy and found to be 5,371 ft (1,637 m) deep.

This extraordinary depth is why Lake Baikal is the **largest freshwater lake by volume** – holding an estimated 23,000 km³ (5,500 cu mi) of water – despite being only the seventh-largest lake by area.

Largest area of calm water
Covering an area of some 6.2 million km² (2.4 million sq mi) in the centre of the North Atlantic, the Sargasso Sea is the world's largest area of calm water. The region is formed by a system of ocean currents called the North Atlantic Gyre, and is named for the sargassum seaweed that covers its surface.

The Sargasso Sea's counterpart at the centre of the North Pacific Gyre has the dubious honour of being the **largest oceanic "garbage patch"**. This roughly Texas-sized region of calm sea has around 5.114 kg of plastic for every 1 km² (29 lb 3 oz per sq mi) of seawater.

Flattest place on Earth
Abyssal plains are vast expanses of flat, featureless terrain found at the deepest parts of the ocean. They cover approximately 40% of the ocean floor. The uniform flatness is caused by the accumulation of sediments, up to 3 mi (5 km) thick in places. This means that there is less than 5 ft (1.5 m) of vertical variation in a square mile (2.78 km²) of seafloor.

Deepest blue hole
"Blue holes" are underwater sinkholes – deep vertical shafts created by the slow erosion of limestone bedrock. The deepest blue hole is the Dragon Hole, situated off the Paracel Islands in the South China Sea. A survey carried out in 2016 by the Sansha Ship Course Research Institute for Coral Protection (CHN) measured its depth at 300.89 m (987 ft). That's deep enough to almost completely submerge the Eiffel Tower.

The survey team used a small VideoRay remotely operated vehicle (pictured above) fitted with a depth sensor to confirm their results.

Largest lake
The largest body of water enclosed entirely by land is the Caspian Sea in Central Asia. It covers 371,000 km² (143,243 sq mi) and measures 1,199 km (745 mi) at its longest from north to south.

Some would argue, however, that the salty Caspian Sea is a sea, not a lake. In that case the title would pass to the **largest freshwater lake**: Lake Superior on the US–Canada border, which covers 82,414 km² (31,820 sq mi).

Shallowest sea
At its deepest point, the Sea of Azov (an area of the northern Black Sea almost completely surrounded by land) is only 14 m (45.9 ft) deep, and it has an average depth of only 7 m (23 ft). The **largest passenger liner**, MS *Harmony of the Seas*, would run aground if it entered the Sea of Azov, as its hull extends some 9.3 m (30 ft 6 in) below the waterline.

Largest ocean
The Pacific Ocean covers approximately 59 million sq mi (152.8 million km²) of Earth's surface, representing around half of the world's oceans by area. The movement of Earth's crust is causing the Pacific to shrink (at a rate of 2–3 cm per year), which means that it will likely lose its record to the slow-growing Atlantic in the far-distant future.

With an area of some 5.4 million sq mi (13.9 million km²), the Arctic is the **smallest ocean**. It has an average depth of 12,000 ft (3,657 m), making it also the **shallowest ocean**.

LEADING LAKES

Largest lake created by a nuclear explosion
On 15 Jan 1965, the Soviet Union detonated a 140-kiloton nuclear bomb under the Chagan River, in what is now north-eastern Kazakhstan. The debris thrown up by this test dammed the river, forming a reservoir. It is now known as Lake Chagan and holds around 100,000 m³ (3,531,000 cu ft) of significantly radioactive water.

◀ Saltiest lake
The Gaet'ale Pond in the Danakil Depression, Ethiopia, has 43.3% salt by weight — nearly twice the salinity of the Dead Sea and more than 12 times the average salinity of the world's oceans (3.5%). The **least salty sea** is the Baltic Sea. The waters in some of its bays have as little as 0.6–0.8% salt by weight, rising to around 3.3% nearer the North Sea.

Largest crater lake
Lake Toba, in the Indonesian island of Sumatra, is the site of a supervolcanic eruption around 75,000 years ago that drove humanity to the brink of extinction. The crater formed by the eruption has since filled with water to form Lake Toba, which is around 100 km (62 mi) by 30 km (18 mi) in extent, and 505 m (1,656 ft) at its deepest point.

Most contaminated lake
Between 1951 and the mid-1970s, Lake Karachay in Chelyabinsk Oblast, Russia, was used as a dumping ground for nuclear waste. In 1968, a drought uncovered the 11-ft-deep (3.4-m) layer of toxic sludge on the lakebed, exposing thousands of local people to dangerous radioactive dust. Today, the lake has been filled in with concrete, but the area is still dangerous.

*Source: National Oceanic and Atmospheric Administration

Pacific
161,760,000 km²
44.7%

Atlantic
85,133,000 km²
23.5%

Indian
70,560,000 km²
19.5%

Southern
21,960,000 km²
6.1%

Arctic
15,558,000 km²
4.3%

GUINNESS WORLD RECORDS

Largest body of fresh water

The Antarctic ice cap is not a sea or a lake, but it is a body of water nonetheless. It holds some 26.92 million km³ (6.45 million cu mi) of fresh water – about 70% of all the fresh water in the world. This body of water also has a body of water under it. Lake Vostok, the **largest subglacial lake**, lies 3,700–4,200 m (12,139–13,779 ft) below the East Antarctic Ice Sheet. It covers an area of some 15,000 km² (5,791 sq mi) and has a depth of at least 100 m (330 ft).

Giant icebergs
In Jul 2017, an iceberg measuring some 5,800 km² (2,200 sq mi) broke away from the Larsen C ice shelf in Antarctica (above). It isn't the **largest iceberg ever recorded**, however; that was B-15, an 11,000-km² (4,200-sq-mi) iceberg that broke away from the Ross Ice Shelf in Mar 2000.

In 1956, the USS *Glacier* sighted an iceberg in the Southern Ocean with an estimated area of 31,000 km² (12,000 sq mi). If true, it would have dwarfed the largest iceberg ever recorded, but there were no satellites back then to confirm the size.

Largest ephemeral lake
Ephemeral lakes are bodies of water created by exceptionally heavy rainfall in areas that typically get very little. The largest is Lake Eyre in Australia, a dry salt flat that is sometimes flooded by heavy rainfall. In 1974, unusually heavy monsoon rains created a temporary inland sea up to 6 m (19 ft 8 in) deep and covering some 8,020 km² (3,100 sq mi).

◀ Largest desert lake
Lake Turkana, located on the edge of Kenya's Chalbi Desert in the Great Rift Valley, has a surface area of 6,405 km² (2,472 sq mi) and an average depth of 100 ft (30.2 m). It is fed by the Omo, Turkwel and Kerio rivers, though its inflow is threatened by irrigation projects. There is no outflow from Lake Turkana, so the only water loss is by evaporation.

▲ Largest pink lake
Retba Lake, better known as Lac Rose (Pink Lake), is a shallow lagoon measuring 1.5 x 5 km (0.9 x 3 mi) located near Dakar in Senegal. Its intense pink colour is the result of a micro-organism called *Dunaliella salina*, which thrives in the lake's highly salty water.

RIVERS

Highest river
The source of the Yarlung Zangbo River lies some 6,020 m (19,750 ft) above sea level at the foot of the Angsi Glacier in Tibet, China. No continuously flowing river has a higher origin. It flows east across the Tibetan Plateau, falling to 3,000 m (9,800 ft) before crossing into India, where it is known as the Brahmaputra River.

Deepest river
The Congo River, which runs 4,700 km (2,920 mi) through central Africa, is the second-largest river by flow rate (see top right). In some places, it has carved a channel 220 m (721 ft) deep – twice as deep as the Amazon at its deepest point.

Largest river basin
The term river basin – or drainage basin – describes an area in which all rainfall (or snowmelt) ends up flowing into the same river. Unsurprisingly, the largest of these is the one that feeds the **largest river** (see right). The Amazon basin covers some 7,045,000 km² (2,720,000 sq mi), including parts of Brazil, Peru, Bolivia, Colombia, Ecuador, Guyana, Suriname and Venezuela.

Largest delta
A delta is a fan-shaped pattern of forked channels, islands and wetlands that forms at the mouth of some large sediment-carrying rivers. The largest is found in Bangladesh, where two massive rivers, the Ganges and the Brahmaputra, meet to form the Ganges-Brahmaputra Delta. This covers an area of 75,000 km² (30,000 sq mi) and stretches from eastern Bangladesh to West Bengal in India.

In areas with a greater tidal range, large rivers form estuaries instead of deltas where they meet the sea. These are areas where the river water and seawater mix to create a partially tidal stretch of river. The **longest estuary** is that of the Ob, in northern Russia. It is 885 km (550 mi) long and some 80 km (50 mi) wide.

Largest subglacial river
Satellite studies of lakes under the Antarctic ice revealed huge rivers of water at its base. A flow of 1.8 km³ (0.43 cu mi) of water over 16 months, roughly three-quarters the discharge rate of the River Thames (UK), could account for changes in the elevation of the ice surface above. The studies were led by University College London and Bristol University (both UK).

Lowest river
The mouth of the Jordan River lies roughly 430 m (1,410 ft) below sea level. It is the only major water source that flows into the Dead Sea, the **lowest exposed body of water**. The Dead Sea is what is known as an endorheic basin, lacking any outlet to the ocean. The hot climate ensures that the water flowing in from the Jordan evaporates before the lake can overflow.

Longest river with its drainage basin in one country
At 6,300 km (3,915 mi) in length, the Chāng Jiāng River (also known as the Yangtze) is the third-longest river and the longest in Asia. Unusually for such a long river, its complete length and entire drainage basin is contained within just one country: China.

China's second-longest river, the Huang He (or "Yellow River"), is also a record holder, though for very different reasons. In Sep 1887, massive flooding on the Huang He killed an estimated 900,000 people – the **highest death toll from a flood** and **highest death toll from a natural disaster**. It flooded again in

Largest river (by flow rate)
The Amazon River discharges an average of 200,000 m³ (7,100,000 cu ft) into the Atlantic Ocean every second – that's enough to fill Lake Geneva in about five days. This increases to more than 340,000 m³ (12,000,000 cu ft) per second in full flood. The flow of the Amazon is 60 times greater than that of the Nile.

The Amazon draws from the world's **largest river basin** (see left). While not in flood, the main stretches of the river (i.e., not its tidal reaches, where an estuary/delta can be much wider) can reach widths of up to 11 km (7 mi), making it the world's **widest river**.

1931, probably with far more fatalities, but no reliable records exist for this catastrophe. Over the course of the 20th century, however, this once fearsome river (nicknamed "China's Sorrow") has been so extensively diverted for irrigation that it holds the dubious honour of being the **largest river to run dry**. For several months each year, its channel becomes choked with silt in Henan Province, some 400 km (250 mi) before it reaches the sea.

Longest underground river
In Mar 2007, cave divers Stephen Bogaerts (UK) and Robbie Schmittner (DEU) reported that two months previously they had discovered a 153-km (95-mi) river beneath the Yucatán Peninsula in Mexico. The river has so many twists and turns that it manages to reach this length despite its source and mouth being only 10 km (6 mi) apart.

The worst of the Citarum's pollution comes from the local textile industry, which uses harmful chemicals and heavy metals to dye and prepare fabrics.

Most polluted river (current)
The Citarum River, which flows through the industrial districts to the east of Jakarta, Indonesia, is the most polluted in the world. According to studies carried out in 2013, the river holds 1,000 times more lead than is considered safe, as well as faecal matter, household waste and various toxic chemicals.

WONDERFUL WATERFALLS

Largest by vertical area
Victoria Falls (also known as Mosi-oa-Tunya) is neither the tallest nor the widest waterfall in the world (see right), but it is the largest. It is here that the wide Zambezi River plunges into a series of zigzagging gorges. The falls are 1,708 m (5,604 ft) wide and 108 m (354 ft) high, creating a sheet of falling water with an area of around 2 million sq ft (184,400 m²).

◀ Greatest annual flow
Inga Falls is a series of rapids and waterfalls located on the Congo River (see above left), some 280 km (174 mi) downstream from Kinshasa in the Democratic Republic of the Congo. The World Waterfall Database estimates that 910,000 cu ft (25,768 m³) of water flows over Inga Falls every second. The largest single drop is 21 m (69 ft) high.

Largest ever
During the last Ice Age, which peaked some 22,000 years ago, a roughly 600-m-high (1,968-ft) ice dam blocked the Clark Fork River in what is now Montana, USA. A lake holding around 2,000 km³ (500 cu mi) of water formed behind it, called Glacial Lake Missoula.

On around 40 occasions, rising temperatures caused the dam to fail, creating monstrous 100-km/h (62-mph) walls of water that tore across what is now Washington and Oregon, draining the lake in 48 hr. On their way to the Pacific, these torrents flowed over a giant waterfall that was 115 m (377 ft) high and 5.6 km (3.4 mi) wide. Its remains, called Dry Falls, can still be seen in the floodwater-scoured region known as the Channeled Scablands, west of Seattle.

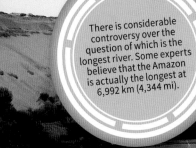

Nile 6,695 km (4,160 mi)

Amazon 6,400 km (3,976 mi)

Chāng Jiāng (Yangtze) 6,300 km (3,915 mi)

There is considerable controversy over the question of which is the longest river. Some experts believe that the Amazon is actually the longest at 6,992 km (4,344 mi).

Longest river

Measured from its delta in Egypt to the headwaters of its most distant tributary in Burundi, the Nile is c. 6,695 km (4,160 mi) long. That's about the same as the straight-line distance from New York, USA, to Helsinki, Finland. The Nile passes through 11 countries in north-eastern Africa – Tanzania, Uganda, Rwanda, Burundi, the Democratic Republic of the Congo, Kenya, Ethiopia, Eritrea, South Sudan, Sudan and Egypt – before emptying into the Mediterranean Sea. Despite its length and vast drainage basin, the Nile has just 1.5% of the flow rate of the Amazon (see opposite).

The Nile (highlighted in red) has two major tributaries: the Blue Nile (light blue), which flows from Lake Tana in Ethiopia, and the longer White Nile (yellow), which flows from Lake Victoria in central Africa.

◄ Widest

With a total average width of 10,783 m (35,377 ft), the Khône Falls on the Mekong River in Laos are around eight times the width of the famous Niagara Falls on the US–Canadian border. The falls comprise a series of rapids and waterfalls – the tallest of which is about 21 m (69 ft) high – which weave between an archipelago of small islands and rocky outcrops.

Tallest (multi-tiered)

The Tugela Falls are near the source of the Tugela River in South Africa's Royal Natal National Park. The falls descend 948 m (3,110 ft) in a series of five drops from a high plateau in the Drakensberg Mountains. Their name is a phonetic spelling of the Zulu word "Thukela", which means "startling" – a reference to the Tugela River's sudden drop from a huge escarpment.

◄ Tallest (single drop)

Most sources regard Angel Falls (known locally as Kerepakupai Merú) in eastern Venezuela as the tallest continuous waterfall. Based on a 1949 survey, it has a total drop of 979 m (3,212 ft). Most of this height is accounted for by what is widely accepted as the **longest single-drop waterfall** (left), plunging 807 m (2,648 ft) from a tepui (table-top mountain) called Auyán-tepui.

ISLANDS

Largest continental island
Australia draws mixed views as to whether it should be classified as an island or a continent (see p.32). It is, in fact, the largest continental island in the world, and is unique in the definition as it has tectonic independence from other tectonic plates and possesses its own distinct species of flora and fauna. With a total land area, excluding offshore islands and territories, of 7,692,024 km² (2,969,907 sq mi), Australia is more than three times the size of Greenland, the **largest island** (see below right).

Largest sand island
Fraser Island stretches for 120 km (75 mi) along the coast of the Australian state of Queensland and covers a total area of 1,840 km² (720 sq mi). It is formed from vast sand deposits that can reach heights of up to 240 m (787 ft) above sea level.

Largest uninhabited island
Devon Island is part of the Canadian archipelago in the Arctic Circle, and lies to the north of Baffin Island (the world's fifth largest island). It has an area of around 55,247 km² (21,331 sq mi). A third of the island is covered with ice while the rest is mostly barren, with glacial meltwater gullies and lakes.

Oldest island
Madagascar, in the Indian Ocean, became an island 80–100 million years ago, when it split off from the Indian subcontinent. An area of 587,041 km² (226,657 sq mi) makes it the fourth-largest island in the world.

Largest raised coral atoll
A raised coral atoll is an island that forms as a normal coral atoll, only to be uplifted by tectonic forces. The largest of these is Lifou Island, which forms part of French New Caledonia in the south-west Pacific Ocean. It measures 1,207 km² (466 sq mi) in area and is the most populous of the Loyalty Islands, with around 9,000 inhabitants as of 2014.

Most islands within an atoll
Huvadhu Atoll, located in the Maldives in the Indian Ocean, covers an area of around 2,900 km² (1,120 sq mi) and contains some 255 islands within its boundary.

Longest barrier island
Formed by wave and current action, barrier islands are narrow and run parallel to mainline coastlines. Padre Island in the Gulf of Mexico, off the coastline of the US state of Texas, measures around 182 km (113 mi) in length.

Tallest island in a lake
Isla Ometepe is an island formed by two volcanoes (Volcán Maderas and Volcán Concepción) on Nicaragua's Lake Nicaragua. The higher of the two volcanoes, Concepción, rises to a height of 1,610 m (5,282 ft) above sea level, making it the tallest island in a lake on Earth.

Most remote inhabited island
Tristan da Cunha (A on map below) lies 2,435 km (1,315 nautical mi) to the south-west of the island of St Helena in the South Atlantic. In 1961, owing to volcanic activity Tristan's inhabitants were evacuated – 198 returned in Nov 1963. It has an area of 98 km² (38 sq mi).

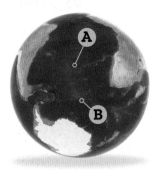

Remotest island
Discovered in the South Atlantic by explorer Jean-Baptiste Bouvet de Lozier on 1 Jan 1739, Bouvet Island (B above) is an uninhabited Norwegian dependency. It lies around 2,600 km (1,404 nautical mi) from the nearest inhabited place – Tristan de Cunha.

Most islands for an archipelago
The Archipelago Sea lies within Finnish territorial waters in the Baltic Sea and contains around 40,000 separate islands. It includes the Åland Islands, an autonomous and Swedish-speaking region of Finland. The archipelago is still gradually rising in the water following the end of the last Ice Age: a process known as "post-glacial rebound".

Lowest island
Situated within Āfrēra Ye'ch'ew lake in Ethiopia, the island of Āfrēra Desēt sits at 103 m (338 ft) below sea level.

The **lowest lake on a sea-level island** is Lake Enriquillo, which lies around 46 m (151 ft) below sea level in a rift valley in the south of the Dominican Republic.

The **highest islands** are located in the Orba Co lake in Tibet, which lies at 17,090 ft (5,209 m) above sea level.

Largest island
Discounting Australia (see above left), the largest island in the world is Greenland, with an area of about 840,000 sq mi (2,175,600 km²). Most of the island is situated north of the Arctic Circle, buried in a permanent ice cap that measures as much as 3 km (1.8 mi) thick. Its coastline is shaped by hundreds of glacial fjords.

RECURSIVE LAKE ISLANDS

The formation of lake islands is due to a number of causes: a build-up of sedimentation, earthquakes, volcanic activity or shoreline erosions.
But when lake islands have their own lakes – and their own islands in turn – things start to get really complicated! Check out our head-spinning list of the largest lakes and islands contained within them. (Diagrams not to scale.)

Largest island
Greenland (see above right) has an area of 840,000 sq mi (2,175,600 km²) – more than three times the size of the US state of Texas. As of 2017, it had a population of around 56,000, ranking it 207th out of 233 countries on Earth.

Largest lake
Situated on the border of south-eastern Europe and the Asian continent, the Caspian Sea is the world's largest inland body of water. It has a total coastline of 7,000 km (4,350 mi) and a surface area of 371,000 km² (143,243 sq mi).

Largest island in a lake
Manitoulin Island, in the Canadian section of Lake Huron, measures 2,766 km² (1,068 sq mi). The 174th largest island in the world, it has four major rivers and 108 freshwater lakes, some of which have their own islands.

Largest lake on an island
A freshwater lake located on Baffin Island, in the Canadian territory of Nunavut, Nettilling Lake measures 5,542 km² (2,140 sq mi) in area. Frozen for long periods of the year, it is home to ring seals and three species of fish.

Top five islands by area
1. Greenland – 2,175,600 km² (840,000 sq mi)
2. New Guinea – 785,753 km² (303,381 sq mi)
3. Borneo – 748,168 km² (288,869 sq mi)
4. Madagascar – 587,041 km² (226,657 sq mi)
5. Baffin Island – 503,944 km² (194,574 sq mi)

Hidden away in the Icelandic Highlands, Lake Langisjór was officially discovered in the late 19th century. It is 20 km (12 mi) long and just 2 km (1.2 mi) wide – hence its name, which translates as "Long Sea".

Largest island created by volcanic eruptions

Measuring 103,000 km² (39,768 sq mi), Iceland was formed about 70 million years ago from volcanic eruptions on the Mid-Atlantic Ridge, a seam under the North Atlantic Ocean where the Eurasian and North American tectonic plates meet. Molten lava poured to the surface and began to cool (artist's impression inset), creating land. There are 35 active volcanoes on Iceland – among the most feared are Hekla and Katla, known as the "Angry Sisters".

Youngest island

Surtsey, off the south coast of Iceland, formed on 14 Nov 1963 when the new land created by an undersea volcano finally breached the ocean surface. By 1967, Surtsey had grown to around 1 sq mi (2.7 km²), although it is gradually shrinking owing to erosion.

Largest island in a lake on an island

The island of Samosir, situated in Lake Toba on Sumatra, Indonesia, has an area of 630 km² (243 sq mi). It is a volcanic island, formed by an erupting supervolcano around 75,000 years ago.

Largest lake on an island in a lake

Manitou Lake has an area of 106 km² (41 sq mi) and is located on Canada's Manitoulin Island, the world's **largest island in a lake** (see left). The lake itself contains a number of islands.

Largest island in a lake on an island in a lake

Treasure Island (or Mindemoya Island) is 1.4 km (0.87 mi) in length and has an area of 0.4 km² (0.15 sq mi). It is found on Lake Mindemoya, on Manitoulin Island in Lake Huron, Canada.

Largest lake on an island in a lake on an island

A nameless 1.5-km² (0.57 sq mi) lake sits on a nameless island within Nettilling Lake on Baffin Island in northern Canada. Nettilling Lake is itself Canada's 11th-largest lake.

Largest island in a lake on an island in a lake on an island

A small islet measuring 0.016 km² (0.006 sq m) lies in a lake on an island within a bigger lake on Canada's Victoria Island. Satellite images have confirmed its size and island status.

BIOMES

Largest biome
The pelagic zone covers the open ocean away from the shore and the seabed, and has a volume of around 1.3 billion km³ (319 million cu mi). This massive biome contains many of the largest animals on Earth, including whales and giant squids.

Largest alpine biome
The Tibetan alpine steppe covers around 875,000 km² (337,839 sq mi). Alpine biomes begin at an altitude of around 10,000 ft (3,048 m) and continue up to the snowline. The harsh conditions have led to an absence of any cold-blooded animals. Plants tend to grow close to the ground because of the wind and cold.

Largest desert
With around 50 mm (2 in) of precipitation per year, Antarctica meets the geographical definition of a desert (see below right). The polar continent has an area of 14 million km² (5.4 million sq mi).

The **largest hot desert** is the Sahara in North Africa, which covers about 9.1 million km² (3.5 million sq mi) and has an east-to-west extent of 5,150 km (3,200 mi).

Largest temperate deciduous forest biome
Temperate deciduous forests lose their leaves each year and receive an average of 30–60 in (76–152 cm) of rainfall annually. The largest example extends for about 1,900 mi (3,057 km) north along the Pacific coast of North America, from San Francisco Bay to Kodiak Island in the Gulf of Alaska. Its total area is around 17,873,700 km² (6,901,074 sq mi).

Greatest mangrove cover by country
According to a report by US scientists Stuart Hamilton and Daniel Casey, Indonesia has the largest area of any country containing mangroves. By analysing data from ecosystem databases, they calculated that, as of 2014, Indonesia had 42,278 km² (16,323 sq mi) of mangrove biome – 25.79% of the global total.

Youngest biome
The Arctic tundra formed only around 10,000 years ago. It is a treeless and windy region encircling the North Pole along the northern coastlines of Russia and Canada, as well as parts of Greenland. Its 48 species of animal include polar bears, foxes, wolves, rodents and caribou.

Deepest marine biome
The hadal zone covers ocean trenches and begins at a depth of around 6,000 m (19,685 ft). This region is characterized by a lack of sunlight and pressures up to 986.9 atmospheres (1.01 tonnes per cm²/ 14,503 psi). Most animals at this depth have evolved to use bioluminescence as a light source.

Largest greenhouse
The Eden Project (see above right), near St Austell in Cornwall, UK, consists of two giant domed biomes. The humid tropics biome covers 25,390 m² (273,295 sq ft) and has a total volume of 415,730 m³ (14.681 million cu ft). The warm temperate biome has 6,540 m² (70,395 sq ft) of floor space and a volume of 85,620 m³ (3.02 million cu ft).

Deepest cold seep
First discovered in the Gulf of Mexico in 1983, cold seeps are an ocean-floor biome sustained by methane- and sulphide-rich fluids seeping from the seabed. The deepest yet discovered lies at a depth of 7,434 m (24,389 ft) in the Japan Trench, off the coast of Japan, in the Pacific Ocean.

Oldest terrestrial biome
Earth's current rainforests have been established for at least a million years. The last Ice Age, which ended around 10,000 years ago, had covered much of the world's forests in ice but left the equatorial forests untouched.

Animals found in the taiga biome include elk, deer, bears, wolverines, rabbits, squirrels and around 32,000 species of insect.

Largest terrestrial biome
The taiga (Russian for "forest") is a boreal, coniferous forest with an area of 16.6 million km² (6.4 million sq mi). It encircles land south of the Arctic tundra biome, covering vast swathes of North America, Russia and Asia. The taiga accounts for around one-third of the world's forested area and is larger than any other major region of desert, tundra or grassland.

BIOMES

The term "biome" refers to communities of plants and animals characterized by their adaptations to a particular environment. Terrestrial biomes are defined by temperature and amount of precipitation, while aquatic biomes are divided into fresh water and marine. Many subdivisions exist in scientific literature. Here are some of the most commonly recognized:

▲ **Marine**
The **largest biome** (see above) covers around 70% of Earth's surface, including estuaries, coral reefs and oceans.

▲ **Freshwater**
Bodies of water with very little salt, such as rivers, lakes, ponds and streams, accounting for some 20% of Earth.

▲ **Temperate grasslands**
Plains and gentle hills where grasses, herbs and flowers grow, such as the US prairies or Argentina's pampas.

▲ **Savanna**
Grasslands that experience very wet and very dry seasons (too dry for forests). Found near the Equator.

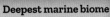

The Eden Project

 Plants: 135,000, from 4,500 species.

 Temperature: 18–35°C (64–95°F), in the humid tropics biome.

 Visitors: 1 million passed through its doors in 2016.

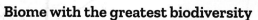 **Height:** the tropics biome is as tall as 11 double-decker buses – and the length of 24.

Biome with the greatest biodiversity

Current-best estimates suggest that as many as 50–75% of all Earth's living species are concentrated in rainforests, which cover around 6–7% of the planet's land.

The **largest tropical rainforest** is the Amazon, which spans nine South American countries and covers between 6.24 and 6.56 million km² (2.4–2.53 million sq mi), depending upon the exact definition. The rainforest represents more than 80% of the Amazon biome, and contains a dazzling array of different animal species (see below).

The biodiversity of terrestrial biomes is mainly due to different species of microbes. Ocean biomes have fewer species but a far higher number of different animal phyla, and thus are more diverse on that level.

Animals of the Amazon

Mammals
The Amazon rainforest is home to many species of monkey, including howlers, spiders, tamarins and capuchins.

Birds
The curl-crested aracari (*Pteroglossus beauharnaesii*) inhabits the south-western zone of the Amazon basin.

Amphibians
The nocturnal Manaus slender-legged tree frog (*Osteocephalus taurinus*) perches in Amazon basin trees and by ponds.

Reptiles
The yellow-spotted Amazon river turtle (*Podocnemis unifilis*) can be sighted in tributaries of the Amazon river.

Insects
The spiny devil katydid (*Panacanthus cuspidatus*) is a predatory insect indigenous to the Amazon basin.

▲ Temperate forest
Wooded areas with moist conditions and four distinct seasons. Home to large, deciduous (leaf-shedding) trees.

▲ Tundra
Very little precipitation, low temperatures, poor soil nutrition and brief growing seasons typify this biome.

▲ Rainforest
Tropical areas occupying 6–7% of the planet, but home to most of the flora and fauna. Produce around 40% of Earth's oxygen.

▲ Taiga/boreal forest
Vast wooded areas in cold climates. Home to conifers, pines and other trees with needles rather than leaves.

▲ Desert
Some 10% of Earth. Defined by annual precipitation – less than 250 mm (9.8 in) – rather than temperature (see above left).

NATURAL DISASTERS

Most powerful earthquake

The Chilean earthquake of 22 May 1960 registered 9.5 on the moment magnitude (M_w) scale. In Chile, it killed more than 2,000 people, injured 3,000 and left some 2 million homeless, with a tsunami (giant wave) that caused great damage and around 200 deaths in Hawaii, Japan and the US west coast.

Deadliest lake

The lake responsible for the most deaths without drowning is Lake Nyos in Cameroon, Central Africa. On the night of 21 Aug 1986, between 1,600 and 1,800 people and countless animals were killed by a large natural release of carbon dioxide gas.

HIGHEST DEATH TOLL CAUSED BY...

Lightning strike (direct)

On 23 Dec 1975, a lightning flash killed 21 people in a hut in Manica Tribal Trust Lands in eastern Rhodesia (now Zimbabwe). The mortality record was confirmed by the World Meteorological Organization (WMO) in May 2017.

The WMO also revealed that on 2 Nov 1994, there were 469 confirmed fatalities in the **highest death toll caused by a lightning strike (indirect)**. During thunderstorms over Dronka in Egypt, a lightning flash had ignited three tanker cars, each holding aircraft or diesel fuel. The railway line under the cars collapsed in a flood, which carried the blazing fuel into the town.

The **highest death toll from an in-flight lightning strike** is 91 people, who died when Peruvian airline LANSA's Flight 508 was hit and crashed into the Amazon rainforest on 24 Dec 1971.

Hailstorm

In May 2017, a WMO committee made public its in-depth investigation of documented mortality records for tropical cyclones, tornadoes, direct and indirect lightning strikes and hailstorms. The report noted that a hailstorm near Moradabad in Uttar Pradesh, India, on 30 Apr 1888 had killed 246 people.

Tornado

On 26 Apr 1989, two towns in Manikganj District in Bangladesh were wiped out by a tornado. This violent storm, with a track of about 1 mi (1.6 km) wide, injured more than 12,000 people and purportedly killed around 1,300 individuals, with as many as 80,000 made homeless, according to the WMO.

Highest earthquake death toll of modern times

At 4:53 p.m. Eastern Standard Time (EST) on 12 Jan 2010, a 7-M_w earthquake struck with an epicentre around 25 km (15.5 mi) west of the Haitian capital Port-au-Prince. Official estimates from the Haitian government one year after the disaster estimated the number of people killed by the quake at 316,000, although other estimates place the death toll at nearer 100,000. Some 1.3 million people were displaced by the earthquake, with 97,294 houses destroyed.

Highest death toll from a tsunami

On 26 Dec 2004, an earthquake with a value of 9 M_w occurred under the Indian Ocean, off the coast of Indonesia. The resulting tsunami inundated the coasts of nine different countries around the Indian Ocean. As of 20 Jan 2005, at least 226,000 people are known to have perished.

Blizzard

From 3 to 9 Feb 1972, a blizzard dropped more than 10 ft (3 m) of snow across parts of rural Iran, ending a four-year drought. Approximately 4,000 people are estimated to have died.

Volcanic eruption

When the Tambora volcano in Sumbawa, Indonesia (then Dutch East Indies), erupted from 5 to 10 Apr 1815, at least 71,000 people were killed.

Tropical cyclone

The WMO's May 2017 study confirmed that the Bangladesh (then East Pakistan) Cyclone, also referred to as the "Great Bhola Cyclone", of 12–13 Nov 1970 had killed an estimated 300,000 people. Most perished in a large storm surge that hit the islands and tidal flats along the shores of the Bay of Bengal.

Earthquake (ever)

The quake that struck China's Shaanxi, Shanxi and Henan provinces on 2 Feb 1556 killed an estimated 830,000 people.

Costliest tropical cyclone

In terms of property damage (not adjusted for inflation), the most costly cyclones are jointly Hurricane Harvey and Hurricane Katrina. Harvey (main picture) hit land on 26 Aug 2017, drifting through central Texas and causing major flooding. A National Oceanic and Atmospheric Administration (NOAA) report of 23 Jan 2018 put the insured losses at $125 bn (£92.6 bn), as of the end of 2017.

Katrina (inset) made landfall on 29 Aug 2005. Winds of 280 km/h (174 mph) ravaged Mississippi, Louisiana and Alabama in particular. The NOAA gauged that it had also caused around $125 bn of damage. Adjusted using the US Consumer Price Index, however, this rises to $161.3 bn (£119.5 bn) in 2017 dollars, making Katrina the **costliest tropical cyclone (inflation-adjusted)**.

THE COST OF A NATURAL DISASTER

▲ Worst damage toll from an ice storm

The North American Ice Storm of 1998 deposited some 5 in (12.7 cm) of freezing rain over much of Quebec and Ontario in Canada, as well as northern New England in the USA. The cost of the damage is thought to have exceeded $4.4 bn (£2.6 bn).

▶ Costliest year for natural disasters

According to a report published by *The Economist* on 31 Mar 2012, and based on figures from insurers Swiss Re, the most expensive year for natural disasters was 2011, with an estimated global loss of $362 bn (£234.2 bn). The worst single event was the Tōhoku earthquake on 11 Mar, the **costliest single natural disaster ever** (see opposite): two-thirds of all the people killed in such events in 2011 died in the Japanese quake and its aftermath. Prior to 2011, the most costly year for natural disasters was 2005, when losses were put at $225 bn (£130.7 bn).

Seen here, a Somali girl carries a water container at the Halabokhad IDP settlement in Galkayo, Somalia, on 20 Jul 2011, when drought in East Africa had given rise to famine and displacement.

As of 2016 – the last year for which complete figures are available – Haiti had suffered the **most fatalities caused by natural disasters per 100,000 inhabitants***. The full top five is as follows:

 Haiti **5.52**

 Fiji **5.12**

 Ecuador **4.19**

 Korea **(DPR) 2.42**

 Zimbabwe **1.72**

*Source: *Annual Disaster Statistical Review 2016: The Numbers and Trends*, from the Centre for Research on the Epidemiology of Disasters (CRED).

With a value of 9.1 M_W, the Tōhoku quake remains the most powerful earthquake to hit Japan and the fourth most powerful quake since modern record-keeping began in 1900.

Costliest natural disaster

According to estimates by *The Economist*, the earthquake and associated tsunami that struck off the Pacific coast of Tōhoku, Japan, on 11 Mar 2011 resulted in an economic loss to the country of $210 bn (£130 bn). Of that total, however, only $35 bn (£21.6 bn) was insured.

◀ The figure in the foreground turns away from what was once his house. It was swept away in the tsunami that struck Kesennuma in Miyagi Prefecture, north Japan, some 400 km (248 mi) north of Tokyo.

▶ Citizens of Natori City in Miyagi Prefecture cycle through the devastation caused by the same earthquake. This photograph was taken nine days after the catastrophic event.

Worst damage toll from a fire disaster

The fire following the earthquake on 18 Apr 1906 in San Francisco, California, USA, cost an estimated $350 m, the equivalent of around $9.22 bn (£6.55 bn) in 2018. The devastating quake registered 7.8 M_W and levelled about 80% of the city. Approximately 3,000 people perished in the disaster.

◀ Worst damage toll from a hailstorm

A massive hailstorm in Munich, Germany, in Jul 1984, which affected around 70,000 homes and destroyed trees, buildings and vehicles, led to insurance costs of $500 m (£378 m). The final bill, which included losses to the economy caused by damage to uninsured buildings and public property, was put at $1 bn (£756.9 m).

Worst damage toll for a snowstorm

Altogether, $5.5 bn (£3.8 bn) worth of damage was caused by a monumental winter storm that traversed the entire east coast of the USA on 11–14 Mar 1993. Approximately 300 people died in the storm, which was described by one meteorologist as "a storm with the heart of a blizzard and the soul of a hurricane".

ROUND-UP

Longest cave system

Mammoth Cave (top) in Kentucky, USA, is a network of linked limestone caves, of which around 640 km (397 mi) has been explored. It took some 25 million years to form, via the weathering action of the Green River and its tributaries.

In Jan 2018, divers confirmed that the 264-km (164-mi) Sistema Sac Actun and the 84-km-long (52-mi) Dos Ojos system in Mexico's Yucatán Peninsula are linked by a previously unexplored channel. This underwater cave complex (above) is 347 km (215.6 mi) long overall, making it the **longest underwater cave system explored**. It is named after the larger of the two systems.

Largest natural gold reserve

The world's oceans contain around 20 million tonnes (22 million US tons) of gold. This is equivalent in value to around 10 times the world's gross domestic product (GDP), as of 2017. However, the concentration of gold in sea water is typically such that one litre of water contains only around 13 billionths of a gram of gold. There are no means of economically extracting gold from sea water, so it will remain in this natural gold reserve unless science can provide a solution.

Largest coral-reef die-off

In 1998, a rise in ocean temperatures saw some 16% of all coral reefs bleach and die. Bleaching is a phenomenon in which damaged reefs shed their symbiotic algae, leaving just the stone-like forms of the coral itself. The 1998 El Niño phenomenon (in which parts of the Pacific Ocean warmed up considerably) probably triggered the event.

Warmest year on record

Overall, the year 2016 was the hottest recorded to date, at 0.83°C (1.49°F) higher than the baseline World Meteorological Organization's (WMO) 1961–90 reference period. This statistic was published by the WMO on 18 Jan 2017.

Highest temperature recorded on Earth

On 13 Sep 2012, the WMO announced that the existing record for the highest temperature – 58°C (136.4°F) at El Azizia in Libya – was invalid, owing to inaccurate

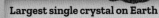

Largest single crystal on Earth

Our planet's inner core is a sphere of mostly iron, some 2,442 km (1,517 mi) across. At 5,000–6,000°C (9,000–10,800°F), it is solid rather than liquid, because of the immense pressures in Earth's interior. Many geologists now believe that this gigantic ball of iron is actually a single crystal, created by differences in the behaviour of seismic waves passing through it in different directions. It is about three-quarters the size of the Moon, and has a mass of around 100 quintillion (1×10^{20}) tonnes.

readings. The declaration came exactly 90 years after it had been established. The official highest temperature is now 56.7°C (134°F), as measured on 10 Jul 1913 at Greenland Ranch in Death Valley, California, USA.

During the Southern Hemisphere winter on 21 Jul 1983, temperatures at Russia's Vostok research station in Antarctica plunged to -89.2°C (-128.6°F), some 54°C (97.2°F) colder than the seasonal average. This is the **lowest temperature ever recorded on Earth**.

As many as four rainbows could be seen at one time during the observations, which included 3,520 time-confirmed photographs.

Longest-lasting rainbow observation

On 30 Nov 2017, a rainbow over Yangmingshan in Chinese Taipei was continuously observed for 8 hr 58 min from the observation decks of the Chinese Culture University (TPE) by members of its Atmospheric Sciences department. It is thought that the phenomenon was caused by the arrival of a seasonal monsoon wind carrying water vapour from the sea.

The celestine crystals that line the walls of this cave are up to 1 ft 6 in (46 cm) across and weigh up to 300 lb (136 kg).

Largest geode

The so-called "Crystal Cave" was discovered in 1897, when the owners of Heineman Winery in Put-in-Bay, Ohio, USA, excavated 40 ft (12.1 m) beneath the property to dig a well. The cave is a single geode (a cavity lined with crystals or minerals) of strontium sulphate ($SrSO_4$), aka celestine. The geode measures approximately 35 ft (10.7 m) at its broadest and is around 10 ft (3 m) high.

added to by a smaller volcanic event around 90 million years ago. Two other south-west Pacific plateaus – the Manihiki and the Hikurangi, which are now separated from the OJP by later ocean basins – are of similar age and composition and are thought to have been formed as a single plateau of lava called the Ontong Java-Manihiki-Hikurangi Plateau. This covered 1% of Earth's surface and comprised 80,000,000 km³ (19,000,000 cubic mi) of basaltic magma.

Largest measured tornado

A tornado with a diameter of 2.6 mi (4.18 km) was measured using Doppler radar by the US National Weather Service on 31 May 2013 in El Reno, Oklahoma, USA.

Most intense rainfall

It can be difficult to produce accurate readings for brief periods of rainfall. That said, the 38.1 mm (1.5 in) of rain that fell in just 1 min at Basse-Terre, Guadeloupe, in the Caribbean on 26 Nov 1970 is widely regarded as the most intense shower ever recorded.

Greatest rainfall in 48 hours

On 15–16 Jun 1995, Cherrapunji in India received 2.493 m (8 ft 2 in) of rain over a two-day period (top), as verified by the WMO. Cherrapunji is a high-altitude town located in the north-east Indian state of Meghalaya. Although its 1,313-m (4,308-ft) elevation contributes to the levels of annual rainfall it experiences, this is by far the most extreme 48-hr period ever recorded.

On 24–27 Feb 2007, Cratère Commerson on Réunion island (above) received total rainfall of 4.936 m (16 ft 2 in) – about as tall as an adult giraffe! This four-day total represents the **greatest rainfall in 96 hours**, as verified by the WMO.

Longest continuously erupting volcano

Mount Stromboli, in the Tyrrhenian Sea off the coast of Italy, has been undergoing continuous volcanic eruptions since at least the 7th century BCE, when its activity was recorded by Greek colonists. Stromboli's regular mild explosions of gas and lava (usually several each hour) have earned it the nickname the "Lighthouse of the Mediterranean".

Largest oceanic lava plateau

During some periods in Earth's history, volcanic magma (molten rock below the surface) has been produced in huge volumes that spread out over large areas of the planet. We have never witnessed one of these events in human history, but evidence for them can be found in huge oceanic lava plateaus. Located in the south-west Pacific Ocean, the Ontong Java Plateau (OJP) was produced around 120 million years ago and

Largest effusive eruption

When streams of runny lava (aka "pāhoehoe") flow from a volcano, rather than violently erupting out of it, it is termed an "effusive eruption". Kīlauea on Hawaii's Big Island (shown) provides a good example: lava has flowed continually from it since 1983. However, it pales in comparison with the largest volumes produced in prehistoric times. Around 64.8 million years ago, a single effusive eruption connected with the Mahabaleshwar–Rajahmundry Traps in Andhra Pradesh, India, is thought to have produced 9,300 km³ (2,231 cubic mi) of pāhoehoe. This is around 3,000–4,000 times more lava than has ever been produced by the current Kīlauea eruption event.

THE WRIGHT FLYER

The "LEGO®-fied" plane you see before you is a slightly truncated version of the original *Wright Flyer**. But all the components are present and correct. In 1892, brothers Orville and Wilbur Wright had opened a bicycle shop in Dayton, Ohio. Repairing as well as selling cycles, they honed their mechanical skills. They also kept up-to-date with the latest experiments in manned flight, such as Otto Lilienthal's work with gliders in Germany.

The Wrights observed the way that birds angled their wings for control in flight. This inspired the brothers' patented "wing warping", whereby the rear edges of an aircraft's wings could be twisted in opposite directions. By late 1902, they had made a glider with a steerable rudder, enabling a pilot to control its flight. The following year saw a new design, with a custom-built gasoline engine and a sprocket bicycle chain to turn the propellers: the *Wright Flyer* (or *Flyer I*). An attempt on 14 Dec 1903, with Wilbur as the pilot, failed. But at 10:35 a.m. on 17 Dec, in the Kill Devil Hills in North Carolina, Orville flew 120 ft (36.5 m) in a flight lasting 12 sec. Three more test flights took place over the next 90 min; the last saw Wilbur airborne for 59 sec, covering 852 ft (259.7 m).

ELEVATOR

The two-wing structure at the front of the aircraft controlled the "pitch" (i.e., the up-and-down angle of the nose). The pilot was able to create more lift (i.e., gain height) by pulling back on the elevator lever (see below).

The wings were covered with muslin to make them smoother and so improve aerodynamic efficiency

Bicycle spoke wire was used as rigging to strengthen the struts

Total length of the Wright Flyer: 21 ft 11 in (6.6 m)

FOR THE RECORD

The **first powered flight** occurred near the Kill Devil Hills in Kitty Hawk, North Carolina, USA, at 10:35 a.m. on 17 Dec 1903, when Orville Wright flew the 9-kW (12-hp) chain-driven *Flyer I* (aka *Wright Flyer*) for 120 ft (36.5 m). He maintained an airspeed of 30 mph (48 km/h), a ground speed of 6.8 mph (10.9 km/h) and an altitude of 8–12 ft (2.4–3.6 m) for about 12 sec. The *Flyer I*, which was constructed by Orville and his brother Wilbur, is now exhibited in the National Air and Space Museum at the Smithsonian Institution in Washington, DC, USA.

ELEVATOR LEVER

The pilot lay flat in a cradle, facing the direction of flight (see above), and controlled the altitude of the aircraft by pulling and pushing a 1-ft (30.5-cm) rod attached by cables to the elevator. By moving his body – and therefore the cradle – the pilot could also reposition the wing tips and rudder. This, in turn, altered the plane's "roll" and "yaw" (twisting), allowing for changes in direction while in the air.

Minifigure and model plane not to scale

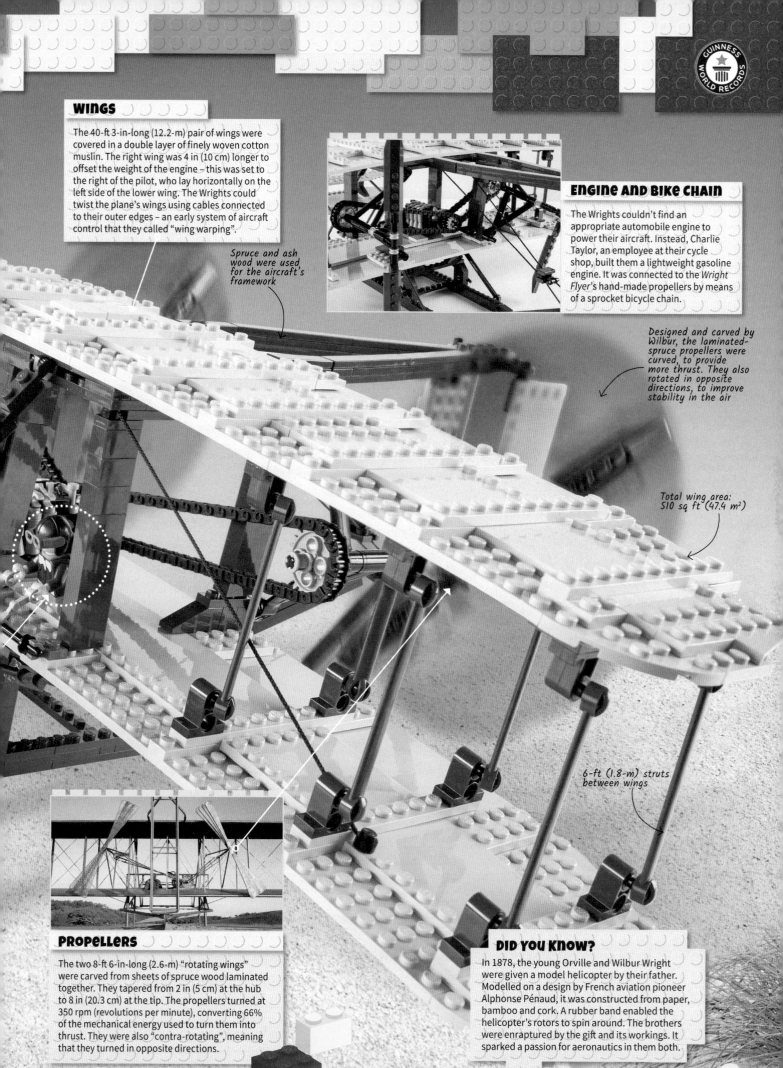

WINGS

The 40-ft 3-in-long (12.2-m) pair of wings were covered in a double layer of finely woven cotton muslin. The right wing was 4 in (10 cm) longer to offset the weight of the engine – this was set to the right of the pilot, who lay horizontally on the left side of the lower wing. The Wrights could twist the plane's wings using cables connected to their outer edges – an early system of aircraft control that they called "wing warping".

Spruce and ash wood were used for the aircraft's framework

ENGINE AND BIKE CHAIN

The Wrights couldn't find an appropriate automobile engine to power their aircraft. Instead, Charlie Taylor, an employee at their cycle shop, built them a lightweight gasoline engine. It was connected to the *Wright Flyer*'s hand-made propellers by means of a sprocket bicycle chain.

Designed and carved by Wilbur, the laminated-spruce propellers were curved, to provide more thrust. They also rotated in opposite directions, to improve stability in the air

Total wing area: 510 sq ft (47.4 m²)

6-ft (1.8-m) struts between wings

PROPELLERS

The two 8-ft 6-in-long (2.6-m) "rotating wings" were carved from sheets of spruce wood laminated together. They tapered from 2 in (5 cm) at the hub to 8 in (20.3 cm) at the tip. The propellers turned at 350 rpm (revolutions per minute), converting 66% of the mechanical energy used to turn them into thrust. They were also "contra-rotating", meaning that they turned in opposite directions.

DID YOU KNOW?

In 1878, the young Orville and Wilbur Wright were given a model helicopter by their father. Modelled on a design by French aviation pioneer Alphonse Pénaud, it was constructed from paper, bamboo and cork. A rubber band enabled the helicopter's rotors to spin around. The brothers were enraptured by the gift and its workings. It sparked a passion for aeronautics in them both.

LIVING PLANET

Greatest insect builder

Mounds built by termites (order Isoptera) in eastern Australia have measured up to 20 ft (6 m) tall and 100 ft (30.5 m) in circumference. These complex structures contain attics, cellars, nurseries and fungus gardens (see below). They are honeycombed with ventilation shafts to regulate temperatures in the brooding chambers and the royal palace, where the queen termite resides. Mounds are made by soldier termites mixing their saliva with particles of sand or clay.

CONTENTS

Termite mounds have complex interiors, with many channels and a central chimney. Air enters the mound via its porous walls. By day, warm air rises up the mound's external "flutes" and sinks down the cooler chimney. At night, the process is reversed. This circulates air and keeps the nest at a comfortable temperature.

100%

Termite nests consist of many galleries separated by thin walls, providing living space, shelter from predators and a site for the insects to cultivate fungal "gardens". The termites eat this fungus, which helps them to decompose the wood and leaves they feed on and so extract nutrients from them. The gardens require a constant temperature, provided by the mounds' complex ventilation systems.

PLANTS

First land plant

Cooksonia appeared approximately 425 million years ago, during the mid-Silurian period. It was a simple plant with a branching stalk that lacked leaves, flowers and roots.

The **first true tree** was the maidenhair (*Ginkgo biloba*) of Zhejiang, China, which first appeared about 160 million years ago, during the Jurassic era.

Deepest plant

Algae were discovered at a depth of 269 m (882 ft) off San Salvador Island in The Bahamas in Oct 1984. The maroon-coloured plants had survived despite the fact that 99.9995% of sunlight had been filtered out by the ocean.

Rarest plant

Only a single specimen of the palm-tree-like cycad *Encephalartos woodii* has ever been found growing wild, in 1895 by John Medley Wood in the Ngoya forest of KwaZulu-Natal, South Africa. It has long since died; others now exist only in botanic gardens and are clones of the original.

Smallest flowering plant

Individual watermeals, an aquatic plant related to duckweed, grow to less than 1 mm long and 0.3 mm wide. They produce a minuscule flower that in turn develops into the **smallest fruit**, weighing about 70 micrograms and measuring 0.25 mm long.

Smelliest plant

Also known as the corpse flower, *Amorphophallus titanum* or titan arum releases an extremely foul odour comparable to that of rotten flesh, which can be smelled 0.5 mi (0.8 km) away.

The same plant boasts the **largest corm** – an underground plant stem that serves as a storage organ. The heaviest example weighed 153.9 kg (339 lb 4 oz).

Largest fungi

An *Armillaria ostoyae*, or honey mushroom fungus, growing in the Malheur National Forest in the Blue Mountains of eastern Oregon, USA, covers 890 ha (2,199 acres). This is roughly the same as 1,220 soccer pitches.

Tallest tree species

Redwoods (genera *Sequoia* and *Sequoiadendron*) and eucalyptuses (genus *Eucalyptus*) have both been recorded growing to heights of more than 113 m (370 ft).

The **tallest living tree** is Hyperion, a coast redwood in Redwood National Park, California, USA. It measured 115.85 m (380 ft 1 in) in 2009.

Most remote tree

A solitary 100-year-old Sitka spruce (*Picea sitchensis*) grows on Campbell Island, New Zealand, where it had been planted by a former governor-general. Its nearest companion is more than 222 km (137.94 mi) away on the Auckland Islands.

Largest meat-eating plant
A giant montane pitcher plant (*Nepenthes rajah*) was measured at 41 cm (16 in) tall on the island of Borneo on 26 Mar 2011. The pitcher uses its fluid-filled trap to capture and drown insects, spiders and even small vertebrates such as frogs and lizards.

Largest single flower
Rafflesia arnoldii has flowers measuring up to 91 cm (3 ft) across and weighing as much as 11 kg (24 lb). Native to south-east Asia, it has no leaves, stem or roots. It grows as a parasite inside jungle vines, from which flower buds burst and expand.

Heaviest organism
A network of quaking aspen trees (*Populus tremuloides*) called "Pando" in the Wasatch Mountains of Utah, USA, grows from a single root system that covers 43 ha (106 acres) – roughly the same size as the Vatican City, the **smallest landlocked country**. The trees (seen from above in the inset) act as a single organism, changing colour in unison.

Largest blossoming plant
Planted in 1892 at Sierra Madre in California, USA, a Chinese wisteria (*Wisteria sinensis*) weighed 220 tonnes (48,500 lb), covered an area of 0.4 ha (1 acre) and had branches measuring 500 ft (152 m) long by 1994. The weighty wisteria produced an estimated 1.5 million blossoms during its five-week blossoming period.

SPEEDY AND SLOW GROWERS

◄ Fastest-growing tree

The empress or foxglove tree (*Paulownia tomentosa*) can grow 6 m (19 ft 8 in) in its first year, and as much as 30 cm (11.8 in) in three weeks. Native to central and western China, and naturalized in the USA, this large species also produces three to four times more oxygen during photosynthesis than any other known species of tree.

Slowest-growing tree

A specimen of the white cedar (*Thuja occidentalis*) located on a cliffside in the Great Lakes region of Canada grew to a height of less than 10.2 cm (4 in) in 155 years – less than twice the size of an average golf tee. The reluctant riser weighed only 17 g (0.5 oz) and averaged a growth rate of 0.11 g (0.003 oz) of wood each year.

► Fastest-growing plant

Certain species of the 45 genera of bamboo have been found to grow up to 91 cm (2 ft 11.8 in) per day, an average of 3.7 cm (1.4 in) every hour. Unusually, bamboo stems or culms emerge from the ground at their full diameter and attain their maximum height in a single growing season of three to four months.

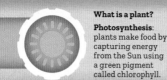

What is a plant?

Photosynthesis: plants make food by capturing energy from the Sun using a green pigment called chlorophyll.

Cells: plant cells possess a distinct nucleus surrounded by a membrane. They are known as eukaryotic cells.

Roots: plants use their root systems to anchor themselves to the ground. They possess limited organs for mobility.

Sugars: plants store the food that they create from photosynthesis (see left) as sugars (pictured) or starches.

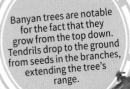

Banyan trees are notable for the fact that they grow from the top down. Tendrils drop to the ground from seeds in the branches, extending the tree's range.

Greatest perimeter length for a tree

Thimmamma Marrimanu, a specimen of the giant banyan tree *Ficus benghalensis* located in Anantapur in Andhra Pradesh, India, has a perimeter circumference measuring 846 m (2,775 ft) – more than the height of the Burj Khalifa, the **tallest building**. The tree, which is thought to be more than 550 years old, has its own dedicated temple where worshippers can pray for fertility.

Captured as a satellite image, Thimmamma Marrimanu looks like a small forest rather than a single tree. It is an epiphyte, i.e., it grows on other trees – hence the banyan's other name: the "strangler fig".

▲ Fastest-growing marine plant
Growing near rocky shores in the Pacific Ocean, giant kelp (*Macrocystis pyrifera*) grows at a speed of up to 34 cm (13.3 in) per day, an average of 1.4 cm (0.5 in) every hour. A single specimen has reached a verified length of 60 m (197 ft). The giant kelp is also the **fastest-growing seaweed**.

Slowest-flowering plant
A rare species of giant bromeliad discovered in the Bolivian mountains in 1870, *Puya raimondii* – also known as queen of the Andes – produces flower clusters after around 80–150 years of its existence. The plant is a monocarp – i.e., upon producing a single immense stalk or panicle bearing numerous flowers, it dies.

▶ Fastest-growing flowering plant
In Jul 1978, a *Hesperoyucca whipplei* planted in Tresco Abbey on the Isles of Scilly, UK, grew 11 ft 11 in (3.63 m) in 14 days – a rate of about 10 in (25.4 cm) per day. Also known as the Spanish bayonet or the Quixote yucca, this plant is native to southern California, USA, and parts of Mexico.

MAMMALS – TERRESTRIAL

First mammal
In 1991, a partial skull of a mammal named *Adelobasileus cromptoni* was discovered in 225-million-year-old rocks in New Mexico, USA. It resembled modern tree shrews.

Largest prehistoric land mammal
Indricotherium (aka *Paraceratherium*) was a long-necked, hornless rhinocerotid that roamed western Asia and Europe c. 35 million years ago. It was an estimated 37 ft (11.27 m) long – the length of a London double-decker bus – and 17 ft 9 in (5.41 m) to the top of its shoulder hump – or around two storeys high. This rhinocerotid did not have horns, but in prehistoric times there were horned rodents, horned armadillos and even horned kangaroos.

Tallest mammal
An adult male giraffe (*Giraffa camelopardalis*) is typically 15–18 ft (4.6–5.5 m) tall. Found in the dry savannah and open woodland areas of sub-Saharan Africa, the giraffe is also the **largest ruminant** (cud-chewing hoofed mammal).

Fastest terrestrial mammal over short distances
The cheetah (*Acinonyx jubatus*) can reach 100 km/h (62 mph) on level ground for brief periods. It is found mostly in eastern and southern Africa and some parts of Asia, including Iran.
   The **fastest terrestrial mammal over long distances** is the pronghorn (*Antilocapra americana*). This antelope-like ungulate, found in North America and parts of Mexico, can travel at 35 mph (56 km/h) for distances of 4 mi (6 km).
   The **slowest mammal** is the three-toed sloth (*Bradypus tridactylus*) of tropical South America. It has an average ground speed of 6–8 ft (1.8–2.4 m) per minute, but in the trees it can accelerate to 15 ft (4.6 m) per minute.

Rarest land mammal
Once widely distributed in south-east Asia, the Javan rhinoceros (*Rhinoceros sondaicus*) has declined to around 60 animals, all confined to the Ujung Kulon National Park in Indonesia.

Most horns on a mammal
Ewes and rams of the rare Jacob sheep typically grow two or four horns, but six are also common. In sheep that have four horns, one pair usually grows vertically, often exceeding 60 cm (2 ft), while the other curls around the side of the head. This "polycerate" (multi-horned) breed is found in the USA and UK.

Largest animal to build a nest
Adult male western gorillas (*Gorilla gorilla*) measure 5 ft 6 in– 6 ft (1.7–1.8 m) tall and weigh 300–500 lb (136–227 kg). Every day, they create a new ground nest from the surrounding vegetation. The nests are circular and have a diameter of up to 1.5 m (4 ft 11 in), making them the **largest mammalian nest**.

Most teeth for a land mammal
The giant armadillo (*Priodontes maximus*) of South America typically has up to 100 teeth. It feeds mostly on ants and termites. Although most mammals do not renew their teeth, those of the pygmy rock wallaby, silvery mole-rat and manatee are continuously replaced.

Largest eyes for a mammal
The Philippine tarsier (*Tarsius syrichta*) is one of the world's smallest primates and lives in the forests of Borneo, Sumatra and the Philippines. Its large, forward-pointing eyes have a diameter of 16 mm (0.6 in) – which would be the equivalent of grapefruit-sized eyes in a human. The tarsier has an overall length of 85–160 mm (3.3–6.3 in).

Newest ape
The Tapanuli orangutan (*Pongo tapanuliensis*) of north-western Sumatra in Indonesia was formally named as a new species on 2 Nov 2017. It was the last mammal to be personally named by eminent anthropologist Prof. Colin Groves, shortly before he passed away.
   On 28 Dec 2017, less than a month after the death of Prof. Groves, a new species was named in his honour. Groves's dwarf lemur (*Cheirogaleus grovesi*) is native to south-eastern Madagascar. As of 29 Jan 2018, it was the **newest species of mammal**.

Largest home range for a terrestrial animal
In a year, the polar bear (*Ursus maritimus*) can typically tramp 30,000 km² (11,580 sq mi) – approximately the size of Belgium – across its Arctic range. Research by the Norwegian Polar Institute, released in Aug 2005, recorded a 74-km (46-mi) swim by a female polar bear from Spitsbergen to Edgeøya island. A home range is defined as the area where animals typically eat, sleep and interact.

MAMMAL GATHERINGS

▼ Largest colony of mammals
The black-tailed prairie dog (*Cynomys ludovicianus*) is found in the western USA and northern Mexico. One prairie-dog colony discovered in 1901 contained about 400 million individuals and was estimated to cover around 61,400 km² (23,705 sq mi) – larger than Croatia.

Greatest concentration of large mammals
One herd of northern fur seals (*Callorhinus ursinus*) breeds mostly on St George and St Paul, two islands in Alaska's Pribilof group with a combined area of 75.1 sq mi (194.5 km²). The group peaked at around 2.5 million animals during the 1950s, although hunting reduced numbers to current levels of just below 1 million.

Longest terrestrial animal migration
The farthest distance travelled by migrating land animals is achieved by Grant's caribou (*Rangifer tarandus granti*), also known as the porcupine caribou. Herds of these animals travel up to 4,800 km (2,982 mi) per year on their way to sheltered wintering grounds. The species is found in Alaska, USA, and Canada's Yukon Territory.

Largest urban bat colony
According to Bat Conservation International, each summer between 750,000 and 1.5 million Mexican free-tailed bats (*Tadarida brasiliensis*) make their home beneath the Ann W Richards Congress Avenue Bridge in Austin, Texas, USA. The colony of bats lives below the bridge's road deck, in gaps between the concrete component structures.

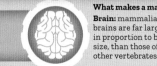

What makes a mammal?
Brain: mammalian brains are far larger, in proportion to body size, than those of other vertebrates.

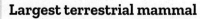

Hair: of all animals, only mammals have hair, although the coverage (and period of cover) varies.

Milk: only mammals produce milk for their offspring, although its composition varies between species.

Temperature: nearly all mammals are warm-blooded and can generate their own body heat.

Largest terrestrial mammal

The adult bull African elephant (*Loxodonta africana*) typically stands 3–3.7 m (9 ft 10 in–12 ft 1 in) at the shoulder and weighs 4–7 tonnes (8,800–15,400 lb).

The brain of a fully grown male African elephant can weigh 5.4 kg (11 lb 14.4 oz) – the **heaviest brain of any terrestrial mammal**. Only the brains of the largest whales are heavier.

African elephants have larger ears than Asian elephants (*Elephas maximus*). Male *and* female African elephants can grow tusks, but female Asian elephants cannot. In fact, Asian elephants are more closely related to the extinct woolly mammoths than to African elephants.

LIVING PLANET

Smallest mammal

The Kitti's hog-nosed bat (*Craseonycteris thonglongyai*) is no larger than a large bumblebee. It has a head–body length of 29–33 mm (1.14–1.29 in), a wingspan of 130–145 mm (5.1–5.7 in) and a weight of 1.7–2 g (0.05–0.07 oz). The tiny bat is found in a few limestone caves on the Khwae Noi River in Kanchanaburi Province, south-west Thailand, and in Burma.

100%

◄ Largest gathering of mammals

Every October, 5–10 million straw-coloured fruit bats (*Eidolon helvum*) converge from all over Africa on 1 ha (2.5 acres) of swamp forest in Zambia's Kasanka National Park. During a six-week stay, they make nocturnal trips to feed on wild fruit. By day, they sleep upside down on branches, which often break under their weight. Resting, however, also leaves them vulnerable to predators such as fish eagles.

▲ Largest herd of mammals (ever)

Herds of springbok (*Antidorcas marsupialis*) in their millions crossed the plains of southern Africa in the 19th century. In 1849, a mass springbok migration, or *trekbokke*, took three days to pass through Beaufort West in the Western Cape, South Africa.

MAMMALS – AQUATIC/SEMI-AQUATIC

Longest walrus tusks
Walruses (*Odobenus rosmarus*, above) have tusks that average 50 cm (1 ft 7.6 in) in length. In 1997, however, a pair of tusks from a walrus were discovered at Bristol Bay in Alaska, USA. The right-hand tusk measured 3 ft 1.875 in (96.202 cm) long; the left-hand tusk was exactly 1 in (2.54 cm) shorter.

Largest pinniped
Of the 34 known species of pinniped (seal), the biggest is the southern elephant seal (*Mirounga leonina*) of the sub-Antarctic islands. Bulls average 5 m (16 ft 5 in) in length from the tip of the inflated snout to the tips of the outstretched tail flippers. They have a maximum girth of 3.7 m (12 ft) and weigh 2,000–3,500 kg (4,400–7,720 lb).

Longest-lived mammal species
In 2007, during a whaling hunt off the coast of Alaska, USA, a group of Iñupiat eskimos reeled in four bowhead whales (*Balaena mysticetus*). Embedded in the neck blubber of one was a late-19th-century explosive harpoon. The whale measured 15 m (49 ft), so had probably been 80–100 years old when it was originally harpooned. Based on this, scientists estimated that the specimen was around 211 years of age in 2007.

Deepest dive by a mammal
In 2013, marine scientists carried out a three-month study of eight Cuvier's beaked whales (*Ziphius cavirostris*) off the coast of southern California, USA. They satellite-linked tags to record the whales' dives, the deepest of which was 2,992 m (9,816 ft) – equivalent to more than nine times the height of Paris's Eiffel Tower.
During the same study, one of the whales recorded the **longest dive by a mammal**, lasting 2 hr 17 min 30 sec.

Smallest aquatic mammal
The American water shrew (*Sorex palustris*) is 130–170 mm (5.1–6.6 in) long, of which its tail accounts for 57–89 mm (2.2–3.5 in). It weighs 8–18 g (0.2–0.6 oz). Adult males are larger than females. While diving, it needs to swim continuously, otherwise its extremely light weight would cause it to rise to the surface. It is native to streams and lake fringes in the mountain ranges of the contiguous USA, Alaska and Canada.

Smallest pinniped
The order Pinnipedia contains meat-eating aquatic mammals including seals and walruses. The smallest pinniped is the Galápagos fur seal (*Arctocephalus galapagoensis*). Adult females average 3 ft 11 in (1.2 m) long and weigh about 60 lb (27 kg). Males are usually considerably larger, averaging 4 ft 11 in (1.5 m) in length and weighing around 141 lb (64 kg).

Most dangerous pinniped
The carnivorous leopard seal (*Hydrurga leptonyx*) is the only seal species with a reputation for apparently unprovoked attacks on humans. There are documented cases of leopard seals lunging through cracks in the ice to snap at people's feet and chasing individuals over the ice.

Densest fur
At its densest regions upon the sides and rump, the fur of the sea otter (*Enhydra lutris*) has around 400,000 hairs per cm² (2,600,000 hairs per sq in). Sea otters do not have blubber and rely on this dense, water-resistant fur to trap and generate warmth. Most of the world's sea otter population is found off the coast of Alaska, USA.

Largest otter ever
The Ethiopian bear otter *Enhydriodon dikikae* is estimated by palaeontologists to have weighed around 200 kg (440 lb). Dating back to the Pliocene epoch, approximately 5.3–2.6 million years ago, it is known principally from a single fossilized partial skull discovered in Ethiopia's Afar Valley.

Rarest freshwater mammal
The Sumatran water shrew (*Chimarrogale sumatrana*) is only known from a single, damaged specimen found in Pagar Alam, southern Sumatra, Indonesia. Based on this, the species was formally described and named in 1921. No confirmed sighting of a living specimen has ever been recorded.

Longest mammal migration
The humpback whale (*Megaptera novaeangliae*) migrates up to 8,200 km (5,095 mi) each way when journeying between its warm breeding waters near the Equator and the colder, food-rich waters of the Arctic and Antarctic regions.

Fastest marine animal
On 12 Oct 1958, a bull killer whale (*Orcinus orca*) was timed at 55.5 km/h (34.5 mph) – around three-quarters the average racing speed of a greyhound – in the north-eastern Pacific. Similar speeds have also been reported for the Dall's porpoise (*Phocoenoides dalli*) in short bursts.

BLUE BEHEMOTH

▶ **Largest mammal**
Based on weight, the **largest animal** on Earth is the blue whale (*Balaenoptera musculus*), which grows to around 160 tonnes (352,740 lb). Its average adult length is 24 m (80 ft), although one huge specimen caught in the Southern Ocean on 20 Mar 1947 weighed 190 tonnes (418,878 lb) and was 27.6 m (90 ft 6 in) long. A blue whale's arteries are so wide that a basketball could float through them. It also has the **heaviest tongue**, at approximately 4 tonnes (8,818 lb) – comparable to an adult African elephant (*Loxodonta africana*), and around the same as a newborn blue whale calf.

The animal's small dorsal fin provides one means of identifying the species.

The fleshy tail, or fluke, helps propel the whale forward. Irregularities in their shape can be used to distinguish individuals.

The blue whale's body appears dark blue when submerged, but greyish-blue at the water's surface.

Not all mammals live on land...
Aquatic and semi-aquatic species include (left to right) manatees, beavers, whales, walruses, otters and hippopotamuses.

Largest freshwater mammal

The common hippopotamus (*Hippopotamus amphibius*) typically weighs 1,300–1,500 kg (2,866–3,306 lb), but can reach 3,630 kg (8,000 lb). Adult males grow in size and weight throughout their lives. By contrast, adult females apparently stop growing at around 25 years old. Hippos are native to rivers, lakes and swamps in much of sub-Saharan Africa, emerging only at night to graze.

The common hippopotamus has the **widest gape of any mammal**. It is able to open its jaws to a remarkable 150° – more than 100° greater than the gape that a human can achieve (45°). The common hippo's mouth can accommodate this huge stretch owing to the fact that its jaws are hinged so far back in its skull.

The term "hippopotamus" can be traced back to an ancient Greek term meaning "river horse". These hefty creatures spend around 16 hr each day in the water, which helps them to keep cool under the hot sun. Despite their weight, they're no slouches on land: a hippo can run at around 30 km/h (19 mph). Their rounded form may suggest they are harmless, but that's not so: hippos kill several hundred people every year.

There are two blowholes on the top of the head, via which the whale inhales air at the surface.

The flippers are 3–4 m (9 ft 10 in–13 ft 1 in) long, with white undersides.

In a whale's upper jaw are plates of baleen, which is made from keratin (a protein found in hooves, wool, hair and nails). It uses them to filter out the tiny krill on which it feeds.

Largest heart

The blue whale has a heart larger than that of any other creature. It may grow to the size of a small car and exceed 1,500 lb (680 kg) – the weight of a dairy cow. The aorta is large enough for an adult to crawl through and pumps some 8,520 litres (2,250 US gal) of blood, compared with 4.5 litres (1.2 US gal) in a human being.

BIRDS

First bird

The earliest fossil bird is known from two partial skeletons found in Texas, USA, dating from 220 million years ago. Named *Protoavis texensis* in 1991, this pheasant-sized creature has proved controversial by pushing the age of birds back many millions of years from the previous record – that of *Archaeopteryx lithographica*, a 153-million-year-old crow-sized flier found in Jurassic sediments in Germany. It is still unclear whether *Protoavis* will be accepted as a true bird, however, making *Archaeopteryx* the earliest unambiguous fossil bird – and the **first flying bird**.

Largest bird ever

The elephant bird or vouron patra (*Aepyornis maximus*) from Madagascar became extinct around 1,000 years ago. This ratite (flightless) bird grew to 10–11 ft (3–3.3 m) tall and weighed about 500 kg (1,100 lb). It produced the **largest bird eggs ever**, measuring 13 in (33 cm) long. Their liquid capacity of 8.5 litres (2.25 US gal) is the equivalent of seven ostrich eggs, 183 chicken eggs or more than 12,000 hummingbird eggs!

The **largest living bird** is the North African ostrich (*Struthio camelus camelus*). Males of this ratite subspecies have been measured at 9 ft (2.74 m) tall and 345 lb (156.5 kg) in weight.

Longest migration by a bird

The Arctic tern (*Sterna paradisaea*) migrates farther than any other bird species. It breeds north of the Arctic Circle, then flies south to the Antarctic for the northern winter and back again, a round trip of about 50,000 mi (80,467 km).

By contrast, the **shortest migration by a bird** is that of North America's blue grouse (*Dendragapus obscurus*). In the winter, it inhabits mountainous pine forests. When nesting begins in springtime, it descends just 300 m (984 ft) to deciduous woods in order to feed upon the early crop of seeds and fresh leaves.

Most airborne bird

After leaving the nesting grounds as a youngster, the sooty tern (*Onychoprion fuscatus*) remains aloft for three to 10 years while maturing, settling on water from time to time before returning to land to breed as an adult.

Smelliest bird

Native to Colombia's rainforest, the hoatzin (*Opisthocomus hoazin*) is a bizarre-looking bird – variously classified with the pheasants, cuckoos, turacos, and even in a taxonomic group of its own – that stinks like cow manure. Its odour is believed to derive from its diet of green leaves and unique (for birds) bovine digestive system that involves a kind of foregut fermentation.

Most poisonous bird

The hooded pitohui (*Pitohui dichrous*) of Papua New Guinea is one of very few poisonous birds. In 1990, scientists discovered that its feathers and skin contain the powerful poison homobatrachotoxin, which affects the nerves of its victims.

Largest hummingbird

The giant hummingbird (*Patagona gigas*) is the only member of its genus and weighs 18–24 g (0.63–0.84 oz). It is roughly the same size as a European starling or North American cardinal and is native to much of the extreme western edge of South America, on both sides of the Andes.

100%

Smallest bird

Male bee hummingbirds (*Mellisuga helenae*) of Cuba and the Isle of Youth measure 57 mm (2.24 in) long, slightly larger than a golf tee. Up to half of this length is taken up by the bill and tail. The males of the species weigh 1.6 g (0.056 oz) – lighter than a single average-sized playing card. Females are slightly larger.

100%

Deepest dive by a bird

The greatest depth definitively recorded for any dive by a bird is 534 m (1,752 ft), by a 29-kg (63-lb 14-oz) emperor penguin (*Aptenodytes forsteri*) at Coulman Island in the Ross Sea, Antarctica. It was measured by Prof Gerald Kooyman of the Scripps Institution of Oceanography (USA) in Nov 1993. Kooyman measured almost 16,000 dives from five different birds, the longest of which lasted 15.8 min.

A pelican uses its pouch to drain off any water before swallowing fish. The pouch can hold 11 litres (2.9 US gal) of water at any one time. The pelican can also flutter its pouch in warm weather to cool down.

Longest bill

At 34–47 cm (1 ft 1 in–1 ft 6.5 in), the largest bill is that of the Australian pelican (*Pelecanus conspicillatus*, left). The bill has a hooked tip and fleshy pouch that changes colour during courtship.

The **longest beak in relation to overall body length** is that of the sword-billed hummingbird (*Ensifera ensifera*). The beak measures 10.2 cm (4 in), making it longer than the bird's body provided that the tail is excluded.

BIRD SPEED

▶ Slowest flying bird

The American woodcock (*Scolopax minor*) and the Eurasian woodcock (*Scolopax rusticola*) have both been timed flying at just 8 km/h (5 mph), without stalling, during their courtship displays.

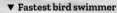

▼ Fastest bird swimmer

The gentoo penguin (*Pygoscelis papua*) has a maximum burst of speed of about 36 km/h (22 mph). By way of comparison, when Usain Bolt set a new world record for the **fastest 100 m** sprint at the 2008 Beijing Olympics in China, his average speed was slightly over 37 km/h (23 mph).

▼ Fastest-running flying bird

The North American roadrunner (*Geococcyx californianus*) is a mainly ground-dwelling species of cuckoo native to the south-western USA. It has been clocked at 42 km/h (26 mph) over a short distance.

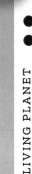

20 cm
Largest bird egg and **smallest bird egg relative to body size** (ostrich)

14 cm
Largest duck egg (white Pekin duck)

12 cm
Largest bird egg relative to body size (brown kiwi)

100%

5.3 cm
Medium-sized hen's egg

1 cm
Smallest bird egg (vervain hummingbird)

Heaviest flying bird

The male kori bustard (*Ardeotis kori*) of South and East Africa can weigh up to 40 lb (18.1 kg) – the weight of the largest confirmed specimen, as documented in 1936. It was shot in South Africa by H T Glynn, who later presented its head and neck to the British Museum in London, UK.

The **largest prehistoric flying bird** was the vulture-like giant teratorn (*Argentavis magnificens*) of 6–8 million years ago. Its wingspan exceeded 6 m (19 ft 8 in) and it weighed c. 80 kg (176 lb).

Highest flying bird

On 29 Nov 1973, a Rüppell's vulture (*Gyps rueppellii*) collided with a commercial aircraft over Abidjan, Ivory Coast, at an altitude of 37,000 ft (11,300 m). Sufficient remains of the bird's feathers were recovered to allow the American Museum of Natural History to make a positive identification of this high flier, which is rarely seen above 20,000 ft (6,100 m).

Largest living bird of prey

Native to the Andes and South America's western coasts, the Andean condor (*Vultur gryphus*) has a wingspan up to 3.2 m (10 ft 6 in). Males, which are heavier than females, can weigh 15 kg (33 lb).

◄ Fastest flightless bird on land

Its powerful legs enable the ostrich (*Struthio camelus*) to reach speeds of 72 km/h (45 mph) when running. Unlike most birds, the ostrich cannot fly.

▶ Fastest bird in level flight

In 2004, French and British researchers reported a mean estimated ground speed of 127 km/h (78.9 mph), sustained for more than 8 hr, by a satellite-tagged grey-headed albatross (*Thalassarche chrysostoma*). It was returning to its nest on Bird Island, South Georgia.

▶ Fastest bird in a dive

The peregrine falcon (*Falco peregrinus*) has been estimated as reaching a terminal velocity of 300 km/h (186 mph) in a dive; at this point, it is the **fastest animal**.

In 2005, "Frightful", a peregrine falcon owned by Ken Franklin (USA), was clocked at 242 mph (389.46 km/h) in a dive after being released from an aircraft at an altitude of 3 mi (4.8 km).

REPTILES

Fastest reptile

The leatherback turtle (*Dermochelys coriacea*) typically swims at speeds of 1.8–10.08 km/h (1.1–6.2 mph), although it can reach 35.28 km/h (21.92 mph) in bursts.

The **fastest reptile on land** is the Costa Rican spiny-tailed iguana (*Ctenosaura similis*), one specimen of which was recorded at 34.6 km/h (21.5 mph). This information was derived from a series of experiments conducted by Prof Raymond Huey from the University of Washington, USA, and colleagues at the University of California, Berkeley, USA, using a specially built lizard racetrack.

The **fastest land snake** is the black mamba (*Dendroaspis polylepis*), which is native to south-eastern tropical Africa. It can reach speeds of 16–19 km/h (10–12 mph) in short bursts over level ground.

Smallest reptile

Three separate species share this title. They are the adult male Madagascan minute leaf chameleon (*Brookesia minima*), Madagascan micro leaf chameleon (*B. micra*) and Mount d'Ambre leaf chameleon (*B. tuberculata*). The full-grown length of all three may be as little as 14 mm (0.5 in) from snout to vent (anus). Females are larger than males.

Oldest reptile fossils

The Joggins Fossil Cliffs are a 15-km-long (9.3-mi) stretch of cliffs on the Bay of Fundy in Canada that represent the richest and most comprehensive record of life in the Carboniferous geological period, c. 354–290 million years ago. It contains fossil remains of 148 species, including *Hylonomus*, which – at around 315 million years old – remains the oldest confirmed reptile on Earth.

The **first aquatic reptile** was *Mesosaurus*, which lived in freshwater areas of present-day South Africa and South America in the early Permian period (298–272 million years ago). Less than 2 m (6 ft 6 in) long at most, it possessed a pair of slender jaws brimming with needle-like teeth, a long tail that was possibly finned and webbed feet.

The **first gliding reptile** was *Coelurosauravus*, which lived some 255 million years ago in the Lopingian epoch of the Upper Permian period. It measured some 40 cm (1 ft 3.7 in) long and looked superficially lizard-like. But its lengthy, flattened body would have been very efficient for gliding purposes, and it possessed a pair of lateral gliding membranes composed of skin stretched across bony rods.

Largest reptile eyes

Based upon estimates derived from studies of fossil remains, palaeontologists consider that the eyeball of one of the largest known ichthyosaurs (or fish-lizards), *Temnodontosaurus*, may have exceeded 300 mm (11.8 in) in diameter. It lived in the deep oceans of what is today Europe (specifically the waters around England, France, Germany and Belgium), during the Early Jurassic period (200–175 million years ago).

Longest lizard

The slender Salvadori's or Papuan monitor (*Varanus salvadorii*) of Papua New Guinea has been reliably measured at 4.75 m (15 ft 7 in) in length. Nearly 70% of this is taken up by the tail. The lizard has a life expectancy of around 15 years.

Longest reptile migration

From 2006 to early 2008, a tagged leatherback sea turtle was tracked by satellite on a 20,558-km (12,774-mi) journey from its nesting site in Papua, Indonesia, to feeding grounds off the coast of the US state of Oregon. In all, the journey took 647 days to complete.

Largest living skink

The Solomon Islands skink (*Corucia zebrata*), also known as the prehensile-tailed or monkey-tailed skink, grows to 81 cm (2 ft 8 in), more than half of which is the tail. This sizeable species occurs on several islands in the Solomon archipelago and feeds upon fruit and vegetables. It is the only member of the genus and is arboreal (tree-living).

Largest chelonian

Turtles, terrapins and tortoises are all commonly described as chelonians. The leatherback turtle averages 6–7 ft (1.83–2.13 m) from the tip of the beak to the end of the tail and 7 ft (2.13 m) across the front flippers. It can weigh as much as 914 kg (2,019 lb).

The **smallest chelonian** is the speckled cape tortoise or speckled padloper (*Homopus signatus*), with a shell 6–9.6 cm (2.3–3.7 in) long. "Padloper" means "road walker" in Afrikaans.

Longest snake

The reticulated python (*Python reticulatus*), which is found in south-east Asia, Indonesia and the Philippines, regularly exceeds 6.25 m (20 ft 6 in) in length, making it also the **longest reptile**. The largest specimen ever recorded measured 10 m (32 ft 9.7 in) – see p.61.

SCALY-SKINNED RECORD-BREAKERS

◄ Largest venomous lizard

In 2009, researchers discovered that a pair of glands in the lower jaw of the Komodo dragon (*Varanus komodoensis*) secrete a venom of different toxic proteins. On average, males grows to 8 ft 6 in (2.59 m) and weigh 175–200 lb (79–91 kg). The Komodo dragon is also the **largest lizard**.

The title of **smallest lizard** is shared by geckos *Sphaerodactylus parthenopion* and *S. ariasae*. Each has an average snout-to-vent length of 16 mm (0.6 in).

▼ Longest venomous snake (species)

Native to India and south-east Asia, the king cobra or hamadryad (*Ophiophagus hannah*) grows to 4 m (13 ft) and weighs about 15 lb (6.8 kg). The **longest venomous snake specimen** on record was captured in Apr 1937 near Port Dickson in Negeri Sembilan, Malaysia. It was put on display at London Zoo, UK, and had attained a length of 5.71 m (18 ft 8 in) by autumn 1939. For the **longest snake ever**, see above right.

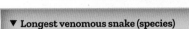

Longest snakes

2.75 m – yellow sea snake (*Hydrophis spiralis*) – **longest sea snake**

4 m – king cobra or hamadryad (*Ophiophagus hannah*) – **longest species of venomous snake**

7.67 m – Medusa, a female reticulated python – **longest snake in captivity**

10 m – reticulated python (*P. reticulatus*) shot in Celebes, Indonesia, in 1912 – **longest snake ever**

This photograph was taken at Crocosaurus Cove in Darwin, Northern Territory, Australia. Visitors have the opportunity to descend into a crocodile pen for 15 min, enclosed within the unsettlingly named Cage of Death.

Heaviest reptile

The saltwater or estuarine crocodile (*Crocodylus porosus*) is found in tropical regions throughout Asia, including India and Indonesia, and the Pacific, including New Guinea and northern Australia. Males may grow up to 1,200 kg (2,645 lb), equivalent to almost 20 adult men, but typically weigh about 408–520 kg (900–1,150 lb). Females are far smaller.

Largest crocodile in captivity (living)

Cassius, an Australian saltwater crocodile, is 5.48 m (17 ft 11.75 in) long. Now an inhabitant of Marineland Crocodile Park on Green Island in Australia, he is seen here being fed by the park's founder, George Craig.

▶ Most venomous lizard

The Gila monster (*Heloderma suspectum*) lives in the south-western USA and north-western Mexico. An LD_{50} value of 0.4 mg/kg has been recorded for its venom when injected intravenously into mice – similar to the toxicity of the venom of the Sumatran spitting cobra (*Naja sumatrana*). The term "LD_{50}" is an abbreviation of "lethal dose, 50%", and represents the dose needed to kill 50% of test animals. The lower the LD_{50} value, the more potent the toxin. The Gila monster's venom is not injected, but seeps into the wound that is created when it bites its victim. Fortunately, human deaths from these species are few, because only relatively small amounts of venom are introduced when the lizard bites.

Most venomous land snake

The inland taipan or small-scaled snake (*Oxyuranus microlepidotus*) is found mainly in Queensland, New South Wales and South Australia. In one strike, it can inject around 60 mg (0.002 oz) of venom, which is toxic enough to kill in excess of 50 average-sized human adults, or 220,000 mice! It has an LD_{50} of around 0.01–03 mg/kg.

Most venomous marine snake

With an LD_{50} of 0.044 mg/kg, the Dubois' sea snake or reef shallows sea snake (*Aipysurus duboisii*) is one of the most venomous snakes in the world. The snake is usually found in shallow waters in coral reef habitats around Papua New Guinea, New Caledonia and the northern, eastern and western coastal areas of Australia.

FISHES

Largest predatory fish

Adult specimens of the rare great white shark (*Carcharodon carcharias*) average 14–15 ft (4.3–4.6 m) in length, and generally weigh 1,150–1,700 lb (520–770 kg). There is plenty of circumstantial evidence to suggest that some great whites grow to more than 20 ft (6 m) long.

Deepest-living fish

Abyssobrotula galatheae, a cusk eel, has been found 8,370 m (27,460 ft) deep in the Puerto Rico Trench. To put that in context, the **deepest point in the sea** – Challenger Deep, within the Mariana Trench in the Pacific Ocean – is 10,994 m (36,070 ft) below sea level.

By contrast, the **highest living fish** is the Tibetan loach (family Cobitidae), which is found at an altitude of 5,200 m (17,060 ft) in the Himalayas.

Smallest fish

The sexually mature adult male *Photocorynus spiniceps* measures 6.2 mm (0.24 in) long and is found in the Atlantic, Pacific and Indian oceans and the Philippine Sea. This species of anglerfish reproduces via sexual parasitism. The male permanently attaches itself to the larger female by biting her back, belly or sides, essentially turning her into a hermaphrodite. It is also the **smallest vertebrate**.

Most venomous fish

Venomous creatures kill their victims by injecting venom into them. *Synanceia horrida*, a species of stonefish found in the tropical waters of the Indo-Pacific, has larger venom glands than any known fish. Just 25 mg of its neurotoxic poison would kill a 70-kg (154-lb) human. Poisonous creatures have poison in their bodies that is passed on when they are eaten, or even touched. The **most poisonous edible fish** is the puffer fish (*Tetraodon* spp.) of the Red Sea and Indo-Pacific region. Its ovaries, eggs, blood, liver, intestines and skin contain the poison tetrodotoxin. A dose of 23.38 mg would prove deadly for a 70-kg human.

Most electric fish

The electric eel or poraquê (*Electrophorus electricus*) is live from head to tail; its electrical apparatus comprises two pairs of longitudinal organs. Up to 6 ft (1.8 m) in length, the eel lives in rivers in Brazil and the Guianas. It stuns prey with shocks of 650 volts.

The **most powerful electric marine fish** is the black torpedo ray (*Torpedo nobiliana*) of the Mediterranean and adjacent parts of the eastern Atlantic. It can discharge 220 volts, yielding up to 1 kW of electricity. As salt water conducts electricity better than fresh water, the ray does not need to create discharges as high as those of the electric eel.

Fish with most eyes

The six-eyed spookfish (*Bathylychnops exilis*) lives 300–3,000 ft (91–914 m) down in the north-eastern Pacific Ocean. A 45-cm-long (1-ft 5-in) pike-like species, it not only has a pair of large, principal eyes, but also a second, smaller pair – known as secondary globes – pointing down within the lower half of its principal eyes. These may help to increase the spookfish's sensitivity to light in its shadowy surroundings. Behind the secondary globes is a third pair of eyes, which divert incoming light into the principal eyes.

Fastest fish

In speed trials at the Long Key Fishing Camp in Florida, USA, a cosmopolitan sailfish (*Istiophorus platypterus*) took out 300 ft (91 m) of line in 3 sec, a velocity of 68 mph (109 km/h). The cheetah, the **fastest land mammal over short distances**, can maintain speeds of c. 100 km/h (62 mph).

Slowest fish

Sea horses' swimming ability is severely limited by a rigid body structure. Some of the smaller species such as the dwarf sea horse (*Hippocampus zosterae*), which reaches a maximum length of only 4.2 cm (1.7 in), probably never attain speeds of more than 0.016 km/h (0.001 mph).

Sea horses are incapable of swimming against the current. To avoid being swept away, they hang on to coral and marine plants with their prehensile tails.

UNDERWATER GIANTS

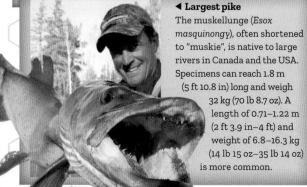

◀ Largest pike

The muskellunge (*Esox masquinongy*), often shortened to "muskie", is native to large rivers in Canada and the USA. Specimens can reach 1.8 m (5 ft 10.8 in) long and weigh 32 kg (70 lb 8.7 oz). A length of 0.71–1.22 m (2 ft 3.9 in–4 ft) and weight of 6.8–16.3 kg (14 lb 15 oz–35 lb 14 oz) is more common.

Largest coelacanths ever

The fossil marine species of the prehistoric genus *Mawsonia* and the fossil marine species *Megalocoelacanthus dobiei* all grew to a length of 3.5–4 m (11 ft 5 in–13 ft 1 in), the largest specimens being roughly the size of a rhinoceros. *Mawsonia* species lived more than 100 million years ago and *Megalocoelacanthus* lived in excess of 65 million years ago.

Largest shark ever

Carcharocles megalodon was c. 16 m (53 ft) long, with a mouth perhaps 2 m (6 ft) wide. Its teeth were serrated and more than 6 in (15.2 cm) long – around twice as large as the teeth of its closest living relative, the great white shark, which is the **largest carnivorous shark** (see above left). It lived during the Pliocene and Miocene epochs some 16–2.6 million years ago.

Largest fish ever

Dating back some 165 million years, the marine fossil species *Leedsichthys problematicus* is thought to have grown to 26–55 ft (7.92–16.76 m). Much of the fish's skeleton would have been cartilage, which did not fossilize. Consequently, no complete specimen has ever been found, and its size must be estimated. It is thought to have been a plankton feeder.

Largest family of fish:
Cyprinidae, the carp family. Contains more than 2,400 species, housed in approximately 220 genera.

Most fertile fish:
the ocean sunfish (*Mola mola*). Ovaries of one female contained 300 million eggs, each about 1.27 mm (0.05 in) long.

Most abundant fish:
the bristlemouth (genus *Cyclothone*). There are thought to be trillions of these tiny oceanic fishes.

Heaviest fish

The elusive whale shark (*Rhincodon typus*) weighs more than any other fish and is also the **largest fish** of all. The greatest confirmed weight for a whale shark is an estimated 21.5 tonnes (47,400 lb) for a specimen captured near Karachi, Pakistan, on 11 Nov 1949. The longest scientifically documented specimen is a female found in the Arabian Sea off Veraval in Gujarat, India, on 8 May 2001; she measured 18.8 m (61 ft 8 in) long. These plankton-feeding giants favour tropical and subtropical waters.

Whale sharks possess the **thickest animal skin**. Typically around 10–14 cm (4–5.5 in), the shark's epidermis has the consistency of rubber and offers it vital protection and insulation.

Heaviest bony fish

Specimens of the ocean sunfish (*Mola mola*) have been recorded with a weight of 2 tonnes (4,400 lb) and measuring 3 m (9 ft 10 in) between fin tips. Sunfish are active in all oceans, both in tropical and temperate climates. They feed on zooplankton, small fishes and algae. Sunfish and oarfish (see below) have a bony skeleton, unlike cartilaginous fish such as sharks and rays.

◄ Largest freshwater fish

The Mekong giant catfish (*Pangasianodon gigas*), mainly of the Mekong River basin in south-east Asia, and *Pangasius sanitwongsei*, principally of the Chao Phraya River basin in Thailand, are both reputed to reach 3 m (9 ft 10.25 in) and weigh 300 kg (660 lb).

Largest fish egg

Perhaps unsurprisingly, the largest fish egg is produced by the **largest fish** – the whale shark (*R. typus*). The greatest specimen on record measured 30.5 x 14 x 8.9 cm (12 x 5.5 x 3.5 in) and contained a live embryo 35 cm (1 ft 1.8 in) long – similar in size to an American football. It was discovered on 29 Jun 1953 by a shrimp trawler fishing in the Gulf of Mexico.

▼ Longest bony fish

The oarfish (*Regalecus glesne*), aka "King of the Herrings", has a worldwide distribution. In c. 1885, a 25-ft-long (7.6-m) specimen weighing 600 lb (272 kg) was caught off Pemaquid Point in Maine, USA. Bony fish (Osteichthyes) account for c. 28,000 fish species. The specimen below was found in 2013 in southern California, USA.

MOLLUSCS

Earliest cephalopods

The ellesmeroceridans are known from certain fossils dating back as far as the Upper Cambrian period, approximately 500 million years ago. They possessed small, slightly curled shells containing several internal chambers arranged in sequence. Cephalopods are a taxonomic class of molluscs that contains squids, octopuses, cuttlefish and extinct forms such as ammonites and belemnites.

Largest ammonite

An incomplete fossil shell of the ammonite *Parapuzosia seppenradensis* discovered in Germany in 1895 measured 1.95 m (6 ft 4 in) across, with the complete shell estimated at around 2.55 m (8 ft 4 in).

Longest-lived mollusc

A quahog clam (*Arctica islandica*) dredged up in 2006 by researchers from the School of Ocean Sciences at Bangor University (UK) is now thought to have been 507 years old – around 100 years older than originally estimated. Sclerochronologists established its age by counting annual growth rings on the shell's exterior, before confirming using the carbon-14 dating method. The clam was nicknamed "Ming", in honour of the Chinese dynasty in power when it was born.

Deepest octopus

The dumbo octopus (*Grimpoteuthis*) lives at depths as low as 16,000 ft (4,865 m), close to the ocean floor. Its soft, semi-gelatinous body is able to resist the great pressure found here.

Largest sea slug

The black sea hare or California black sea hare (*Aplysia vaccaria*) has been known to grow to 99 cm (3 ft 3 in) in length and weigh nearly 14 kg (30 lb 14 oz).

Largest abalone

The red abalone (*Haliotis rufescens*) can attain a maximum shell length of 31 cm (1 ft). It occurs from British Columbia in Canada to Baja California in Mexico, inhabiting rocky creviced areas containing the kelp upon which it feeds.

Smallest species of squid

Currently known only from two specimens, *Parateuthis tunicata* was collected by the German South Polar Expedition of 1901–03. The larger of the two specimens measured 1.27 cm (0.5 in) in length, including its tentacles.

Most venomous mollusc

Found off the coasts of Australia and parts of south-east Asia, the blue-ringed octopus species *Hapalochlaena maculosa* and *H. lunulata* carry a neurotoxic venom that can kill victims within minutes of being bitten. Each octopus is estimated to carry sufficient venom to paralyse 10 adult humans.

Largest clam
Found on Indo-Pacific coral reefs, the marine giant clam (*Tridacna gigas*) is the largest of all existing bivalve shells. A specimen measuring 115 cm (3 ft 9.2 in) long and weighing 333 kg (734 lb) was collected off Ishigaki Island, Japan, in 1956 and scientifically examined in Aug 1984.

Largest cuttlefish
The giant cuttlefish (*Sepia apama*) can grow to 1 m (3 ft) in total length with a 50-cm (1-ft 7.6-in) mantle. Occurring along the south-eastern coast of Australia, it lives as deep as 100 m (328 ft), favouring rocky coral reefs, seagrass beds and the seafloor. It can weigh more than 10.5 kg (23 lb).

Largest cowry
The Atlantic deer cowry (*Macrocypraea cervus*) can attain a total length of 19.05 cm (7.5 in). The marine sea snail is most widely distributed in the tropical Atlantic Ocean, especially the Caribbean Sea. As an adult, the cowry's shell is pale brown in colour, dappled with distinctive white spots (see left) similar to those on a young deer hide, hence its name. These spots are lacking in juveniles.

Largest land snail
The largest known land gastropod is the African giant snail (*Achatina achatina*). In Dec 1978, the largest recorded specimen measured 39.3 cm (1 ft 3.5 in) from snout to tail when fully extended, with a shell length of 27.3 cm (10.75 in). It weighed 900 g (2 lb). Named Gee Geronimo, it was collected in Sierra Leone in Jun 1976 and owned by Christoper Hudson of Hove in East Sussex, UK.

SUPER-SIZED SQUIDS

▶ **Heaviest colossal squid**
An adult male colossal squid (*Mesonychoteuthis hamiltoni*) weighing around 450 kg (990 lb) and measuring 10 m (33 ft) long was caught by fishermen in the Ross Sea of Antarctica. It was taken to New Zealand for research, and the catch was announced on 22 Feb 2007. Despite their vast size, colossal squids – and their close relatives, the giant squid – are strangely elusive creatures, rarely captured alive or even on film.

The underside of each tentacle bears hundreds of chitin-lined suction cups.

In 1996, a giant squid caught off the coast of New Zealand was displayed in Wellington. In 2002, seven juveniles became the **first capture of living giant squids**, also off New Zealand.

Squids possess two tentacles even longer than their eight arms.

Each tentacle is divided into three regions: carpus, manus and dactylus.

Molluscs
Three notable extant classes of molluscs are bivalves (clams, mussels and oysters),
gastropods (snails and slugs) and cephalopods (octopuses, squids and cuttlefish).

Largest octopus

A live specimen of the Pacific giant octopus (*Enteroctopus
dofleini*) measured almost 4 m (13 ft 1 in) long and weighed
71 kg (156 lb 8 oz), although there are records of an even
larger specimen with a tentacle span of 9.6 m (31 ft 6 in) and
an estimated weight of 600 lb (272 kg). These underwater
behemoths snare their prey – other molluscs,
fish and lobsters – with suckers that
measure up to 6.4 cm (2.5 in) and can
support a weight of 16 kg (35 lb).

*The Pacific giant octopus is found
in the cold waters of the North Pacific,
off the west coast of America and
Canada, and the east coast of Korea
and Japan. It only lives to around
four years old, with both males and
females dying soon after breeding.*

Giant and colossal squids have the
largest eye of any animal – up to
40 cm (1 ft 3.75 in) in diameter.

The fin (or wing) projects out
from the squid's mantle and
aids locomotion.

The squid moves by pulling water into its
mantle cavity and out through a fleshy,
tube-like structure called a siphon.

CRUSTACEANS & MYRIAPODS

Oldest land animal

The fossil of a 1-cm-long (0.39-in) myriapod found near Stonehaven, UK, by bus driver and amateur palaeontologist Mike Newman (UK) is thought to be 428 million years old and the earliest evidence of a creature living on land rather than in the sea. Formally named *Pneumodesmus newmani* in 2004, it had spiracles – air-breathing structures on the outside of its body.

Most heat-tolerant animal

Tardigrades or water bears are a group of tiny, near-indestructible animals that can survive temperatures exceeding 150°C (302°F). They are able to halt their metabolism in challenging environments. These 1-mm-long (0.04-in) invertebrates have even survived in outer space.

Deepest-living crustacean

In Nov 1980, live amphipods were taken from 10,500 m (34,450 ft) down in the Challenger Deep (Mariana Trench), in the west Pacific Ocean, by the US research vessel *Thomas Washington*. Amphipods are shrimp-like animals.

First known venomous crustacean

Xibalbanus tulumensis is a blind crustacean that inhabits underwater caves in the Caribbean, off Mexico's Yucatán Peninsula, and feeds upon other crustaceans. Its front claws inject into its prey a toxin similar to rattlesnake venom that breaks down the victim's internal body tissues, turning it into liquid that the *X. tulumensis* then sucks up and ingests.

Furriest crustacean

The yeti lobster (*Kiwa hirsuta*) lives on hydrothermal vents on the seafloor in the South Pacific Ocean. Its long claws and shorter thoracic limbs are covered in long, silky, blond-coloured filaments called setae. These distinctive hair-like structures are intertwined with bacteria.

Most abundant animal types

Copepods are crustaceans that live in almost every aquatic environment. They include more than 12,000 species and, with krill, represent the most important zooplankton. Their groups can number a trillion individuals. Most copepods are very small, measuring less than 1 mm (0.04 in) long.

Fastest-swimming crustacean

Henslow's swimming crab (*Polybius henslowii*) has been timed at 1.3 m/s (4.26 ft/s) in captivity. It is likely that it can swim even faster under natural conditions in the wild, however.

The **fastest-moving crustaceans on land** are the tropical ghost crabs of the genus *Ocypode*. Named for their nocturnality and often pale colouration, they have been timed at speeds of up to 4 m/s (13.12 ft/s).

Longest marine crustacean

The taka-ashi-gani or giant spider crab (*Macrocheira kaempferi*) is found off the south-eastern coast of Japan. It has an average body size of 10 x 12 in (25.4 x 30.5 cm) and a leg span of 8–9 ft (2.43–2.74 m). The largest specimen ever found had a leg span of 12 ft 1.5 in (3.69 m) – around the same length as a tiger shark – and weighed 41 lb (18.6 kg).

First barnacle

The fossil species deemed by many palaeontologists to be the earliest-known barnacle is *Priscansermarinus barnetti*. Specimens found in the Middle Cambrian Burgess Shale of British Columbia in Canada have been estimated to be 509–497 million years old. Discovered in 1975, *P. barnetti* was probably a species of stalked or lepadomorph barnacle.

The **largest barnacle** is the giant acorn barnacle (*Balanus nubilus*), reaching 12.7 cm (5 in) high – about two-and-a-half times the height of a golf tee – and 7 cm (2.76 in) across.

AMAZING MYRIAPODS

◀ Most venomous centipede

Known by a variety of names including the Vietnamese centipede, *Scolopendra subspinipes* is an aggressive predator that injects venom via a modified pair of front limbs. This venom contains an ingredient scientists call "Ssm Spooky Toxin", and has an LD_{50} of 130 mg/kg. It enables the centipede to kill animals 15 times its own size.

Most legs of any animal

Centipedes do not have 100 legs and millipedes do not have 1,000, but millipedes do have more legs than centipedes. They have two pairs per body segment, whereas centipedes have just one pair. Millipedes have about 300 pairs of legs, but a millipede formally named *Illacme plenipes* and found in California, USA, has 375 pairs (750 legs).

▼ Largest millipede

The average length of the African giant black millipede (*Archispirostreptus gigas*) is 16–28 cm (6.2–11 in). However, the **largest millipede specimen** ever recorded was an adult named Millie, owned by Jim Klinger (USA), which measured 38.7 cm (1 ft 3.2 in) long, with a circumference of 6.7 cm (2.6 in) and a total of 256 legs.

Crustaceans
Comprising mostly aquatic creatures, the class Crustacea includes lobsters, crabs, barnacles, shrimp and woodlice.

Myriapods
Mostly terrestrial, myriapods include centipedes and millipedes. Like crustaceans, they are arthropods, with an outer skeleton, pairs of jointed appendages and a segmented body.

GUINNESS WORLD RECORDS

Heaviest marine crustacean

The American or North Atlantic lobster (*Homarus americanus*) is the weightiest of all sea-living crustaceans. On 11 Feb 1977, a specimen weighing 20.14 kg (44 lb 6 oz) – about two-thirds of the weight of a Dalmatian dog – and measuring 1.06 m (3 ft 6 in) from the end of the tail-fan to the tip of the largest claw was caught off Nova Scotia in Canada.

The **smallest crustacean** (and **smallest arthropod**) is *Stygotantulus stocki*, a tantulocarid, or parasitic crustacean. Only 0.094 mm long, it lives on the exterior of harpacticoid copepods (which are also crustaceans).

Largest crustacean on land
Also the **heaviest crustacean on land**, the robber or coconut crab (*Birgus latro*) lives on Indo-Pacific tropical islands and atolls. Weights of up to 9 lb (4.1 kg) and a leg span of up to 1 m (3 ft 3 in) have been recorded, although they average around 2.5 kg (5 lb 8 oz) and 3 ft (91 cm).

Largest freshwater crustacean
Native to small streams in Tasmania, the Tasmanian or Gould's giant crayfish (*Astacopsis gouldi*) can grow to 80 cm (2 ft 7.4 in) – longer than Jyoti Amge, the **shortest living woman** – and weigh 5 kg (11 lb). This crayfish is also the **largest freshwater invertebrate** of any kind.

First amphibious centipede
Scolopendra cataracta was formally described and named in May 2016. Native to south-east Asia and some 20 cm (7.8 in) long, this large, venomous, carnivorous species was discovered by Dr George Beccaloni in Thailand in 2001. Unlike all previously known centipedes, it swims powerfully like an eel, via horizontal undulations of its body.

Largest class of myriapods
Diplopoda contains the millipedes, of which approximately 12,000 species have currently been described by science. However, there may be many more still awaiting discovery, with estimates of the total number of millipede species in existence worldwide ranging from 15,000 to 80,000. They exist on all continents except for Antarctica.

▶ Largest centipede
The giant centipede (*Scolopendra gigantea*) of Central and South America is 26 cm (10.2 in) long. Also known as the Peruvian giant yellowleg centipede, it has modified jaws on its head, which can trap and deliver venom to prey such as mice, lizards and frogs.

The **smallest centipede** is Hoffman's dwarf centipede (*Nannarrup hoffmani*). It is 10.3 mm (0.4 in) long and has 41 pairs of legs.

100%

INSECTS & ARACHNIDS

Earliest insect
A fossilized head section of the *Rhyniognatha hirsti* insect – known from the Rhynie chert rock deposits in Aberdeenshire, UK – dates back approximately 410 million years, to the Early Devonian period.

Largest taxonomic order of insects
Coleoptera, the taxonomic order containing the beetles, comprises approximately 40% of all living insect species. This equates to between 350,000 and 400,000 species. Beetles are of almost global distribution, absent only from Antarctica, northern polar regions and marine habitats.

Heaviest insect
A series of male goliath beetles (family Scarabaeidae) of equatorial Africa weighed 70–100 g (2.5–3.5 oz), with lengths of up to 11 cm (4.33 in) from the tips of the small frontal horns to the abdomen's end. The largest species are *Goliathus regius*, *G. meleagris*, *G. goliatus* (=*G. giganteus*) and *G. druryi*.

The **heaviest insect larva** specimen was a full-grown larva of the actaeon beetle *Megasoma actaeon*, bred in Japan in 2009, which weighed 228 g (8 oz). This is almost as heavy as an adult female common rat!

Smallest insect
The "feather-winged" beetles of the family Ptiliidae (or Trichopterygidae) and the taxonomic tribe Nanosellini measure 0.25 mm (0.01 in). Some of these minute insects live inside the spore tubes on the underside of shelf fungi (Polyporaceae).

The **lightest insects** are the male blood-sucking banded louse (*Enderleinellus zonatus*) and the parasitic wasp *Caraphractus cinctus*, which can weigh as little as 0.005 mg, or 5,670,000th of an ounce.

Fastest wing-beat of an insect
The tiny midge of the genus *Forcipomyia* can beat its wings 62,760 times per minute – or 1,046 times per second! This requires a muscular contraction–expansion cycle of 0.00045 sec, the **fastest muscle movement** ever measured.

Fastest arachnid
Inhabiting arid areas of north Africa and the Middle East, solifugids of the genus *Solpuga* have an estimated burst sprint capability of 16 km/h (10 mph). Despite alternative names of camel spider or sun spider, solifugids are not true spiders as they have separate head, thorax and abdomen sections.

Fastest insect on land
A species of Australian tiger beetle named *Cicindela hudsoni* is capable of running at speeds of up to 2.5 m/s (5.6 mph; 9 km/h) – faster than any other insect. At full speed, the beetle's visual system struggles to keep up, which means it has to slow down if it wants to see properly!

Longest insect
Made public in Aug 2017, the longest recorded specimen of the *Phryganistria chinensis* stick insect measured 640 mm (25.19 in) with legs fully outstretched. The specimen – bred at the Insect Museum of West China in Chengdu – is the descendent of the previous record holder, which was discovered on a road during a field inspection in 2014.

Most destructive insect
Native to dry regions of Africa, the Middle East and western Asia, the desert locust (*Schistocerca gregaria*) measures only 4.5–6 cm (1.77–2.36 in) long but can eat its own weight in food every day. Certain weather conditions induce vast swarms to gather and devour almost all vegetation in their path.

Biggest vinegaroon
The giant vinegaroon *Mastigoproctus giganteus* of southern USA and Mexico can grow to 6 cm (2.36 in) in length and weigh up to 12.4 g (0.4 oz). Vinegaroons are arachnids that spray chemicals from their anal glands to ward off predators.

100%

Largest aquatic insect by wingspan
A dobsonfly (*Acanthacorydalis fruhstorferi*) discovered on 12 Jul 2015 in Chengdu in Sichuan Province, China, had a wingspan of 21.6 cm (8.5 in). Dobsonflies are members of the Pterygota subclass of winged insects. Despite the males' fearsome-looking mandibles, they are so large in proportion to the body that they are relatively weak. Their main form of defence is a strong odour they can emit.

SUPER SPIDERS

◄ Heaviest arachnid
A two-year-old specimen of the goliath bird-eating spider *Theraphosa blondi*, bred by Robert Bustard and reared by Brian Burnett (both UK), weighed 170 g (6 oz) – the same as three tennis balls. The heavyweight spider is native to the coastal rainforests of Suriname, Guyana, French Guiana, southern Venezuela and northern Brazil.

Most venomous spider
Just 0.2 mg/kg of venom from the male Sydney funnel-web spider *Atrax robustus* is a lethal dose for primates, including humans. Native to Sydney and its environs in New South Wales, Australia, the spider can be found in moist habitats, under logs or foliage, and also frequents gardens. The female's venom is far less dangerous.

Strongest spider
The California trap-door spider *Bothriocyrtum californicum* can exert a force 38 times its own weight while resisting attempts to open its trapdoor – a silken structure covering the entrance to its underground burrow. This equates to a man trying to keep a door closed while it is being pulled on the other side by a small jet plane!

Highest-living spider
In 1924, a species of jumping spider belonging to the taxonomic family Salticidae was found living at a height of 6,700 m (21,981 ft) on Everest in Nepal. It wasn't until 1975 that the aerodynamic arachnid was formally described and named the Himalayan jumping spider *Euophrys omnisuperstes* – which translates as "highest of all".

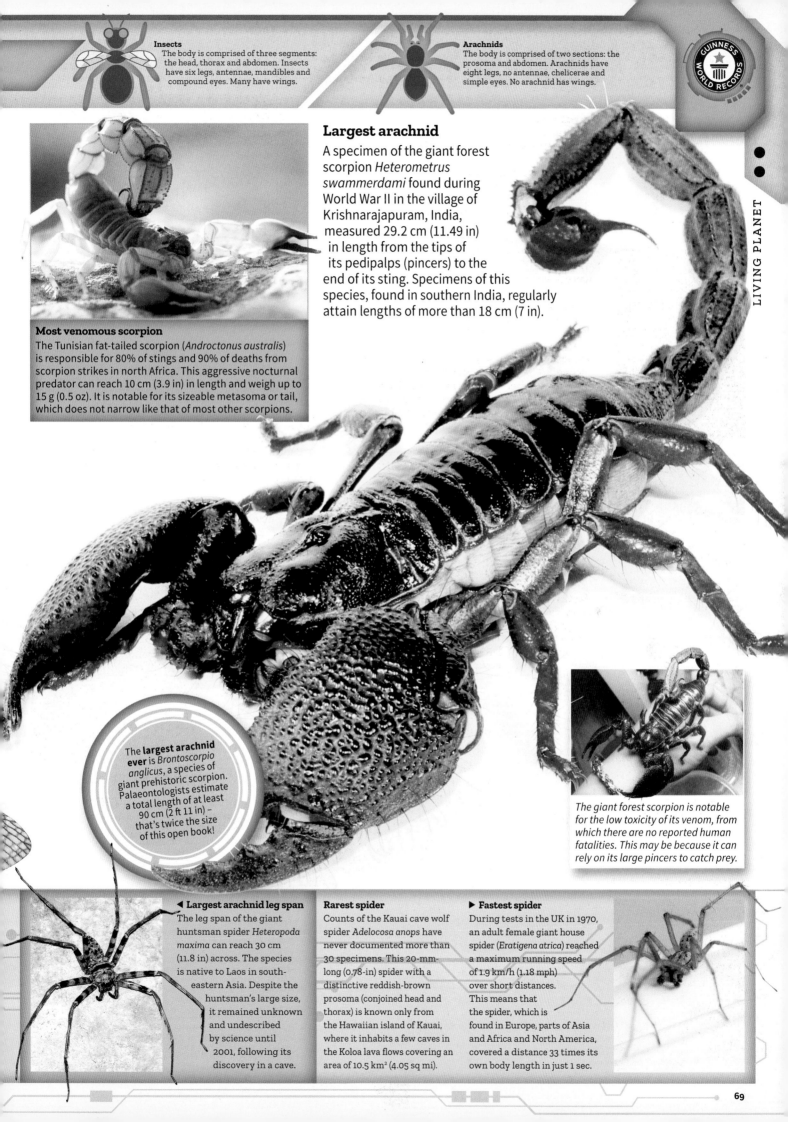

Insects
The body is comprised of three segments: the head, thorax and abdomen. Insects have six legs, antennae, mandibles and compound eyes. Many have wings.

Arachnids
The body is comprised of two sections: the prosoma and abdomen. Arachnids have eight legs, no antennae, chelicerae and simple eyes. No arachnid has wings.

GUINNESS WORLD RECORDS

LIVING PLANET

Largest arachnid

A specimen of the giant forest scorpion *Heterometrus swammerdami* found during World War II in the village of Krishnarajapuram, India, measured 29.2 cm (11.49 in) in length from the tips of its pedipalps (pincers) to the end of its sting. Specimens of this species, found in southern India, regularly attain lengths of more than 18 cm (7 in).

Most venomous scorpion
The Tunisian fat-tailed scorpion (*Androctonus australis*) is responsible for 80% of stings and 90% of deaths from scorpion strikes in north Africa. This aggressive nocturnal predator can reach 10 cm (3.9 in) in length and weigh up to 15 g (0.5 oz). It is notable for its sizeable metasoma or tail, which does not narrow like that of most other scorpions.

The **largest arachnid ever** is *Brontoscorpio anglicus*, a species of giant prehistoric scorpion. Palaeontologists estimate a total length of at least 90 cm (2 ft 11 in) – that's twice the size of this open book!

The giant forest scorpion is notable for the low toxicity of its venom, from which there are no reported human fatalities. This may be because it can rely on its large pincers to catch prey.

◄ Largest arachnid leg span
The leg span of the giant huntsman spider *Heteropoda maxima* can reach 30 cm (11.8 in) across. The species is native to Laos in south-eastern Asia. Despite the huntsman's large size, it remained unknown and undescribed by science until 2001, following its discovery in a cave.

Rarest spider
Counts of the Kauai cave wolf spider *Adelocosa anops* have never documented more than 30 specimens. This 20-mm-long (0.78-in) spider with a distinctive reddish-brown prosoma (conjoined head and thorax) is known only from the Hawaiian island of Kauai, where it inhabits a few caves in the Koloa lava flows covering an area of 10.5 km² (4.05 sq mi).

► Fastest spider
During tests in the UK in 1970, an adult female giant house spider (*Eratigena atrica*) reached a maximum running speed of 1.9 km/h (1.18 mph) over short distances. This means that the spider, which is found in Europe, parts of Asia and Africa and North America, covered a distance 33 times its own body length in just 1 sec.

JELLYFISHES & SPONGES

Largest jellyfish

Most jellyfishes have a bell or body diameter ranging from 2 to 40 cm (0.8 in–1 ft 3.7 in), but some species grow far larger. The largest is the Arctic giant jellyfish (*Cyanea capillata arctica*). An Arctic giant of the north-western Atlantic that washed up in Massachusetts Bay, USA, in 1870 had a bell diameter of 7 ft 6 in (2.28 m) and tentacles stretching 120 ft (36.5 m).

Smallest jellyfish

There are around 16 species of irukandji box jellies. They are predominantly native to Australia's marine waters, especially those off Queensland, but also turn up elsewhere, including Japan, the US state of Florida and occasionally even off the English coast. They sport a bell that can be as little as 5 cm (1.9 in) across and boast a volume as small as 1 cm³ (0.06 cu in). Irukandji box jellies have four tentacles, which may measure only a few centimetres long. Despite their tiny size, however, they are extremely venomous, occasionally having proven fatal to humans. Unlike all other jellyfishes, they bear nematocysts (stinging cells) not only on their tentacles but also on their bell.

Largest box jellyfish

Also the most venomous jellyfish (see below left), the largest species of box jelly is Flecker's sea wasp (*Chironex fleckeri*). It is composed of a cuboidal bell (hence "box" in its common name) with a diameter that can reach 30 cm (11.8 in) and 60 tentacles that may grow to 3 m (9 ft 10 in) long in fully extended form when hunting. Native to the waters off Australia, particularly Queensland, Flecker's sea wasp is one of the most venomous of all creatures.

Largest stalked jellyfish

These creatures are distinguished by a stalk, with which they anchor themselves to surfaces. With a calyx (cup-shaped cavity) diameter of 10 cm (3.9 in) and a height of 3 cm (1.1 in) when living, Janet's stalked jellyfish (*Lucernaria janetae*) is larger than all others of this group. (Preserved specimens shrink.) First discovered in 2003, it was formally described in 2005 and is the only species of stalked jellyfish (or stauromedusan) known from the Pacific Ocean, where it lives in association with hydrothermal vents on the ocean floor. It was named after American marine biologist Dr Janet Voight, in recognition of her commitment to discovering and describing new species of deep-sea invertebrates.

Longest siphonophore

Siphonophores are related to true jellyfishes (scyphozoans). Some, like the Portuguese man o' war (*Physalia physalis*), greatly resemble them and are often mistakenly identified as such, but in reality belong to a separate taxonomic class, Hydrozoa. The longest species is the giant siphonophore (*Praya dubia*), distributed through the European Atlantic and the Gulf of Mexico off California, USA. Following a study conducted in 1987 by the Monterey Bay Aquarium Research Institute in California, it is now known that this serpentine, bioluminescent species can grow longer than 40 m (131 ft).

Most venomous jellyfish

The striking but deadly Flecker's sea wasp or box jellyfish (*C. fleckeri*) is usually found off the coasts of northern Australia. It has enough poison to kill 60 humans, and on average is responsible for one death a year. Symptoms prior to death include vomiting, nausea, diarrhoea, shivering, sweating, and aches and pains. The inset above shows sting scars from a box jellyfish encountered in the waters around Queensland, Australia.

Longest-lived jellyfish

The immortal jellyfish (*Turritopsis dohrnii*) is native to the Mediterranean Sea and the waters off Japan. If an adult *T. dohrnii* is threatened, injured or faces an inhospitable environment, it will simply transform back into a polyp and then reproduce asexually, budding off a series of genetically identical specimens that can each then mature into an adult. This cycle can continue indefinitely. Despite its name, this species is not a true jellyfish (scyphozoan) but a hydromedusan (class Hydrozoa).

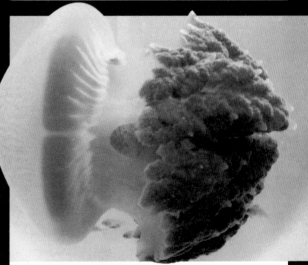

Rarest jellyfish

The Cookii monster (*Crambione cookii*) – a very large, pink and venomous jellyfish – was seen and sketched by American scientist Alfred Gainsborough Mayor in the sea off Cooktown in Queensland, Australia, in 1910. It was not reported again until 2013, when a specimen was spotted and captured off Queensland's Sunshine Coast.

SUPERLATIVE SPONGES

◀ Largest sponge

The barrel-shaped loggerhead sponge (*Spheciospongia vesparium*) measures up to 105 cm (3 ft 5 in) tall and 91 cm (3 ft) in diameter. It is found in the Caribbean and the waters off Florida, USA.

The **smallest sponge** is the widely distributed *Leucosolenia blanca*, which reaches just 3 mm (0.11 in) tall when fully grown.

Longest-lived sponge species

Scolymastra joubini is an Antarctic hexactinellid or glass sponge. It grows very slowly in this region's exceedingly cold waters, and one 2-m-tall (6-ft 6-in) specimen in the Ross Sea had an estimated age of at least 15,000 years. Its extraordinary lifespan makes *S. joubini* one of the oldest animal specimens on Earth.

▼ First reef-building animals

The archaeocyathids were primitive cup-shaped organisms resembling hollow horn corals ("archaeocyathid" translates as "ancient cup"). These constitute the **first sponges** or poriferans. Their reefs (known as bioherms) may have been as deep as 10 m (32 ft). Their fossils date back to the beginning of the Tommotian Age, 525 million years ago.

Jellyfishes
These marine creatures have saucer- or bell-shaped bodies, often transparent, and are fringed with stinging tentacles.

Sponges
Primitive invertebrates with a soft, porous structure and harder skeleton, sponges filter oxygen and nutrients from water currents.

GUINNESS WORLD RECORDS

At 100 ft (30.4 m) or more, the tentacles of the lion's mane jellyfish can be longer than a blue whale. Eight bunches of tentacles (sometimes more than 150 per bunch) surround its mouth.

LIVING PLANET

Heaviest jellyfish

As they are composed almost entirely of water and soft parts, with no heart, blood, skeleton, respiratory organs or brain, it is not readily possible to obtain precise weights for jellyfishes. However, based upon its huge body size, volume and tentacle mass, the lion's mane jellyfish (*Cyanea capillata*) has been estimated to weigh in excess of 1 tonne (2,200 lb). The species is found mainly in the North Atlantic, North Pacific and North Sea, and around southern Australia.

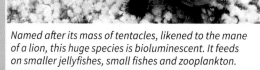

Named after its mass of tentacles, likened to the mane of a lion, this huge species is bioluminescent. It feeds on smaller jellyfishes, small fishes and zooplankton.

▶ **Heaviest sponge**
In 1909, a wool sponge (*Hippospongia canaliculata*) 6 ft (1.83 m) in circumference was collected off The Bahamas. It initially weighed 80–90 lb (36–41 kg), but this fell to 12 lb (5.44 kg) after it had been dried and relieved of all excrescences. It is now preserved in the National Museum of Natural History in Washington, DC, USA.

Largest reef system ever
Around 160 million years ago, during the Late Jurassic period of the Mesozoic Era, the Tethys Ocean was host to a discontinuous system of glass sponge reefs that was around 7,000 km (4,350 mi) long. The Tethys Ocean once existed between the continents Laurasia and Gondwana, before either the Atlantic or Indian oceans began to form.

▶ **First carnivorous sponge**
Asbestopluma hypogea was discovered in Jan 1995 within a shallow-water Mediterranean cave off La Ciotat in France, by researchers from France's Centre d'Océanologie de Marseille. It uses novel tendril-like structures not previously reported in sponges to seize tiny crustaceans swimming nearby. These are then hauled inside its body and digested (pictured).

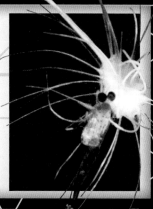

DINOSAURS

They lived millions of years ago and were the largest creatures to ever walk Earth. But just how big were the dinosaurs, and how can we be sure? What can individual bone fragments tell us about the size of these "terrible lizards"?

Spinosaurus
The **largest carnivorous dinosaur** – and probably the **largest land-based predator ever** – was *Spinosaurus*. The analysis of skull fragments suggests that this creature was 17 m (56 ft) long and weighed up to 9 tonnes (19,850 lb).

Tyrannosaurus rex
T. rex may not have been the largest dinosaur, but it did have the **strongest bite for a land animal**. The maximum force generated at the back teeth has been calculated to have reached 57,000 N (12,814 lb/f) – equivalent to the force of a medium-sized elephant sitting on the ground.

Dinosaurs were among our planet's most visibly diverse land animals. They ranged in size from the chicken-sized *Microraptor zhaoianus* – at 39 cm (15.3 in) in length, the **smallest dinosaur** – to the titanic, 100-tonne (220,00-lb) sauropods (see right)… a weight difference of 100,000:1.

Ever since these prehistoric beasts were first identified – the **first scientific description of a dinosaur** was in 1824, when skeletal remains found in Oxfordshire, UK, were classified as belonging to *Megalosaurus bucklandii* – palaeontologists have faced the challenge of estimating these creatures' sizes. It's fine when the remains are more or less complete: the **most complete** *Tyrannosaurus rex*, for example, is "Sue", who was unearthed in 1990 in South Dakota, USA, and found to be 90% complete. But many dinosaurs – such as the longest, *Amphicoelias* (right) – are known from incomplete, fragmentary remains.

Over 2,000 species of non-avian dinosaur have so far been recognized and named, but many are known from just a single bone. In cases such as these, the dinosaurs' total sizes can only be estimated by comparing the size of their bones with those from closely related species known from much more complete skeletal remains.

Argentinosaurus – probably the **heaviest dinosaur** (right) – is known from only a small number of bones found in Argentina

Diplodocus had the **longest tail** of any animal, stretching up to 14 m (46 ft) in length – about three times the length of a London black taxi cab!

Diplodocus
Sauropoda were herbivorous dinosaurs that first appeared in the late Triassic (c. 200 mya) and included the well-known *Diplodocus* (above) and *Brachiosaurus*. There is some debate as to the **longest dinosaur**, but the most likely contender is *Amphicoelias*, estimated at around 60 m (197 ft) – longer than an Olympic swimming pool!

in the early 1990s. One vertebra (neck bone) was 1.59 m (5 ft 3 in) long, indicative of a giant sauropod, so to estimate its final size, palaeontologists compared it with vertebrae in the skeletons of more complete members of the sauropod clade, namely *Saltasaurus* and *Rapetosaurus*. From this, the final weight of *Argentinosaurus* was estimated at 100 tonnes.

Such estimates can be accurate, but problems may sometimes arise. Mongolia's *Therizinosaurus*, for instance, was found with claws measuring up to 3 ft (91 cm) along their outer edge. Estimates of its total body size using only its claw dimensions would suggest an enormous creature. However, partial skeletal remains revealed that its claws were disproportionately long – indeed, the **longest dinosaur claws** (see below) – so caution is always needed when assessing the true size of these megabeasts.

Dinosaurs are not a thing of the past: we continue to make new discoveries that reshape our understanding of these magnificent creatures and how they grew to such epic proportions. The non-avian dinosaurs may have died out 65 million years ago, but they continue to fascinate and intrigue us.

DINOSAUR DEFENCES

▼ Largest armoured dinosaur
Big beasts need big defences, and few dinosaurs had defences as effective as *Ankylosaurus*. This 2.5-m-wide (8-ft) herbivore (the **widest dinosaur**, relative to length) was clad in protective plates, studs and spikes, and wielded a heavy club-like tail.

Longest dinosaur spikes
Loricatosaurus, a herbivorous stegosaur that lived in England during the middle Jurassic, had tail spikes up to 1 m (3 ft 3 in) in length. (They may also have been covered in a horny sheath, making them twice as long as this.) These formidable spikes were probably used as weapons against potential attackers, and may also have served to attract or impress mates.

▶ Longest dinosaur claws
The therizinosaurids ("scythe lizards") had long claws – the purpose of which remains unclear but would have surely helped with defence. In the case of *Therizinosaurus cheloniformis*, the claws measured a record 3 ft (91 cm) along the outer curve (compared with "just" 20 cm (8 in) for *T. rex*).

Argentinosaurus

The **largest-ever land-based animal** was the sauropod dinosaur *Argentinosaurus huinculensis* (pictured). This long-necked, long-tailed, four-legged herbivore lived in the Late Cretaceous period (97–93.5 mya). Some estimates put its weight at 124 tonnes (273,373 lb), but most palaeontologists favour a range of 60–90 tonnes (132,277–198,416 lb). At the very least, that makes it around 10 times heavier than an adult African elephant.

From the tip of its nose to the tip of its tail, *A. huinculensis* was an estimated 30–40 m (98–131 ft) long, making it around twice the length of a bowling alley.

The Naturmuseum Senckenberg in Germany houses a reconstruction of an Argentinosaurus *skeleton. The actual dinosaur's record-breaking weight was estimated in 1994, following a study of its vast vertebrae, one of which was 1.59 m (5 ft 3 in) long.*

Thickest dinosaur skull

Pachycephalosaurus, a dome-headed herbivore that lived during the late Cretaceous, had a 65-cm-long (2-ft) skull with a bone dome measuring 20 cm (8 in) thick. By comparison, an average male skull is around 0.65 cm (0.25 in) thick. *Pachycephalosaurus* may have used head-butting as a last-ditch attempt to deter predators.

◀ Longest dinosaur horns

The paired brow horns borne above the eyes by three genera of ceratopsian or horned dinosaur – the North American *Triceratops* (left), the North American *Torosaurus* and the Mexican *Coahuilaceratops* – measured up to 1.2 m (3 ft 11 in) long. The horns were likely used in defence and in courtship jousting bouts, just as antlers are used by modern-day deer.

The ceratopsids had the **largest dinosaur skulls**; a *Pentaceratops* on display at the Sam Noble Museum of Natural History in Norman, Oklahoma, USA, has a skull measuring 3.2 m (10 ft 6 in) in height – the **largest individual dinosaur skull** on record.

Fastest dinosaur

If the best defence is running away, the most successful dinosaurs would have been the ornithomimosaurs (bird-mimics). The fastest ornithomimosaur was *Gallimimus* ("chicken mimic") of Mongolia, whose light bodies, long legs and slender toes enabled them to cruise for some time at speeds of 40–60 km/h (24–37 mph).

PETS

Oldest dog ever

The greatest reliable age recorded for a dog is 29 years 5 months, for an Australian cattle-dog named Bluey. Owned by Les Hall of Rochester in Victoria, Australia, Bluey was obtained as a puppy in 1910 and worked among cattle and sheep for nearly 20 years before being put to sleep on 14 Nov 1939.

The **oldest cat ever** was Creme Puff, who was born on 3 Aug 1967 and lived until 6 Aug 2005 – an amazing 38 years 3 days! She lived with her owner, Jake Perry, in Austin, Texas, USA.

Oldest rabbit ever

A wild rabbit named Flopsy was caught on 6 Aug 1964 and died 18 years 327 days later at the home of L B Walker of Longford in Tasmania, Australia.

The **oldest guinea pig ever** was Snowball, owned by M A Wall of Bingham in Nottinghamshire, UK. Snowball died on 14 Feb 1979, aged 14 years 10 months 2 weeks.

Most treats balanced on a dog's nose

Husky cross-breed George balanced 29 treats on his nose with handler Dima Yeremenko (UK) for a *GWR LIVE!* record challenge during the London Pet Show at ExCeL London, UK, on 9 May 2015. George is a rescue dog from the RSPCA.

Longest human tunnel travelled through on a skateboard by a cat

On 9 Feb 2017, Bengal feline Boomer propelled himself on a skateboard between the legs of 13 people in Coolangatta, Queensland, Australia. He was under the watchful eye of his owner, animal trainer Robert Dollwet (USA/AUS).

The **longest human tunnel travelled through on a skateboard by a dog** is 33 people, achieved by five-year-old bulldog Dai-chan on the set of *Gyouretsunodekiru Houritsu Soudanjyo* in Chiyoda, Tokyo, Japan, on 17 Sep 2017.

Loudest purr by a domestic cat

On 2 Apr 2015, Merlin purred at 67.8 dB at his home with owner Tracy Westwood (UK) in Torquay, Devon, UK. This is about the same volume as a flushing toilet!

The **loudest bark by a dog** measured 113.1 dB – louder than a revving motorcycle – and was produced by golden retriever Charlie at the "Bark in the Park" event, which took place in Rymill Park in Adelaide, Australia, on 20 Oct 2012.

Most tricks performed by a pig in one minute

Guided by her owner, Dawn Bleeker (USA), mini-pig Joy completed 13 tricks in Newton, Iowa, USA, on 16 Jan 2018. The tricks included sitting, reverse-walking and honking a horn.

Tallest donkey

Romulus, a nine-year-old American Mammoth Jackstock owned by Cara and Phil Yellott of Red Oak, Texas, USA, stood 17 hands (172.7 cm; 5 ft 8 in) tall on 8 Feb 2013.

The **shortest donkey** is KneeHi, a brown jack miniature Mediterranean donkey who measured 64.2 cm (2 ft 1 in) to the withers in Gainesville, Florida, USA, on 26 Jul 2011.

Highest jump by a dog

On 14 Sep 2017, Feather, a two-year-old female greyhound owned by Samantha Valle (USA, see opposite), cleared a jump of 191.7 cm (6 ft 3.5 in) in Frederick, Maryland, USA. Feather smashed the record of 172.7 cm (5 ft 7.9 in), set by Cinderella May a Holly Grey in 2006.

Longest fur on a rabbit

An English Angora rabbit named Franchesca, owned by Betty Chu (USA), had fur 36.5 cm (1 ft 2.37 in) long when measured in Morgan Hill, California, USA, on 17 Aug 2014. This measurement was an average based on various lengths of fur on Franchesca's body.

Most dice stacked on a cat's paw

On 18 Jun 2017, a domestic short-haired cat named Bibi balanced a total of 10 dice on a single steady paw (here, he is pictured with nine). He can also hold up all 13 playing cards in a suit in one paw. A YouTube video of Bibi in action had 37,250 views as of 9 Feb 2018. He lives with his owner Siew Lian Chui (MYS) in Puchong, Selangor, Malaysia.

Tallest cat scratching tree

A cat scratching tree rising 5.93 m (19 ft 5.5 in) was created by Diane Less (USA) at the Angels for Animals shelter in Canfield, Ohio, USA, as verified on 2 Dec 2017. Diane used pipe cleaners to model her design, inspired by saguaro cacti. The tree has 35 branches and is made from steel pipes, plywood and AstroTurf.

REIGNING CATS AND DOGS

◀ Tallest dog living

Freddy, owned by Claire Stoneman (UK), was 1.035 m (3 ft 4.75 in) tall when measured in Leigh-on-Sea, Essex, UK, on 13 Sep 2016. It took GWR Editor-in-Chief Craig Glenday and vet Emma Norris almost a day – and a few of Freddy's favourite liver-flavoured treats – to measure him. The runt of a litter of 13, as a pup Freddy shredded 26 sofas! His favourite meal? A whole roast chicken.

◀ Smallest dog living

A female Chihuahua called Milly measured 9.65 cm (3.8 in) tall on 21 Feb 2013. She is owned by Vanesa Semler of Dorado in Puerto Rico. Born on 1 Dec 2011, Milly was so small that she could fit in a teaspoon, and had to be fed milk every two hours with an eye-dropper. She loves having her picture taken and often sticks out her tiny tongue for the camera.

Pet ownership internationally*

33% dog **23%** cat **12%** fish **6%** bird **6%** other **43%** no pets

Percentage of people living with different pets across 22 countries (multiple answers possible)   *Source: GfK Global Studies*

Most skips by a dog in one minute

Geronimo, a two-year-old female border collie and kelpie cross, achieved 91 skips with her owner Samantha Valle (USA) on 13 May 2012. A New York-based travelling performer, Samantha adopted Geronimo from a facility in Missouri. The dog also enjoys double-dutch skipping and Frisbee.

Spring-heeled Jessica can jump on to a horse's back and also push a shopping trolley. She performs as part of the "CrackerJacks" with another terrier called Jacob.

Most skips by a dog and person in one minute (single rope)

On 1 Dec 2016, Rachael Grylls (UK) and her Jack Russell terrier Jessica skipped over a rope 59 times in 60 sec in Lewdown, Devon, UK. The pair – who have trained together since Jessica was one – regularly perform at animal shows. They spent 15 min a day practising skipping in the hope of eclipsing the existing record of 58. When they beat it by a single skip, Jessica was rewarded with "sausages and lots of hugs".

▶ Shortest domestic cat living

A nine-year-old female Munchkin cat called Lilieput measured 13.34 cm (5.25 in) from the floor to the shoulders on 19 Jul 2013. Lilieput was discovered as a stray by Christel Young of Napa in California, USA. In Aug 2014, she survived the South Napa earthquake.

Longest dog ever

Aicama Zorba of La-Susa, an old English mastiff owned by Chris Eraclides of London, UK, had a nose-to-tail length of 254.4 cm (8 ft 4 in) in Sep 1987. The huge dog, known as Zorba, stood 94 cm (3 ft 1 in) at the shoulder and by Nov 1989 had reached a peak weight of 343 lb (155.5 kg) – roughly the same as five Dalmatian dogs.

▶ Longest domestic cat ever

Mymains Stewart Gilligan – also known as Stewie – was measured at 123 cm (4 ft) long on 28 Aug 2010. He was owned by Robin Hendrickson and Erik Brandsness (USA). Stewie, a Maine Coon, was a therapy cat who frequented a local senior centre. Sadly, he passed away in Jan 2013.

ROUND-UP

Fastest time to pop 100 balloons by a dog
On 9 Apr 2017, Loughren Christmas Star – aka Toby – popped 100 balloons with his teeth and claws in 28.22 sec in Calgary, Alberta, Canada. The whippet, owned by Christie Springs (CAN), celebrated his ninth birthday with a new GWR title.

Earliest example of brood care

Brood care describes when an animal actively looks after its offspring, rather than leaving them to fend for themselves. In 2015, five female specimens of an archaic relative of shrimps and other crustaceans known as *Waptia fieldensis* were uncovered in Canada's Burgess Shale fossil deposits. Each specimen was found to contain a clutch of up to 24 eggs tucked inside its carapace. These eggs contained embryos and were relatively large, each egg measuring at least 2 mm

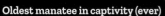

Oldest manatee in captivity (ever)
Born on 21 Jul 1948, Snooty the manatee became a star attraction at the South Florida Museum in Bradenton, Florida, USA. "Baby Snoots" was transferred there in 1949, and went on to greet more than a million visitors. In 1979, he was made Manatee County's official mascot. Sadly, Snooty died on 23 Jul 2017, aged 69 years 2 days.

(0.078 in) – or around one-fortieth the length of the mother (80 mm; 3.15 in). This is an example of a specific type of reproductive strategy known as K selection, in which an animal only produces a small number of offspring but takes care of them for an extended period of time. This makes *Waptia fieldensis* – who existed approximately 508 million years ago, during the mid-Cambrian period – the first-known caring parents.

Earliest modern baboon

A fossilized partial skull of a baboon specimen dating back 2.02–2.36 million years was found at Malapa, near Johannesburg in South Africa, by a team of researchers from the Evolutionary Studies Institute at Wits University. The skull was believed to belong to the present-day species known as the hamadryas or sacred baboon *Papio hamadryas*. The team formally published their research in Aug 2015.

Newest insect order

Formally described and named in 2017, Aethiocarenodea contains only a single, long-extinct species, *Aethiocarenus burmanicus*. It is known from just one tiny specimen, found embedded inside a sample of amber from Myanmar's Hukawng Valley and dating back almost 100 million years. *A. burmanicus* possessed a triangular head, giving it an "E.T.-like" appearance. Uniquely, the longest side occurred at the apex of the head, rather than connecting to its neck.

Largest thaliacean
A member of the Thaliacea class of free-floating filter feeders, the giant fire salp *Pyrostremma spinosum* is in fact a colony composed of thousands of tiny individual organisms known as zooids. They exist together as a "super-organism", a hollow tube that can measure 20–30 m (65–98 ft) in length and more than 1 m (3 ft) in width.

Most carnivorous bat

A large prehistoric species known from fossil remains obtained in France's Quercy Phosphorites Formation, the death-eater *Necromantis adhicaster* dates back approximately 40 million years. Unique among all bats, present and past, were its carnassials – paired upper and lower teeth modified to permit enlarged and often self-sharpening edges to pass by each other in a shearing manner, thus enabling the animal to slice through flesh with ease. Only truly carnivorous mammals possess carnassials, although whether the death-eater killed and devoured live prey or merely scavenged upon already dead carcasses is presently unclear.

Largest population of camels in the wild
Estimated in 2013 at 300,000 individuals – and increasing at roughly 10% per year – the largest population of camels in the wild is in Australia. They are the descendents of camels imported for desert transportation purposes from the 1840s until the early 1900s, whereupon they were released or escaped from captivity.

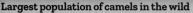

Because it can go for days without eating any food, a Siberian tiger can eat about 100 lb (45 kg) of meat at one sitting – the same as half a kangaroo!

Largest feline carnivore

The male Siberian tiger (*Panthera tigris altaica*) averages 3.15 m (10 ft 4 in) from nose to tail, stands 99–107 cm (3 ft 3 in–3 ft 6 in) to its shoulder and weighs around 265 kg (584 lb). Roaming the birch forests of eastern Russia and parts of China and North Korea, the giant carnivore eats deer, moose, boar and even bears! There are more than 550 individual tigers in existence – a recovery from a low of 20–30 in the 1930s.

Largest triclad worm

An adult specimen of the flatworm *Rimacephalus arecepta* can measure 60 cm (1 ft 11 in) in length. Native to Lake Baikal in Russia – at 5,371 ft (1,637 m), the **deepest lake** – the worm feeds upon the dead and dying specimens of fish that it encounters in the icy waters.

Longest bird of paradise

Adult male specimens of the black sicklebill (*Epimachus fastosus*) measure up to 110 cm (3 ft 7 in) in length. The species is native to mid-mountain forests on the island of New Guinea, and is one of several closely related sicklebills. Like most other birds of paradise, the adult female is smaller than the male and has much plainer plumage.

Deadliest animal

Based on the number of human deaths from the diseases that they transmit – an estimated 725,000 to 1 million every year – *Anopheles* mosquitoes are by far the most lethal animals on Earth. These insects are vectors (carriers/transmitters) of various parasites, which the mosquitoes pass on when feeding on our blood. The most dangerous of these parasites belong to the genus *Plasmodium* and cause malaria.

Rarest swallowtail butterfly

The Ceylon or Sri Lankan rose *Pachliopta* (=*Atrophaneura*) *jophon* is the only species of swallowtail butterfly categorized as Critically Endangered by the IUCN. Its grave state is the result of habitat destruction, and although precise numbers of specimens are not currently confirmed, it is presently confined to the rainforests of the central hill country in south-western Sri Lanka.

Rarest crane

The Siberian crane (*Leucogeranus leucogeranus*) is estimated at roughly 3,000 birds and is categorized as Critically Endangered by the IUCN. Two populations remain – one in the Arctic tundra of eastern Russia, and one in the Arctic tundra of western Russia (of which only 10 or so survive). The eastern population migrates to China for the winter, while the western heads to Iran.

Smallest echinoderm

A member of the Echinoderm phylum of marine invertebrates, the sea cucumber or holothuriid *Psammothuria ganapatii* measures no more than 4 mm (0.15 in) long. It is so small that it exists between individual grains of beach sand on India's Waltair coast, and remained undescribed by science until May 1968. It is so different from all other sea cucumber species that it is housed within its own genus.

Longest tongue on a dog (current)

Mochi, a female St Bernard living in Sioux Falls, South Dakota, USA, has an 18.58-cm-long (7.31-in) tongue, as measured on 25 Aug 2016. She was rescued by owners Carla and Craig Rickert (USA) when she was two years old. Mochi's tongue was measured at the vet clinic while under anaesthesia for dental care.

Wild Things

Take a trip with GWR's *Wild Things* as it tracks down the weirdest and most wonderful wildlife in the record books – from blood-sucking bats to fearsome frogs and the *real* angry birds...

In 2015, April Gould appeared as a contestant on the TV show *American Ninja Warrior*. She was dubbed the "Goat Whisperer".

Fastest time to climb over a human tunnel by a goat

On 30 Jun 2017, Ninja the goat ran along the backs of 25 people forming a human tunnel in 9.40 sec in Gilbert, Arizona, USA. Ninja lives with owner April Gould (USA), a former professional waterskiier who now farms goats and trains them for acrobatic participation in her "goat yoga" classes.

SATURN V

If a malfunction were to take place at launch, this escape system would pull the command module (located beneath it) to safety

DID YOU KNOW?

Despite its size, Saturn V wasn't the **most powerful rocket ever**. That record goes to the former USSR's N1 booster, with a lift-off thrust of around 40,000 kN (9.89 million lbf). It launched on 21 Feb 1969, but never flew successfully. By contrast, the Falcon Heavy, launched on 6 Feb 2018 by SpaceX (USA), had a lift-off thrust of 22,819 kN (5.13 million lbf). It could take a payload of some 64 tonnes (141,096 lb) into low-Earth orbit. See pp.176–77.

The secon[d] powered b[y] J-2 engine[s] hydrogen [and] Its purpose[...] the sp[...]

In Jul 1969, humans first set foot on the Moon as part of NASA's Apollo 11 mission. The rocket that had taken them there was the Saturn V. So successful was it that the same rocket design would be used on all future Apollo missions, the last of which (Apollo 17) took place in Dec 1972. Saturn V would also be employed to launch the USA's first space station, *Skylab*, in 1973.

The third stage had one rocket engine, to put the Apollo spacecraft into Earth orbit. Later it reignited, boosting the craft to an escape velocity of around 10.4 km/sec (6.4 mi/sec) and propelling it towards the Moon

The **largest rocket**, Saturn V stood 110.6 m (363 ft) tall – similar to the height of St Paul's Cathedral in London, UK – and weighed as much as 2,965 tonnes (6.5 million lb) when fully fuelled. It had a lift-off thrust of 33,803 kN (7.6 million lbf), and could boost 118,000 kg (260,145 lb) of payload to low-Earth orbit in around 12 min – the **most powerful rocket by lift capacity (ever)**. Its development was led by German engineer Wernher von Braun, who had designed the Jupiter-C rocket that took the USA's first satellite into orbit in 1958. Work began in 1961, but the first Saturn V wasn't launched until 9 Nov 1967, as part of the Apollo 4 mission. Today, the cost of the project would be around $73 billion (£51 billion).

1 2 3 4 5 6 7

1: APOLLO 11 – FROM EARTH TO THE MOON

1: Lift-off takes place on 16 Jul 1969 at 9:32 a.m. EDT (Eastern Daylight Time).
2: Saturn V has three main sections, or "stages". Around 2 min 41 sec after launch, at an altitude of 42 mi (67 km), the rockets shut down and stage one is cast off. The stage-two rockets kick in at around 2 min 44 sec. Some 33 sec later, the launch escape system atop the rocket is ejected.
3: At around 9 min, the second stage is ejected and the third stage – equipped with one J-2 engine – ignites. It shuts down at 11 min 39 sec into the mission – by which time the craft is in Earth's orbit – but kicks in again at around 2 hr 44 min, to propel the spacecraft out of orbit and towards the Moon.
4–6: Some 4 hr 17 min into the flight, the command-and-service module *Columbia* separates from the third stage, turns 180° and pulls the lunar module *Eagle* away, leaving the third stage to float off.
7: At 100 hr 12 min into the mission, the lunar module undocks from *Columbia*, thereafter to enter the Moon's orbit and descend to the lunar surface, touching down at 4:17 p.m. EDT on 20 Jul 1969.

2: ON THE MOON

The lunar module comprises two sections. The upper "ascent" stage houses the crew in a pressurized compartment and its movement is controlled by rockets. The lower "descent" stage has a central rocket and contains equipment for exploration of the lunar surface. The lower stage remains on the Moon when the astronauts take off in the "ascent" stage to rejoin the *Columbia* command-and-service module in lunar orbit.

FOR THE RECORD

The first stage of the Saturn V launch was powered by five Rocketdyne F-1s – the **most powerful single-chamber liquid-fuelled rocket engine**. Each had a thrust of 6,770 kN (1.52 million lbf). Lasting some 2 min 30 sec, this initial stage required 203,400 US gal (770,000 litres) of kerosene fuel and 318,000 US gal (1,204,000 litres) of liquid oxygen. By comparison, it takes 861 US gal (3,272 litres) of fuel to get a Boeing 747 off the ground.

APOLLO 11

NASA's emblem for the Apollo 11 mission featured a bald eagle (the USA's national bird) and an olive branch to denote peaceful aims

The first stage
was jettisoned after the F-1 engines shut off at an altitude of 42 mi (67 km)

3: THE JOURNEY HOME

1: While astronaut Michael Collins stays in *Columbia*, his colleagues Buzz Aldrin and Neil Armstrong conduct experiments on the Moon.
2: *Eagle* takes off from the lunar surface 124 hr 22 min into the mission.
3–4: Nearly 4 hr later, it docks with *Columbia*, which Aldrin and Armstrong then enter. *Eagle* is jettisoned some 2 hr later.
5: Just before Earth re-entry, *Columbia*'s command module casts off its service module (housing oxygen, water and electricity for the command module, as well as the rocket that propels it to and from the Moon).
6–7: The command module re-enters Earth's atmosphere. Its parachutes open and it splashes down in the Pacific Ocean at around 12:50 p.m. EDT on 24 Jul 1969.

Five Rocketdyne F-1 engines (see "For the Record")

| 1 | 2 | 3 | 4 | 5 | 6 | 7 |

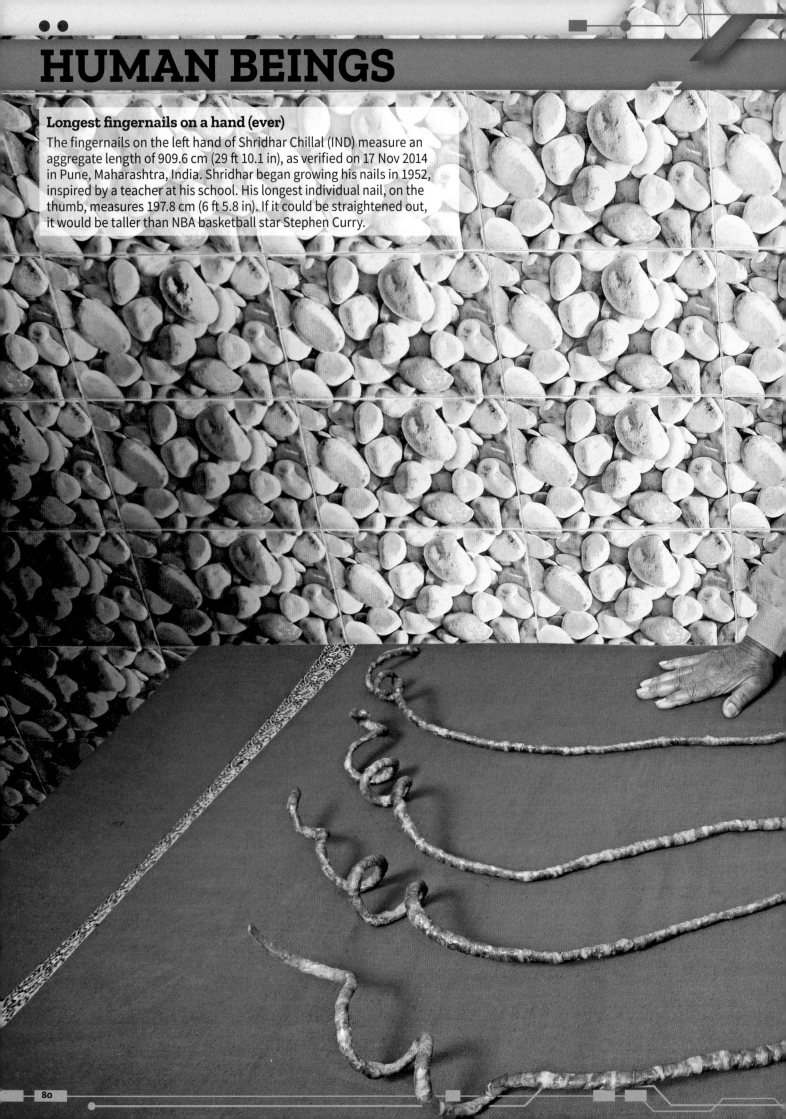

HUMAN BEINGS

Longest fingernails on a hand (ever)

The fingernails on the left hand of Shridhar Chillal (IND) measure an aggregate length of 909.6 cm (29 ft 10.1 in), as verified on 17 Nov 2014 in Pune, Maharashtra, India. Shridhar began growing his nails in 1952, inspired by a teacher at his school. His longest individual nail, on the thumb, measures 197.8 cm (6 ft 5.8 in). If it could be straightened out, it would be taller than NBA basketball star Stephen Curry.

Shridhar's nails have grown more fragile with age, making their accurate measurement a delicate process. GWR adjudicators used string to mark off the nails' lengths before gauging the string against a normal tape measure.

HEAVIEST HUMANS

The story of the heaviest humans on Earth is by turns turbulent, tragic and even uplifting. Record holders face a constant struggle, not only with their extreme size and fluctuating waistlines, but also the life-threatening health issues that accompany them.

Jon Brower Minnoch
A rare photograph of the **heaviest man ever**. At his peak of more than 1,400 lb (635 kg; 100 st), he weighed more than seven average adult men.

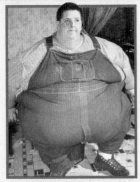

Robert Earl Hughes
This outsize American registered the **largest chest measurement**: 3.15 m (10 ft 4 in). He died in 1958.

The heaviest human category is not one that's challenged very often. Few individuals wish to publicize their extreme obesity, although occasionally a new story breaks when someone seeks help for what is a very serious medical condition. This is the case with the most recent man to be verified as the world's **heaviest human**: Juan Pedro Franco Salas of the central Mexican city of Aguascalientes. In Nov 2016, Juan Pedro made headlines around the world when he was hospitalized for life-saving treatment. Initially reported to weigh 1,105 lb (501 kg; 79 st), he actually tipped the scales at 594.8 kg (1,311 lb 4.9 oz; 93 st 9 lb).

Prior to Juan Pedro, the **heaviest man** was fellow Mexican Manuel "Meme" Uribe Garza of Monterrey, who reached a peak weight of 560 kg (1,235 lb; 88 st) – heavier than six average men – in Jan 2006. He made a televised plea for help and slimmed down to 840 lb (381 kg; 60 st) with the guidance of obesity experts. Manuel was hospitalized in May 2014 suffering from cardiac arrhythmia (irregular heartbeat) and liver failure, and passed away three weeks later at the age of 48.

Other heaviest men of recent times include Michael Hebranko (USA, 1953–2013), who suffered from morbid obesity his entire life and whose weight peaked at 1,100 lb (499 kg; 78 st) in 1999. The wall of Michael's home had to be removed in order to get him to hospital and a whale sling used to manoeuvre him into bed. T J Albert Jackson (USA, 1941–88), meanwhile, peaked at 890 lb (404 kg; 63 st 9 lb). "Fat Albert", as he was known, had a chest measurement of 305 cm (120 in), a waist of 294 cm (116 in) and a 75-cm (29-in) neck.

The **heaviest man ever** was Jon Brower Minnoch (USA), who had suffered from obesity since childhood. In Sep 1976, he measured 185 cm (6 ft 1 in) tall and weighed 442 kg (974 lb; 69 st 9 lb). But just two years later, in Mar 1978, Jon was admitted to University Hospital, Seattle, USA, where consultant endocrinologist Dr Robert Schwartz calculated that he must have weighed in excess of 1,400 lb (635 kg; 100 st). A great deal of this was due to water accumulation – a result of his congestive heart failure. In order to get Jon to hospital, a dozen firemen and an improvised stretcher were required to move him from his home to a ferry boat. When he arrived at University Hospital, saturated with fluid and suffering from heart and respiratory failure, Jon was put in two beds lashed together. It took 13 people to roll him over.

After nearly two years on a diet of 1,200 calories per day, Jon was discharged at 216 kg (476 lb; 34 st). In Oct 1981, however, he had to be readmitted after putting on more than 89 kg (196 lb; 14 st). When he passed away on 10 Sep 1983, the **heaviest ever human** weighed more than 362 kg (798 lb; 57 st).

Manuel Uribe
Peaking at 560 kg (1,234 lb 9 oz), Mexico's Manuel was the **heaviest man** from 2006 to his death in 2014.

HIGHEST OBESITY RATES (INDUSTRIALIZED NATIONS)

COUNTRY	CONTINENT	PERCENTAGE
USA	North America	38.2
Mexico	North America	32.4
New Zealand	Australia	30.7
Hungary	Europe	30
Australia	Australia	27.9

Source: OECD Obesity Update 2017

Billy and Benny McCrary
The **heaviest twins (male)**: in Nov 1978, Billy weighed 337 kg (743 lb; 53 st) and Benny was 328 kg (723 lb; 51 st 9 lb).

Billy and Benny McCrary (both USA) found fame as professional wrestling duo the McGuire Twins. Each boasted a waist measuring 2.13 m (6 ft 11.8 in). Billy died in a motorcycle accident in 1979, while Benny suffered heart failure in 2001.

LARGER-THAN-LIFE LADIES

▶ **Heaviest living woman**
Pauline Potter (USA) weighed 293.6 kg (647 lb; 46 st) when measured in Sacramento, California, USA, in Jul 2012. She attributes her weight problems to her childhood, when she regularly had to go without food. Following gastric bypass surgery, Pauline shed almost 150 lb (68 kg; 10 st), but continues to battle with her weight.

Heaviest woman to give birth
Donna Simpson of New Jersey, USA, weighed 532 lb (241 kg; 38 st) when she delivered daughter Jacqueline in Feb 2007. The birth took place at Akron City Hospital in Ohio, USA, carried out by a team of 30 medical professionals. Jacqueline weighed 8 lb 7 oz (3.8 kg) at birth – around 1/60th of her mother's weight.

Heaviest quadruplets ever born
Tina Saunders (UK) gave birth to two girls and two boys weighing a combined total of 10.4 kg (22 lb 15.7 oz) at St Peter's Hospital in Chertsey, Surrey, UK, on 7 Feb 1989.

The **heaviest triplets ever born** weighed a total of 24 lb (10.9 kg) and were born to Mary McDermott (UK) on 18 Nov 1914.

Highest rate of female obesity
According to the World Health Organization, 63.3% of the female population of Nauru are classed as clinically obese, as of 2016. The next-highest nation on the list is the Cook Islands on 59.2%, with Palau third on 58.8%. The Marshall Islands and Tuvalu make up the top five, with 57.3% and 56.2% respectively.

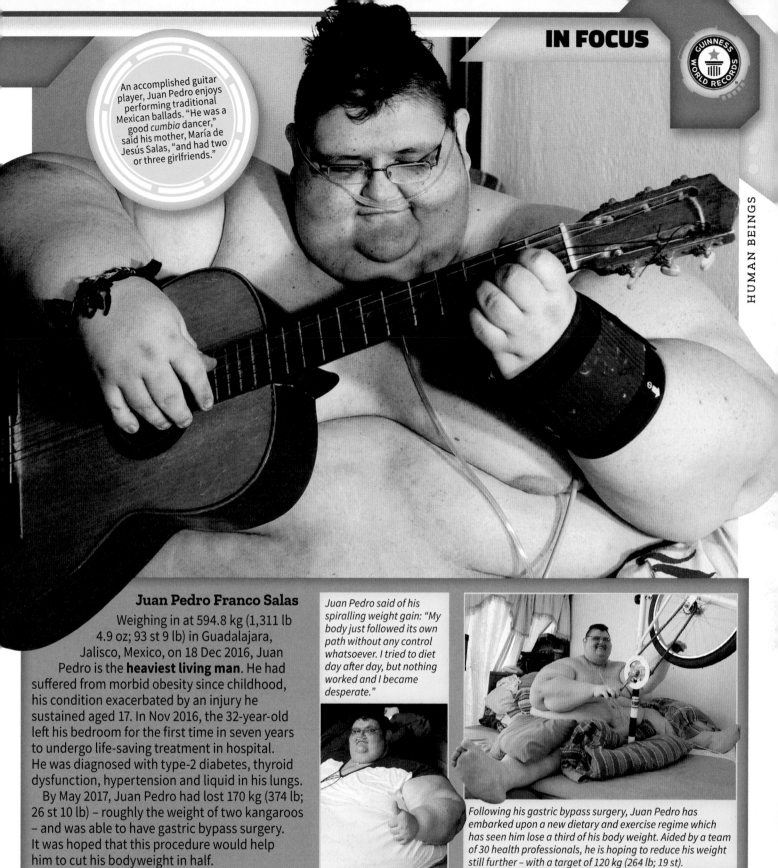

An accomplished guitar player, Juan Pedro enjoys performing traditional Mexican ballads. "He was a good *cumbia* dancer," said his mother, María de Jesús Salas, "and had two or three girlfriends."

Juan Pedro Franco Salas

Weighing in at 594.8 kg (1,311 lb 4.9 oz; 93 st 9 lb) in Guadalajara, Jalisco, Mexico, on 18 Dec 2016, Juan Pedro is the **heaviest living man**. He had suffered from morbid obesity since childhood, his condition exacerbated by an injury he sustained aged 17. In Nov 2016, the 32-year-old left his bedroom for the first time in seven years to undergo life-saving treatment in hospital. He was diagnosed with type-2 diabetes, thyroid dysfunction, hypertension and liquid in his lungs.

By May 2017, Juan Pedro had lost 170 kg (374 lb; 26 st 10 lb) – roughly the weight of two kangaroos – and was able to have gastric bypass surgery. It was hoped that this procedure would help him to cut his bodyweight in half.

Juan Pedro said of his spiralling weight gain: "My body just followed its own path without any control whatsoever. I tried to diet day after day, but nothing worked and I became desperate."

Following his gastric bypass surgery, Juan Pedro has embarked upon a new dietary and exercise regime which has seen him lose a third of his body weight. Aided by a team of 30 health professionals, he is hoping to reduce his weight still further – with a target of 120 kg (264 lb; 19 st).

Heaviest Ms Olympia contestant

Nicole Bass (USA) weighed 92.5 kg (204 lb; 14 st 8 lb) when she participated in the 1997 international bodybuilding contest. Bass, a bodybuilder and professional wrestler who starred in the WWF (now WWE) in the late 1990s, was also the **tallest Ms Olympia contestant**, at 188 cm (6 ft 2 in). She passed away in Feb 2017.

◄ Heaviest woman ever

Rosalie Bradford (USA) is claimed to have reached a peak weight of 1,200 lb (544 kg; 85 st) in Jan 1987. In Aug that year, she was rushed to hospital having developed congestive heart failure. Through a combination of carefully controlled dieting and exercise – including clapping her hands – Rosalie was able to bring her weight down to 283 lb (128 kg; 20 st) by Feb 1994. She went back to higher education and toured the USA, making motivational speeches at weight-loss seminars. Despite her success in controlling her size, however, it continued to be a problem throughout Rosalie's life. She finally passed away on 29 Nov 2006 at the age of 63, owing to weight-related complications.

Heaviest sportswoman

Sumo wrestler Sharran Alexander (UK) weighed 448 lb (203.2 kg; 32 st) on 15 Dec 2011. She took up the sport in her early 40s, participating in the Sumo World Championships having won a 2006 reality TV show. Sharran went on to compete in competitions around the world, winning four gold medals and attaining second Kyū grade.

SIZE MATTERS

Tallest teenager ever
By the age of 17, Robert Wadlow (USA, 1918–40) had grown to a height of 245 cm (8 ft 0.5 in). Find out more about this remarkable man on p.85.

The **tallest teenager ever (female)** is Anna Haining Swan (CAN, 1846–88), whose height peaked at 241.3 cm (7 ft 11 in) when she was 17. On 17 Jun 1871, Anna married Martin van Buren Bates, who stood 236.22 cm (7 ft 9 in) tall. See also p.90.

Largest hands on a teenager
The right hand belonging to Mathu-Andrew Budge (UK, b. 28 Dec 2001) is 22.5 cm (8.85 in) long from the wrist to the tip of the middle finger, while his left is 22.2 cm (8.74 in). He was measured on 13 Feb 2018 in London, UK, aged 16 years 47 days.

Mathu-Andrew also has the **largest feet on a teenager (male)**. His left foot is 32.95 cm (12.97 in) long, and his right 32.85 cm (12.93 in). He wears a UK shoe size 18.

SHORTEST...

Man ever
Chandra Bahadur Dangi (NPL, 1939–2015) measured 54.6 cm (1 ft 9.5 in) tall, as verified in Lainchaur, Kathmandu, Nepal, on 26 Feb 2012. At the time, Chandra weighed 14.5 kg (31 lb 15.47 oz) and claimed to be 72 years old.

Woman ever
Pauline Musters (NLD, aka "Princess Pauline") was born on 26 Feb 1876 and measured just over 1 ft (30 cm) at birth. She died of pneumonia with meningitis in New York City, USA, on 1 Mar 1895. A post-mortem examination showed her to be exactly 2 ft (61 cm) tall.

Tallest married couple
Sun Mingming and his wife Xu Yan (both CHN) stand 236.17 cm (7 ft 8.98 in) and 187.3 cm (6 ft 1.74 in) tall respectively. They had a combined height of 423.47 cm (13 ft 10.72 in) on 14 Nov 2013 when measured in Beijing, China. They had married there on 4 Aug that year.

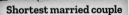

Shortest married couple
Paulo Gabriel da Silva Barros and Katyucia Lie Hoshino (both BRA), who married on 17 Sep 2016, have a combined height of 181.41 cm (5 ft 11.42 in). Paulo is 90.28 cm (2 ft 11.54 in) tall and Katyucia measures 91.13 cm (2 ft 11.88 in), as verified in Itapeva, São Paulo, Brazil, on 3 Nov 2016.

Shortest men and women
Jyoti Amge (IND, above left) was 62.8 cm (2 ft 0.7 in) tall when measured in Nagpur, India, on 16 Dec 2011, making her the **shortest living woman**.

The **shortest living man** is Khagendra Thapa Magar (NPL, above right), who stands 67.08 cm (2 ft 2.41 in) tall, as confirmed at Fewa City Hospital in Pokhara, Nepal, on 14 Oct 2010.

Madge Bester (ZAF) is just 65 cm (2 ft 1.5 in) tall, making her the **shortest living non-mobile woman**. She suffers from *Osteogenesis imperfecta*, or brittle bone disease, and is confined to a wheelchair.

The **shortest living non-mobile man** is Junrey Balawing (PHL, left), who was 59.93 cm (1 ft 11.5 in) tall when measured at Sindangan Health Centre in Zamboanga del Norte, Philippines, on 12 Jun 2011.

Twins ever
Béla and Matyus Matina (1903–c. 1935) of Budapest, Hungary, who later became naturalized American citizens, each stood 76 cm (2 ft 6 in) tall. They appeared in *The Wizard of Oz* (USA, 1939), billed as Mike and Ike Rogers.

Longest legs (female)
Russia's Ekaterina Lisina has legs that measure 132.8 cm (4 ft 4.2 in) and 132.2 cm (4 ft 4 in) for the left leg and right leg respectively, taken from the heel to the top of the hip. That's more than twice the height of the **shortest woman ever** (see above left). Their length was confirmed in Penza, Russia, on 13 Jun 2017. Ekaterina is also the **tallest professional model**, with a height confirmed at 205.16 cm (6 ft 8.77 in) in Labinsk, Russia, on 20 Jul 2017.

TALL AND SHORT STORIES

◀ Shortest stuntman
Kiran Shah (UK) stood 126.3 cm (4 ft 1.7 in) tall when measured on 20 Oct 2003. In a career dating back to 1976, Kiran has worked on many blockbusters. He was the perspective stunt double (for long shots in action scenes) for Elijah Wood in the *Lord of the Rings* (NZ/USA, 2001–03) trilogy and worked on three of the recent Star Wars movies.

Shortest spy
The smallest recorded spy was Richebourg (FRA, 1768–1858), who measured 58 cm (1 ft 11 in) as an adult. He was employed by the aristocracy to act as a secret agent during the French Revolution (1789–99), dispatching messages into and out of Paris while disguised as an infant, wrapped up and carried by an accomplice posing as a "nurse".

◀ Tallest athlete at the Paralympic Games (male)
Morteza Mehrzad Selakjani (IRN), who is 246 cm (8 ft 0.85 in) tall, competed as a sitting volleyball player at the 2016 Paralympic Games in Rio de Janeiro, Brazil, from 7 to 18 Sep. He has a condition known as acromegaly, caused by an overactive pituitary gland. Symptoms include enlarged hands, feet and facial features.

Shortest nationalities
According to a survey published in the journal *eLife* on 26 Jul 2016, the **shortest women** were those of Guatemala, with an average height of 149.4 cm (4 ft 10.8 in). The **shortest men** were those from East Timor, whose height averaged just under 160 cm (5 ft 3 in).

Average height
166 cm (5 ft 5 in)

Tallest nationalities
As of the same date, *eLife* reported that the Netherlands had the **tallest men**, with an average height exceeding 182.5 cm (5 ft 11.85 in). The **tallest women** lived in Latvia and reached an average height in excess of 168 cm (5 ft 6.14 in).

Tallest living man

Sultan Kösen (TUR) stood 251 cm (8 ft 2.8 in) tall when measured in Ankara, Turkey, on 8 Feb 2011. On 26 Oct 2013, his dream of finding a soulmate came true: he married 175-cm-tall (5-ft 9-in) Merve Dibo in Mardin, Turkey. He also has the **largest hands for a living person**, verified at 28.5 cm (11.22 in) from the wrist to the tip of the middle finger when last measured on 8 Feb 2011.

Tallest living woman
Siddiqa Parveen (IND) measured at least 222.2 cm (7 ft 3.4 in) tall in Dec 2012. Owing to ill health, she has been unable to stand upright, so it has proved impossible to ascertain her exact stature. However, Dr Debashish Saha – of the Fortis Hospital in Kolkata, India – who performed the measurements, estimated her standing height to be at least 233.6 cm (7 ft 8 in).

Tallest man ever
Robert Pershing Wadlow (USA, 1918–40) was found to be 272 cm (8 ft 11.1 in) tall when last measured on 27 Jun 1940. He remains the tallest man in medical history for whom there is irrefutable evidence.

The **tallest woman ever** was Zeng Jinlian (CHN, 1964–82), who measured 246.3 cm (8 ft 1 in) when she died on 13 Feb 1982.

*On 26 Jan 2018, visitors to the ancient Giza pyramid complex in Cairo, Egypt, had an unexpected treat in the form of the **tallest living man** and the **shortest living woman**. The record-breaking duo had been officially invited by the Egyptian Tourism Promotion Board to visit some of the country's renowned historic sites.*

Sultan is 76 cm (2 ft 6 in) taller than Merve, but the **greatest height difference in a married couple** is 94.5 cm (3 ft 1 in) for France's Fabien and Natalie Pretou.

◄ **Shortest comedian**
Imaan Hadchiti (LBN/AUS), who is 102.5 cm (3 ft 4.3 in) tall, has been on the comedy circuit in Australia and the UK since 2005. Imaan and his sister Rima are the only known people with Rima Syndrome, resulting in short stature but usual-sized proportions. He began his career, aged 15, by winning Australia's Class Clown national stand-up contest.

Tallest ballet dancer
Fabrice Calmels (FRA) measured 199.73 cm (6 ft 6.63 in) in Chicago, Illinois, USA, on 25 Sep 2014. He began ballet training at the age of three, and when he was 11 entered the Paris Opera Ballet School. In 2002, Fabrice joined Chicago's Joffrey Ballet and went on to become a lead dancer there two years later. He remains with the Joffrey Ballet company today.

◄ **Tallest astronaut**
Former US astronauts James Wetherbee (near left) and James van Hoften are both 193 cm (6 ft 4 in) tall. Astronauts grow slightly when they spend time in orbit, however. Although they were the same height on Earth, in space Wetherbee (whose lengthiest mission lasted nearly 14 days) would have been taller than van Hoften (whose longest mission lasted six days).

BODY MODS

Most piercings in the tongue
Francesco Vacca (USA) has 20 tongue piercings, as confirmed at Invisibleself, a piercing and jewellery studio located in Lyndhurst, New Jersey, USA, on 5 Jan 2017.

As of 17 Feb 2012, Axel Rosales (ARG) had the **most piercings on the face**, with 280.

Longest neck
The maximum known extension of a human neck is 40 cm (1 ft 3.75 in), created by the successive fitting of copper coils. This is practised by the women of the Padaung or Karenni tribe of Burma, among whom it is considered a sign of beauty. In time, the necks become so long and weak that they cannot support the women's heads without the coils.

Longest earlobes (stretched)
Monte Pierce (USA) can stretch his earlobes to a length of 5 in (12.7 cm) for his left and 4.5 in (11.43 cm) for his right. When not stretched, his earlobes measure just under 1 in (2.54 cm).

Monte currently also holds the record for the **farthest ear sling-shot**, having propelled an American dime (10-cent) coin 3.55 m (11 ft 8 in) on the set of *Lo Show dei Record* in Madrid, Spain, on 16 Feb 2008.

Narrowest waist (current)
Cathie Jung (USA) has a corseted waist measuring 15 in (38.1 cm). Un-corseted, it measures 21 in (53.34 cm). Cathie's enthusiasm for Victorian fashions led her, at the age of 38, to begin wearing a 6-in-wide (15.24-cm) training belt to gradually reduce her then 26-in (66-cm) waist. She has never had surgery to define her waist.

Most flesh tunnels in the face
Joel Miggler (DEU) had 11 flesh tunnels (hollow, tube-like jewellery) in his face, as verified in Küssaberg, Germany, on 27 Nov 2014. They ranged from 3 mm to 34 mm (0.1–1.3 in), although Joel has plans to further increase their size.

FIRST...

Implanted antenna
In 2004, British-born artist Neil Harbisson had an antenna installed in the back of his head. He was born with a rare form of colour blindness and cannot perceive any colours other than black and white. The antenna is fixed to a camera that hangs in front of Harbisson's eyes and converts colour, in the form of light waves, into sound waves that he can experience as musical notes. The spectrum he can now hear runs from low notes (dark red) to high notes (purple).

Harbisson wears this "eyeborg" at all times. It is even pictured in his passport photograph, making him the **first officially recognized cyborg**.

Sealed magnet finger implants
Steve Haworth (USA) performed the first sealed magnetic implant in 2005. He created the insert in collaboration with

Most pierced senior citizen (male)
John Lynch (UK, b. 9 Nov 1930; above right), aka "Prince Albert", had 241 piercings, including 151 in his head and neck, as of 17 Oct 2008. The count took place in Hammersmith, London, UK. Before he retired, John worked for 30 years as a bank manager.

Most tattooed man
Circus performer Lucky Diamond Rich (AUS, b. NZ) has spent more than 1,000 hr being tattooed, and boasts more than 200% skin coverage. He overlaid his first layer of colourful tattoos with a total covering of black ink, and is now adding white designs on top of that.

fellow body-mod artist Jesse Jarrell and Todd Huffman, a graduate student at Arizona State University. The implant – a neodymium magnet coated in gold and silicone to seal it from the rest of the body – was fitted beneath the skin of one of Huffman's fingers. A similar design is now one of the most popular technological body modifications, enabling the finger to lift small metal objects; it can also vibrate in the presence of invisible magnetic fields.

Most body modifications (married couple)
As of 7 Jul 2014, Victor Hugo Peralta (URY) and his wife Gabriela Peralta (ARG) had 84 body mods between them, as verified on the set of *Lo Show dei Record* in Milan, Italy. These augmentations consist of 50 piercings, eight microdermals, 14 body implants, five dental implants, four ear expanders, two ear bolts and one forked tongue.

INK-REDIBLE NEEDLEWORK

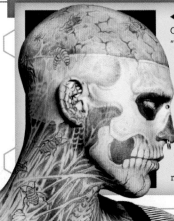

◀ Most insect tattoos
Canada's Rick Genest, aka "Rico", has 176 insects tattooed on his arms, torso, back and head. The count was verified on *Lo Show dei Record* in Milan, Italy, on 27 Apr 2011.

Rick also has the **most bones tattooed on the body** – 139 – as confirmed at the same time and the same location. The tattoos reproduce part of his skeleton.

Most skull tattoos
Charles "Chuck" Helmke (USA) has 376 skulls tattooed across his body. The designs are featured both as pieces of artwork in their own right and as background and shading. Helmke – the **most tattooed senior citizen (male)**, with 97.5% coverage – is the life partner of Charlotte Guttenberg, who herself holds several GWR titles (see right).

▶ Most tattoos of the same name
Mark Evans (UK) has one name tattooed 267 times on his skin, as verified on 25 Jan 2017 in Wrexham, UK. It took two tattooists an hour to ink "Lucy" on Mark's back, in celebration of the birth of his daughter of the same name. The record attempt was also made to raise funds for the hospital that had assisted with Lucy at the time.

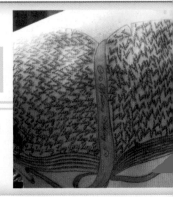

What is a body mod?

Tattoos: ancient form of body decoration in which patterns are inked into the skin by means of a needle.

Implants: inserts beneath the skin (e.g., horns). "Transdermal" implants sit partly above and partly below the skin.

Piercings: adornments inserted into body parts. And earrings, nose rings and lip piercings are only the beginning...

Splitting: also known as "bifurcation", this mod involves dividing the tongue from the tip to the base, giving a forked appearance.

HUMAN BEINGS

Most body modifications

Rolf Buchholz (DEU) has 516 body mods, as verified on 16 Dec 2012 in Dortmund, Germany. Rolf's body adornments include 481 piercings – with 37 in his eyebrows and 111 around his mouth – two subdermal horn implants, a split tongue and five magnetic implants in the fingertips of his right hand. He also has approximately 90% tattoo coverage. IT consultant Rolf has been modifying his body for almost 20 years. He had his first piercing and tattoo on the same day, aged 40.

Rolf sported a brand-new look for our exclusive *GWR* photo shoot. He has run four marathons in the past two years and lost around a third of his body weight.

Most body modifications (female)

María José Cristerna (MEX) has 49 body modifications altogether. These include significant tattoo coverage, a range of transdermal implants on her forehead (including titanium horns), chest and arms, and multiple piercings in her eyebrows, lips, nose, tongue, ear lobes, belly button and nipples. This former lawyer also owns a tattoo parlour and is a mother of four.

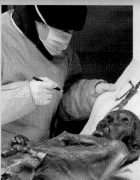

◄ Oldest tattoos

Discovered in 1991 in the Italian Alps, a mummified man dubbed "Ötzi" has a total of 61 tattoos on his body. Located on his back, ribs, lower legs and left wrist, the tattoos were created by slicing open the skin and rubbing in charcoal dust. Ötzi is thought to have died around 5,300 years ago. He was probably killed by an arrowhead found in his back.

Most tattoos of the same cartoon character

Lee Weir (NZ) has 41 tattoos of Homer Simpson on his left arm, as verified in Auckland, New Zealand, on 5 Jun 2014. A diehard fan of *The Simpsons*, Lee has a tattoo sleeve boasting multiple versions of the iconic character, including Homer in an elephant suit, as a jack-in-the-box, the Grim Reaper, the Hulk and even a doughnut.

▶ Most tattooed woman

Charlotte Guttenberg (USA) has 98.75% of her body tattooed, as verified in Melbourne, Florida, USA, on 7 Nov 2017. At the time of approval, Charlotte also held the Guinness World Records titles for the **most tattooed senior citizen** and the **most feathers tattooed on the body** (216). Only the palms of her hands, her fingers and some parts of her face remain bare.

OLDEST PEOPLE

Oldest living person (male)

Masazō Nonaka (JPN, b. 25 Jul 1905) was 112 years 282 days old as of 3 May 2018. A resident of Ashoro in Hokkaido, Japan, he is one of 67,800 centenarians in Japan. Masazō puts his longevity down to soaking in thermal baths (his family owns a hot-springs inn) and eating sweets. The record for **oldest living woman** – and **person** – is pending approval. According to the Gerontology Research Group (see table below), Japan's Chiyo Miyako (b. 2 May 1901) was aged 117 years 1 day old as of 3 May 2018, and the most likely contender for the title at the time of going to press.

LONGEST CAREER AS...

A motor racing driver

As of 29 Oct 2017, Alan Baillie (UK, b. 17 Jan 1937) had been motor racing for 55 years 135 days. His first race was in an Austin-Healey at Nottingham Sports Car Club's 10th Annual Motor Race Meeting at Silverstone, UK, on 16 Jun 1962. He has raced every year since then.

A comics artist

Al Jaffee (USA) had worked for 73 years 3 months from the first publication of his artwork in *Joker Comics* in Dec 1942 through to the Apr 2016 issue of *MAD* magazine.

An airline mechanic

As of 17 Jul 2017, Azriel "Al" Blackman (USA, b. Aug 1925) had worked for American Airlines for exactly 75 years. He was 91 years old at the time, just a month shy of his 92nd birthday.

OLDEST...

Radio talk-show host (living)

Walter Bingham (ISR, b. 5 Jan 1924) was aged 94 years 116 days as of 1 May 2018. He presents two programmes – *Walter's World* on Israel National News and *The Walter Bingham File* on Israel News Talk Radio – both of which are broadcast from Jerusalem.

Person to ride a zip wire

On 6 Apr 2018, Jack Reynolds (UK, b. 6 Apr 1912) celebrated his 106th birthday by gliding down a 347-m-long (1,138-ft) line c. 50 m (160 ft) up in the air. The feat took place at the Go Ape! adventure centre in Grizedale, Cumbria, UK.

Person ever

The greatest age to which any human has lived is 122 years 164 days by Jeanne Louise Calment. Born in Arles, France, on 21 Feb 1875, she died in a nursing home there on 4 Aug 1997.

The **oldest man ever** was Jiroemon Kimura (JPN, b. 19 Apr 1897), who died on 12 Jun 2013 aged 116 years 54 days.

Oldest performing flying trapeze artist (female)

Aerial gymnast Betty Goedhart (USA, b. 25 Oct 1932) was 84 years 249 days old on 1 Jul 2017, as confirmed in San Diego, California, USA. She performs four times a week at Trapeze High in Escondido. Although she loved watching circus trapeze artists as a child, Betty didn't become a "flyer" herself until she was 78 years old.

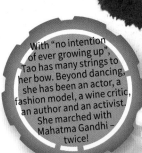

Oldest competitive ballroom dancer (female)

Tao Porchon-Lynch (FRA, b. 13 Aug 1918) was still enjoying competitive ballroom dancing at the age of 98 years 302 days, as confirmed in White Plains, New York, USA, on 11 Jun 2017. Tao has been performing in dance contests since the age of 87. She is also a yoga master and has been practising this ancient discipline for 70 years.

With "no intention of ever growing up", Tao has many strings to her bow. Beyond dancing, she has been an actor, a fashion model, a wine critic, an author and an activist. She marched with Mahatma Gandhi – twice!

TOP 10 OLDEST LIVING PEOPLE

NAME	RESIDENCE	BORN	AGE
Chiyo Miyako (JPN)	Kanagawa, Japan	2 May 1901	117 years 1 day
Giuseppina Projetto-Frau (ITA)	Florence, Italy	30 May 1902	115 years 338 days
Kane Tanaka (JPN)	Fukuoka, Japan	2 Jan 1903	115 years 121 days
Maria-Giuseppa Robucci-Nargiso (ITA)	Apricena, Italy	20 Mar 1903	115 years 44 days
Shimoe Akiyama (JPN)	Aichi, Japan	15 May 1903	114 years 353 days
Delphine Gibson (USA)	Pennsylvania, USA	17 Aug 1903	114 years 259 days
Lucile Randon (FRA)	Toulon, France	11 Feb 1904	114 years 81 days
Shin Matsushita (JPN)	Miyagi, Japan	30 Mar 1904	114 years 34 days
Tane Yonekura (JPN)	Kagoshima, Japan	2 May 1904	114 years 1 days
Gabrielle Valentine des Robert (FRA)	Nantes, France	4 Jun 1904	113 years 333 days

Source: Gerontology Research Group & gerontology.wikia.com, as of 3 May 2018; all female

OLDEST...

◀ Boxer

Stephen "Steve" Ward (UK, b. 12 Aug 1956) was 60 years 337 days old at the time of a bout in Nottinghamshire, UK, on 15 Jul 2017. This was to be Steve's last competitive fight. Germany's Andreas Sidon knocked him down in the seventh round of the first WBC Veteran Heavyweight title contest and he retired afterwards.

▲ Active fighter pilot

Squadron Leader Phillip Frawley (AUS, b. 8 Mar 1952) was 65 years 146 days old as of 1 Aug 2017. He is a fully operational fighter pilot and flying instructor.

◀ Person to cross America by bicycle (female)

Lynnea C Salvo (USA) was 67 years 32 days old when she finished her trip from Oceanside, California, to Bethany Beach, Delaware, USA, on 23 Oct 2016. A retired teacher, she cycled 3,163 mi (5,090.35 km) through temperatures that sometimes exceeded 100°F (37.78°C). Lynnea rode in support of a mental-health charity.

 Japan 17 | **USA** 6 | **Italy** 6 | **France** 3 | **UK** 2 | **Canada** 1 | **Netherlands** 1 | **Australia** 1

HUMAN BEINGS

Oldest tandem parachute jump (male)

On 14 May 2017, Bryson William Verdun Hayes (UK, b. 6 Apr 1916) performed a parachute jump from a height of 15,000 ft (4,572 m) at the age of 101 years 38 days. He's seen here, wearing a yellow jump suit, accompanied by chief instructor Jason Farrant. The attempt took place at Dunkeswell Aerodrome in Honiton, Devon, UK. Verdun performed his first tandem parachute jump aged 100.

The **oldest tandem parachute jump (female)** was by Estrid Geertsen (DNK, b. 1 Aug 1904; d. 25 Jun 2012). On 30 Sep 2004, aged 100 years 60 days, she parachuted from an altitude of 4,000 m (13,120 ft) over Roskilde in Denmark.

Verdun is a World War II veteran and former member of the Royal Corps of Signals. He was joined by 10 members of his family on his jump, which raised money for The Royal British Legion.

Oldest person to paraglide (male)

On 22 Jul 2017, Janusz Orłowski (POL, b. 14 Jan 1926) performed a paraglide at the age of 91 years 189 days in Brzeska Wola, Poland. Nicknamed "Praszczur" ("Grandpa"), Janusz soared solo above the ground for 12 min, during which he reached a maximum altitude of 332 m (1,089 ft).

▼ Married couple to scuba dive (aggregate age)

Philip (b. 1 Jul 1931) and Grace Hampton (b. 12 Aug 1931, both USA) had a total age of 171 years 329 days when they dived in the Cayman Islands on 4 Jul 2017.

▲ Solo helicopter pilot

On 14 Sep 2017, David Marks (UK, b. 5 Aug 1930) flew between Northampton Sywell Aerodrome and Fenland Aerodrome, UK, aged 87 years 40 days.

▼ Scuba diver

Wallace Raymond Woolley (UK, b. 28 Aug 1923) completed a dive to the *Zenobia* wreck in Larnaca Bay, Cyprus, on 28 Aug 2017, at the age of 94 years. The event was organized for his birthday.

◄ Ice hockey player

On 20 Jul 2017, Mark Sertich (USA, b. 18 Jul 1921) was aged 96 years 2 days when he competed in the Snoopy's Senior World Hockey Tournament in Santa Rosa, California, USA. As of Apr 2018, he was still on the ice every week. Mark has been playing for around 85 years, but feels that he only became truly serious about the sport when he reached 80 years old.

FAMILY MATTERS

Heaviest birth
Giantess Anna Bates (née Swan, CAN), who stood 7 ft 11 in (241.3 cm) tall, gave birth to a boy weighing 22 lb (9.98 kg) at her home in Seville, Ohio, USA, on 19 Jan 1879. The baby was 2 ft 4 in (71.12 cm) long, making him the **longest baby** ever recorded.

Oldest mother to conceive naturally
On 20 Aug 1997, Dawn Brooke (UK) gave birth to a son by Caesarean section at the age of 59 years. She conceived accidentally, without the aid of fertility treatment.

Oldest adoptive parent
Muriel Banks Clayton (USA, b. 22 Jul 1922) was aged 92 years 322 days when she officially adopted Mary Banks Smith (USA) in Dallas, Texas, USA, on 9 Jun 2015.
    Mary was 76 years 96 days of age at the time, making her the **oldest person officially adopted**.

Most living generations (ever)
The greatest number of generations that have been alive at the same time in a single family is seven. On the birth of her great-great-great-great-grandson on 21 Jan 1989, Augusta Bunge (USA) was aged 109 years 97 days – making her the **youngest great-great-great-great-grandparent**. Also alive at the time were her daughter (aged 89), granddaughter (70), great-granddaughter (52), great-great-granddaughter (33) and great-great-great-granddaughter (15).

Largest family reunion
On 12 Aug 2012, a total of 4,514 members of the Porteau-Boileve family assembled at Saint-Paul-Mont-Penit in Vendée, France.

FIRST...

Mother-child supercentenarians
Supercentenarians are people who have attained an age greater than 110. (See pp.88–9 for more.) Mary P Romero Zielke Cota (USA, b. 1870) died in 1982 at the age of 112 years 17 days. Her daughter, Rosabell Zielke Champion Fenstermaker (USA, b. 1893), was similarly long-lived, finally passing away in 2005 aged 111 years 344 days.

Married man to give birth
A controversial figure, Thomas Beatie (USA) was born female but legally became a man in his home state of Oregon, USA. He underwent sex-reassignment surgery in 2002 but did not have his female reproductive organs removed. As a man, Beatie was legally able to marry Nancy, his female partner, in 2003. Nancy had previously had a hysterectomy, so when the couple wanted to start a family it was Thomas, who, with the help of an anonymous sperm donor, conceived and carried the child. The couple's daughter, Susan, was born on 29 Jun 2008.

Conjoined twins to identify as mixed gender
Lori Lynn and Dori Schappell (USA, b. 18 Sep 1961) were born as conjoined – and therefore genetically identical – twin sisters. They became the first such twins to describe themselves as mixed gender when, in 2007, Dori declared that he was transgender, identifying himself as a male named George. The craniopagus twins have separate bodies but partially fused skulls, and share bone, vital blood vessels and 30% of their brain (the frontal lobe and the parietal lobe).

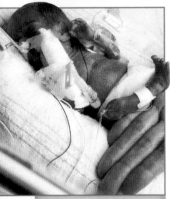

Lightest birth
Rumaisa Rahman (USA) weighed 260 g (9.17 oz) when she was born prematurely in Maywood, Illinois, USA, on 19 Sep 2004. The **shortest baby** was Nisa Juarez (USA), who was 24 cm (9.44 in) long when born prematurely on 20 Jul 2002 in Minneapolis, Minnesota, USA.

Fastest marathon run by a married couple
Paul Kipchumba Lonyangata and Purity Cherotich Rionoripo (both KEN) ran an aggregate time of 4 hr 27 min 5 sec at the Marathon de Paris in France on 9 Apr 2017. Purity set a record of her own on the day – find out more on our Marathons spread (pp.224–25).

Identical twin transplant surgeons to operate on identical twins
Doctors Rafael and Robert Mendez (USA) are identical twins who perform organ transplants as a team. Rafael removes the organ, while Robert places it in the new recipient. In Jan 1999, at the University of Southern California Hospital in Los Angeles, USA, the brothers performed a kidney transplant on identical twins Anna Cortez and Petra Martinez. Identical twins are genetically perfect donors and recipients for one another because of their genetic identity. The only risk from such a procedure is infection.

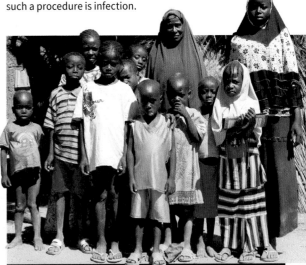

Highest fertility rate (country)
Measured in terms of the average number of children born to each woman, Niger remains the country with the highest fertility rate, with 7.3 children born per woman. This is according to figures from the World Bank, as of Jan 2018.

SAME-DAY DELIVERY

◀ Most siblings born on Leap Day
The children of Karin and Henry Henriksen (both NOR) – Heidi (b. 1960), Olav (b. 1964) and Leif-Martin (b. 1968) – all have infrequent birthdays, as they are on Leap Day: 29 Feb. This extra day usually falls once every four years. Its addition resets the Gregorian calendar to align with Earth's orbit around the Sun.

Most generations born on Leap Day
The only verified example of a family with three consecutive generations born on 29 Feb is that of the Keoghs. Peter Anthony (IRL, b. 1940), his son Peter Eric (UK, b. 1964) and his granddaughter Bethany Wealth (UK, b. 1996) all celebrate their birthdays less often than most. The chances of this have been put at around one in 3 billion.

▲ Most siblings born on the same day
The sole confirmed instance of a family producing five single children with coincident birthdays –excluding multiple births – is that of Catherine (1952), Carol (1953), Charles (1956), Claudia (1961) and Cecilia (1966) Cummins. All five siblings were born on 20 Feb to Carolyn and Ralph Cummins (USA).

Most prolific mother
Valentina Vassilyev (RUS) had 69 children: four sets of quads (16), seven sets of triplets (21) and 16 sets of twins (32).

Most children delivered in a single birth to survive

Nadya Suleman (USA) claimed headlines across the world on 26 Jan 2009 when she gave birth to six boys and two girls at the Kaiser Permanente Medical Center in Bellflower, California, USA. The babies were conceived with the aid of *in vitro* fertilization (IVF) treatment and delivered by Caesarean section. The record-breaking multiple birth proved highly controversial, not least because Nadya already had six young children, who had also been born following IVF treatment.

This photograph of Nadya Suleman was taken when she was around 29 weeks pregnant. She went on to give birth just a week later – her eight babies were nine weeks premature.

Seen here are Nadya's famous octet: Noah, Jonah, Jeremiah, Josiah, Isaiah, Makai, Maliyah and Nariyah.

Largest same-birthday gathering

Apenheul Primate Park (NLD) brought together 228 people, all of whom were born on 4 Jul, at an event in Apeldoorn, Netherlands, on 4 Jul 2012. The attempt was held partly in celebration of the birth of five new gorillas at the park, but also to highlight awareness of the critical state of gorilla populations in the wild.

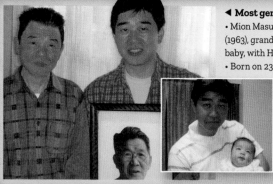

◀ **Most generations born on the same day**
• Mion Masuda (JPN), born in 2005, shares her birthday of 26 Mar with her father Hiroshi (1963), grandfather Minao (1933) and great-grandfather Kanamori (1899). She is seen as a baby, with Hiroshi; the main image shows Hiroshi with Minao and a photo of Kanamori.
• Born on 23 Aug 2001, Jacob Camren Hildebrandt (USA) shares his birthday with his father (1966), grandmother (1944) and great-grandmother (1919).
• Maureen Werner (USA), born on 13 Oct 1998, shares her birthday with her mother (1970), grandfather (1938) and great-grandmother (1912).
• Veera Tuulia Tuijantyär Kivistö (FIN, b. 1997) was born on 21 Mar, as were her mother (1967), grandfather (1940) and great-grandfather (1903).
• Ralph Bertram Williams (USA) was born on 4 Jul 1982 in Wilmington, North Carolina, USA, the same day as his father, grandfather and (in 1876) great-grandfather.

ROUND-UP

Longest time to live with a bullet in the head

William Lawlis Pace (USA, b. 27 Feb 1909) was accidentally shot in Oct 1917, at the age of eight, in Wheeler, Texas, USA. The gunshot caused facial disfigurement, total hearing loss in the right ear and near blindness in the right eye. He died on 23 Apr 2012, aged 103, by which time the bullet had remained in his head for 94 years and at least 175 days.

verified in Himatnagar, Gujarat, India, on 11 Nov 2014. As a carpenter, he has to be particularly careful not to damage them at work.

Largest object removed from a human skull

On 15 Aug 2003, builder Ron Hunt (USA) fell off a ladder while using a drill and fell face-first on to the still-revolving 46-cm (1-ft 6-in) drill bit. It passed through his right eye and exited through his skull above his right ear. Surgeons at Washoe Medical Center in Nevada, USA, found that it had pushed his brain aside rather than penetrating it, thereby saving his life.

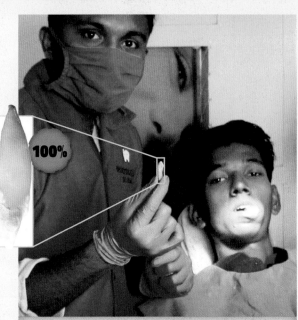

100%

Longest human tooth extracted

A 3.67-cm-long (1.44-in) tooth was removed from Urvil Patel (IND) in Gujarat, India, on 3 Feb 2017. Almost twice the average size for this type of tooth, it was extracted by Dr Jaimin Patel in an operation that lasted some 30 min.

> The super-flexible Mohammed stands only 4 ft 6 in (1.37 m) tall and weighs around 29 kg (64 lb). He hones his natural gifts by practising for 3 hr every day at a sports club in Gaza City.

Longest nose on a living person

Mehmet Özyürek (TUR) has a nose that measures 8.8 cm (3.46 in) from the bridge to the tip, as confirmed on the set of *Lo Show dei Record* in Rome, Italy, on 18 Mar 2010.

Most quarters held in the nose

On 29 Jun 2012, Thomas Gartin (USA) successfully kept 14 quarters in his nose on the set of *Guinness World Records Gone Wild!* in Los Angeles, California, USA. As stipulated in GWR guidelines, the quarters had to remain in the nose for 10 sec without being held in with the hands.

Farthest eyeball pop

Kim Goodman (USA) can pop her eyeballs to a protrusion of 12 mm (0.47 in) beyond her eye sockets. Her eyes were measured in Istanbul, Turkey, on 2 Nov 2007.

Most fingers and toes (polydactylism) on a living person

Devendra Suthar (IND) has 28 digits (comprising 14 fingers and 14 toes), as

Most full-body revolutions maintaining a chest stand in one minute

With his chest flat on the ground and his arms stretched behind him, Mohammed al-Sheikh (PSE) completed 38 rotations of his legs around his torso in 60 sec in Amman, Jordan, on 8 Feb 2017. Nicknamed "Spider-Boy", the youthful contortionist had been one of the final three contenders on reality show *Arabs Got Talent* the previous year.

Most hula-hoop revolutions in one minute

Gregory Sean Dillon (USA) completed 243 rotations of a hula hoop around his body in 60 sec at Vivos Fitness in California, USA, on 20 Mar 2012. He used a 3-ft (91.4-cm) aluminium hoop for the record attempt.

Youngest person to have a wisdom tooth extracted

At the age of 9 years 339 days, Matthew Adams (USA, b. 19 Nov 1992) had his lower two wisdom teeth removed, owing to lack of space. The operation took place at Midland Oral and Maxillofacial Surgery in Michigan, USA, on 24 Oct 2002.

Youngest person to wear a full set of dentures

On 25 Feb 2005, Daniel Sanchez-Ruiz (UK) was given dentures at the age of 3 years 301 days. He suffers from a genetic disorder known as hypohydrotic ectodermal dysplasia, the symptoms of which include abnormal development of the teeth.

Hairiest teenager

According to the Ferriman-Gallwey method, which grades hair density on nine areas of

Oldest false teeth

Based on discoveries made in Etruscan tombs, partial dentures of bridge-work (above) were worn in what is now Tuscany, Italy, as early as 700 BCE. Some were permanently attached to existing teeth, while others were removable.

The **most expensive false teeth sold at auction** (below) had belonged to British prime minister Winston Churchill. They sold for £15,200 ($23,700) to an anonymous bidder on 29 Jul 2010 at an auction staged by Keys Fine Art Auctioneers in Aylsham, Norfolk, UK.

Longest moustache (ever)

India's Ram Singh Chauhan had a moustache measuring 14 ft (4.26 m) – about the length of a London black cab – as verified on the set of *Lo Show dei Record* in Rome, Italy, on 4 Mar 2010.

LONGEST SURVIVAL...

Without a pulse

Julie Mills (UK) was at the point of death owing to severe heart failure and viral myocarditis when, on 14 Aug 1998, cardiac surgeons at The John Radcliffe Hospital in Oxford, UK, used a non-pulsatile blood pump (AB180) to support her for a week. For three days during that period, she had no pulse. Her heart recovered and the pump was removed. She was the first person to survive this procedure.

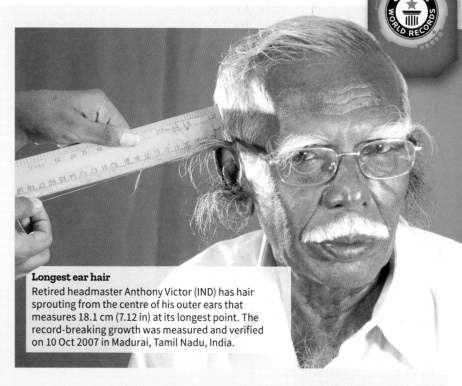

Longest ear hair

Retired headmaster Anthony Victor (IND) has hair sprouting from the centre of his outer ears that measures 18.1 cm (7.12 in) at its longest point. The record-breaking growth was measured and verified on 10 Oct 2007 in Madurai, Tamil Nadu, India.

Most tongue-to-nose touches in one minute

Ashish Peri (IND) brought the tip of his tongue up to touch his nose 142 times in 60 sec in Mumbai, India, on 12 Jun 2017.

the body from 0 (little) to 4 (heavy coverage) Supatra "Nat" Sasuphan (THA, b. 5 Aug 2000) was the most hirsute adolescent when measured on 4 Mar 2010. She scored 4 in four areas: face, neck, chest and upper back. In 2018, Nat revealed on social media that she had fallen in love and shaved her face.

Longest beard on a living person

Sarwan Singh (CAN) had grown his beard to a length of 8 ft 2.5 in (2.5 m) when measured in Surrey, British Columbia, Canada, on 8 Sep 2011. It had initially been measured on the set of *Lo Show dei Record* in Rome, Italy, on 4 Mar 2010, at which time it was 7 ft 9 in (2.36 m) long.

After a single-lung transplant

As of 25 Sep 2017, Veronica Dwyer (IRE, b. 22 Mar 1941) had lived 29 years 129 days following her lung transplant on 19 May 1988 in Harefield, Middlesex, UK.

After a heart transplant

Ted Nowakowski (USA, b. 23 Nov 1948) died on 11 Jan 2018, a total of 34 years 261 days after his heart transplant on 25 Apr 1983.

With diabetes

Hazel Davies (AUS, 1902–2002) had type 1 diabetes for 81 years, having been diagnosed at the age of 19 in 1921. At the time, she was forced to rely on a strict diet to control her condition, because insulin was not yet used as a treatment.

Most clothes pegs clipped on a face

On 17 Jul 2013, Garry Turner (UK) attached 161 clothes pegs to his face on the set of *Rekorlar Dünyası* in Istanbul, Turkey.

Garry possesses the **stretchiest skin** and is able to pull the skin of his stomach to a distended length of 15.8 cm (6.22 in). He has a rare medical condition called Ehlers-Danlos syndrome. With this condition, the collagen that strengthens the skin and determines its elasticity becomes defective, resulting in (among other things) loose skin and hypermobile joints.

DISNEY CASTLE

The elaborate turrets and royal-blue rooftops of Cinderella Castle have become an enduring symbol of The Walt Disney Company and its celluloid fairy tales. Dreamed up by artist Herbert Ryman, the castle sits surrounded by a moat in the heart of the Magic Kingdom theme park in Florida, USA. At night, the building comes alive with 16 million coloured lights and regular firework displays.

The design for Cinderella Castle was inspired by Disney's own animated version and real-life fortresses such as the Alcázar of Segovia in Spain, Moszna Castle in Poland and Neuschwanstein in Germany (see right). Thanks to an architectural trick known as forced perspective, the castle appears even taller than it really is. The proportions of the doors and windows at the top of the castle are smaller than those at the bottom, fooling the eye into thinking that they are even higher in the air. The entire castle took around 18 months to build, and was completed in Jul 1971.

FOR THE RECORD

Cinderella Castle at the Walt Disney World Resort in Florida, USA, measures 189 ft (57.6 m) in height and is the **tallest castle in a theme park**. The structure is made from concrete and fibreglass and does not – despite appearances – feature a single brick. It is the third-tallest structure in the resort after The Twilight Zone Tower of Terror and Expedition Everest – all of which are kept under 200 ft (61 m) to prevent them from having to carry aircraft-warning lights.

Cinderella Castle is taller than Nelson's Column in London, UK, and the Leaning Tower of Pisa in Italy

MONARCH'S MANOR

The royal residence of Windsor Castle in Berkshire, UK, is designed in the shape of a waisted parallelogram measuring 576 x 164 m (1,890 x 538 ft) and is the **largest inhabited castle**. It was built in the 11th century, in the aftermath of the Norman invasion of England. Forty kings and queens have called Windsor Castle home since Henry I (c. 1068–1135).

An 18-min firework show is launched from the castle every night

FORTRESS OF FAIRY TALES

Perched atop an Alpine crag overlooking the village of Hohenschwangau in Bavaria, Germany, Neuschwanstein Castle looks as though it has sprung straight from the pages of a storybook. Its northern tower rises 213 ft (65 m) into the air, making it the **tallest castle**. Neuschwanstein was commissioned at great expense by Ludwig II of Bavaria, who moved into the still-incomplete building in 1884. He lived there for only 172 days before dying in mysterious circumstances on 13 Jun 1886.

The castle boasts 27 towers, numbered 1–29 (towers 13 and 17 were scrapped before construction)

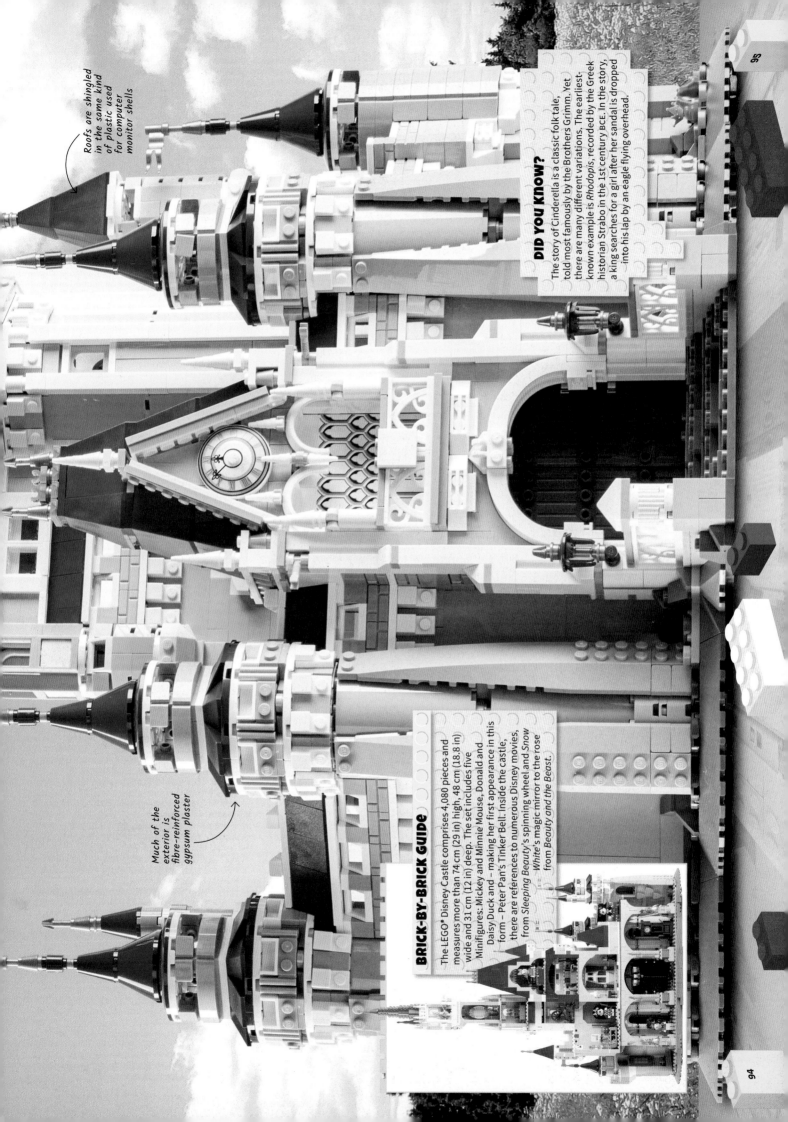

Roofs are shingled in the same kind of plastic used for computer monitor shells

DID YOU KNOW?

The story of Cinderella is a classic folk tale, told most famously by the Brothers Grimm. Yet there are many different variations. The earliest-known example is *Rhodopis*, recorded by the Greek historian Strabo in the 1st century BCE. In the story, a king searches for a girl after her sandal is dropped into his lap by an eagle flying overhead.

Much of the exterior is fibre-reinforced gypsum plaster

BRICK-BY-BRICK GUIDE

The LEGO® Disney Castle comprises 4,080 pieces and measures more than 74 cm (29 in) high, 48 cm (18.8 in) wide and 31 cm (12 in) deep. The set includes five Minifigures: Mickey and Minnie Mouse, Donald and Daisy Duck and – making her first appearance in this form – Peter Pan's Tinker Bell. Inside the castle, there are references to numerous Disney movies, from *Sleeping Beauty*'s spinning wheel and *Snow White*'s magic mirror to the rose from *Beauty and the Beast*.

Fastest speed in a body-controlled jet-engine-powered suit
Inventor Richard Browning (UK) reached an airborne speed of 32.02 mph (51.53 km/h) using his Gravity Flight Suit at Lagoona Park in Reading, Berkshire, UK, on 7 Nov 2017. Inspired by the cinematic exploits of *Iron Man*'s Tony Stark, Browning achieved his dreams of flight by constructing a light exoskeleton suit attached to six kerosene-fuelled micro gas turbines with a combined thrust of 1,274 N (130 kgf, or 286.6 lbf). The £40,000 ($52,449) outfit is completed by ultra-light snake-resistant walking boots. Once in the air, Browning uses his body to adjust his speed and direction – to go faster, he pulls in his arms and pushes out his chest.

CONTENTS

FANTASTIC FEATS

The Gravity Flight Suit – named Daedalus, after the ancient Greek inventor – has a potential top speed of 450 km/h (279 mph). However, Richard has been unable to try his suit at top speed owing to the one thing his invention is missing... a parachute.

FOOD FEATS

Largest M&M's mosaic (logo)

Mars Incorporated (BGR) created a mosaic of the M&M's logo measuring 533 sq ft (49.51 m²) in Sofia, Bulgaria, as verified on 29 Sep 2017. Consisting of approximately 291,500 M&M's, the mosaic was constructed by 27 people and took 17 hr 30 min to assemble.

Largest candy mosaic

On 16 Apr 2017, CYE-Ningbo Cultural Square Development (CHN) unveiled a candy mosaic measuring 160.22 m² (1,724 sq ft) in Ningbo, Zhejiang Province, China. The image, which was created by 60 people, used almost 300,000 lollipops and took 11 hr to complete.

Tallest tower of cupcakes

On 23 Sep 2017, Cupcakes of Hope (ZAF) built a tower of sweet treats measuring 10.77 m (35 ft 4 in) in height in Vereeniging, Gauteng Province, South Africa.

Most people grilling/barbecuing simultaneously

Yuca Expoeventos (MEX) brought together 394 barbecuers to do their stuff on the Plaza de la Mexicanidad in Ciudad Juárez, Chihuahua, Mexico, on 19 Aug 2017.

Most flautas served in eight hours

Financial institution BBVA Bancomer (MEX) served 12,000 flautas (rolled tacos) on 9 Oct 2017 in Mexico City, Mexico. They required 396 kg (873 lb) of tortillas, 495 kg (1,091 lb) of beef, 165 kg (363 lb) of panela cheese, 429 kg (945 lb) of guacamole and 200 litres (52.8 US gal) of cream.

Largest serving of plov

On 8 Sep 2017, Uzbek entertainment TV channel Milliy TV cooked up a serving of plov weighing 7,360 kg (16,226 lb) in Tashkent, Uzbekistan. Plov is a traditional rice-and-meat dish, often served from a cauldron known as a *kazan*.

Most blueberries stuffed in the mouth in one minute

Dinesh Shivnath Upadhyaya (IND) crammed 86 blueberries in his mouth in 60 sec on 16 Jan 2018 in Mumbai, India. Dinesh is the holder of multiple GWR food-related titles (see below) – this was the fourth time he had broken this particular record.

Most juice extracted from grapes by treading in one minute

Martina Servaty (DEU) squeezed out 12.76 litres (3.37 US gal) of juice by treading grapes in 60 sec live on Gordon Ramsay's *The F Word* in Los Angeles, California, USA, on 26 Jul 2017.

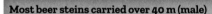

Most beer steins carried over 40 m (male)

Michael Sturm (DEU) carried 26 steins containing 26 litres (6.9 US gal) of beer along a 40-m (130-ft) course at the Oktoberfest Brahma Extra São Paulo in Brazil on 27 Sep 2017. He managed to retain 98.33% of the total weight – well above the 90% lowest permitted rate. Michael had tried 28 steins, but was unable to complete the course.

Largest locro de papa soup

Sixteen-year-old Paulina Baum (ECU) made a traditional Ecuadorian potato soup weighing 12,760 lb (5,787.84 kg) with 20,000 servings in Quito, Ecuador, on 5 Mar 2017.

Largest ceviche

On 14 Apr 2017, the Universidad Tecnológica de Manzanillo (MEX) prepared a fresh seafood dish weighing 11,480 kg (25,309 lb) in Manzanillo, Colima, Mexico.

Largest cake ball

To celebrate their 150th anniversary, on 3 Sep 2017 Sheffield Wednesday Football Club (UK) built a cake in the shape of a soccer ball weighing 285 kg (628 lb 5 oz). It was decorated with the club crest.

Most sausages produced in a minute

On 3 Apr 2017, Barry John Crowe (IRL) made 78 sausages in 60 sec on the set of RTÉ's *Big Week on the Farm* in Cavan, Ireland. World champion butcher Barry has been making sausages since the age of 13. Each one he produced had to be at least 4 in (10.16 cm) long. He smashed the previous record of 60, set in 2016.

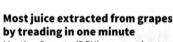

FASTEST TIME TO...

Drink a bottle of ketchup

On 7 Sep 2017, Dinesh Shivnath Upadhyaya (IND) downed a 500-g (17.6-oz) bottle of ketchup in 25.37 sec in Mumbai, India. The gastronomic guzzler (see above, and right) beat the previous best by more than 4 sec.

Peel and eat a grapefruit

On 16 Mar 2017, multi-record holder Dinesh (see left) peeled and ate a grapefruit in 14.22 sec in Mumbai, India.

Eat 500 g of mozzarella

On 12 Apr 2016, Ashrita Furman (USA) ate half a kilo (1 lb 1 oz) of cheese in New York City, USA, in 1 min 34.44 sec.

Eat a KitKat (no hands)

Daniel Dickinson (UK) ate two fingers of chocolate in 22.52 sec at Lakeland Leisure Park in Cumbria, UK, on 31 Aug 2016.

Assemble a yule log

TV chef James Martin (UK) built a yule log in 1 min 17 sec on *Saturday Morning with James Martin* on 8 Dec 2017.

Tallest stack of...
M&M's: Silvio Sabba (ITA) balanced four M&M's on top of one another in Rodano, Milan, Italy, on 21 Dec 2016.

Doughnuts in one minute: On 17 Jan 2018, Steven Ruppel (USA) stacked 11 doughnuts in 60 sec in Wausau, Wisconsin, USA.

Macarons: A 2.07-m-high (6-ft 9.4-in) tower of macarons was built by the Vocational School of Visionary Arts in Tokyo, Japan, on 22–23 Aug 2014.

FANTASTIC FEATS

Fastest time to eat three pickled eggs

On 7 Dec 2017, Kevin "L.A. Beast" Strahle (USA) wolfed down three pickled eggs in just 21.09 sec in Ridgewood, New Jersey, USA. Kevin is a competitive eater who thinks nothing of knocking back 12 raw eggs in a single serving, drinking a gallon of honey while covered in bees or eating 10 cacti. In 2017, he devoured one GWR title after another – see below and right, if you're hungry for more...

The activities on these pages are strictly for experts only – **don't try them at home!**

Kevin's extreme eating challenges had earned his YouTube channel "skippy62able" more than 2 million subscribers as of Mar 2018.

*On 3 May 2017, Kevin achieved the **most bhut jolokia chillies eaten in two minutes**, munching down 121 g (4.3 oz) of the fearsomely hot peppers – formerly the **hottest chilli**.*

*On 12 May 2017, Kevin gobbled up the **most powdered doughnuts in three minutes** – nine. He could not lick his lips at any time during the attempt.*

*On 12 May 2017, Kevin stopped by the GWR office in New York City, USA, and set the **fastest time to drink a bottle of maple syrup** – 10.84 sec.*

*Kevin battled to avoid the dreaded "brain freeze" while achieving the **most ice lollies (popsicles) eaten in one minute** – six – on 7 Dec 2017.*

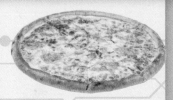

Eat a 12-in pizza
Kelvin Medina (PHL) put away a pizza in 23.62 sec in Taguig, Metro Manila, Philippines, on 12 Apr 2015.

Eat 500 g of cranberry sauce
André Ortolf (DEU) ate 500 g (17.6 oz) of cranberry sauce in 42.94 sec in Augsburg, Germany, on 19 Aug 2016.

Eat a hot dog (no hands)
On 16 May 2016, Peter Czerwinski (CAN) ate a hot dog with no hands in 23.12 sec in New York City, USA.

Eat a bowl of pasta
Michelle Lesco (USA) downed a 150-g (5.2-oz) serving of pasta in 26.69 sec in Scottsdale, Arizona, USA, on 18 Sep 2017.

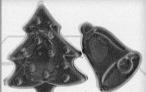

Eat all chocolates from an advent calendar
Kevin Strahle (see above) ate all the festive chocolates in 1 min 27.84 sec on 4 Dec 2017.

BIG FOOD

LARGEST...

Jam-filled biscuit

Frances Quinn – winner of the 2013 *Great British Bake Off* TV show – and Hambleton Bakery (both UK) designed and baked a giant jam-filled biscuit weighing 26.76 kg (58 lb 15 oz). The "Grand Slammy Dodger", as it was named, was sculpted into the shape of a tennis racket to celebrate the 2017 Wimbledon Championships. Unveiled on 14 Jul 2017, it weighed about the same as a Dalmatian dog.

Bread dumpling

A 170-lb (77.1-kg) dumpling was prepared by Andrea, Filippo and Matteo Bettega, Andrea Nascimbene, Andrea Andrighetti in an event organized by Gruppo G.A.R.I. (all ITA) in Imer, Trento, Italy, on 10 Jun 2017. The traditional Italian *canederlo* or *knödel* contained flour, parsley, speck, chives and sage.

Ice-cream-scoop pyramid

A total of 5,435 scoops of ice-cream were piled into a 23-layer pyramid by Diplom-Is (NOR) in Strömstad, Sweden, on 28 Jan 2017. The final structure weighed 500 kg (1,102 lb) and measured 1.1 m (3 ft 7 in) tall.

Dulce de leche candy

A *cajeta de Sayula* weighing 1,615.5 kg (3,561 lb 9 oz) was made by Cajeteros de Sayula (MEX) in Jalisco, Mexico, on 28 Feb 2017. This dish, a regional variation on *dulce de leche* ("sweet milk"), was made from milk, sugar, vanilla and rice flour, which was poured into a wooden case and cooked with a blowtorch.

Chili con carne

A rhinoceros-sized serving of chili con carne weighing 4,800 lb (2,177 kg) was prepared by the Spirit of Texas Festival in College Station, Texas, USA, on 4 Mar 2017.

Chocolate rabbit

The largest rabbit made of chocolate weighed 4,245.5 kg (9,359 lb 11 oz) – more than 4,000 times heavier than the average pet bunny. It was sculpted by Equipe da Casa do Chocolate at Shopping Uberaba in Minas Gerais, Brazil, on 25 Feb 2017. The giraffe-sized confection stood 4.52 m (14 ft 9.9 in) tall and contained an estimated 21.2 million calories.

Cachupa stew

The national dish of Cape Verde in West Africa, cachupa stew typically comprises meats cooked with corn, sweet potato, beans and cabbage. On 9 Jul 2017, 6,360 kg (14,021 lb) of it – equivalent in weight to a large African elephant – was cooked by Cavibel SA and Grupo Mirage (both CPV) in the country's capital, Praia. No elephants were involved: the meats used were pork and chicken.

Largest serving of guacamole
A 2,980-kg (6,569-lb) serving of guacamole – heavier than four average dairy cows – was dished up by Empacadora de Aguacates Sierra del Tigre (MEX) in Concepción de Buenos Aires, Jalisco, Mexico, on 3 Sep 2017.

Largest chocolate truffle
On 21 Apr 2017, Sweet Shop USA of Mount Pleasant, Texas, produced a giant chocolate truffle weighing 1,074.33 kg (2,368 lb 8 oz). The "Milk Swiss Mint Truffle" – about 5.5 million calories – was equivalent in weight to 12 adult men!

Longest French strawberry cake
On 14 May 2017, five professional pastry chefs at the Strawberry Festival in Beaulieu-sur-Dordogne, France, prepared a *fraisier pâtissier* that stretched 32.24 m (105 ft 9 in). The confection – about the same length as a blue whale – was built from layers of pastry, *crème pâtissiere* (a thick custard) and strawberries.

Largest samosa
A samosa weighing 153.1 kg (337 lb 8.4 oz) was made by Muslim Aid in London, UK, on 22 Aug 2017. The triangular – and vegetarian – treat measured 1.4 m (4 ft 7 in) along its longest side and weighed more than two average adult women. It was made as part of the 2017 Eid celebrations to raise awareness of global poverty and starvation.

MOST EXPENSIVE...

*Sold at auction

◀ Hot dog

The "Juuni Ban" hot dog at Tokyo Dog in Seattle, Washington, USA, sells for $169 (£101.69), as verified on 23 Feb 2014. For this, you get smoked-cheese bratwurst, butter-teriyaki-grilled onions, maitake mushrooms, wagyu beef, foie gras, shaved black truffles and caviar.

Slice of wedding cake*

A box containing a piece of the Duke and Duchess of Windsor's 1937 wedding cake was sold at Sotheby's in New York, USA, on 27 Feb 1998 for $29,900 (£18,152) to Benjamin and Amanda Yin of San Francisco, USA. When asked if they would be exhibiting the cake, the buyers replied, "We're sure not going to eat it! It represents the epitome of a great romance."

Imperial bottle of wine*

A bottle of 1947 French Cheval-Blanc was sold at Christie's in Geneva, Switzerland, on 16 Nov 2010 for £192,000 ($307,805). "Imperial" bottles contain the equivalent of eight standard 75-cl (750-ml; 25.36-fl-oz) bottles.

The **most expensive wine by the glass** cost FF8,600 (£983; $1,453.07), paid by Robert Denby (UK) for the first glass of Beaujolais Nouveau 1993.

Bottle of whisky*

The Macallan M Decanter "Constantine" sold at Sotheby's in Hong Kong, China, on 23 Jan 2014 for $628,000 (£380,169). The 6-litre (1.59-US-gal) decanter stands 70 cm (2 ft 4 in) tall and was created as part of a four-bottle "Imperiales" range named after Roman emperors. The whisky for the M Decanter was created by Bob Dalgarno, whisky-maker at The Macallan.

The **longest kebab** – of meat and vegetables – was skewered by staff of ArcelorMittal in Newcastle, South Africa, on 17 Oct 2008 and measured 2.04 km (1.26 mi).

The **longest sushi roll** measured 2.84 km (1.76 mi) and was made by 400 volunteers for the Tamana Otawara Festival in Kumamoto, Japan, on 20 Nov 2016.

The **longest sausage chain** stretched 3.54 km (2.2 mi) and was linked together by Worstenfeesten (BEL) at Kerkhofstraat in Vlimmeren, Belgium, on 15 Aug 2013.

The prodigious pizza was prepared at California's Auto Club Speedway. After the event, all of the remaining slices were donated to food banks and homeless charities.

Longest pizza

A mega-sized margherita pizza measuring 1.2 mi (1.93 km) in length was made by Pizzaovens.com, Venice Bakery, Orlando Foods, AT-PAC, Sysco, TFX NonStick!, Capstone Scaffold Services, Scaffold Works, SoCalGas, Tony Gemignani, Giulio Adriani, John Arena (all USA) and Italforni (ITA) in Fontana, California, USA, on 10 Jun 2017. It took eight hours to cook the pizza: the raw dough and its toppings were passed through three industrial ovens using a conveyor belt.

More than 100 people took 54 hr to create the pizza and top it with some 5,000 lb (2,267 kg) of tomato sauce.

After 3,900 lb (1,769 kg) of cheese was added, the pizza travelled 7,000 ft (2,133 m) along a conveyor belt and into the three ovens used to bake it.

▶ Sandwich

The "Quintessential Grilled Cheese" sells for $214 (£132.64) at Serendipity 3 in New York, USA. The cheese used in the toastie is made from the milk of the Podolico cow, which grazes in southern Italy on aromatic plants such as fennel, liquorice, juniper, bay laurel and wild strawberries. Only around 25,000 such cows exist.

MAKE YOUR OWN
I. Bake bread with Dom Pérignon Champagne and 23-carat edible gold flakes.
2. Cut two slices and cover with truffle butter. Add caciocavallo Podolico cheese, toast until golden and dip edges in more gold flakes.
3. Serve with lobster bisque, crème fraîche and truffle oil.

Mangoes*

The most expensive mangoes in the world cost AUS$2,562.50 (£888; $1,284) each! They were purchased by Sam Coco (AUS) when he bought a tray of 16 Top End mangoes at the Brisbane Produce Markets Charity Auction in Australia for AUS$41,000 (£14,212; $20,544) on 12 Oct 2001. The mangoes were donated to Brisbane's Mater Children's Hospital.

Hamburger

Since 2 Jul 2011, the most that you can spend on a commercially available hamburger – as listed on a restaurant menu – is $5,000 (£3,115.86), for the burger served at Juicys Outlaw Grill in Corvallis, Oregon, USA. The hamburger weighs 777 lb (352.44 kg) and is available for ordering with 48 hours' notice for preparation time.

COLLECTIONS

Whether it's yo-yos or fishing lures, bus tickets or ballpoint pens, once you've got the collecting bug it's hard to stop! These record holders have spent time, effort and money pursuing the ultimate assemblages. What will you start collecting?

Recent record-worthy collections

Advertising statues: 8,917
Michael Pollack (USA)

Brandy bottles: 1,057
Manuel Bru Vicente (ESP)

Computers (single brand): 250
Wang Zhaoyu (CHN)

Ear trumpets (below): 359
Myk Briggs (UK)

Fishing lures: 3,563
Will "Spike" Yocum (USA)

Irons: 30,071
Ion Chirescu (ROM)

Jigsaw puzzles: 1,047
Luiza Figueiredo (BRA)

Lip balms: 730
Bailey Leigh Sheppard (UK)

Miniature books: 3,137
Sathar Adhoor (IND)

Model cars: 37,777
Nabil Karam (LBN)

Model trains: 2,956
Bernd Schumacher (USA)

Paper cups: 736
V Sankaranarayanan (IND)

Postcards: 15,089
Marina Noutsou (GRC)

Snow globes: 4,059
Wendy Suen (CHN)

Ties: 21,321
Irene Sparks (NZ)

Toy soldiers: 1,020
Jonathan Perry Waters (USA)

Collections are among the most popular and recognizable GWR categories. They can be fun, such as the **largest collection of banana-related memorabilia** – 17,000, amassed by Ken Bannister (USA), owner of the International Banana Club Museum. They can be wonderfully eccentric: Rainer Weichert (DEU) amassed the **largest collection of "Do Not Disturb" signs** – 11,570. They can even be a little bit gruesome: the **largest collection of human teeth** numbered 2,000,744, and was collected by an Italian monk named Brother Giovanni Battista Orsenigo (1837–1904).

Almost any object can form the basis of a collection, but it definitely helps to have a passion for it. Maybe that's why animal-related collections are so popular, although few people can rival the **largest collection of mouse- and rat-related items** – a staggering 47,398, owned by Christa Behmenburg (DEU). See below for other notable examples.

Sport fans and TV show aficionados can also assemble huge hoards, such as the **largest collection of sporting memorabilia** – 40,669 items, by Philippos Stavrou Platini (CYP). No object is too humble or too small: witness Ed Brassard's (USA) amazing **largest collection of matchbook covers**, totalling 3,159,119. Then there's the **largest collection of espionage-related items**, which includes more than 7,000 items of spying equipment and belongs to military and intelligence historian and author Keith Melton (USA). It's so secret that we cannot reveal where it's located!

If you have a collection that you think might be eligible for a Guinness World Records title, follow our top tips to give yourself the best possible chance:

Largest collection of clown-related items
F M Kahn (DEU) has been collecting clown memorabilia since 1989, and as of 11 Apr 2017 had amassed 4,348 items in Hoogvliet, Netherlands. He has opened his own clown museum, which includes figurines of comic creations made from Murano glass, porcelain and 24-carat gold.

- You must provide a clear inventory of all your items in a spreadsheet or logbook, together with photographic evidence of every single object.
- You'll also need to video a count of the collection, which must be attended by two witnesses. Both witnesses must produce a signed statement confirming what they have seen.
- Remember that records are based on the number of *different* individual items – duplicates will not be counted. If items are usually paired, such as earrings or cufflinks, the number of pairs must be given.
- You'll also need a covering letter, in which you can give a brief history of your collection, and tell us how and why you got started.

For full guidelines concerning collections and all other records, go to **guinnessworldrecords.com**. Good luck!

Largest collection of Sylvanian Families
Dance teacher Jacc Batch (UK) owns 3,489 items connected to the popular woodland animal toy range in Kettering, Northamptonshire, UK, as verified on 19 May 2017. He began collecting aged seven, with the hedgehog brother becoming his first figurine.

ANIMALS ASSEMBLE!

◀ Largest collection of hippopotamus-related items
On 12 Jul 2016, Rebecca Fusco of Meriden in Connecticut, USA, had her collection of unique hippo-related memorabilia verified at 604. Rebecca began her hippo haul almost 20 years ago. It ranges from figurines and toys to Russian nesting dolls and salt and pepper shakers.

Largest collection of frog-related items
Sheila Crown (UK) began collecting frog items in 1979, when she bought a frog for her green-painted study. She added to her "hopping list" until they numbered 10,502, and she had to move to a bigger property to house them all. On 12 May 2002, the frogs were put on display at the FrogsGalore Museum in Marlborough, Wiltshire, UK.

◀ Largest collection of rubber ducks
Charlotte Lee (USA) had 5,631 different rubber ducks as of 10 Apr 2011, which she displayed in glass showcases on the walls of her dedicated duck room. Charlotte is an associate professor at the University of Washington, and has given talks on "Collecting Rubber Ducks and the Path to Mastery".

Frank's favourite LEGO set is a Batcave from the classic *Batman* 1960s TV series. He loves it for the iconic characters and vehicles.

Largest collection of LEGO® sets

Frank Smoes (AUS) and his family have been stockpiling and building LEGO® sets since 1980. On 9 May 2017, their private collection of interlocking plastic brick sets was verified at 3,837 in Melbourne, Victoria, Australia. Frank's collection has at least 1.2 million individual bricks and pieces, and includes more than 8,000 LEGO Minifigures.

◄ **Largest collection of penguin-related items**

Birgit Berends (DEU) had amassed a collection of 11,062 different penguin-themed objects in Cuxhaven, Germany, as of 14 Mar 2011. She began collecting in earnest at the age of 18, inspired by the animated series *Pingu*. Besides stuffed toys, Birgit owns penguin books, mugs, posters, ties, towels and even underwear!

▶ **Largest collection of sheep-related items**

Alessia Citti (ITA) had amassed 1,822 sheep-related items in Ciampino, Rome, Italy, as of 19 Feb 2017. She was given her first toy sheep by her mother when she was just six months old. Most of Alessia's collection is kept in her bedroom, which she has dubbed her "Sacred Temple for Sheep" (Il Vittoriale delle Pecore).

ODD TALENTS

Farthest distance to limbo-skate under bars

G Devisri Prasad (IND) travelled 184 m (603 ft 8 in) on skates beneath 10-in-high (25.4-cm) bars at Ramakrishna Housing in Amaravati, Andhra Pradesh, India, on 31 Aug 2017. A national skating champion, he was 10 years old at the time.

Longest underwater walk with one breath (female)

On 27 Oct 2017, Marina Kazankova (ITA) walked 69.4 m (227 ft 8 in) underwater on one breath inside an aquarium tank filled with fish in Dubai, UAE. Kazankova is a freediver and actress who in 2015 starred in a single-shot, real-time music video that was filmed entirely underwater.

Fastest time to make an origami boat with the mouth

Gao Guangli (CHN) took just 3 min 34 sec to fold a paper sheet into the shape of a boat using only his mouth. The feat took place in Jining, Shandong Province, China, on 2 Dec 2017. Guangli suffered from polio as a child and wanted to break the record to show that he can still achieve amazing feats.

Fastest time to deposit 20 coins into a piggy bank using chopsticks

On 8 Nov 2017, Rocco Mercurio (ITA) took only 38.94 sec to drop 20 coins into a piggy bank with a pair of chopsticks in Villa San Giovanni, Calabria, Italy.

The **most coffee beans moved in a minute using chopsticks** is 48, by Silvio Sabba (ITA) on 10 Aug 2017 in Rodano, Lombardy, Italy.

Longest duration spinning a basketball on a toothbrush

On 25 Dec 2017, Sandeep Singh Kaila (IND) spun a basketball on a toothbrush for 60.50 sec in British Columbia, Canada.

Most walnuts crushed by hand in one minute

Prabhakar Reddy (IND) crushed 251 walnuts with his right hand in 60 sec in Andhra Pradesh, India, on 5 Jan 2018.

Most consecutive pinky pull-ups

On 27 Nov 2017, Tazio Gavioli (ITA) completed 23 pull-ups in a row using just his little fingers in Carpi, Modena, Italy. Tazio began strength training when his cat Kali lost a paw – he learned to climb with one arm to show "solidarity".

Fastest 50 m on hand skates

Mirko Hanssen (DEU) covered a distance of 50 m (164 ft) on hand skates in 8.55 sec in Bocholt, North Rhine-Westphalia, Germany, on 16 Nov 2017. Mirko wore K2 Mach 100 skates to achieve the new speed record, which was measured using light sensors.

Most balls thrown into a target from a jumping motorcycle in one minute (team)

On 5 Sep 2017, the BoldogFMX Team (UK) performed a series of ramp jumps up to a 6-m-high (19-ft 8-in) ring, slotting home 10 balls in 60 sec for CBBC's *Officially Amazing* in York, North Yorkshire, UK. The daredevil riders were Arran Powley, Samson Eaton and Dan Whitby.

Most bō staff rotations around the body on one leg in one minute

Chloé Bruce (UK) rotated a Japanese martial arts staff around her body 51 times in 60 sec, while standing on one leg, on CBBC's *Officially Amazing* in Bracknell, Berkshire, UK, on 9 Sep 2017. Martial artist Chloé has worked as a stunt double on blockbusters such as *Star Wars: The Force Awakens* (USA, 2015).

Fastest speed for a snowboarder towed by a vehicle

Jamie Barrow (UK) reached 149.65 km/h (92.98 mph) while being towed behind a Maserati Levante in St Moritz, Switzerland, on 19 Feb 2018. He broke his own record of 99.84 km/h (62.03 mph), set back in 2016 (pictured below). A bad back injury forced Jamie to retire from Britain's snowboard cross team in 2013, but it clearly hasn't slowed down his appetite for breaking records!

The **fastest speed for a skier towed by a vehicle** is 189.07 km/h (117.48 mph), by Graham Bell and Jaguar Land Rover (both UK) in Arjeplog, Sweden, on 7 Mar 2017.

JUMPING FOR JOY

◀ **Fastest 100 m on a space hopper (female)**

Ali Spagnola (USA) covered 100 m (328 ft) on a space hopper in a mere 38.22 sec at UCLA's Drake Track & Field Stadium in Los Angeles, California, USA, on 9 Mar 2017.

Ashrita Furman (USA) holds the overall record for the **fastest 100 m on a space hopper**, with a time of 30.2 sec set on 16 Nov 2004.

Highest jump above one's own head

Franklin Jacobs (USA) cleared the height of his head by 1 ft 11.75 in (59 cm) via a 7-ft 7.25-in (2.32-m) high jump in New York City, USA, on 27 Jan 1978.

The **highest jump above one's own head (female)** is 32 cm (12.60 in) by Yolanda Henry (USA). She reached 2 m (6 ft 6.74 in) with a jump in Seville, Spain, on 30 May 1990.

▶ **Fastest time to bunny hop 15 hurdles on a trials bicycle**

Joe Oakley (UK) hopped over 15 hurdles on a trials bicycle in 13.88 sec at the Urban Games in Newcastle, UK, on 19 Aug 2012.

He also set the record for the **fastest time to complete an oil barrel course on a trials bicycle**: 10.63 sec. He crossed nine barrels on the set of *Officially Amazing* (CBBC) at Wollaton Hall in Nottingham, UK, on 12 Jun 2014.

Extreme juggling...
Most bowling balls juggled: Milan Roskopf (SVK) kept three 10-lb (4.53-kg) bowling balls in the air for 28.69 sec at the Prague juggling marathon in Prague, Czech Republic, on 19 Nov 2011.

Most times to juggle hats on to the head in one minute: on 7 Jul 2015, while juggling three hats, Marcos Ruiz Ceballos (ESP) caught one on his head 71 times in 60 seconds.

Greatest combined weight juggled: on 17 Jul 2013, Ukraine's Denys Ilchenko juggled three tyres with an overall weight of 26.98 kg (59 lb 7.6 oz) on the set of *Officially Amazing* in Nairn, UK.

GUINNESS WORLD RECORDS

Josh risked getting the chop when he completed the **most consecutive axe juggling catches** – 604, at Art Factory on 3 Nov 2017.

Also on 3 Nov 2017, Josh achieved the **longest duration juggling five soccer balls** with a time of 1 min 15.02 sec.

Most samurai swords juggled

Josh Horton (USA) kept four samurai swords rotating in the air at once at Art Factory Studios in Paterson, New Jersey, USA, on 3 Nov 2017. His successful attempt was recorded as part of the ongoing *Chronicles of a Record Breaker* series by sports entertainment network Whistle Sports. Look left and you'll find five other records that Josh has also achieved.

The **most toilet rolls balanced on the head in 30 sec** is 12, by Josh in Malibu, California, USA, on 16 May 2017.

On 17 Nov 2017, Josh set the **longest duration balancing a guitar on the forehead** (7 min 3.9 sec) in Dallas, Texas, USA.

Josh kept his cool while achieving the **most torches juggled on a balance board** (5) at Art Factory on 3 Nov 2017.

In all, Josh has picked up nine gold medals from the World Juggling Federation and International Jugglers' Association.

The activities on these pages are strictly for experts only – **don't try them at home!**

▼ Longest reverse vault (parkour)
Ryan Luney (UK, below) covered an unprecedented 4.06 m (13 ft 3.8 in) with a reverse vault in Carrickfergus Gym & Trampoline Club, County Antrim, UK, on 22 Jun 2016.

The **longest distance vaulted between two objects (parkour)** is 4 m (13 ft 1.48 in), by Toby Segar (UK) on 15 Aug 2014.

Farthest forward-flip trampoline slam dunk
In this feat, an individual attempts to thrust a basketball through a hoop having first completed a front flip from a trampoline. Kerim Daghistani (HUN) performed an 8.1-m (26-ft 6.89-in) forward-flip trampoline slam dunk – measured from the centre of the trampoline to the backboard – in Budapest, Hungary, on 4 Nov 2017.

▶ Highest standing jump
Canada's Evan Ungar made a 1.616-m (5-ft 3.6-in) jump from a standing position in Oakville, Ontario, Canada, on 13 May 2016. He broke the record at One Health Clubs, with 100 people cheering him on.

A year to the day later, Evan also achieved the **highest standing jump on one leg** – 1.346 m (4 ft 4.99 in) – in Mississauga, Ontario, Canada.

MASS PARTICIPATION

Largest gathering of people dressed as Peter Pan
"The Boy Who Never Grew Up" inspired the Cancer Research UK Relay for Life, held in Kirriemuir, UK, on 12 Aug 2017. Altogether, 534 runners dressed as Peter Pan joined the race, which was staged in the birthplace of J M Barrie – creator of the famous literary character.

Largest cricket lesson (single venue)
Sports charity Chance to Shine (UK) brought together 580 people to learn more about cricket at Lord's Cricket Ground, in London, UK, on 17 Jul 2017. Charlotte Edwards, a former captain of the England women's team and Chance to Shine ambassador, led the lesson, assisted by 25 cricket coaches.

Most people wolf-howling
To mark 150 years since Canada was established, on 1 Jul 2017 the Great Wolf Lodge (CAN) gathered 803 people to howl like wolves in Niagara Falls, Ontario.

Largest gathering of people with the same forename
No introductions had to be made at this same-name party, which was held in Kupres, Bosnia and Herzegovina, on 30 Jul 2017. That's because all 2,325 people in attendance were called Ivan. The event was arranged by Kupreški kosci (BIH).
   The **largest gathering of people with the same surname**, meanwhile, is 1,488 Gallaghers, who met in Letterkenny, Ireland, on 9 Sep 2007, beating 1,224 Joneses from Wales.

Largest Peruvian folk dance
A total of 3,170 people paired up on 24 Jun 2017 to perform the *pandilla moyobambina*, a traditional dance from the San Martín region of northern Peru. The record was part of the feast of San Juan festivities, when locals gather in Moyobamba, Peru, to take a dip in natural thermal pools – a custom known as the "Baño Bendito" ("Blessed Bath").

Most people dancing with swords
It sounds dangerous, but sword-dancing is a traditional art form in many cultures, including several regions of India. Vijayalakshmi Bhoopathi (IND) organized a sword dance by 798 students of the Mayuri Academy of Performing Arts in Chennai, Tamil Nadu, India, on 29 Jul 2017.

Largest yoga lesson
On 21 Jun 2017 – International Yoga Day – 55,506 yogis came together to practise spiritual and physical well-being in Mysuru, Karnataka, India. The session was organized by the District Administration of Mysuru (IND).

Most people modelling on a catwalk
On 4 Jul 2015, a crowd of 3,651 fashion models and members of the public took to a 40-m-long (131-ft) catwalk in Pier Head, Liverpool, UK. The event was organized by Culture Liverpool in association with very.co.uk (both UK). It took a full 3 hr 50 min for all the participants to strut their stuff.

Most people dressed in traditional Romanian clothing
A gathering of 9,643 people wearing historic Romanian dress assembled in Năsăud, Romania, on 14 May 2017 in an event arranged by the Bistriţa-Năsăud community (ROM). They were celebrating National Day of Folk Costume in Romania, which aims to preserve the country's cultural values, with an emphasis on traditional folk costume, music and dance.

> Wally has many different names around the world, including Waldo in the USA, Willy in Norway, Charlie in France and Văn-lang in Vietnam.

Largest gathering of people dressed as Wally
Where's Wally? It wasn't very difficult to find the iconic book character in his stripy red jumper at the Huis Ten Bosch theme park in Sasebo, Nagasaki, Japan, on 8 Oct 2017: there were 4,626 of him! It was a case of third time lucky for the amusement park, having previously failed to break this record twice before.

LARGEST HUMAN IMAGE OF A...

Letter
Give us a "C"! On 15 Aug 2017, the University of California, Berkeley (USA) formed a colossal letter "C" with 7,194 students at the California Memorial Stadium. This smashed the mark set just a few months before by the University of Tennessee, who – not surprisingly – created a giant "T" with 4,223 people.

Mouth
The University of Glasgow Dental School in Scotland, UK, must have raised a few smiles on 9 Jun 2017... A supersized mouth was made up of 756 students and other locals from the Glasgow area – all wearing either red or white ponchos to recreate lips and teeth. They were seeking to raise awareness for good oral hygiene.

▼ Bicycle
Hoping to inspire "the future generation of commuters to make the choice to travel in an active way", Auckland Transport (NZ) created a bike with 1,799 students, parents and staff at Glen Eden Intermediate School in Auckland, New Zealand, on 9 Jun 2017.

Flower
Country Garden Crape Myrtle Real Estate (CHN) amassed 2,567 people to form a humongous human bloom on 10 Sep 2017. The red flower was created outside the Shaoyang Cultural and Art Center in Shaoyang, Hunan, China, and surpassed the previous record – a lotus formed in California, USA, on 15 Jul 2017 – by 162 people.

Celebrating local culture, the Câmara Municipal de Ponte da Barca in Portugal staged the **largest Portuguese folk dance** on 20 Aug 2017. There were 661 dancers involved.

The Andhra Pradesh Social Welfare Residential Educational Institutions Society (IND) organized the **largest Kuchipudi dance** on 11 Apr 2017, bringing together 7,002 dancers.

Welcoming the spirits of deceased ancestors, 2,872 people took part in the **largest bon dance**, on 9 Sep 2017. The event was organized by Yao Kawachi Ondo Festival Association (JPN) and held in Yao, Osaka, Japan.

Harry Potter and the Philosopher's Stone was first published on 26 Jun 1997, as part of a 500-copy run. *The Cursed Child*, by contrast, had an initial print run in 2016 of 4.5 million in the USA alone!

Largest gathering of people dressed as Harry Potter

The date 10 Nov 2017 was a spellbinding day for 823 students from Wembley Primary School (AUS) in Perth, Australia. They achieved a new GWR title for the greatest number of people assembled together wearing Harry Potter's iconic school uniform and zigzag scar. Year 6 student Charlotte Raston (centre) had the magic idea.

Largest gathering of people dressed as sunflowers
To encourage outdoor activities, Chinese realtors Mayland City hosted 889 people dressed as sunflowers in Guangzhou, Guangdong, China, on 4 Nov 2017.

Largest gathering of people dressed as emojis (multiple locations)
Sony Pictures convinced 531 people to get in touch with their emotions in five different countries on 15 Jul 2017 to celebrate the release of *The Emoji Movie*.

▶ Camera
Marking the centenary of camera-maker Nikon, NITAL (ITA) – the firm's official distributor in Italy – snapped 1,454 people standing in the shape of a camera on 17 Jun 2017. Participants dressed in black, grey, red or white, and gathered in formation outside the castle at Stupinigi, near Turin in northern Italy.

Maple leaf
Gamania Digital Entertainment (TPE) created a massive maple leaf with 1,558 people during a family fun day at the EXPO Dome in Taipei, Chinese Taipei, on 25 Jun 2017. Although this plant is most commonly associated with Canada, the giant leaf design was chosen in honour of Gamania's best-selling online role-playing game, *MapleStory*.

▼ Motorcycle
It took 1,325 participants to recreate a Yamaha Exciter on 30 Jul 2017, recognizing the millionth sale of this model. At the same event, put on by Yamaha Motor Vietnam, they also achieved the **largest motorcycle logo**, using 554 motorbikes.

SDRAWKCAB

Longest journey walking backwards
The greatest-ever exponent of reverse pedestrianism has to be Plennie L Wingo (USA), who between 15 Apr 1931 and 24 Oct 1932 completed an 8,000-mi (12,875-km) transcontinental walk from Santa Monica in California, USA, to Istanbul in Turkey. Plennie wore special glasses with rear-view mirrors to help him see where he was going, and funded his trek by selling postcards of himself.

Longest distance walking backwards in 24 hours
Anthony Thornton (USA) walked 153.52 km (95.4 mi) backwards from 31 Dec 1988 to 1 Jan 1989 in Minneapolis, Minnesota, USA. He averaged a speed of 6.4 km/h (3.9 mph).

Longest distance driving in reverse
Brian "Cub" Keene and James "Wilbur" Wright (both USA) drove their Chevrolet Blazer 14,534 km (9,031 mi) in reverse for 37 days between 1 Aug and 6 Sep 1984. They passed through 15 US states and parts of Canada.

Fastest mile driven in reverse
Terry Grant (UK) drove a mile backwards in 1 min 37.02 sec at the Goodwood Festival of Speed in West Sussex, UK, on 1 Jul 2012. He steered an electric Nissan Leaf along an uphill course at an average speed of 55 mph (88 km/h).

Fastest run backwards mile
Aaron Yoder (USA) ran a mile backwards in 5 min 54.25 sec in Lindsborg, Kansas, USA, on 23 Nov 2015. He trained by running backwards for 45 min a day for eight weeks.
On 25 Jul 1991, Ferdie Ato Adoboe (GHA) ran the **fastest backwards 100 m (male)** in 13.6 sec in Northampton, Massachusetts, USA.

Fastest 50 m using backflips
Vitaly Scherbo (BLR) backwards-somersaulted 50 m (164 ft) in 10.22 sec at Makuhari Messe Event Hall in Chiba, Japan, on 31 Aug 1995.

Most backwards rolls in one minute
On 16 Apr 2012, Jack Leonard Riley (AUS) completed 56 backwards rolls in 60 sec in Calwell, Australia.

Longest jump backwards from standing
Jan Hempel (DEU) leapt backwards a total distance of 2.01 m (6 ft 7 in) in Munich, Germany, for *Guinness – Die Show der Rekorde* on 22 Feb 2002.

Farthest basketball shot made backwards
Thunder Law of the Harlem Globetrotters (both USA) sunk a basketball shot backwards from 25 m (82 ft) at the US Airways Center in Phoenix, Arizona, USA, on 3 Nov 2014.

Longest backflip into a pair of trousers
On 5 Sep 2016, Raymond Butler (USA) reclaimed his record for acrobatic attire on the set of *The Today Show* in New York City, USA. Cheered on by a watching crowd, he backflipped a distance of 8 ft 6 in (2.59 m) into a pair of trousers. Raymond, a self-taught acrobat, had first set the record in 2013, only to be outbounced three months later.

Most books typed backwards
As of 10 Apr 2017, Michele Santelia (ITA) had re-typed 76 books from back to front in Campobasso, Italy. Each book was copied in its original language using a computer with four blank keyboards and without looking at the screen. Michele's most recent work, *The Indian Vedas Backwards*, was typed using the ancient characters of the Sanskrit alphabet. It is composed of 1,153 pages, 9,277 paragraphs, 20,924 lines, 107,216 words and 635,995 characters.

Longest palindrome
The longest known palindrome – a word that reads the same forwards or backwards – is the 19-letter "saippuakivikauppias". It is a Finnish term for a dealer in lye (caustic soda).

The **longest backflip** is 4.26 m (13 ft 11.71 in), by Lukas Steiner (AUT) on the set of *Lo Show dei Record* in Milan, Italy, on 28 Apr 2011.

SLEEHW DEKCIW

◀ Longest distance riding backwards on a motorcycle
On 7 Oct 2014, Dipayan Choudhury (IND) rode backwards for 202 km (125.5 mi) in Jabalpur, India. A Lance Havildar in the Indian Army Corps of Signals, Dipayan is part of the "Dare Devils" motorcycle display team. He more than trebled the distance achieved by the previous record holder.

Longest distance cycling backwards on a unicycle
Steve Gordon (USA) rode backwards on a unicycle for a distance of 68 mi (109.4 km) at Southwest Missouri State University in Springfield, USA, on 24 Jun 1999.
The **longest distance by unicycle on a line of bottles backwards** is 8.5 m (27 ft 10 in), achieved by Chen Zhong Qin (CHN) on 7 Jan 2015.

◀ Longest distance cycling backwards
On 7–8 Oct 2013, charity fundraiser Andrew Hellinga (AUS) cycled backwards while sat on the handlebars for 337.6 km (209.7 mi) at the Holden Performance Driving Centre in Norwell, Queensland, Australia. This is also the **longest distance cycling backwards in 24 hours**.

The **fastest marathon backwards on inline skates** is 1 hr 39 min 59 sec, achieved by Tomasz Kwiecień (POL) in Warsaw, Poland, on 22 Sep 2013.

The **fastest marathon joggling backwards (three objects)** is 5 hr 51 min 25 sec, by Joe Salter (USA) atthe Quad Cities Marathon in Moline, Illinois, USA, on 22 Sep 2013.

The **fastest marathon running backwards (male)** is 3 hr 43 min 39 sec, by Xu Zhenjun (CHN) at the Beijing International Marathon in China on 17 Oct 2004.

Fastest speed downhill skiing backwards (female)

On 27 Mar 2017, freestyle skier Emilie Cruz (FRA) reached a speed of 107.143 km/h (66.57 mph) skiing backwards at Les Carroz in the French resort of Grand Massif. She was inspired to attempt the record after she saw Elias Ambüehl (CHE) achieve the **fastest speed downhill skiing backwards (male)** – 131.23 km/h (81.54 mph), on 27 Feb 2017 – and learned that there was no female equivalent.

In 2012, Emilie qualified for the FIS Freestyle Ski Junior World Championships. She finished fifth in the Slopestyle event.

Ski instructor Emilie Cruz lives in a village at the base of an alpine resort. She began skiing at the age of two-and-a-half, and was introduced to the freestyle discipline – in which competitors perform aerial flips and spins – at 14.

Longest distance driving in reverse in 24 hours

John and Brian Smith (both USA) drove backwards for 1,369.95 km (851.25 mi) at the I-94 Speedway in Sauk Centre, Minnesota, USA, from 13 to 14 Jun 1999.

The **longest distance reversing a tractor and trailer** is 20.16 km (12.52 mi), by Patrick Shalvey (IRE) on 29 Mar 2017 in Cavan, Ireland.

▼ Farthest reverse ramp jump by car

On 13 Feb 2014, ex-pro skateboarder and multiple GWR title holder Rob Dyrdek (USA) celebrated the series finale of MTV's *Rob Dyrdek's Fantasy Factory* with a reverse ramp jump of 27.2 m (89 ft 2.8 in) at Six Flags Magic Mountain in Valencia, California, USA. He drove a 2014 Chevrolet Sonic RS Turbo.

Longest distance reversing an articulated truck (team)

On 3 Oct 2009, a team of 11 drivers reversed a 19-m (62-ft) semi-trailer (articulated lorry) a distance of 109.76 km (68.2 mi) in Cessnock, New South Wales, Australia.

The **longest distance driving in reverse in an articulated truck (individual)** is 64 km (39.7 mi), by Marco Hellgrewe (DEU) on 22 Sep 2008.

FIGHT!

Largest snowball fight

The town of Saskatoon in Saskatchewan, Canada, played host to a snowball fight between 7,681 people on 31 Jan 2016. The event was staged by the PotashCorp WinterShines Festival to send off Team Canada for the Yukigassen ("Snow Battle") World Championships – an annual professional snowball-fighting competition held in Hokkaido, Japan.

Largest streamer-string fight

A fight between 629 participants armed with cans of streamer string was organized by the Funatorium Explorium at the CE Centre in Ottawa, Ontario, Canada, on 20 Feb 2012.

At the same venue on 18 Feb 2013, the Funatorium was also responsible for the world's **largest paper-ball fight**. A total of 282 combatants took part in the brawl, which was billed as an "indoor paper snowball fight".

Largest pillow fight

Bedding manufacturer MyPillow (USA) hosted a fluffy fight between 6,261 pillow-wielding pugilists on 21 Jul 2015. The battle was staged during a St Paul Saints' baseball game at CHS Field in Minnesota, USA, and was introduced by actor Stephen Baldwin, who also took part.

The **longest-running pillow-fight contest** is the annual World Pillow Fight Championships, which were staged in Kenwood, California, USA, between 1964 and 2006. Approximately 100 pillow-fighters battled it out with wet pillows while sitting astride a steel pole placed over a mud-filled creek. The event was revived on 4 Jul 2014, and another Championship was planned for 2018.

Largest toy-pistol fight

"Jared's Epic NERF Battle" took place at the AT&T Stadium in Arlington, Texas, USA, on 12 Mar 2016. In all, 2,289 sharp-shooters took part, raising money for the Rebuild Rowlett Foundation for Long Term Relief, on behalf of victims of a devastating tornado. Participants were also urged to leave their NERF blasters behind at the end of the attempt so that they could be donated to the Buckner Children's Home (USA).

Largest water-balloon fight

The Christian Student Fellowship at the University of Kentucky in Lexington, USA, staged a water-balloon fight between 8,957 participants on 26 Aug 2011. A total of 175,141 water balloons were lobbed in the conflict.

The **most hits with water balloons in one minute** is 42, by Ashrita Furman (victim) and Bipin Larkin (both USA) in Jamaica, New York City, USA, on 21 Sep 2016.

Largest laser-tag survival match

The most participants in a laser-tag survival match is 307 and was achieved by ECombat (UK) at the NEC in Birmingham, UK, on 6 Apr 2013. The attempt took place during *The Gadget Show LIVE,* and after the two-hour battle was up, the last man standing was Marcus van Wiml.

Most custard pies thrown in a movie sequence

The Laurel and Hardy silent two-reeler *The Battle of the Century* (USA, 1927) saw 3,000 custard pies flung in a single scene. The producer, Hal Roach, bought the entire day's stock from the Los Angeles Pie Company. (See also above right.) *Guinness World Records no longer accepts claims for custard-pie throwing owing to concerns about food wastage.*

Largest shaving-cream pie fight

Ulverston in Cumbria, UK, was the birthplace of Stan Laurel, one half of the comedy partnership Laurel and Hardy (see below left). On 18 Jun 2016, at the town's Another Fine Fest event, celebrating Laurel's birth, 1,180 people took part in a pie fight using paper plates loaded with shaving cream.

Largest robots to fight

In the summer of 2015, US robotics collective MegaBots challenged Japan's Suidobashi Heavy Industry to a fight... using giant mecha robots! The robot rumble finally took place and was aired on 17 Oct 2017, when Suidobashi's 4-m-tall (13-ft) *Kuratas* – the **largest mecha robot controlled by smartphone** – battled with MegaBots' 4.8-m-tall (16-ft) *Eagle Prime*. The 16.78-tonne (18.5-ton) cataclysmic clash ended with *Eagle Prime* flooring *Kuratas*.

Largest water-pistol fight

Two teams from the University of California, Irvine, USA, faced off for a water-pistol fight on 24 Sep 2013. The battle, organized by NLA Sports (USA), saw 3,875 shooters get soaked in the 12-min conflict on the campus's sports field. See right for the **largest toy-pistol fight**.

MORE WACKY WORLD CHAMPIONSHIPS

◄ Toe-wrestling

Alan "Nasty" Nash (UK, left) has secured the **most wins of the Toe Wrestling World Championships (men)**, taking home the trophy for the 14th time on 19 Aug 2017 in Fenny Bentley, Derbyshire, UK. The **most wins by a woman** is four by Karen Davies (UK), in 1999–2002. Men never wrestle women, owing to a risk of "myxomatoesis"!

◄ Redneck Games

In 1996, radio DJ Mac Davis of station Y96 in East Dublin, Georgia, USA, started the **first Redneck Games** as an antidote to that year's Olympic Games in nearby Atlanta. The annual charity event features disciplines such as redneck horseshoes (aka toilet-seat throwing, left), bobbing for pigs' trotters and the mud-pit belly flop.

Phone-throwing

The Mobile Phone Throwing World Championships was founded in 2000 in Savonlinna, Finland. The **farthest distance to throw a mobile phone** is 110.42 m (362 ft 3 in) – the length of a soccer pitch – by javelin thrower Dries Feremans (BEL) at the national championships in Kessel-Lo, Belgium, on 27 Aug 2014.

The Spanish enjoy flinging meringue! The Festival of Vilanova i la Geltrú – a town near Barcelona – features a day-long food fight known as La Merengada.

Over in Italy, the Battle of the Oranges is staged annually in the town of Ivrea. The three-day fight pits nine teams of *aranceri* (orange throwers) against each other.

Oranges are not the only fruit to be thrown around: the normally quiet town of Binissalem in Mallorca, Spain, plays host to an annual grape-throwing festival.

Strangely, the main industry in Buñol isn't tomatoes but concrete! Tomatoes aren't even grown in the area, at least not on a large scale. Luckily, locals refrain from throwing concrete at each other.

Largest annual food fight

On the last Wednesday in August, the town of Buñol, near Valencia, Spain, holds its annual tomato festival, La Tomatina. The origins of the food fight are unknown, but each year tens of thousands of participants gather to throw tomatoes at each other. At the peak of the event's popularity in 2012 – the last time that attendance was free – an estimated 40,000 visitors descended on the small village to take part, throwing at least 40 tonnes (88,185 lb) of tomatoes.

The tomatoes are trucked into Buñol, often from as far away as Extremadura, 550 km (341 mi) to the west. Tourists pay extra to ride in the trucks and throw the first tomatoes.

Buñol's streets run with tomato pulp during La Tomatina. The fruit acid actually helps clean the pavements – after the pulp is hosed away, they're left sparklingly clean.

Bog-snorkelling
The **most entrants at a World Bog Snorkelling Championships** is 200, for the event on 31 Aug 2009 at Waen Rhydd peat bog in Llanwrtyd Wells, Powys, UK. Bog-snorkelling requires entrants to negotiate two lengths of a 60-yard-long (180-ft; 55-m) waterlogged trench cut into a peat bog... wearing obligatory snorkels and flippers.

▶ Wife-carrying
Despite its name, the sport of wife-carrying does not require competitors to carry their wives – any male may carry any willing female, as long as she is more than 49 kg (108 lb) and at least 17 years old. World Championships have been held annually in Sonkajärvi, Finland, since 1992. The **most Wife Carrying World**

Championships won is six, by Taisto Miettinen and his "wife" Kristiina Haapanen (both FIN) in 2009–13 and 2017. The "couple" are pictured here from the 2017 competition, held on 30 Jun and 1 Jul.

Shin-kicking
First held in England in 1612, Robert Dover's Cotswold Olimpicks have hosted the **longest-running shin-kicking competition** since 1636. Modern competitors wear white coats to represent shepherds' smocks and can use straw to cushion their shins. Steel toe caps are strictly forbidden!

SLACKLINING

INTERNATIONAL SLACKLINE ASSOCIATION

The International Slackline Association (ISA) aims to support and develop slackline communities of all sizes, including the urban-alpine activity of slacklining as well as competitive slackline sports. The ISA is devoted to increasing safety in all forms of slacklining through education and active risk management. All records in this section have been approved by the ISA, except for those in the "Balance Skills" section below.

Fastest 100 m slackline walk
French funambulist Lucas Milliard completed a 100-m (328-ft) slackline walk in 1 min 59.73 sec at an event organized by Hailuogou National Glacier Forest Park in Luding, Sichuan Province, China, on 12 Jun 2016.

Fastest 200 m slackline walk
On 17 Jul 2017, Daniel Ivan Laruelle (BEL) walked a 200-m (256-ft) slackline in just 4 min 17 sec at Shenxianju Scenic Spot in Taizhou, Zhejiang Province, China. In his successful record attempt, he went head-to-head with Lucas Milliard (4 min 26 sec) and Alexander Helmut Schulz (4 min 36 sec).

First triple buttflip on a slackline
The first ever official triple buttflip – a triple front flip starting and finishing in a sitting position – was achieved by French gymnast-turned-slackliner Louis Boniface in Apr 2017.

Longest urban highline walk with harness (male)
On 9 Dec 2017, Nathan Paulin (FRA) crossed the 670 m (2,198 ft 1.9 in) between the Eiffel Tower and the Place du Trocadéro in Paris, France, along a 2.5-cm-wide (1-in) highline suspended 60 m (196 ft 10.2 in) above the ground.

Longest free solo highline (male)
On 19 Sep 2017, Friedi Kühne (DEU) walked without a safety harness across a 110-m-long (360-ft 10.7-in) line suspended around 200 m (656 ft) above the ground in the Verdon Gorge in France. He beat his own mark of 72 m (236 ft 2.6 in), established at Hunlen Falls in British Columbia, Canada.

The **longest free solo highline (female)** is 28 m (91 ft 10.3 in), by Faith Dickey (USA) in Sep 2012 on a highline rigged 25 m (82 ft) above the ground in Ostrov, Czech Republic.

Longest waterline without harness (male)
On 13 Jul 2013, Mich Kemeter (AUT) walked a 250-m (820-ft 2.5-in) slackline installed over Grüner See (Green Lake) in Tragöss, Austria, without a safety harness. He kept his arms extended from his sides for the duration of the walk, which lasted for 20 min. He beat his own record of 222 m (728 ft 4.1 in), set the previous year over the same lake.

The 1,662-m walk by the Sangle Dessus-Dessous (SDD) team was also the **longest slackline walk ever**.

Longest highline walk with harness (female)
Mia Noblet (CAN) shattered her own world record with a highline walk of 493 m (1,617 ft 5.4 in) on 13 Nov 2017. The line was rigged 120 m (393 ft 8.4 in) high between Castleton Tower and the Rectory rock formations in Castle Valley, Utah, USA.

Longest waterline walk with harness (male)
The team of Samuel Volery (CHE), Lukas Irmler (DEU) and Tijmen van Dieren (NLD) crossed a 750-m-long (2,460-ft 7.5-in) waterline suspended 35 m (114 ft 9.9 in) above Kalterer See (Lake Kaltern) in South Tyrol, Italy, on 29 Apr 2017.

Longest longline without harness (male)
On 9 May 2015, Alexander Schulz (DEU) traversed a 610-m (2,001-ft 3.7-in) longline rigged between two dunes in the Inner Mongolia deserts of China. He completed the feat in fading light on his final attempt of the day. The line sagged to a maximum of 30 m (98 ft) during Schulz's epic walk.

The **longest longline without harness (female)** is 230 m (754 ft 7.1 in), by Laetitia Gonnon (CHE/FRA) on 28 Sep 2014. The line was installed over a field in Lausanne, Switzerland.

Longest highline walk with harness (male)
On 9 Jun 2017, Pablo Signoret (inset left) and Nathan Paulin (inset right, both FRA) – members of the slackline team SDD – walked 1,662 m (5,452 ft) along a highline suspended 340 m (1,115 ft) above the Cirque de Navacelles valley in the Massif Central mountains of France. The next day, SDD's Lucas Milliard (FRA, main image) also completed the walk, recording the fastest time of 1 hr 6 min. A fourth SDD team member, Antony Newton, attempted the feat on the same day but fell just 152 m (499 ft) from the end of the line.

BALANCE SKILLS (VERIFIED BY GWR)

◄ **Greatest distance travelled on a slackline while juggling three objects**
Lyle Bennett (ZAF) travelled 33.35 m (109 ft 4 in) while juggling three balls at the Wild Clover Farm in Stellenbosch, South Africa, on 4 Oct 2014. He covered almost four times the distance of the previous record during his charity performance, which took him 4 min 2 sec.

Longest distance travelled on a slackline by unicycle
Lutz Eichholz (DEU) covered 15.66 m (51 ft 4 in) across a slackline on his unicycle on the set of CCTV – *Guinness World Records Special* in Beijing, China, on 9 Sep 2013.

Eichholz has also achieved the **most 180° jumps (switches) on a unicycle in one minute** – 26 – in Cannes, France, on 18 Jun 2016.

◄ **Greatest distance travelled on a slackline by bicycle**
On 11 May 2014, Vittorio Brumotti (ITA) travelled 10.05 m (32 ft 11.6 in) on a bicycle across a slackline at Parco Leonardo in Fiumicino, Rome, Italy. It took the free-wheeling funambulist 20 sec to cross the line, which was suspended 1.05 m (3 ft 5 in) above the ground.

Slackline: a 2.5-cm (1-in) piece of synthetic fabric strung between anchor points for the purposes of balancing.

Highline: a slackline high above the ground, from where an unmitigated fall would cause major injuries or fatality.

Longline: a long slackline from which a safe landing on solid ground is still possible.

Waterline: a slackline strung over a body of water, not usually at a great height.

Highest highline (male)

On 28 Feb 2014, Andy "Sketchy" Lewis (USA) walked a 40-ft (12.19-m) line stretched between two hot-air balloons floating 4,000 ft (1,219 m) above the Mojave Desert in Nevada, USA. Upon the successful completion of his mid-air highline, daredevil Lewis leapt from the balloon and parachuted to Earth.

In 1999, Stephan Siegrist featured in *Eiger Live*, a live 30-hr broadcast on Swiss TV that followed a climbing team's successful ascent of the north face of the Eiger.

Highest elevation highline with harness (male)

Stephan Siegrist (CHE) walked a 21-m-long (69-ft) highline on Mount Kilimanjaro in Tanzania at an altitude of 5,700 m (18,700 ft) on 29 Jun 2016. The low oxygen content of the air at such high altitude made it even harder to ward off dizziness and maintain balance, while the unexpected snow on Kilimanjaro only increased the difficulty of Siegrist's record attempt.

Most side surfs on a slackline in one minute

Slackline legend Andy Lewis (USA, see above) achieved 143 side surfs on a slackline in 60 sec at the Diaoshuilou Waterfall at Jingpo Lake, Mudanjiang City, China, on 28 Aug 2011. Side surfs are when the slackline is rocked back and forth at great speed, in the same way a surfer might carve their surfboard through the waves.

◄ Longest duration controlling a soccer ball on a slackline

Football freestyler John Farnworth (UK) performed mid-air "keepie-uppies" with a soccer ball while balancing on a slackline for 29.82 sec in Preston, Lancashire, UK, on 14 Jan 2016. Farnworth has achieved numerous GWR titles thanks to his supreme freestyling skills.

Most Korean butt bounces on a slackline in one minute

Lukas Irmler (DEU) achieved 29 Korean butt bounces on a slackline in 60 sec on the set of *CCTV – Guinness World Records Special* in Beijing, China, on 9 Dec 2012. A Korean butt bounce begins with the slackliner standing on their feet, before they drop down to their backside and bounce back to their feet.

EXTREME PERFORMERS

Most hula hoops spun simultaneously on multi-body parts

Dunja Kuhn (DEU) spun 59 hula hoops around her body in London, UK, on 24 May 2017. It was one of three hula-hoop attempts on the same day broadcast by GWR on *Facebook Live*.

Longest duration performing a six-hula-hoop box split

On 10 Feb 2018, "Queen of the Rings" Brookelynn Bley (USA) spun six hula hoops on her body while simultaneously performing a box split position for 1 min 13 sec – an epic feat of hooping endurance.

Most knives thrown around a human target in one minute

On 26 Dec 2007, "The Great Throwdini" (aka Dr David R Adamovich, USA) hurled 102 throwing knives – each 14 in (35.5 cm) long – around "Target Girl", aka Tina Nagy (USA), in 60 sec in Freeport, New York, USA.

Most nails inserted into the nose in 30 seconds

Burnaby Q Orbax (CAN) – one half of the Monsters of Schlock duo – inserted 15 nails into his nose in half a minute in Saint John, New Brunswick, Canada, on 16 Jul 2015.

The next day, Orbax reclaimed the record for the **heaviest weight lifted using hooks through the forearms** – 45.18 kg (99 lb 9.6 oz).

Fastest time to escape from a straitjacket while suspended from a hot-air balloon

On 22 Jul 2017, Super Ning (CHN) freed herself from a straitjacket in 53.70 sec while hanging from a hot-air balloon flying 30 m (98 ft) above the ground in Weihai, Shandong Province, China.

Longest time spent on a bed of nails

The duration record for lying on a bed of nails with 6-in (15.2-cm) nails placed 2 in (5 cm) apart is 300 hr, by Ken Owen (UK) from 3 to 14 May 1986. His longest uninterrupted stretch lasted 132 hr 30 min!

Heaviest concrete-block break on a bed of nails (male)

On 12 Feb 2012, kung fu master Neal Hardy (AUS) had 15 blocks weighing 774.99 kg (1,708 lb 8 oz) – about the same as nine adult men – placed on his chest and broken while he lay on a bed of nails at Petrie Plaza in Canberra, ACT, Australia.

Most nails hammered with the head in one minute

Wrestler and strongman John Ferraro (USA) knocked 13 nails into a block of wood with his head in 60 sec on the set of *Guinness World Records Gone Wild!* in Los Angeles, California, USA, on 3 Jul 2012. MRI scans suggest that Ferraro's skull is almost two-and-a-half times thicker than average.

Most apples held in own mouth and cut by chainsaw in one minute

The "Space Cowboy" (aka Chayne Hultgren, AUS) cut 21 apples held in his mouth with a chainsaw in 60 sec in Sydney, New South Wales, Australia, on 19 Apr 2017.

On 10 May 2017, Chayne followed up with the **most consecutive under-leg chainsaw-juggling catches** – 14.

Fastest 10 m walked *en pointe* on a slackline

On 16 Aug 2017, Olga Henry (RUS/USA) walked 10 m (32 ft 9 in) along a slackline *en pointe* (i.e., on the tips of the toes) in 2 min 33.71 sec in Carlson Park, Culver City, California, USA. The line was 5.08 cm (2 in) wide and raised more than 1 m (3 ft 3.3 in) above the ground.

Farthest distance by a human cannonball

On 13 Mar 2018, "The Bullet" (aka David Smith Jr, USA) flew 195 ft (59.43 m) from a cannon on behalf of Xbox and *Sea of Thieves* at Raymond James Stadium in Tampa, Florida, USA.

"The Bullet" also achieved the **greatest height by a human cannonball** – 26 m (85 ft 4 in) – on *Guinness World Records Unleashed* in California, USA, on 8 Jul 2013.

Longest time controlling a football with the soles while on the roof of a moving car

Football freestyler Ash Randall (UK) juggled a ball on the soles of his feet while lying on the roof of a moving car for 93 sec at Cardiff Airport, UK, on 15 Nov 2014. During the attempt, Ash battled cross-winds and cramp in his legs as he was carried along at a speed of more than 10 mph (16 km/h).

POGO-A-GO-GO

◀ Fewest pogo-stick jumps in one minute

On 11 Jul 2016, Henry Cabelus (USA) managed to jump just 38 times in 60 sec in New York City, USA – beating Biff Hutchison's previous record by one. In order to minimize the number of jumps, pogo performers have to gain as much height as possible, without stalling or stepping down from the stick.

▶ Fastest mile on a pogo stick

On 24 Jun 2017, Drew McQuiston (USA) covered a mile on a pogo stick in 7 min 40 sec at an athletics track in Pittsburgh, Pennsylvania, USA. He didn't fall from his stick once during his four-lap dash. Drew's soundtrack for his attempt included "Jump Around" by House of Pain and Van Halen's "Jump".

Death-defying stunts...

Lowest death dive escape: Robert Gallup (AUS) escaped from a chained mailbag inside a locked cage, having being thrown out of a plane at 18,000 ft (5,486 m).

Most magic tricks performed in a single skydive: 11, by Martin Rees (UK) at GoSkydive in Salisbury, Wiltshire, UK, on 15 Oct 2016.

Most deadly magic trick: at least 12 people (eight magicians and four bystanders) have been killed during the bullet-catch trick, in which a magician appears to catch a marked bullet in his teeth.

Heaviest Strongman deadlift

Eddie "The Beast" Hall (UK) achieved a deadlift of 500 kg (1,102 lb 4.9 oz) – around the same weight as an adult male polar bear – at the World Deadlift Championships in Leeds, UK, on 9 Jul 2016. Eddie had set a new record of 465 kg (1,025 lb 2.3 oz) earlier that day, but he went on to obliterate that mark, becoming the first human to deadlift half a tonne. He collapsed soon after his winning lift, having burst blood vessels in his head with his superhuman effort.

The rules for a deadlift in a Strongman competition are notable for allowing the use of double loop straps, ultra-tight lifting suits and unlimited "hitching" of the bar up the thighs.

In the run-up to a contest, Eddie super-sizes his meals. Every day, he consumes 12,500 calories – including a full English breakfast, steak, cheesecake and protein shakes.

The activities on these pages are strictly for experts only – **don't try them at home!**

▶ **Fastest mile on a pogo stick while juggling three balls**
Ashrita Furman (USA) covered a mile on a pogo stick while juggling three balls in 23 min 28 sec in New York City, USA, on 26 Sep 2007. He shaved more than a minute off his own record.

On 28 Jan 2010, Ashrita set the **greatest distance juggling on a pogo stick:** 4 mi (6.44 km) on Easter Island, Chile.

Highest jump on a pogo stick
Twenty-year-old Dmitry Arsenyev (RUS) cleared a bar set at 3.378 m (11 ft 0.99 in) on his pogo stick in Wilkinsburg, Pennsylvania, USA, on 5 Nov 2017.

On the same day, Michael Mena (USA) achieved the **highest forward-flip pogo-stick jump** – 3.086 m (10 ft 1.49 in) – also in Wilkinsburg.

▲ **Most consecutive cars jumped over on a pogo stick**
Xpogo Stunt Team member Dalton Smith (USA) leaped over three cars lined up by Nissan (JPN) in consecutive jumps on the roof of a car park in Croydon, Greater London, UK, on 6 Jun 2017. Not content with clearing the three vehicles, Smith rounded off the feat by dismounting from his stick with a somersault.

ENDURANCE

Longest duration on a balance board
Tatum Braun (USA) maintained her equilibrium on a balance board for 7 hr 25 min 30.86 sec in Charlotte, Vermont, USA, on 10 Jul 2015. It must be something in the genes: her mother, Cricket Braun, held this record in 2005.

LONGEST DURATION...

Balancing an umbrella on one finger
Himanshu Gupta (IND) kept an umbrella aloft on the middle finger of his right hand for a total of 2 hr 22 min 22 sec in Bangalore, India, on 7 Oct 2017.

Underwater live radio broadcasting (unsupported)
On 13 May 2017, New Zealand's Stu Tolan hosted a submarine radio broadcast lasting 5 hr 25 min 25 sec for 104.8 Channel 4. He was stationed at a depth of 3 m (9 ft 10 in) in the 11-million-litre Atlantis Ambassador Lagoon aquarium at the Palm resort in Dubai, UAE. During the attempt, Stu underwent 11 air-tank changes, which were carried out by a team of six scuba divers.

Standing on a Swiss ball
Garrett Lam (USA) kept his footing on a Swiss ball for 5 hr 25 min 36.98 sec in Boston, Massachusetts, USA, on 18 Sep 2015.

Indoor freefalling
Stef Millet and Manu Sarrazin (both FRA) jointly achieved a 7-hr 15-min 18-sec freefall at the Windoor wind tunnel in Empuriabrava, Spain, on 7 Jul 2017. They beat the previous attempt, set the previous year, by more than 15 min.

Balancing a soccer ball on the head
On 27 Jan 2017, Arash Ahmadi Tifakani (IRN) kept a soccer ball balanced on his head for 8 hr 42 min 12 sec without letting it drop in Bandar Abbas, Hormozgan, Iran.

Standing motionless
Om Prakash Singh (IND) stood motionless, except for involuntary blinking, for 20 hr 10 min 6 sec in Allahabad, India, on 13–14 Aug 1997. He was recovering from chicken pox when he made the record attempt and claimed afterwards that he would have lasted longer if doctors had not advised him to stop.

Trampolining by a team
The eight-strong Autism Together (UK) team trampolined for 25 hr in Birkenhead, in the Metropolitan Borough of Wirral, UK, from 2 to 3 Apr 2017. The octet, who took turns to bounce in 20-min shifts, began the session on World Autism Awareness Day to raise awareness of the condition.

Skipping
On 4–5 Dec 2009, Joey Motsay (USA) skipped rope for 33 hr 20 min at Positive Stress Workout in Greensboro, North Carolina, USA. His record attempt raised $38,000 (£22,949) for Smile Train, a charity providing free cleft lip and palate surgeries for children worldwide.

Playing futsal
From 30 Jun to 2 Jul 2017, the Lee Knight Foundation (UK) completed a non-stop 50-hr futsal marathon in Birkenhead, UK. The teams – the Green Knights and the White Knights – took part in the event to raise funds for disabled supporters' facilities.

Longest marathon on a dance videogame
Carrie Swidecki (USA) completed a 138-hr 34-sec session of *Just Dance 2015* (Ubisoft, 2014) at Otto's Video Games & More! in Bakersfield, California, USA, from 11 to 17 Jul 2015. She live-streamed the attempt on Twitch and raised $7,305 (£4,677) for the charity ExtraLife4Kids.

Longest marathon on a roller-coaster
Richard Rodriguez (USA) rode the Pepsi Max Big One and Big Dipper roller-coasters at Pleasure Beach in Blackpool, Lancashire, UK, for 405 hr 40 min from 27 Jul to 13 Aug 2007. For the duration of his 17-day attempt, he was allowed only a five-minute rest break between rides to get something to eat, shower or change his clothes.

Longest marathon in a bumper car
On 10–11 Aug 2016, Manuela Benus and Jan Spekker (both DEU) carried out a 28-hr marathon bumper-car session at the Hamburger Dom festival in Hamburg, Germany. The event was organized by TV channel RTL Nord. Manuela and Jan both work for the channel and rode the cars for exactly 28 hr to mark its 28th anniversary.

MARATHON MUSIC

Sitar
Renuka Punwani (IND) played sitar for an unbroken stretch of exactly 25 hr at the Pancham Academy of Indian Music in Ahmedabad, Gujarat, India, from 26 to 27 Nov 2011. Renuka was a sprightly 76 years old at the time. She has also accompanied other members of the academy in marathon music-making attempts.

▼ Piano
From 11 to 17 Oct 2015, India's Mrityunjay Sharma performed a 127-hr 8-min 38-sec keyboard recital in Delhi, India. His instrument of choice was a Korg professional arranger Pa300 keyboard. He dedicated his achievement to record-breaking Indian cricketer Sachin Tendulkar.

Guitar
Ireland's David Browne played guitar continuously for 114 hr 6 min 30 sec at the Temple Bar pub in Dublin, Ireland, from 12 to 17 Jun 2011. David was allowed a 30-sec break between songs, and a 40-min break after 8 hr, during which time he had the chance to catch up on sleep, freshen up, change his clothes and eat a protein snack.

Ukulele
Between 26 and 27 Nov 2016, Robin Evans (UK) completed a 30-hr 2-min ukulele marathon at the Duke of Uke music shop in London, UK. Robin had a playlist of 129 songs – including numbers by Rick Astley, The Bangles and Justin Bieber – that he played through a total of six times. He was allowed only a 30-sec break between numbers.

Continuous football control
21 hr 1 min
Abraham Muñoz
(MEX)

Table-tennis-bat-and-ball duration
5 hr 2 min 37 sec
Aryan Raj
(IND)

Tennis-racket-and-ball duration
4 hr 30 min
Aswin Sridhar
(IND)

Golf-club-and-ball duration
1 hr 37 min 58 sec
Brad Weston
(USA)

GUINNESS WORLD RECORDS

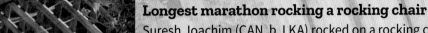

Longest marathon rocking a rocking chair

Suresh Joachim (CAN, b. LKA) rocked on a rocking chair continuously for 75 hr 3 min from 24 to 27 Aug 2005 at the Hilton Garden Inn in Mississauga, Ontario, Canada. To stay awake, he played guitar, read about golf and interacted with his family, who were present in the room for the entire time. You'll find two more of his record-breaking feats below.

Suresh declared himself to be "very comfortable" after an hour and a half. "But maybe too comfortable. I'm rocking back and forth, so I'm going to get sleepy. That could be a very difficult problem!" He managed another 73 hr 33 min.

Longest duration balancing on one foot
Suresh stood on just one foot for 76 hr 40 min in Colombo, Sri Lanka, on 22–25 May 1997.

Longest continuous crawl
On 18–19 May 2001, Suresh crawled 56.62 km (35.18 mi), with at least one knee grounded at all times. He completed more than 2,500 laps of a circuit 66 ft (20.1 m) in circumference outside the Queen Victoria Building in Sydney, Australia.

◀ Violin
Nikolay Madoyan (ARM) played violin for 33 hr 2 min 41 sec continuously (apart from 30-sec breaks between pieces) at Komitas Chamber Music House in Yerevan, Armenia, from 11 to 12 Feb 2017. His repertoire included works by J S Bach, Beethoven, Mozart and Paganini.

Accordion
America's Cory Pesaturo carried out a 32-hr 14-min 52-sec session on the accordion from 4 to 5 Aug 2017 at Optik Neuroth in Graz, Austria. Cory's record-breaking performance included renditions of classical compositions such as Pachelbel's "Canon in D" alongside techno songs such as Darude's "Sandstorm".

◀ Bagpipes
From 12 to 13 Aug 2015, Rikki Evans (UK) performed a lung-bursting 26-hr 5-min 32-sec bagpipe marathon at The National Piping Centre in Glasgow, UK. Rikki used his record attempt to raise money for a number of good causes, including CLAN Cancer Support, Cash for Kids and the Gordon Duncan Memorial Trust.

EPIC JOURNEYS

First recorded walk from John O'Groats to Land's End
In 1871, brothers John and Robert Naylor (both UK) walked the length of the UK from John O'Groats to Land's End. They covered 1,372 mi (2,208 km) in two months – more than twice the distance of the journey as the crow flies – owing to diversions for sightseeing.

First circumnavigation by walking
The first person reputed to have walked around the world is George Matthew Schilling (USA), from 1897 to 1904. However, the first verified ambulatory circumnavigation was by David Kunst (USA), who walked 23,250 km (14,450 mi) across four continents between 20 Jun 1970 and 5 Oct 1974.

Longest journey by bicycle (individual)
Itinerant lecturer Walter Stolle (CZE) cycled 402,000 mi (646,960 km) in an 18-year tour through 159 countries that lasted from 24 Jan 1959 to 12 Dec 1976. Five of Stolle's bikes were stolen and six broke down, while he suffered 1,000 flat tyres. He was robbed more than 200 times and gored by a gazelle in Africa, but claimed to have never once fallen ill.

First person to sail around the world (solo and non-stop)
Robin Knox-Johnston (UK) circumnavigated the globe single-handedly in his yacht *Suhaili* between 14 Jun 1968 and 22 Apr 1969. Having entered the Sunday Times Golden Globe Race, he was the only remaining competitor by the time he reached the finishing line at Falmouth in Cornwall, UK.

First surface circumnavigation via both poles
On 29 Aug 1982, Sir Ranulph Fiennes and Charles Burton (both UK) of the British Trans-Globe Expedition arrived back at Greenwich in London, UK, after a three-year journey covering some 35,000 mi (56,300 km). Having left Greenwich on 2 Sep 1979, they crossed the South Pole on 15 Dec 1980 and the North Pole on 10 Apr 1982.

Fastest circumnavigation by scheduled flights (six continents)
Michael Quandt (DEU), travel editor of the *Bild am Sonntag* newspaper, flew around the world in 66 hr 31 min on 6–8 Jul 2004. Taking only scheduled flights, he flew from Singapore to Australia, the USA, Venezuela, the UK, Egypt and Malaysia before returning to Singapore.

Fastest circumnavigation by car
The record for the **first and fastest man and woman to have circumnavigated the Earth by car** covering six continents under the rules applicable in 1989 and 1991 embracing more than an equator's length of driving (24,901 road miles; 40,075 km) is held by Saloo Choudhury and his wife Neena Choudhury (both India). The journey took 69 days 19 hours 5 minutes from 9 September to 17 November 1989. The couple drove a 1989 Hindustan "Contessa Classic" starting and finishing in Delhi, India.

Longest journey by aquabike (jetski)
South Africans Marinus du Plessis (above) and Adriaan Marais survived choppy seas, mechanical issues and a dock-leaping sea lion to complete a 95-day 17,266.69-km (10,729-mi) aquabike odyssey. Starting in Anchorage, Alaska, USA, they reached Panama City, Panama, on 19 Sep 2006, having followed the west coast of North America.

Longest journey by taxi
Leigh Purnell, Paul Archer and Johno Ellison (all UK) travelled 69,716.12 km (43,319.58 mi) around the globe in a 1992 LTI Fairway FX4 London black taxi cab named *Hannah* from 17 Feb 2011 to 11 May 2012. Their journey clocked up a charge on the meter of £79,006.80 ($127,530) – excluding tip.

Fastest circumnavigation sailing solo
Francois Gabart (FRA) sailed alone around the world in 42 days 16 hr 40 min 35 sec on board his 100-ft (30.48-m) trimaran *MACIF*, completing his epic journey on 17 Dec 2017. On 13–14 Nov 2007, he achieved the **greatest distance sailed in 24 hours single-handedly** – 850.68 nautical mi (1,575.45 km) in the South Atlantic. Both records were ratified by the World Sailing Speed Record Council.

Longest journey by wheelchair
From 21 Mar 1985 to 22 May 1987, Rick Hansen (CAN) wheeled his way through four continents and 34 countries on an epic journey totalling 40,075.16 km (24,901.55 mi). Hansen, who was paralysed from the waist down in 1973 as a result of a motor accident, started and finished in Vancouver, British Columbia, Canada.

POLES APART

First person to reach the South Pole
A party of five Norwegian explorers led by Captain Roald Amundsen reached the South Pole at 11 a.m. on 14 Dec 1911. They had endured a 53-day march with dog sledges from the Bay of Whales.

The **first women to reach the South Pole by land** were Tori Murden and Shirley Metz (both USA), on 17 Jan 1989.

▶ First undisputed overland journey to the North Pole
At 3 p.m. on 19 Apr 1968, expedition leader Ralph Plaisted (USA) arrived at the North Pole accompanied by a three-man team. They had travelled for 42 days on snowmobiles. Earlier claims to have reached the pole have proved unverifiable.

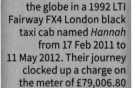

▶ First person to walk to both poles
Robert Swan (UK) headed the eight-man "Icewalk" expedition that arrived at the North Pole on 14 May 1989. He had previously led the three-man "In the Footsteps of Scott" trek that reached the South Pole on 11 Jan 1986.

The **first person to visit both poles** was Dr Albert Crary (USA), completed on 12 Feb 1961.

Longest journey....

Walking on hands: 1,400 km (870 mi), by Johann Hurlinger (AUT) between Vienna and Paris over 55 days in 1900.

On stilts: 4,840 km (3,008 mi), by Joe Bowen (USA) from Los Angeles, California, USA, to Bowen, Kentucky, USA, in 1980.

By skateboard: 12,159 km (7,555 mi), by Rob Thomson (NZ) in 2007–08 – from Leysin in Switzerland to Shanghai in China.

Pushing a wheelbarrow: around 14,500 km (9,000 mi), by Bob Hanley (AUS) across Australia from Apr 1975 to May 1978.

Fastest circumnavigation by bicycle

Between 2 Jul and 18 Sep 2017, Mark Beaumont (UK) cycled around the world in 78 days 14 hr 40 min, starting and ending at the Arc de Triomphe in Paris, France. Beaumont – who had first held this record in 2008 – completed his "Around the World in 80 Days Challenge" ahead of schedule, beating the previous record holder by more than 40 days. Between 2 Jul and 31 Jul, he covered 11,315.29 km (7,031 mi) – the **farthest distance cycled in one month (male)**.

Mark Beaumont is no stranger to endurance cycling. In 2015, he achieved the **fastest bicycle journey from Cairo to Cape Town (male)** – 41 days 10 hr 22 min.

Beaumont's 18,000-mi (28,968-km) route took him through 16 countries in total, ending in a final "sprint finish" from Lisbon, Portugal, back to his starting point in Paris, France.

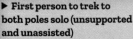
Fastest circumnavigation by bicycle (female)
Paola Gianotti (ITA) cycled around the world in 144 days between 8 Mar and 30 Nov 2014. Starting and ending in Turin, Italy, her journey comprised a distance of 29,595 km (18,389 mi). She overcame 32 punctures, a fractured vertebra, a flood, an earthquake, a tsunami and 16 attacks by stray dogs during the course of her marathon adventure.

▶ **First person to trek to both poles solo (unsupported and unassisted)**
In 1995, Marek Kamiński (USA, b. POL) skiied to both poles with no external assistance. He reached the North Pole from Cape Columbia on 23 May after a 70-day, 770-km (478-mi) journey. On 27 Dec, he reached the South Pole from Berkner Island after a 53-day, 1,300-km (807-mi) trek.

First women to reach both poles
Catherine Hartley and Fiona Thornewill (both UK) reached the geographic North Pole on 5 May 2001, having set out from Ward Hunt Island, Northwest Territories, Canada, on 11 Mar. Both women had previously skiied to the South Pole on 4 Jan 2000, setting out from Hercules Inlet.

▶ **First winter expedition to the North Pole**
Matvey Shparo and Boris Smolin (left to right, both RUS) began their winter expedition on 22 Dec 2007, arriving at the North Pole on 14 Mar 2008. They travelled in complete darkness, hauling sleds of 160 kg (352 lb 11 oz) each and navigating by the light of their headlamps.

FANTASTIC FEATS

MULTI-DISCIPLINARIANS

First person to complete the Adventurers Grand Slam

On these pages, we celebrate multi-talented record holders who have excelled in more than one field. One of them is David Hempleman-Adams (UK), who completed the Adventurers Grand Slam by climbing the highest peak on every continent (Seven Summits) and trekking to the North and South poles. He began his quest in 1980, climbing Denali (also known as Mount McKinley) in Alaska, USA, and completed it 18 years later by reaching the North Pole with Rune Gjeldnes in May 1998.

The **first person to complete the Explorers Grand Slam** was Park Young-seok (KOR), upon reaching the North Pole on 30 Apr 2005. This challenge involves climbing the Seven Summits, all 14 mountains over 8,000 m (26,246 ft), and reaching both poles on foot.

Fastest electric motorcycle

Inventor and green-technology pioneer Chip Yates (USA) reached a speed of 316.899 km/h (196.912 mph) on his SWIGZ Electric Superbike Protoype at Bonneville Salt Flats in Utah, USA, on 30 Aug 2011. On 24 Nov 2013, Chip achieved the **fastest time to climb to 3,000 m in an electric aircraft** – 5 min 32 sec, in a modified Rutan Long-EZ aircraft in Inyokern, California, USA.

First Atlantic crossing by hot-air balloon

On 2–3 Jul 1987, Richard Branson (UK) and Per Lindstrand (SWE) flew from Sugarloaf in Maine, USA, to Limavady in Northern Ireland, UK. They covered 4,947 km (3,074 mi) in 31 hr 41 min. The same duo went on to achieve the **first Pacific crossing by hot-air balloon**, piloting the *Virgin Otsuka Pacific Flyer* from Japan to Lac la Martre in Yukon, Canada, on 15–17 Jan 1991.

Entrepreneur Branson (b. 18 Jul 1950) is also the **oldest person to kiteboard the English Channel**. On 1 Jul 2012, he crossed from Dymchurch in Kent, UK, to Wimereux in France aged 61 years 349 days.

First person to sail and row the Indian and Atlantic oceans

James Kayll (UK) sailed the Indian Ocean from Thailand to the African country of Djibouti on board *Ocean Song* on 8 Jan–13 Feb 2005, before rowing across it from Geraldton in Western Australia to Mauritius on *Indian Runner 4* on 21 Apr–6 Jul 2011.

The former army captain has done the same across the Atlantic, sailing from Gran Canaria to St Lucia on board *Polyphagus* (19 Nov–6 Dec 2000), and rowing on board *Row 2 Recovery* from La Gomera to Antigua (4 Dec 2013–21 Jan 2014).

Fastest journey from the lowest to the highest point on Earth (Dead Sea to summit of Everest)

On 21 May 2006, Pauline Sanderson, Dominic Faulkner, Jamie Rouan (all UK) and Geri Winkler (AUT) summitted Everest having travelled from the Dead Sea after a journey of 150 days 19 hr 15 min.

Longest ramp jump in a car

On 31 Dec 2009, Travis Pastrana (USA) jumped 269 ft (81.99 m) at the "Red Bull: New Year. No Limits" event in Long Beach, California, USA. Pastrana, a stunt performer and professional motocross competitor who has won the **most medals for Moto X at the Summer X Games** – 13 – jumped in his rally car off a pier on to a floating barge in the harbour.

Pastrana is also responsible for the **longest tandem motorcycle backflip** – 4.99 m (16 ft 5 in), together with Jolene Van Vugt (CAN) at Godfrey Trucking/Rocky Mountain Raceway in Salt Lake City, Utah, USA, on 17 Nov 2008.

Fastest circumnavigation by balloon (FAI-approved)

On 12–23 Jul 2016, Fedor Konyukhov (RUS) flew around the world in a balloon named *Morton* in 11 days 4 hr 20 min. He took off from Northam in Western Australia and landed at Bonnie Rock in the same state. Konyukhov has also set the **fastest time to row across the South Pacific east to west (solo)** – 159 days 16 hr 58 min, from 22 Dec 2013 to 31 May 2014. He rowed 7,393 mi (6,424 nautical mi; 11,897.9 km) from Concón, Chile, to Mooloolaba in Queensland, Australia, on board *Tourgoyak*.

This accomplished explorer has also completed the Seven Summits challenge, scaling each continent's greatest peak between 1992 and 1997.

Longest non-stop flight by any aircraft (FAI-approved)

Steve Fossett (USA) flew 41,467.53 km (25,766.72 mi) in the *Virgin Atlantic GlobalFlyer* airplane on 8–11 Feb 2006. He took off from the Kennedy Space Center in Florida, USA, breaking the previous record over Shannon in Ireland.

The millionaire owned the **largest racing catamaran (yacht)**, the *Cheyenne*, which was 125 ft (38.1 m) long and 60 ft (18.3 m) wide. In 2004, Fossett and crew set a then-record circumnavigation time of 58 days 9 hr 32 min.

THREE POLES CHALLENGE (NORTH POLE/SOUTH POLE/EVEREST)

◄ First person to complete the Three Poles Challenge
On 8 May 1994, Erling Kagge (NOR) summitted Everest to complete the Three Poles Challenge. On 4 May 1990, he and Børge Ousland (NOR) had become the **first people to reach the North Pole unsupported (emergency-assisted)**, while on 7 Jan 1993 Kagge completed the **first solo expedition to the South Pole**.

First female to complete the Three Poles Challenge
Tina Sjögren (SWE, b. CZE) reached the North Pole on 29 May 2002 to become the first woman to complete the Three Poles Challenge. She had summitted Everest on 26 May 1999 and made the South Pole on 2 Feb 2002, accompanied by her husband Tom Sjögren. Only 35 days separated their polar trips.

◄ First person to complete the Three Poles Challenge without supplementary oxygen on Everest
Of the 22 explorers to have completed the challenge, only Antoine De Choudens (FRA) summitted Everest without supplementary oxygen. De Choudens, who was lost on Shishapangma in 2003, finished the trio at the South Pole on 10 Jan 1999.

Number of people who have...
Climbed Everest:
4,834
(as of 15 Mar 2018)

Rowed an ocean:
885
(as of 16 Feb 2018)

Reached a pole:
North Pole: 247
South Pole: 399
(as of Jan 2017)

All three:
2: Maxime Chaya (LBN)
and Fedor Konyukhov
(RUS)

GUINNESS WORLD RECORDS

FANTASTIC FEATS

A veteran of extreme environments, Parazynski has also dived into the summit lake on the Licancabur volcano in Bolivia and climbed down into the Masaya volcano in Nicaragua!

A medical officer for the US Antarctic Program, Parazynski visited the South Pole, where he posed for an "Atlas photo", i.e., with the world on his shoulders.

First astronaut to summit Everest

On 20 May 2009, NASA astronaut Scott Parazynski (USA) climbed Everest, becoming the first person to travel in space and summit Earth's **highest mountain**. Parazynski spent 1,381 hr in space between 1994 and 2007, participating in five spaceflights. He took a Moon rock to Everest that had been collected by the crew of *Apollo 11*, and returned with a summit rock; both rocks now reside on the *International Space Station*.

First Three Poles Challenge – North Pole to land

Johan Ernst Nilson (SWE) topped Everest in May 2007, then commenced the polar stages by being dropped at the North Pole on 6 May 2011. He walked 775 km (481.56 mi) unsupported in 48 days before reaching land on 22 Jun. Nilson went on to successfully complete a trek to the South Pole on 19 Jan 2012.

▶ Fastest time to complete the Three Poles Challenge (female)

Cecilie Skog (NOR) completed the Three Poles Challenge in 1 year 336 days. She summitted Everest on 23 May 2004, reached the South Pole on 27 Dec 2005, and arrived at the North Pole on 24 Apr 2006. As of 11 Dec 2017, she remains one of only two women to have finished the challenge.

▶ Fastest time to complete the Three Poles Challenge (male)

It took Adrian Hayes (UK) just 1 year 217 days to finish this demanding feat. He summitted Everest on 25 May 2006, reached the North Pole on 25 Apr 2007 from Ward Hunt Island in Canada, and finally claimed the South Pole on 28 Dec 2007, making the journey from the Hercules Inlet.

MOUNTAINEERING

First ascent of Everest

Everest (8,848 m; 29,029 ft), on the border between Nepal and China, was first climbed at 11:30 a.m. on 29 May 1953 by Edmund Percival Hillary (NZ) and Tenzing Norgay (IND/Tibet). The successful expedition was led by Col (later Hon. Brigadier) Henry Cecil John Hunt (UK).

On 16 May 1975, Junko Tabei (JPN) became the **first woman to ascend Everest**. She also became the **first woman to climb the Seven Summits** when she topped Elbrus (5,642 m; 18,510 ft) on 28 Jul 1992, completing the Carstensz and Kosciuszko lists (see opposite).

Reinhold Messner (ITA) and Peter Habeler (AUT) made the **first ascent of Everest without supplementary oxygen**, on 8 May 1978. This feat is regarded by some purist mountaineers as the first "true" ascent of Everest, since overcoming the effects of altitude (i.e., the low oxygen content of the air) is the greatest challenge for high-altitude climbers.

First ascent of K2

Achille Compagnoni and Lino Lacedelli (both ITA) scaled K2 (8,611 m; 28,251 ft) – the world's second-highest mountain – on 31 Jul 1954. The mountain is situated in the Karakoram range on the border between Pakistan and China.

Wanda Rutkiewicz (POL) became the **first woman to climb K2** when she reached the summit on 23 Jun 1986.

First ascent of Annapurna I

Maurice Herzog and Louis Lachenal (both FRA) scaled Annapurna I (8,091 m; 26,545 ft) in Nepal on 3 Jun 1950.

Annapurna I is the **deadliest mountain to climb**. As of 31 Jan 2018, only 251 people had reached the top of the mountain during a total of 261 ascents, and 69 people had died on its slopes – 11 of them on their descent. For every three climbers who make it safely up and down, one dies trying.

First married couple to climb all 8,000-m mountains

Nives Meroi and Romano Benet (both ITA) summitted all 14 mountains higher than 8,000 m (26,246 ft) between 20 Jul 1998 – when they climbed Nanga Parbat (8,125 m; 26,656 ft) in Pakistan – and 11 May 2017, when they topped Annapurna I in Nepal. The couple always climb together, without high-altitude porters or supplementary oxygen.

Fastest ascent of Everest and K2 without supplementary oxygen

Karl Unterkircher (ITA) summitted Everest on 24 May 2004 and K2 on 26 Jul 2004, with only 63 days between the two ascents.

The **fastest ascent of Everest and K2 without supplementary oxygen by a woman** is 92 days, by Alison Hargreaves (UK). She climbed Everest on 13 May 1995 and K2 on 13 Aug 1995. Sadly, she was killed during her K2 descent.

Fastest ascent of the three highest mountains without supplementary oxygen

Silvio Mondinelli (ITA) climbed Everest on 23 May 2001, Kangchenjunga (8,586 m; 28,169 ft), between Nepal and India, on 20 May 2003, and K2 on 26 Jul 2004. It took 3 years 64 days in all.

Gerlinde Kaltenbrunner (AUT) was the **first** and **fastest woman to ascend the three highest mountains without supplementary oxygen**. She climbed Kangchenjunga on 14 May 2006, Everest on 24 May 2010 and K2 on 23 Aug 2011. It took her 5 years 101 days to summit all three mountains.

Fastest time to climb the north face of the Eiger solo

On 16 Nov 2015, Ueli Steck (CHE) ascended the north face of the Eiger in Switzerland's Bernese Alps in 2 hr 22 min 50 sec, via the Heckmair route. He first set a speed record for topping this 1,800-m (5,905-ft) expanse in 2007, with a time of 3 hr 54 min.

Fastest time to climb El Capitan

On 21 Oct 2017, Brad Gobright and Jim Reynolds (both USA) completed the 883-m (2,900-ft) "Nose" route of El Capitan in California, USA, in 2 hr 19 min 44 sec. They broke the previous record – set in 2012 by Alex Honnold and Hans Florine, and once thought "unbeatable" – by just under 4 min.

Most nationalities on Everest in one season

In all, climbers from 46 nations made 667 ascents of Everest from 10 to 25 May 2013. Of these, 44 were women. The largest group was the Nepalese, with 363 climbers, followed by India with 66. Some ascents were repeats by the same climbers. This also represents the **most ascents of Everest in one year**.

OLDEST PERSON TO CLIMB...

◀ An 8,000-m mountain without bottled oxygen

The undisputed record goes to Carlos Soria (ESP, b. 5 Feb 1939), who summitted Manaslu (8,163 m; 26,781 ft) on 1 Oct 2010, aged 71 years 238 days. Boris Korshunov (RUS, b. 31 Aug 1935) has stated that he topped Cho Oyu (8,188 m; 26,863 ft) on 2 Oct 2007, aged 72 years 32 days, but some alpinists dispute this.

The Seven Summits (Carstensz list)

On 21 Nov 2013, aged 76 years 128 days, Werner Berger (ZAF/CAN, b. 16 Jul 1937) climbed Carstensz Pyramid, thereby completing the Carstensz list. Some six-and-a-half years earlier, on 22 May 2007, Wenger had completed the Kosciuszko list for the Seven Summits when he conquered Everest at the age of 69 years 310 days.

▶ Everest (female)

On 19 May 2012, following an all-night climb, Japan's Tamae Watanabe (b. 21 Nov 1938) summitted Everest for the second time, at the age of 73 years 180 days. Watanabe reclaimed a record that she had originally held 10 years earlier, when she completed her initial conquest of the world's **highest mountain** at the age of 63.

The Death Zone
Above 7,500 m (24,606 ft), oxygen levels are around a third of those at sea level. Loss of appetite and dizziness kick in – often with fatal consequences...

Frostbite: low oxygen levels and icy cold make the skin's blood vessels contract. The body's extremities quickly get cold.

Pulmonary edema: the lungs begin to fail and fill with body fluids. As a result, climbers may drown in their own liquids.

Cerebral edema: at high altitudes, blood leaks into the brain. This swells, leading to hallucinations and impaired judgement.

The Seven Summits are the highest mountains on each continent. There are two versions of what these constitute, however. The Kosciuszko list includes Mt Kosciuszko (2,228 m; 7,309 ft) in Australia. The Carstensz list replaces this with the more challenging Carstensz Pyramid, aka Puncak Jaya (4,884 m; 16,023 ft), in New Guinea.

First blind person to climb Everest

Erik Weihenmayer (USA) was born with retinoschisis, an eye condition that left him totally blind by the age of 13. Despite this, on 25 May 2001, he reached the summit of Everest, becoming the first – and so far only – blind man ever to have done so. He is also the **first blind person to climb the Seven Summits (Carstensz list)**, a feat achieved when he topped that mountain on 26 Aug 2008.

Most ascents of Everest by a woman

Lakpa Sherpa (NPL) reached the summit of Everest for the eighth time on 13 May 2017, more than any other female climber. She made her first ascent via the south side on 18 May 2000, while the eighth came on 13 May 2017 via the north side. All of her ascents were completed during the spring climbing season.

Most ascents of Everest

On 27 May 2017, Kami Rita I (aka "Topke", left) scaled Everest for the 21st time in his career. In doing so, he equalled the record first set by Apa Sherpa (b. 20 Jan 1960) – who topped Everest for the 21st time on 11 May 2011 – and matched by Phurba Tashi Sherpa (b. 24 May 1971), whose 21st ascent came on 23 May 2013. All three men are Nepalese.

▶ Everest

Yuichiro Miura (JPN, b. 12 Oct 1932) summitted Everest on 23 May 2013 aged 80 years 223 days. It was the third time that Miura had held this record: he topped the same mountain as the world's oldest summiteer in 2003 and again in 2008. Understandably, the climb took its toll: "Three times is enough!" he told a press conference after the 2013 trek.

The Seven Summits (Kosciuszko list)

Spanish climber Ramón Blanco (b. 30 Apr 1933) summitted Kosciuszko in Australia on 29 Dec 2003, at the age of 70 years 243 days.

The **oldest woman to climb the Seven Summits (Kosciuszko list)** is Carol Masheter (USA, b. 10 Oct 1946, right), who completed the feat on 17 Mar 2012, aged 65 years 159 days.

▶ The Seven Summits (Carstensz list, female)

Carol Masheter completed her final Seven Summits climb by ascending Carstensz Pyramid on 12 Jul 2012, at the age of 65 years 276 days. She had completed the Kosciuszko list on 17 Mar 2012 (see opposite). Carol – who is afraid of heights! – is a keen advocate of what she dubs "optimal aging", through regular activity.

ROUND-UP

Most consecutive pogo-stick jumps without using hands

Oliver Galbraith (UK) jumped 4,530 times on a pogo stick, balancing on his legs and feet, in Bangor, UK, on 21 May 2017. It took him 38 min.

Most casino chips shuffled into one stack

Using one hand, Saar Kessel (ISR) combined two columns of different-coloured casino chips into a stack 20 chips tall, alternating the colours, in Mishmar HaShiv'a, Israel, on 9 Nov 2017.

Most basketball half-court shots in one hour

Buckets Blakes, Hammer Harrison, Thunder Law, Bull Bullard and Spider Sharpless (all USA) of the Harlem Globetrotters netted 348 shots from the court's halfway line in 60 min in New York City, USA, on 11 Oct 2017.

Youngest person to row any ocean solo

Oliver Crane (USA, b. 19 Jul 1998) was 19 years 148 days old when he embarked on the Talisker Whisky Atlantic Challenge in his craft *SS4*. His voyage lasted from 14 Dec 2017 to 28 Jan 2018 – 44 days 16 hr 9 min in all – taking him from La Gomera in the Spanish Canary Islands to Antigua in the Caribbean. See below for more records set during this gruelling race.

Longest time to hold the breath voluntarily

Spain's Aleix Segura Vendrell held his breath for 24 min 3.45 sec in Barcelona, Spain, on 28 Feb 2016. Aleix is a professional free diver.

The **longest time to hold the breath underwater (female)** is 18 min 32.59 sec, by Karoline Mariechen Meyer (BRA) at the Racer Academy swimming pool in Florianopolis, Brazil, on 10 Jul 2009. Also a professional free diver, Karoline trained for four months beforehand and inhaled oxygen for 24 min prior to her attempt.

TALISKER WHISKY ATLANTIC CHALLENGE

Record	Date/Time	Holder(s)
First all-female trio to row any ocean	13 Feb 2018	Dianne Carrington, Sharon Magrath, Elaine Theaker (all UK)
Highest average age for an all-female team to row the Atlantic	57 years 40 days	
First sisters to row an ocean together	19 Jan 2018	Camilla and Cornelia Bull (both NOR)
Fastest open-class solo row of the Atlantic east to west	30 days 7 hr 49 min	Mark Slats (NLD)
Fastest open-class pair to row the Atlantic east to west	37 days 8 hr 8 min	Jon Armstrong, Jordan Beecher (both UK)
Fastest all-female open-class four to row the Atlantic east to west	34 days 13 hr 13 min	Amber Li Xiaobing, Sarah Meng Yajie, Cloris Chen Yuli, Tina Liang Mintian (all CHN)
Lowest average age for an all-female team to row any ocean	22 years 236 days	
Oldest woman to row any ocean	61 years 349 days	Dianne Carrington (UK)

Fastest 100 m wearing ski boots (female)

Emma Kirk-Odunubi (UK) took just 16.86 sec to run 100 m in a pair of ski boots on 2 Jun 2016. The event was held at the Barn Elms track in Barnes, Greater London, UK. Each of her ski boots weighed around 1.16 kg (2 lb 8.9 oz). On the same day, and at the same venue, Max Willcocks (UK) ran the outright **fastest 100 m wearing ski boots** in 14.09 sec.

Most blunt to fakies (ollie blunts) in one hour

On 17 Jan 2011, Kyle Decot (USA) performed 849 blunt to fakies in 60 min on a skateboard at The Flow Skatepark in Columbus, Ohio, USA.

Highest altitude skateboarding

Aleks Stocki (AUS) skated at an altitude of 5,355 m (17,569 ft) in Leh, a city in the Jammu and Kashmir state of India, on 29 Aug 2017.

Oldest person to swim the English Channel

On 6 Sep 2014, at the age of 73 years 177 days, Otto Thaning (ZAF, b. 13 Mar 1941) crossed from Shakespeare Beach in Dover, UK, to Wissant Bay near Calais in France. It took him 12 hr 52 min to complete the swim.

The **oldest woman to swim the English Channel** is Pat Gallant-Charette (USA, b. 2 Feb 1951). Aged 66 years 135 days, she crossed from England to France in 17 hr 55 min on 17 Jun 2017.

Sally Anne Minty-Gravett (UK, b. 16 Jul 1957) is the **oldest person to complete a two-way English Channel swim**. On 30 Aug 2016, aged 59 years 45 days, she swam from Dover to Calais and back again in 36 hr 26 min.

Longest time to spin a plate on the finger

On 18 Dec 2016, Himanshu Gupta (IND) kept a plate spinning on his finger for 1 hr 10 min 39 sec in Bangalore, India.

Himanshu also used his revolutionary skills to achieve a new GWR title for the **longest time to spin a Swiss ball on one finger (using one hand)**: 5 min 38 sec, in Bangalore, on 12 Sep 2016.

Longest paperclip chain (individual)

Ben Mooney (UK) strung together a 1,997.9-m-long (6,554-ft 9-in) chain of paperclips, as verified in Belfast, UK, on 8 Apr 2017. Comprising around 66,000 individual paperclips, the chain was so long that it had to be measured on the ground of the car park of Ben's school. Ben's feat was sponsored: he raised around £400 ($497) for a local Marie Curie cancer hospice.

Oldest person to swim the Oceans Seven

Aged 58 years 110 days, Antonio Argüelles Díaz-González (MEX, b. 15 Apr 1959) completed the Oceans Seven open-water swimming challenge on 3 Aug 2017. Participants swim the North Channel between Northern Ireland and Scotland. The Oceans Seven is the open-water swimming community's equivalent of the Seven Summits challenge (for more, see p.122).

Farthest barrel roll in a car

On 11 Jul 2017, Terry Grant (UK) performed an aerial roll in a Jaguar E-PACE across a distance of 15.3 m (50 ft 2 in) in London, UK.

Fastest hole of golf by a team of four

Tom Lovelady, Lanto Griffin, Stephan Jaeger and Andrew Yun (all USA) finished a hole of golf in 27.875 sec at the Palm Desert Resort Country Club in California, USA, on 4 Jan 2018.

Most head spins in one minute (male)

Cirque du Soleil performer Youssef El Toufali (BEL) completed 137 rotations on his head in 60 sec in Las Vegas, Nevada, USA, on 6 May 2012.

The **most head spins in one minute (female)** is 101 by "B-girl Roxy" (aka Roxanne Milliner, UK), on the set of *Officially Amazing* in Edinburgh, UK, on 18 Jul 2013.

Heaviest aircraft pulled

Kevin Fast (CAN) pulled a CC-177 Globemaster III weighing 188.83 tonnes (416,299 lb) for 8.8 m (28 ft 10 in) at Canadian Forces Base Trenton in Ontario, Canada, on 17 Sep 2009.

Most swords swallowed simultaneously (male)

On 10 Sep 2017, Franz Huber (DEU) held 28 swords in his throat at the same time in Eggenfelden, Germany. The blades were 51.3 cm (1 ft 8.1 in) long and 1.2 cm (0.4 in) wide.

Franz has several throat-stretching GWR records to his name, including the **largest curve in a swallowed sword** – 133° – in Burghausen, Germany, on 9 Jan 2017 (see right). He has also recorded the **most push-ups while sword swallowing** (20) and the **most swords swallowed and twisted** (15), both achieved on 9 Sep 2017.

Longest duration balancing on a 6-m ladder

On 7 Jan 2016, Uzeyer Novruzov (RUS) balanced atop an unsupported 6-m-tall (19-ft 8-in) ladder for 7 min 15 sec on the set of *CCTV – Guinness World Records Special* in Beijing, China.

Most binary digits memorized in 30 minutes

The simplest number system is binary, comprising just the digits 1 and 0. At the World Memory Championships in Shenzhen, Guangdong Province, China, on 6–8 Dec 2017, Enkhshur Narmandakh (MNG) memorized a binary sequence of 5,445 digits.

The **most Pi places memorized** is 70,000, by Rajveer Meena (IND) at VIT University in Vellore, India, on 21 Mar 2015. The recall took him almost 10 hr.

Highest shallow dive into fire

On 21 Jun 2014, "Professor Splash" (aka Darren Taylor, USA) plunged 8 m (26 ft 3 in) into 10 in (25.4 cm) of water that was covered in flames. The feat took place on NBC's *Show Stopping Sunday* special at Universal Studios in Los Angeles, California, USA.

Highest BMX vertical air

Mat Hoffman (USA) achieved a 26-ft 6-in (8.07-m) vertical jump on a BMX bicycle from a 24-ft-tall (7.31-m) quarterpipe on 20 Mar 2001 in Oklahoma City, Oklahoma, USA.

Longest BMX backflip

On 3 Aug 2005, Mike Escamilla (USA) performed a 62-ft 2-in (18.94-m) backflip on a BMX bike off the Mega Ramp at X Games 11 in Los Angeles, California, USA.

Franz secured his first GWR title in 2015, when he achieved the **most swords swallowed and twisted**. He's since broken his own record by adding a couple more swords (see below)…

Longest duration balancing a chainsaw on the chin

On 4 Oct 2017, juggler and multiple GWR record holder David Rush (USA) successfully kept a chainsaw balanced on his chin for a total of 10 min 0.78 sec at the Cradlepoint Block Party in Boise, Idaho, USA.

The next day, David achieved the **longest duration balancing a chainsaw on the forehead** – 5 min 1 sec.

Please do not attempt either of the above two records yourself at home!

MEET THE MAKERS

The GWR archive is packed with record holders who embody the spirit of the "Maker Movement" – inventors, artists, hobbyists and DIY-ers behind some super-sized or super-fast creations. In this special chapter, British inventor, engineer and TV star Edd China selects some of his favourite Maker projects...

Think fast. Think big. Think the unthinkable!

That's my starting point whenever I'm working on a new project. I've got a passion for creating things that make people look twice – inventions that seem to have stepped straight out of a dream or a cartoon. In fact, you can see my latest project here: a diesel ice-cream van that I'm converting into electric, making it more friendly to the environment. I've also been testing it out on the race track at the Bruntingthorpe Proving Ground – I love breaking records, so I'm souping it up for an attempt at the **fastest electric ice-cream van**. I've had a lot of success in the past (you'll find my current and former records below), but I still need you to wish me luck!

BE INSPIRED

In this chapter, you'll meet 10 other inventors and designers who share my passion for records. These Makers are individuals who combine active imaginations, practical skills and perseverance to create extraordinary, one-of-a-kind objects. These larger-than-life inventions, and their passionate designers, are an example to us all. I'm sure that at some point, a few people told the creative folk who came up with these fantastic ideas that it couldn't be done. There must have been times when they doubted it themselves, too. But they pushed on until they succeeded – and earned themselves a place in the pages of Guinness World Records.

Hopefully, these projects will inspire you to come up with a record-breaking design of your own one of these days!

Edd

The first part of my project involved swapping out the original diesel engine from a Whitby Morrison ice-cream van.

...and replacing it with this electric engine – much better for the environment!

I've had a passion for engineering since I was young; it inspired me to become an inventor. I also co-hosted Discovery Channel's Wheeler Dealers show.

EDD'S INGENIOUS INVENTIONS

My **fastest office** has a top speed of 140 km/h (86.9 mph).

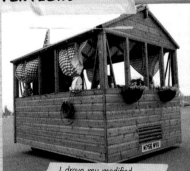
I drove my modified garden shed to a speed of 94 km/h (58.4 mph)!

Myself and GWR's Craig Glenday relax in a 111-km/h (69-mph) bed.

On board my 140-km/h (86.9-mph) "Casual Lofa".

Here's me at Bruntingthorpe Proving Ground – an airport in Leicestershire, UK, where I test out my record-breaking inventions. I've been zipping up and down the 2-mi (3.2-km) race track here, trying out my new electric ice-cream van. It's a challenging project, but I hope that by summer 2018 I'll have it going fast enough to secure the GWR title for **fastest electric ice-cream van**. You can follow my progress at **www.guinnessworldrecords.com/makers** – you'll also find galleries and video clips of other record-breakers to inspire you to get involved in your own Maker projects. Have fun!

CONTENTS

EDD'S *Electric* ICES

My next challenge is hooking up the "Whippy" ice-cream machine to the electric engine.

Marek Turowski reached a speed of 148 km/h (92 mph) in my super-fast sofa.

My 124.77-km/h (77.53-mph) milk float takes the chequered flag.

My fleet bathroom suite reaches 68 km/h (42.25 mph).

Myself, "Mario" and "Lara Croft" ride the 92-km/h (57-mph) **fastest mobile gaming rig**.

MEET THE MAKERS

LARGEST YO-YO

How do you make a yo-yo that's as big as a Volkswagen Beetle and heavier than an adult male rhinoceros? And how do you spin it? Say "yo!" to Beth Johnson, who explains the how and why of her titanic toy...

The journey to a new Guinness World Records title can begin in a host of different ways. Beth Johnson (USA) began hers in 2001, when she was having chemotherapy treatment and surgery for cancer. Having survived, "I decided to do something – something that would get my name all over the world!" That "something" was building the world's largest yo-yo...

UPS AND DOWNS

From design to construction and the patriotic paint job, Beth's giant-sized toy – which she dubbed the "Whoa-Yo" – was pretty much all her own work. She spent more than three years building it, only for the yo-yo to crash in a trio of successive tests. Undeterred, Beth spent 5–6 hr per day over eight to nine weeks producing a new design.

On 15 Sep 2012 – more than 10 years after first deciding to build it – Beth demonstrated her giant yo-yo for a fourth time in Cincinnati, Ohio, USA. Measuring 11 ft 10.75 in (3.62 m) in diameter and weighing a hefty 4,620 lb (2,095.6 kg), the gadget plunged 120 ft (36.5 m) on a rope attached to a 150,000-lb (68-tonne) crane before successfully rebounding – just like a conventional yo-yo!

"I couldn't believe it. I was just so excited," she admitted afterwards. "I was so nervous, my heart was beating 100 times a minute. But I was so happy and I am still so excited." It took patience, perseverance and perfectionism, but Beth Johnson got what she'd wanted: global recognition and a place in the record books.

MEET THE MAKER: BETH JOHNSON

What inspired you to create your record-breaking yo-yo?
I wanted to show people you can do anything you put your mind to. If you try hard enough, anything is possible.

Have you made anything else on such an outsize scale?
No, the yo-yo is the only thing I've ever made this large. I really like to make things – if I see something I'd like to have and it's too much money, I'll try to make it.

Did it cost a lot to construct such a colossal object?
Yes, the yo-yo wound up being an expensive project. I think we spent somewhere around $3,000 [£1,850], and that was just making it.

How difficult was it to put the yo-yo together?
The most challenging part, I think, other than lifting one side and putting it on to the other, was making sure that I had both sides the same. Since I was using a sander to shape it, it was time-consuming. We also had to build a customized cart for it.

Then we drove it 1,000 mi [1,600 km] to Jacksonville, Florida, three times – and it failed each time! [Beth is shown above preparing for an earlier record attempt.]

Yes, it took a few attempts for you to get that GWR title! The rope snapped on the third attempt and the yo-yo was damaged when it landed. Did you feel like giving up?
The first time we tried it, in Florida, when it did the "sleeper" [a common yo-yo throw] and then fell to the ground, I was really upset. The news reporter who was there asked me what I thought. All I could do was cry and shake my head.

After the third time, I had major repairs to carry out, and had to strip all the paint off and repaint it. Everyone thought I was crazy, but I'm not a quitter.

And when we finally got it to work, at the fourth try, it was so rewarding. It was awesome!

The **first yo-yo patent** was filed by Haven & Hettrick (USA) on 20 Nov 1866. But the basic design dates back to ancient Greece, as seen on this vase from 440 BCE.

– SPEC –

WEIGHT 4,620 LB
2,095.6 KG

DIAMETER 11 FT 10.75 IN
3.62 M

LENGTH 120 FT
OF ROPE 36.5 M

AS HEAVY
AS A RHINO!

LARGEST RUBIK'S CUBE

There's no shortage of record-breaking super-size toys. Tony Fisher (UK) created a Rubik's Cube with 1.57-m (5-ft 1.8-in) sides, as confirmed on 5 Apr 2016 in Ipswich, Suffolk, UK. It took lifelong puzzle fan Tony a mere two months to construct the fully functional cube at home, and visitors from as far away as Japan have come to see it for themselves.

MEET THE MAKERS
LARGEST HAMBURGER

How long does it take to prepare and cook a 1-tonne burger? How do you move it onto the bun? And what do you do with it afterwards? Welcome to the world of giant-sized fast food.

On the day, around 300 assistants were on hand to help. Here, the patty is being eased on to the bun.

Burgers have made regular appearances in the pages of Guinness World Records over the years, from the **most eaten in one minute** (five, by Rix Terabite, aka Ricardo Francisco, of the Philippines) to the **longest line of hamburgers** (475.10 m; 1,558 ft 8.6 in). And then there's the grandaddy of them all: the **largest hamburger**. Step forward six men on a mission to max out the meat...

On 9 Jul 2017, Germany's Wolfgang Leeb, Tom Reicheneder, Rudi Dietl, Josef Zellner, Hans Maurer and Christian Dischinger (all DEU) took more than an hour to assemble this super-sized snack in the Bavarian town of Pilsting, Germany.

It comprised three meat patties, cheese, salad and a bun, and weighed in at a scales-straining 1,164.2 kg (2,566 lb 9 oz). A hungry crowd of 6,000 onlookers came along to watch the burger being put together, along with a film crew from TV station Kabel Eins who were making a documentary.

The whole preparation process was observed by a local food-hygiene expert – naturally, all that food wasn't going to be wasted. Once the record had been officially confirmed by GWR's Lena Kuhlmann, the record-breaking burger was chopped up and sold, with all proceeds donated to kindergartens in Bavaria.

Even after they had prepared the burger, it took the team nearly an entire day to cook the raw meat.

The 360 kg (793 lb) of mixed salad and cheese used is the weight of about 50 bowling balls.

RECIPE

Beef Patty
1,000 kg Bavarian beef
18 kg salt
2 kg black pepper
60 kg onions
80 kg tomatoes
60 kg cucumbers
60 kg iceberg salad
100 kg cheese
20 kg hamburger sauce
10 kg mustard

Bun
60 kg flour (type 550)
0.6 kg sugar
1.2 kg salt
4.2 kg oil
1.8 kg baking agent
4.2 kg eggs
1.2 kg malt
1.8 kg yeast
32.4 litres water

Method
1. Mix the mince, salt and pepper and pack into the patty mould. 2. Cook for 10 hr 30 min at 100–120°C (212–248°F). 3. Meanwhile, make the bun by mixing the water and sugar in a large tub and dissolving in the yeast. 4. Leave for a few minutes, then mix in all other ingredients. 5. Leave the dough covered for 1 hr in a warm place. 6. Afterwards, thoroughly knead the dough and shape it. 7. Bake at approx. 200°C (392°F) in a stone oven for 45 min. Then assemble remaining ingredients.

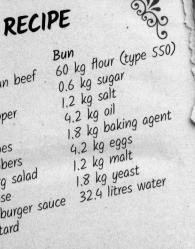

MEET THE MAKER: JOSEF ZELLNER

What inspired you to go for this record in the first place?
We are a group of friends who wanted to put together a special event for our homeland.

What were the most difficult elements of the process?
The trickiest part was putting the hamburger together. Each patty weighed about 260 kg [573 lb]. We needed a 36-tonne [79,366-lb] Autokran [mobile crane] to move the meat.

How long did it take you to prepare the burger?
We made the burger the day before it was cooked. It took about 8 hr.

How long did it take to cook the burger itself?
The meat was cooked on Sunday, 9 Jul 2017, from 8:00 a.m. to 6:30 p.m. After cooking, it took about another hour to put the burger together.

Did anything go wrong on the day?
In the morning we had bad weather, with rain and wind. So our barbecue oven was not hot enough. It took a longer time than expected to cook the burger.

What happened to it afterwards?
The burger was cut up into more than 3,000 "small burgers" and was sold to the spectators [about 6,000 people]. We donated the money we received to kindergartens here in Bavaria.

Are there any other GWR records that you would like to attempt in the future?
After this event, we'll surely think about the possibility of doing another world record. To cook the largest burger in the world was really exhausting for all of us, but it was also very exciting!

Finally: how does it feel to be a Guinness World Records title holder?
It is great to be in the Guinness World Records book, of course! We're very, very proud to belong to this exclusive circle and hope we can do this another time.

Largest meatball
Between 5 and 8 Oct 2011, seven members of the Columbus Italian Club (USA) prepared a colossal meatball weighing 503.71 kg (1,110 lb 7.84 oz) – around the same as a grand piano – with a 1.38-m (4-ft 6.3-in) diameter. The meat and spices were mixed in batches of 50 lb (22.6 kg), then refrigerated, transported to another location, packed into a vessel and cooked in a specially made oven. It was presented at the St John's Italian Festival in Columbus, Ohio, USA.

4

AS HEAVY AS A WALRUS

The finished burger was more than twice as heavy as a full-grown Arabian horse. Or to put it another way...

LARGEST RUBBER-BAND BALL

How long does it take to create a rubber-band ball that weighs more than a hippo? Where do you get the materials? And why is it best to work on it at night? Let Joel Waul put you in the loop.

"Sometimes I would wake up in the morning and I couldn't even believe it was in my driveway," says Joel Waul (USA) of his Guinness World Records achievement. The **largest rubber-band ball** that he patiently assembled weighs 4,097 kg (9,032 lb), as verified in Lauderhill, Florida, USA, on 13 Nov 2008. It took more than 700,000 rubber bands of all sizes to make the 2-m-tall (6-ft 7-in) sphere.

ROUNDING IT ALL UP

Joel – aka the "Rubba Ban Man" – was inspired when he saw the then-largest rubber-band ball being dropped out of a plane for a TV stunt. He set to work in Apr 2004, calling his fledgling ball "Nugget". By late summer, it was up to his waist. Joel realized it was getting too big for his house, so he rolled it into his back yard. By Apr 2007, it weighed more than 5,000 lb (2,268 kg) and Joel once again decided to move it. This time, he smashed it through his fence and rolled it into his driveway, where he continued to add more and more rubber bands. Deciding the name "Nugget" didn't suit his beast of a ball, Joel renamed it "Megaton".

Largest ball made of stickers

Made from around 100,000 stickers and labels, this huge globe weighs 105.052 kg (231 lb 9.6 oz) and was created by John Fischer (USA) and staff at printers StickerGiant, which John founded. Named "Saul" (simply because it rhymes with "ball"), it was weighed in Longmont, Colorado, USA, on 13 Jan 2016. The record was completed in honour of the first National Sticker Day, which was held on that date.

– SPEC –

WEIGHT 4,097 KG
(9,032 LB)

HEIGHT 2.0 M
(6 FT 7 IN)

NUMBER OF BANDS 700,000-PLUS

AS HEAVY AS A MALE HIPPOPOTAMUS

MEET THE MAKER: JOEL WAUL

This record has been broken a few times since the 1990s. Did you always believe you were destined to be the record holder?
Yes, I knew from the moment I first saw the world record in the 2000 edition of Guinness World Records.

When did you get started and how long did it take to complete?
I started on 10 Apr 2004 and it took four years and seven months to complete.

Where did all those bands come from? Did you have to buy them?
Up to 3,200 lb [1,451 kg] came from the internet, and after I'd used up all of those my ball was sponsored by [physical therapy specialists] Stretchwell. In the beginning I spent $7,000 [£3,800] of my own money on rubber bands before "Megaton" was sponsored.

With such a big size, some of the bands must have been enormous. What are they used for other than helping you to break records?
Therapy bands – they're used for sports injury rehabilitation.

When "Megaton" was still small, did you use more conventional-sized rubber bands?
Yes, I used size-32 rubber bands.

"Megaton" was constructed in your driveway. Was it affected by the hot Florida sun or other weather conditions?
It was mostly the sun that affected "Megaton". When I wasn't working on it, I had it covered with a tarpaulin to protect it. I did a lot of work on it at night.

You smashed the previous world record by an incredible 4,438 lb (2,013 kg)! Did you monitor the ball's weight as you made it, or did you simply stop when you ran out of steam?
Yes, I monitored the weight of "Megaton". And no, I certainly didn't run out of steam! Actually, I ran out of time. If I had had two more weeks before the Guinness World Records adjudicator came to weigh "Megaton", it would have been 10,000 lb [4,536 kg].

LET'S GET YOU STARTED...

Want to make a band ball of your own? Begin by folding one ordinary rubber band over itself, so that it bunches up.

Next, carefully wrap a second band over the widest section of the first one, thus pinning down the original set of loops.

Wrap another rubber band tightly over the second one. Continue the process, making sure that you are developing both the width and the length evenly.

As you continue to add layers, the shape will begin to balloon outwards.

Eventually, if you have alternated your rubber bands correctly, they should start to take on a spherical shape. Now all you have to do is add another band. Then another. Then another...

MEET THE MAKERS
LARGEST ORIGAMI RHINO

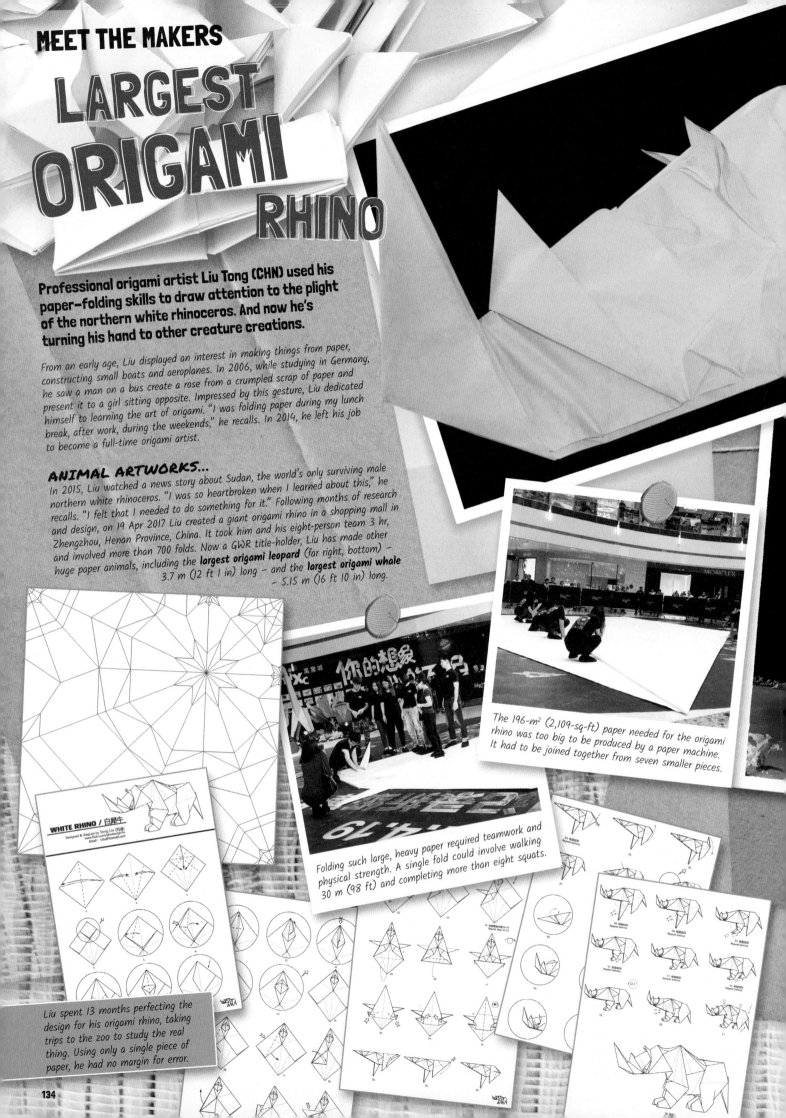

Professional origami artist Liu Tong (CHN) used his paper-folding skills to draw attention to the plight of the northern white rhinoceros. And now he's turning his hand to other creature creations.

From an early age, Liu displayed an interest in making things from paper, constructing small boats and aeroplanes. In 2006, while studying in Germany, he saw a man on a bus create a rose from a crumpled scrap of paper and present it to a girl sitting opposite. Impressed by this gesture, Liu dedicated himself to learning the art of origami. "I was folding paper during my lunch break, after work, during the weekends," he recalls. In 2014, he left his job to become a full-time origami artist.

ANIMAL ARTWORKS...
In 2015, Liu watched a news story about Sudan, the world's only surviving male northern white rhinoceros. "I was so heartbroken when I learned about this," he recalls. "I felt that I needed to do something for it." Following months of research and design, on 19 Apr 2017 Liu created a giant origami rhino in a shopping mall in Zhengzhou, Henan Province, China. It took him and his eight-person team 3 hr, and involved more than 700 folds. Now a GWR title-holder, Liu has made other huge paper animals, including the **largest origami leopard** (far right, bottom) – 3.7 m (12 ft 1 in) long – and the **largest origami whale** – 5.15 m (16 ft 10 in) long.

The 196-m² (2,109-sq-ft) paper needed for the origami rhino was too big to be produced by a paper machine. It had to be joined together from seven smaller pieces.

Folding such large, heavy paper required teamwork and physical strength. A single fold could involve walking 30 m (98 ft) and completing more than eight squats.

WHITE RHINO / 白犀牛
Designed & diagram by Tong Liu (刘通)
www.flickr.com/photos/ljliu
Email : Liu@foxmail.com

Liu spent 13 months perfecting the design for his origami rhino, taking trips to the zoo to study the real thing. Using only a single piece of paper, he had no margin for error.

Another of Liu Tong's creations is the **largest origami dove**, which measures 4.64 m (15 ft 2 in) high, 1.90 m (6 ft 2 in) long and 2.92 m (9 ft 6 in) wide.

-SPEC-

WEIGHT 110 LB (50 KG)

LENGTH 25 FT 8 IN (7.83 M)

HEIGHT 13 FT 4 IN (4.06 M)

LIU'S RHINO IS TWICE AS TALL AS A REAL RHINO!

MEET THE MAKER: LIU TONG

What role does accurate planning and precise calculation play in your origami creations?

Design is the first and most difficult part of the project. You need to make calculations carefully to achieve a reasonable distribution of the paper, which guarantees that the final work's structure and proportions are perfect.

What tools are involved?

I use both pens and computers during my design, but computers are mainly for verifying whether my design is correct or not, and whether or not it can be folded successfully. So mostly my design is completed by using pens and paper. The tools for folding are simply a pen, one piece of paper, a ruler, a protractor... and that's it.

What are the rules of origami?

Modern origami requires that no matter how complicated or how simple the work is, it needs to be done with a completely square piece of paper, without cutting or additional collage. In other words, if we unfold the work it could be restored to the original square piece of paper.

What's special about the origami paper used in this record?

It needs to be very tough, as well as able to handle pressure, which means that after repeated times of folding it's still not broken. In the meantime, the paper should be very thick and soft enough, because hard or fragile paper isn't suitable for folding.

What's your favourite thing to make?

Every work is like my own child – I created them, I'm attached to all of them. If I must pick one, I would still pick the white rhino.

What's the next big project?

My next project is to work with the China Capital Museum to restore some cultural relics. I will fold some origami replica works of the relics for the museum to display.

LARGEST DISPLAY OF TOOTHPICK SCULPTURES

Stan Munro (USA) painstakingly makes art out of an oral-hygiene tool. But can it really take five years to plan just one of these awesome sculptures?

Stan Munro has been "toothpicking" since fifth grade. On 15 May 2014, he earned a GWR title for the **largest display of toothpick sculptures**, with a group of 101 sculptures in New York City, USA. He spent more than 10 years creating these sculptures and figures, using in excess of 3 million toothpicks and 75 US gallons (284 litres) of glue. His display includes buildings from 37 countries, built to 1:164 scale, including China's Temple of Heaven, the Eiffel Tower in France, India's Taj Mahal, the Chrysler Building and Seattle Space Needle (both USA), the UK's MI6 headquarters and La Sagrada Familia in Spain. "The exhibit was just meant to compare buildings side by side, mostly skyscrapers," he explains. "The more I got into it, the more I fell in love with it, and the more intricate the structures became."

His replica of the Golden Gate Bridge is a tribute to Stan's skill and patience. "I spent five years planning how I could build a transportable 12-m-long [39-ft 4-in] version," he explains. "That meant testing different methods and learning new techniques. I eventually came up with an idea for a bridge that came apart into 18 main sections: two towers, two anchors, six deck sections, eight main cables and hundreds of supporting cables – all assembled with a pin-and-groove system in two days." One glance at the finished bridge tells you that all that planning was worth it.

- INSPIRATION -
GOLDEN GATE BRIDGE

Stan's detailed *Star Wars* recreations include the iconic All Terrain Scout Transport (AT-ST) and Imperial Shuttle. Both are shown above, along with a toothpick Darth Vader and stormtroopers.

Stan has also created a display of 125 sci-fi spaceships, including this Star Destroyer – the **largest Star Wars toothpick sculpture**. Incorporating some 15,000 toothpicks, it is 39 cm tall, 1.98 m long and 80 cm wide (1 ft 3.3 in x 4 ft 10.2 in x 2 ft 7.4 in) and weighs 7 lb 6.4 oz (3.4 kg).

MEET THE MAKER: STAN MUNRO

Your toothpick structures are an amazing blend of engineering and art. How did you get started?
The truth is, I had a box of toothpicks, a bottle of glue and a free afternoon. I had no intention of it getting this big. In the beginning, I just wanted to create a little city of 10 world landmarks built to the same scale. And that's all I really do – copy someone else's engineering and art, but I do it as faithfully as possible.

What's the hardest part of building your structures?
The hardest part is just starting. There may be some sections I'm not sure how to do when I start, but I don't worry about that until I get there.

Can you tell us about the structural engineering of your creations?
I'm not allowed to use anything but toothpicks and glue – that's not just a GWR rule, that's my rule. But it turns out the tiny toothpick doesn't just make the structures look good on the outside, it's the perfect tool to make them strong on the inside. The strength of wood and the lightweight material is the perfect combination.

How much planning goes into a build?
Nowadays I can download satellite photos, blueprints and photos from every angle, but I still do everything by hand – no laser-cutting, no computer-generated window cutouts.

What tools are typically involved?
I use various cutting tools, rulers, clamps and masking tape to hold pieces together until the glue dries. The most advanced tool I use is a hand-held rotary device [above] – I smooth edges and cut out windows with it, but mostly I use a pair of scissors. As long as you cut with the grain, it's not much different than cutting paper or cardboard.

What's the next challenge?
The next challenge is not so much one building, but one country: India. Akshardham, Lotus Temple and the Taj Mahal were just the beginning. I could probably spend the rest of my life just building temples from India...

Tallest toothpick sculpture
On 22 Jun 2013, Stan's 1:164-scale model of the Burj Khalifa in Dubai, UAE, was measured at 5.09 m (16 ft 8.4 in) at the Phelps Art Center in Phelps, New York, USA. It contains at least 300,000 toothpicks. "The first structure I built at this scale was the Chrysler Building in NYC for my wife, and it had to fit in the game room downstairs," he explains. "I stuck with the 1:164 scale, thinking I would only keep the one building for her. That was 16 years ago…"

MEET THE MAKERS

FASTEST JET-POWERED GO-KART

Tom Bagnall wanted to drive a fast go-kart, so he turned to his friend and engineer Andy Morris (both UK), who gave him a *really* fast go-kart – and a *Guinness World Records* title too!

← TEST 1 – NEW TYRES! LOL

Tom Bagnall comes from Cheadle in Staffordshire, UK. On 5 Sep 2017, he drove the **fastest jet-powered go-kart** at 112.29 mph (180.71 km/h) for CBBC's *Officially Amazing* at RAF Elvington airfield near York, UK.

THE ROAD TO A RECORD

Although it was Andy Morris who designed and constructed this record-breaking go-kart, Tom himself is a qualified mechanical engineer. "I've had a passion for engineering since a young age," he explains. "I started to design and build jet engines a long time ago. I first started on pulse-jet engines. They're fun and simple to build, but they produce a lot of noise and are not that practical for the applications that I used them for! So I moved on to gas-turbine engines. They produce more power and are far more practical."

His other great passions are drag racing and land-speed records. Tom's been a huge drag-racing fan for years, and has been going to race meetings since he was just 15 years old. It was only a question of time before he built his own jet-powered vehicles and began racing them. He joined a jet-car team as one of the pit crew...and a few years later he owned that very car and was racing it! Tom's hoping to set a new record with his latest project – a gas turbine-powered kayak with afterburner: "You can't beat the look on people's faces when they expect to see a fighter jet flying over their head and instead they see a kayak shredding past them!"

– SPEC –

WEIGHT 70 KG
(154 LB 5 OZ)

LENGTH 3 M (9 FT 10.1 IN)
WITH AFTERBURNER
2.1 M (6 FT 10.6 IN)
WITHOUT AFTERBURNER

WIDTH 1.2 M (3 FT 11.2 IN)

SPEED 112.29 MPH
(180.71 KM/H)

Fastest jet-powered fire truck
On 11 Jul 1998, *Hawaiian Eagle*, a jet-powered fire truck owned by Shannen Seydel (USA), reached a speed of 655 km/h (407 mph) in Ontario, Canada. The vehicle, a red 1940 Ford, was powered by two Rolls-Royce Bristol Viper Mk 633-41 full after-burning engines. Each engine could produce 6,000 hp (4,474 kW), generating a combined thrust of 53.37 kN (12,000 lbf).

Afterburner fuel pump

12-V gear pump for oil

Main engine fuel pump

Turbocharger

Oil filter

Afterburner

Turbo inlet

Oil tank/cooler

50-mm axle

E.C.U.

24-V igniter

NEARLY TWICE AS FAST AS A CHEETAH

-PARTS LIST-

- 12-V gear pump for oil
- Two Bosch 044 motorsport fuel pumps
- Custom-made heat-exchange oil tank
- 24-V aircraft igniter for main engine
- Spark-gap igniter for afterburner
- Custom-made engine control unit (E.C.U.) to control and monitor engine
- Design and make combustion chamber (BIG JOB)
- Design and make afterburner
- Stainless-steel hose (hydraulic type) – enough for oil and fuel system
- Find a Monster Turbo and buy or make inlet/outlet flanges
- Buy needle valve to control fuel flow
- Fuel and oil filters

MEET THE MAKER: ANDY MORRIS

How long have you been interested in engineering?

All my life. My father and both grandfathers were engineers: one was a director at the Brough Superior motorcycles firm, and the other worked on the gliders used at the D-Day landings. As a boy, I loved to take things apart to see what made them tick.

But it wasn't until seeing an episode of Channel 4's *Scrapheap Challenge* featuring Nick Haddock – now a friend – that I realized I could make a jet engine. I built my first one about 10 years ago, just to see if I could do it; it ended up in a go-kart. The oil reservoir was a stainless-steel biscuit barrel! I like to repurpose materials when I can. The combustion chamber on Tom's go-kart was the casing from an old fire extinguisher.

Tom is the ideal driver for speed runs. He's got a small frame and he's light, so the vehicle can accelerate quickly with him in it. Plus, he has great spatial awareness.

How long did it take to build Tom's go-kart?

Six months, but after about three years of working out how to obtain optimum performance. At one point, I totally rewired it and changed the type of battery supply. That saved 6 kg [13 lb 3 oz] or more, and weight is crucial in speed records: vehicles must be as light as possible.

Could it have gone faster?

Yes! We didn't have the time or fuel to do any more runs on the day. And a longer track would have helped, as the go-kart could have built up more speed. For some reason, the afterburner

wasn't working well on the day either. Thrust jet engines are a very inefficient way of producing drive; our engines are far smaller than those in drag-racing jet cars.

What else are you working on right now?

Well, I've got a jet-powered bike in my shed, with a home-made jet engine. That took about three months to make. I'm also working on another jet engine – hopefully one of the most powerful DIY gas turbines yet built, reaching 300 lbf [36 kgf] with an afterburner. I'm going to put it in a go-kart, then put Tom in it – although I haven't told him that yet...!

LARGEST SKATEBOARD

How long does it take to build the biggest skateboard in the world? And how fast can it travel? Step forward Joe Ciaglia, one half of the creative partnership behind the board of your dreams.

Around 10 years ago, Joe Ciaglia – director of California Skateparks – began working with entrepreneur Rob Dyrdek (both USA) to design and construct the latter's Fantasy Factory – a hybrid skatepark/warehouse/office complex and home to Rob's eponymous MTV reality show. Soon, Joe and Rob had come up with the idea of creating the ultimate in outsize skateboards. California Skateparks' craftsmen took it from there. Unveiled on MTV's *Rob Dyrdek's Fantasy Factory* in Los Angeles, California, USA, on 25 Feb 2009, the **largest skateboard** is 36 ft 7 in (11.15 m) long, 8 ft 8 in (2.64 m) wide and 3 ft 7.5 in (1.10 m) high.

TAKING IT TO THE STREET

In 2010, Joe took the board out for a solo ride in Pennsylvania's Woodward Skate Camp. So what happened next? "Well, I decided to ride the board solo after trying it a few times with kids from the camp," he recalls. "I got on and the board began picking up speed, and it started drifting left towards dangerous terrain. As I was flying down the hill, I realized there was no way I could steer the board away from launching off this huge dirt pile. I knew I had to bail before it hit the dirt. So I got low to the edge and jumped off, but I didn't jump far enough out and the back tyre hit my foot and took my shoe off. Luckily I didn't get hurt, but it was definitely one of the crazier experiences I've had!"

The supersized skateboard weighs in at more than 3,600 lb (1,630 kg), but was designed to exactly the same specifications as a normal-sized board.

– SPEC –

LENGTH 36 FT 7 IN
(11.15 M)

WIDTH 8 FT 8 IN
(2.64 M)

HEIGHT 3 FT 7.5 IN
(1.10 M)

AS LONG AS ONE OF LONDON'S NEW ROUTEMASTER BUSES!

MEET THE MAKER: JOE CIAGLIA

What is your background in skateboarding?
I casually skateboarded as a kid growing up in Southern California. I started California Skateparks in 1998, and we've built and designed more than 350 skateparks across the world as well as skateboarding events such as X Games, Street League and Vans Park Series.

Is the board in proportion and fully functional? If you were big enough, could you steer it and do tricks?
The skateboard is to scale. It's actually 12.5 times the size of a normal skateboard. So yes, if you were 12.5 times your size, you could definitely skate it!

How long did it take to build?
About 10 weeks, with three guys working on it.

What's the top speed the skateboard has reached?
The fastest the board has gone is probably 56 km/h

[35 mph] down a grass hill at Camp Woodward in Pennsylvania.

What was the most difficult aspect of the construction?
The hardest part was not having any directions or blueprints. We just started and figured it out as we progressed with its construction. Everything was custom-built and fabricated for the skateboard.

What did setting the record mean to you?
I've always liked pushing the boundaries and building things people never thought were possible. As soon as the idea to build the skateboard came up, I couldn't wait to get started. I wanted to make sure to not only set the record, but break the old record by a long way.

Do you have any plans to attempt more Guinness World Records titles?
Not currently, but I believe down the road there's a chance we could potentially build another world record-breaker.

2

The seven-ply (layer) wooden deck is 5.5 in (13.97 cm) thick. Inside is a supporting frame made out of steel.

3

The wheels are racing car tyres with a 2-ft 6-in (76.2-cm) diameter. The steel trucks were custom-made and the rubber bushings (which allow the board to turn and pivot) are adjustable.

4

In 2011, rapper Nas performed his tracks "It Ain't Hard to Tell" and "Made You Look" from atop the record-breaking board in New York City, USA.

LARGEST RUBE GOLDBERG

Why must inventions always be efficient? Is the quickest way always the best? And is there a place for humour in engineering? One man thought so...

Reuben Garrett Lucius "Rube" Goldberg (1883–1970) was a US Pulitzer Prize-winning cartoonist with a degree in engineering from the University of California. He is famous for drawing ridiculously complex machines that used multiple steps – the more the better – to achieve a simple goal. (In the UK, William Heath Robinson became famous for sketching similar designs.) In fact, Rube Goldberg is the only person ever to be listed in Merriam-Webster's American English dictionary as an adjective, defined as "accomplishing by complex means what seemingly could be done simply". Animals, cogs, rockets, springs, gravity, flowing water, power tools and countless animate or inanimate objects can be used to achieve something as straightforward as turning on a light, popping a balloon or turning the pages of a book.

KEEP IT COMPLICATED!

Today, the spirit of Rube Goldberg lives on in a series of annual contests. Competitors from all over the world strive to design, build and demonstrate entertaining machines that achieve silly things in complex, long-winded ways. As Rube himself stated, his machines were a "symbol of man's capacity for exerting maximum effort to accomplish minimal results".

Largest Rube Goldberg in competition

More than 5,000 hr in the making, the most complicated Rube Goldberg machine built under the pressure of a competition is a 300-step device submitted by the Purdue Society of Professional Engineers Rube Goldberg Team (all USA, pictured right and above). Activated at the National Rube Goldberg Machine Contest at Purdue University in West Lafayette, Indiana, USA, on 31 Mar 2012, its goal was to blow up and pop a balloon! As per official rules, the machine finished one run in under 2 min (actually 1 min 56 sec). It also completed each of the annual tasks set in the contest's history up to that point, including sharpening a pencil, juicing an orange and making a hamburger.

A chain-reaction machine is painstakingly erected in Detroit, Michigan, USA, in 2015. It featured around half a million objects, including some 250,000 dominoes.

The green-shirted team Rubicon X from Arlington, Massachusetts, and Bath, Michigan (both USA), put their entry to the test at the 2011 competition.

WHAT EXACTLY IS AN RGMC?

In the words of the Director of Rube Goldberg Inc.: "A Rube Goldberg Machine Contest [RGMC] is an event where students of all ages compete with the machines they have imagined, designed and created in a fun and competitive forum. The competitions encourage teamwork, critical thinking and out-of-the-box problem-solving in a fresh learning environment and on a level playing field. To compete in an RGMC, all you need is a good imagination and a pile of junk!" To find out more, see opposite page.

Schoolchildren carefully assemble their link in a chain-reaction event held at the Rockwell Cage gymnasium in Cambridge, Massachusetts, USA, on 25 Nov 2016.

MEET THE MAKER'S GRANDDAUGHTER: JENNIFER GEORGE

Who are you?
I'm Jennifer George, Rube Goldberg's granddaughter, and for the last decade I've been the legacy Director of Rube Goldberg Inc.

Why do you put on these contests?
Since 1988, thousands of students have celebrated Rube's legacy by creating Rube Goldberg machines in our annual contest and they've learned – and laughed – a lot. On a formal basis, this learning experience now falls under the category STEM/STEAM (Science, Technology Engineering, Art and Maths) education – something that came naturally to Rube, who was trained as an engineer but was an inventor and artist at heart. [He is seen above in 1964 at home in New York, drawing his last cartoon. Seen left is Rube's design for a self-operating napkin from 1931.]

What are the rules?
Students need to build a Rube Goldberg machine [RGM] based on the task determined by Rube Goldberg Inc. There are a maximum number of steps and size for the machine, and we encourage the repurposing of recycled items and everyday household objects. In addition to the RGM itself, teams need to present step lists and narratives. And, of course, the machines must be funny!

How do people take part?
Contest registration is done on our website: **rubegoldberg.com**. Students from ages eight through to 22 may enter our contest, guided by a Team Leader. Together they build an RGM to our specifications and rules.
· Team Leaders register a team and invite students to take part.
· Teams design and build a machine to accomplish the task.
· Teams compete in either the live or online contest.
· The live contest culminates in regional championships, competing for top place in their division at the live finals.
· The online competition culminates in individual teams from around the world vying for top place in their division.

LARGEST WATER PISTOL

Can water really smash through glass? And what has the planet Mars got to do with soaking your friends from head to foot? Step forward YouTuber, inventor and former NASA engineer Mark Rober.

On 6 Nov 2017, Mark Rober and his friends Ken Glazebrook, Bob Clagett and Dani Yuan (all USA) presented the world's **largest water pistol**. Based on the classic Super Soaker, it measures 1.22 m (4 ft) tall by 2.22 m (7 ft 3.4 in) long by 0.25 m (9.8 in) wide and is powered by a tank of pressurized nitrogen. It's capable of firing a powerful jet of water that can smash glass! Mark is an engineer and inventor who worked at NASA's Jet Propulsion Laboratory for seven years and helped to put the *Curiosity* rover on Mars. His YouTube channel is dedicated to researching and testing quirky scientific projects, and currently has 3 million subscribers.

SPACE TECH AND THE SUPER SOAKER

So, did Mark's NASA background come in useful when he was creating his giant water pistol? "Absolutely," he says. "Of the seven years working on the *Curiosity* rover, three years were spent on the Descent Stage, which is the jet pack that safely lowered the rover to the ground. That jet pack relied on the exact same principles as the Super Soaker. In the case of the rover, we had two pressurized helium tanks that pushed hydrazine fuel to the eight thrusters. For the Super Soaker, we used pressurized nitrogen to push the water to the nozzle.

"Sometimes I'll be sitting in my back yard and I'll look up at the sky and see the dot that has a red tinge [Mars]. It gives me goosebumps to think that little red dot, 50 million miles [80.4 million km] away, has hardware that I've designed and built and tested on its surface." But is it as cool as building a giant water pistol...?

Largest Nerf gun
Mark knows all about outsized toy weaponry. He has also built a 6-ft-long (1.82-m) Nerf gun, as verified in Sunnyvale, California, USA, on 22 Jun 2016. For ammunition, Mark created scaled-up foam darts from pool noodles (foam floats) and sink plungers, which the gun ejects at a speed of around 40 mph (64 km/h).

– COMPARISON –

HEIGHT 1.22 M
(4 FT)

LENGTH 2.22 M
(7 FT 3.4 IN)

WIDTH 0.25 M
(9.8 IN)

MAXIMUM WATER SPEED 272 MPH
(437.7 KM/H)

HOW IT WORKS...

(1) Mark fills a tank inside the handle of the water pistol with high-pressure nitrogen gas. Also in the handle is a 2-US-gal (7.5-litre) tank of water. When the trigger is pulled, the gas flows into the water tank, forcing the water down through a tube and out of the nozzle. **(2)** He also adjusts the nozzle on the pistol's barrel. A 0.07-mm (0.003-in) diameter is terrific for halving watermelons, but that kind of power can do serious damage. As Mark says, "It's not good to shoot at people in that mode because the water volume flow rate is low and it's generally considered poor form to slice your friend's arm off!" With a nozzle diameter of 6.3 mm (0.25 in), however, the water flow is perfect for a safe and comprehensive soaking

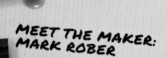

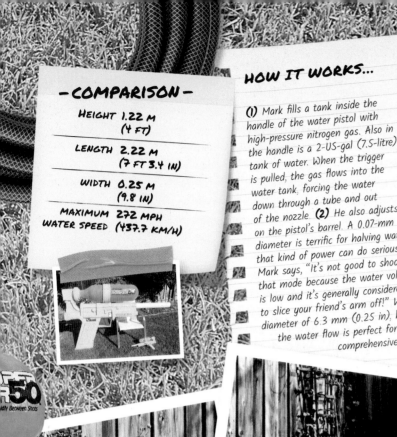

MEET THE MAKER: MARK ROBER

Which features of the water pistol are you most proud of?
I love its two modes. If you use a narrow-opening nozzle [diameter: 0.07 mm], the water is a powerful, concentrated stream that can slice a watermelon in half or rip open a soda can. The second mode has a nozzle that is 6.3 mm wide and has a really high volumetric flow rate, so your friends get drenched immediately. It's like a fire hose with lots of force, and that's the nozzle we broke the glass with.

How long did it take you to build the pistol?
It took about three months and we built it in three phases. The first phase was engineering experimentation, which took the longest. We used the same principles as our original Super Soaker, which uses a pressurized tank to push the water out. In the case of the original Super Soaker, you built up that pressure by pumping the handle, but we needed this to be much more powerful, so we experimented with a bunch of different pressurant tanks and nozzle sizes to find the optimal way to shoot the water the farthest. We settled on a system that's pressurized at 2,400 psi, which is seven times higher than a fire hose.

The second phase was building the wooden frame structure to contain the optimized tank and hose system. This took about a day and we scaled up all the dimensions, making the gun 2.22 m long.

The third phase was adding the extra EVA foam to get the shape right and then painting it to look awesome. EVA foam is a great choice because it's strong but also lightweight, so it's still relatively easy to move the gun around.

What did setting the record mean to you?
My earliest memory of going to the school library involves racing to be the first to get to the school copy of Guinness World Records. My friends and I loved reading about all the crazy and cool things people had accomplished. I never, ever imagined I would one day be in the book myself! Maybe there's some future engineer or builder sitting in a school library reading this right now who'll also be in here one day.

You also hold the record for the largest Nerf gun [see opposite]. Are you planning to set more?
Yes. It's addictive! I've decided to set at least one record every year. I already have my ideas for the next three years...but I'm not telling yet.

LARGEST RIDEABLE HEXAPOD

What inspired Star Wars fan Matt Denton (UK) to build a six-legged mechanical marvel? And how did it lead to him working on *Episode VII: The Force Awakens*? *Guinness World Records* meets the man who turns science fiction into jaw-dropping reality.

Named *Mantis*, the **largest rideable hexapod** robot stands 2.8 m (9 ft 2 in) tall and has a 5-m (16-ft 4-in) diameter, as verified on 15 Nov 2017 in Wickham, Hampshire, UK. Powered by a 2.2-litre (0.58-US-gal) turbo-diesel Perkins engine, it can be driven from its cockpit or operated remotely by wi-fi. *Mantis* weighs 1.9 tonnes (4,188 lb), has 18 degrees of freedom and a top speed of just over 1 km/h (0.6 mph). Walking machines have been a passion of Matt's for years now – but where did it all start? The answer lies a long time ago, in a galaxy far, far away...

FIRST STEPS

Matt saw *Star Wars Episode V: The Empire Strikes Back* (USA, 1980) when he was seven. He was immediately struck by the AT-AT walkers: "Machines that walk – that's cool!" he thought to himself. "Why use wheels when you can have legs?" After school, he began an electronics apprenticeship, which eventually led to him working on TV show *Space Precinct*, creating software for robotic machinery. But three weeks' work at Jim Henson's Creature Shop made him realize just how much he needed to improve his skills.

His expertise with hexapods saw Matt go on to work with animatronic engineer Joshua Lee on the Harry Potter movies. One day, Joshua told him about a top-secret new film that he might be interested in... (see right for more!). But away from the day job, Matt was working hard on a labour of love: *Mantis*!

Drawing up plans
Mantis took three years to build – and it was a MK II version. Matt noticed that the MK I model (a year-and-a-half in the making) had mechanical problems – particularly issues with the hydraulic systems – as soon as he got it to stand up.

The "brain"
The leg-coordination system of *Mantis* is the "HexEngine" box. Its Linux PC uses HexEngine software to control the movements of the machine. The unit receives commands from the hexapod's Operator Interface (see above right) and sends feedback to it.

– SPEC –

HEIGHT 2.8 M (9 FT 2 IN)

WEIGHT 1.9 TONNES (4,188 LB)

DIAMETER 5 M (16 FT 4 IN)

ENGINE 2.2 LITRES (0.58 US GAL)

TOP SPEED 1 KM/H (0.6 MPH)

AS HEAVY AS THREE COWS!

146

On each arm of the driver's seat is a joystick and 14 buttons to control Mantis's movements.

The Operator Interface houses a 6.5-in (16.5-cm) touch-screen display showing the position of the six legs.

MANTIS

The birth of BB-8
The loveable spheroid droid BB-8 debuted in *Star Wars VII: The Force Awakens*. Matt got a dream job on the film as creature FX electronic design and development supervisor. As part of a team, he worked on seven versions of BB-8, from a static robot to two radio-controlled models. Handling those controls could be hair-raising, though: "It's very powerful, and it's quite heavy – and you're [moving it] around some pretty key actors," he explains. "You don't want to hurt anyone!"

MEET THE MAKER: MATT DENTON

How many hexapods have you built?
More than 20, with various shapes and made from different materials. Most were less than 50 cm [1 ft 7.6 in] in diameter. One ended up in a Harry Potter movie as a six-legged tortoise!

Does it have a practical purpose?
One company approached me to ask if I could make a 200-tonne [440,925-lb] hexapod for underwater use. I wound up making this 1.9-tonne version partly to "road test" the problems I'd face. Also, a South American mining company was interested in *Mantis* as they are operating within the rainforest – regarded as "sensitive terrain". The pressure of each of *Mantis*'s feet is no more than that of a human footprint, so they don't damage landscape.

Did you have many challenges to overcome in making Mantis?
Lots! I had very little experience with hydraulics, but had to figure out how the engine, hydraulic pump and

tank would work together. The system generates so much heat that initially I would've needed a 0.5-tonne [1,100-lb] cooling tank. Just think: a JCB digger has one arm, but *Mantis* has six, meaning six times the flow and six times the cooling capacity. At that weight, *Mantis* wouldn't have been very mobile, so I had to scale the tank right down. In fact, I had to become an expert in multiple areas, so I spent a lot of evenings reading!

What are you working on now?
Nothing as ambitious as *Mantis*! My friend James Bruton lent me a 3D printer while I was working on a half-scale BB-8 prototype, and that got me started on printing giant LEGO® kits, based on the original designs. I've built one of a go-kart (98 pieces), a fork-lift truck (216 pieces) and a bulldozer (372 pieces – and 600 hr of 3D printing!). It's my homage to LEGO Technic sets, which fired up my imagination as a child. I probably wouldn't be doing what I do now without them.

BUCKET-WHEEL EXCAVATOR

Bucket-wheel excavators are mechanical behemoths that churn up the earth at a staggering rate. They are used in large-scale open-pit mining operations to clear what is known as "overburden" – the material that lies above valuable mining seams. These continuous digging machines are marvels of complex engineering that can take up to five years to construct, and cost as much as $100 million (£80 million). But once they get to work, look out!

The first bucket-wheel excavators were developed in the early 20th century, and evolved from water dredgers. The machines may be massive, but the basic principle is very simple: when the huge wheel at the front of the excavator rotates, it turns buckets that scoop up earth and drop it on to a conveyor belt to be carried away. Modern bucket-wheel excavators perform this operation on a literally earth-shaking scale: the biggest of all is Bagger 293, a 14,196-tonne (31.3-million-lb) monster that is simultaneously the **largest** and **heaviest land vehicle**.

3,000,000

VOLUME CONTROL

The Bagger 293 has 18 buckets, each with a volume of 6,600 litres (1,743 US gal). Working continuously, the excavator is capable of shifting 240,000 m³ (8.475 million cu ft) of earth in a single day. This is the equivalent of around 3 million bathtubs' worth of soil.

Excavators can reach 310 ft (94 m) in height – making them taller than the Statue of Liberty

These durable machines are made for inhospitable conditions. They can function at temperatures of −45°C (−49°F) and altitudes of more than 5,000 m (16,400 ft)

A counterweight boom gives the excavator stability

MAKING TRACKS

As powerful as bucket-wheel excavators are, they are unlikely to win many races. Moving on three rows of caterpillar-track assemblies, Bagger 293 has a top speed of around 0.33 mph (0.53 km/h). Any roads it crosses have to be rebuilt afterwards, as its sheer weight is enough to crush the concrete.

Conveyor belts carry the earth to a discharge point

BUCKET LIST

Bagger 293 had a cameo role in Episode 4 of the first season of the HBO drama *Westworld* (2016). Under the guidance of Dr Ford (Anthony Hopkins), it laid waste to an entire city.

FOR THE RECORD

The **largest land vehicle** capable of moving under its own power is the 14,196-tonne (31.3 million-lb) Bagger 293 bucket-wheel excavator, an earth-moving machine manufactured by MAN TAKRAF of Leipzig, Germany. Employed in an open-cast coal mine in the German state of North-Rhine Westphalia, it is 220 m (722 ft) long, 94.5 m (310 ft) tall at its highest point, and is capable of shifting 240,000 m³ (8.475 million cu ft) of earth per day. Bagger 293 is also the **heaviest land vehicle** and the **largest mobile industrial machine**.

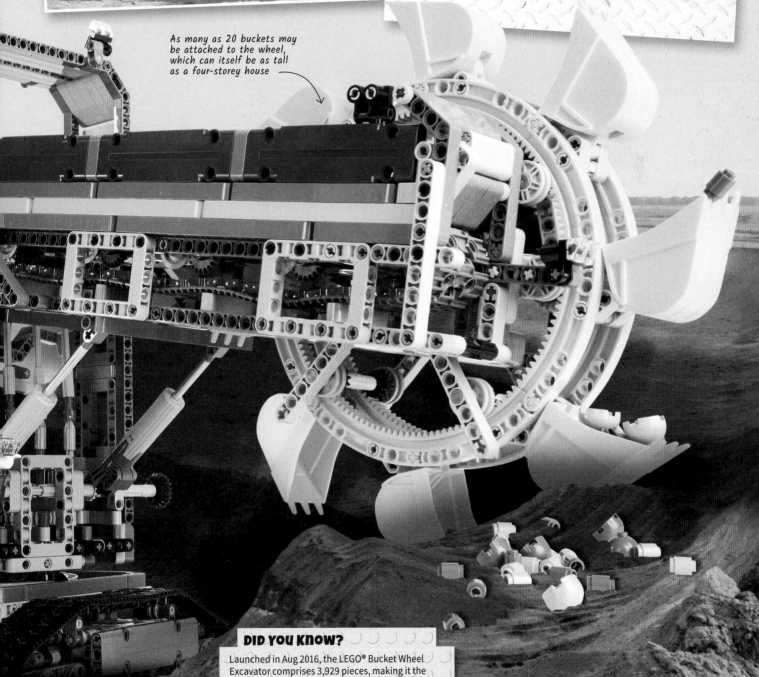

As many as 20 buckets may be attached to the wheel, which can itself be as tall as a four-storey house

DID YOU KNOW?

Launched in Aug 2016, the LEGO® Bucket Wheel Excavator comprises 3,929 pieces, making it the **largest commercially available LEGO Technic set**. Its approximate dimensions are 28 in (72 cm) long, 16 in (41 cm) high and 11 in (29 cm) wide. Thanks to a number of motorized elements, including caterpillar tracks, conveyor belts and a rotating bucket wheel, the model works just like a real mining vehicle.

SCIENCE & TECHNOLOGY

Highest footbridge

Suspended some 260 m (853 ft) above the ground between two mountain cliffs, the Zhangjiajie Grand Canyon Glass Bridge in Sanguansixiang, Hunan Province, China, offers breathtaking views for those with a head for heights. Before opening the bridge to the public on 20 Aug 2016, officials took sledgehammers to the panels (above) to reassure visitors that they could cross the glass-bottomed gangway in complete safety. Just 13 days after opening, however, the bridge was closed by the authorities: it was attracting 80,000 visitors daily (rather than the 8,000 anticipated) and the facilities required urgent improvement. It reopened on 30 Sep 2016.

CONTENTS

GUINNESS
WORLD RECORDS

Designed by architect Haim Dotan, the Zhangjiajie bridge spans 430 m (1,411 ft) and tapers to a width of just 6 m (19 ft 8 in) at its centre. It is located in the Zhangjiajie National Forest Park, whose famous quartz-sandstone pillars were said to have inspired the Hallelujah Mountains in the 2009 film *Avatar*.

BIG STUFF

LARGEST...

Bean bag

Created by Comfort Research (USA). "Big Joe's World's Largest Bean Bag Chair" measured 147.9 m³ (5,223 cu ft) and weighed more than 4,000 lb (1,814 kg) on 20 Sep 2017. It was installed on the roof of a building in Grand Rapids, Michigan, USA, as an entry in the 2017 ArtPrize contest.

Set of bingo balls

On 3 Jun 2017, Sun Bingo (UK) hosted a game of bingo in Blackpool, Lancashire, UK, with balls each measuring 73 cm (2 ft 4 in) in diameter – three times bigger than bowling balls! There was also the **largest bingo ticket/card** to match: 171 sq ft (15.912 m²) – the size of a parking space.

Inflatable pool toy

On 3 Jun 2017, an inflatable swan measuring 21.49 m (70 ft 6 in) tall, 16.58 m (54 ft 4 in) wide and 15.33 m (50 ft 3 in) long was unveiled by AT&T (USA) in Hermosa Beach, California, USA. The swan, which took a month to fabricate, was rendered in the company colour of blue.

The **largest inflatable beach ball** had a diameter of 19.97 m (65 ft 6 in) and was displayed on 31 May 2017. It was placed on a barge on the River Thames in London, UK, to promote the movie *Baywatch* (USA, 2017).

Underpants

Cottonil (EGY) displayed a pair of underpants measuring 25.36 m (83 ft 2 in) across the waist and 18.09 m (59 ft 4 in) from waistband to crotch on 7 Mar 2018 in Cairo, Egypt.

At the same event, they unveiled the **largest tank top**: 36.49 m (119 ft 8 in) from shoulder to hem and 27.65 m (90 ft 8 in) between armpits.

Largest game of JENGA

On 11 Dec 2015, Caterpillar Inc. (USA) used five of its construction vehicles to build and play a super-sized version of the popular game JENGA. Made out of solid pine, each of the 27 blocks measured 8 ft (243.8 cm) long, 2 ft 8 in (81.2 cm) wide and 1 ft 4 in (40.6 cm) high. The tower began with nine layers and ended with 13 after a total of 16 blocks were added over the course of 28 hr.

Largest knitting needles

Student Elizabeth Bond (UK) fashioned a pair of knitting needles measuring 4.42 m (14 ft 6.01 in) long with a diameter of 9.01 cm (3.54 in). She presented them for measurement at Wiltshire College in Chippenham, UK, on 13 Jun 2017. Elizabeth created the needles as part of her final-year Art and Design project.

Object unboxed

On 11 May 2017, three-year-old truck fan Joel Jovine (USA) unboxed a huge 80 x 40 x 18-ft (24.3 x 12.1 x 5.4-m) cardboard and cellophane box in Charlotte, North Carolina, USA, to find a Volvo VNL truck model measuring 21.95 m (72 ft) long inside! It was a surprise sent by Volvo Trucks (USA).

Batch of slime

A massive pool of slime weighing 13,820 lb (6,268.64 kg) – heavier than an African bull elephant – was mixed by Madison Greenspan and Team Maddie Rae's Slime Glue (both USA) at the Play Fair convention in New York City, USA, on 4 Nov 2017. The slime contained liquid starch, purple pigment powder, glitter and Madison's proprietary slime glue.

Eye chart

On 19 May 2017, opticians Louis Nielsen (DNK) constructed an unmissable eye chart measuring 23.07 m² (248.32 sq ft) in Copenhagen, Denmark.

Among the other records Florian set at the Gorilla Cafe was the **fastest time to jump-pot 15 pool balls (US table)** – 6.78 sec

Longest usable pool cue

On 13 Mar 2017, trick-shot maestro Florian Kohler (FRA) played pool with a cue measuring 5.37 m (17 ft 7.4 in) – almost four times the length of an average cue! He demonstrated its usability by breaking off and potting seven balls before sinking the 8 ball. It was one of six pool records Florian achieved in one day at the Gorilla Cafe in Las Vegas, Nevada, USA.

SUPER-SIZED STATIONERY

▼ Largest crayon

Serial record-breaker Ashrita Furman (USA, right) created a crayon measuring 5.21 m (17 ft 1.1 in) long and 0.45 m (1 ft 5.7 in) in diameter. It was verified on 10 Oct 2017 in Jamaica, New York City, USA.

Longest pencil

To celebrate the opening of their new factory, BiC (FRA) displayed a pencil measuring 1,091.99 m (3,582 ft 7.64 in) in Samer, France, on 10 Oct 2017. The pencil was made out of a graphite centre and recycled polystyrene, which made it bendable. BiC more than doubled the length of the previous record holder, created in 2015.

◀ Largest marker pen

On 5 Sep 2017, Zebra Co. (JPN) unveiled a marker pen measuring 1.68 m (5 ft 6.1 in) long and 25.6 cm (10.08 in) wide in Shinjuku, Tokyo, Japan. The pen was made to commemorate the company's 120-year anniversary. The huge marker pen is exactly 12 times larger than Zebra Co.'s regular-sized commercial Hi-Mckie marker pen.

Trousers: 40 ft (12.19 m) long, with a 26-ft (7.92-m) waist. Made by Rishi Thobhani (UK) and displayed in Leicester, East Midlands, UK, on 23 May 2009.

Socks: 45 ft (13.72 m) from top to toes, and 10 ft (3.05 m) wide. Constructed in Oct 1986 by Michael Roy Layne (USA) in Boston, Massachusetts, USA.

T-shirt: 96.86 m (317 ft 9.38 in) long and 69.77 m (228 ft 10.84 in) wide. Created on 5 Jan 2018 by Plastindia Foundation (IND) in Mumbai, India.

The wagon was inspired by "Coaster Boy", a 45-ft (13.7-m) statue of a child in a Radio Flyer wagon at the 1933 World's Fair in Chicago, Illinois, USA.

Largest toy wagon

To celebrate their 100th anniversary in 2017, US toy company Radio Flyer displayed a giant version of their iconic red wagon in Chicago, Illinois, USA. It measured 8.05 m (26 ft 5 in) long, 3.54 m (11 ft 8 in) tall and 3.59 m (11 ft 9 in) wide, as verified on 20 Dec 2016. The wagon, which was originally created for Radio Flyer's 80th anniversary, is more than eight times the size of the normal toy and weighs 15,000 lb (6,800 kg). It can comfortably carry more than 75 children.

Largest Santa

The Portuguese municipality of Águeda created a Santa Claus measuring 21.08 m (69 ft 1.9 in) tall, 9.18 m (30 ft 1.4 in) wide and 12.62 m (41 ft 4.8 in) deep, as verified on 12 Dec 2016. It was hoped that the 16,000-lb (7.25-tonne) statue would draw festive tourists.

◀ **Largest ballpoint pen**

Acharya Makunuri Srinivasa (IND) created a ballpoint pen measuring 5.5 m (18 ft 0.53 in) long and weighing 37.23 kg (82 lb 1.24 oz). It was presented and measured in Hyderabad, India, on 24 Apr 2011.

The **largest fountain pen** was 7 ft (2.13 m) long and was created by Zbigniew Różanek (POL) in 1991.

▶ **Largest paperclip**

A paperclip measuring 9.28 m (30 ft 5 in) in height and 2.72 m (8 ft 11 in) in width was created by Evgeny Stepovik (RUS) in Miass, Russia. Created from stainless steel, it weighed 530 kg (1,168 lb 7 oz) and was unveiled on 29 May 2010.

▶ **Largest pair of scissors**

Memory expert Neerja Roy Chowdhury (IND) created a pair of scissors measuring 2.31 m (7 ft 7 in) from tip to handle. They were used to cut the ribbon wrapping on her memory-training comic book, launched at the Air Force Auditorium in New Delhi, India, on 16 Aug 2009.

COMPUTING

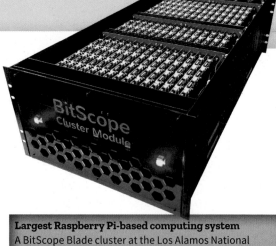

Oldest analogue computer

The 2,000-year-old Antikythera mechanism was found near the Greek island of Antikythera in 1900–01. Now encrusted with sea accretions, this collection of bronze gears was built with a mechanical complexity that has not been demonstrated in any other object prior to the 14th century. It is believed that the device was used to anticipate eclipses.

First microchip

In 1958, two American electrical engineers – Jack Kilby and Robert Noyce – independently devised techniques that allowed multiple transistors and the connections between them to be etched into a single wafer-thin piece of semiconductor material.

Fastest internet connection

In Jan 2014, scientists in the UK achieved a real-world internet connection speed of 1.4 terabits/sec using commercial-grade fibre-optic cable. (A bit – short for "binary unit" – is a basic element of information used by computers; there are eight bits to a byte.) The test was performed on a 410-km-long (255-mi) underground link between the cities of London and Ipswich, with the cooperation of BT and Alcatel-Lucent.

Greatest storage device capacity (prototype)

In 2016, the US data-storage company Seagate Technology revealed that they had created a 60-terabyte solid-state drive (SSD). A terabyte (TB) is 1 trillion bytes – in terms of data storage, the equivalent of approximately 210 DVDs or 1,423 CDs full of data.

Largest online social network

As of 4 Jan 2018, Facebook had 2.07 billion monthly users. Of these, 1.15 billion were mobile users. Facebook reached the 2-billion monthly-user milestone on 30 Jun 2017.

Lightest commercially available 14-inch laptop

Weighing 826 g (1 lb 13 oz), the LG Gram 14 was found to be lighter than any of its closest competitors in a comparison carried out by SGS Testing Services in Seoul, South Korea, on 14 Dec 2016. Manufactured by LG (KOR), the laptop is about twice the weight of a FIFA standard size-5 soccer ball.

Oldest working digital computer

The Harwell Dekatron Computer (aka WITCH, or Wolverhampton Instrument for Teaching Computation from Harwell) was first used in Apr 1951. After lying dismantled in storage for 20 years, it underwent a complete restoration between Sep 2009 and Nov 2012 and is currently at The National Museum of Computing at Bletchley Park in Buckinghamshire, UK.

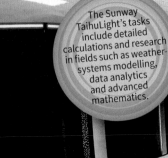

Largest Raspberry Pi-based computing system

A BitScope Blade cluster at the Los Alamos National Laboratory in New Mexico, USA, joins up 750 Raspberry Pi single-board computers to give it a total of 3,000 working cores. The module was built by scientific hardware manufacturer BitScope (AUS) and IT services provider SICORP (USA) and delivered on 13 Nov 2017. The BitScope Blade provides an accessible and affordable testing environment for students and software developers, enabling users to practise and try out new ideas in the notoriously challenging field of supercomputer programming.

Fastest data-sorting operation in a cloud competition

Data plays a crucial role in our lives and it is very important to be able to rapidly process large amounts of it. "Sorting" is a key step in data-processing, which can be costly and time-consuming. In 2016, Tencent Corporation (CHN) designed and implemented a procedure capable of sorting 100 TB in 98.8 sec in the Indy GraySort category competition – a sort rate of 60.7 TB/min. They used a 512-node OpenPOWER cluster for the task.

Fastest computer

As announced on 20 Jun 2016, the Sunway TaihuLight at the National Supercomputing Center in Wuxi, China, performs at 93.01 petaflops on the Linpack benchmark. (A petaflop represents 1 quadrillion floating-point operations per second; the Linpack benchmark is a means of measuring a computer's power in terms of how quickly it is able to solve a series of equations.) It features 40,960 separate processors operating in tandem with one another, allowing it to perform at nearly three times the speed of the previous record holder.

The Sunway TaihuLight's tasks include detailed calculations and research in fields such as weather-systems modelling, data analytics and advanced mathematics.

FIRST...

▲ Personal computer

Known as "Simon", the earliest PC was developed by Edmund Berkeley (USA) and released in 1950. It cost around $600 (£214) to build and contained an overall memory capacity of 12 bits.

▲ Computer with integrated circuits

In 1964, IBM's System/360 incorporated a type of integrated circuit. Its modules combined discrete transistors with printed circuits and resistors.

▲ Computer mouse

Douglas Engelbart (USA) invented the computer mouse in 1964 and was awarded a US patent in 1970. It was nicknamed a "mouse" because of the resemblance of the wire to a tail.

▲ Microprocessor

The 4004 chip, by Intel (USA), dates from 1971. A thumbnail-sized single-processor CPU, it had the same power as ENIAC, the room-sized **first general-purpose electronic computer**, completed in 1946.

Top 5 PC brands
Based on total sales between 2013 and 2017, these are the **best-selling desktop PC brands (cumulative units)**, as of 4 Apr 2018.

Source: Euromonitor

1 Lenovo
37,399,900 units

2 DELL
32,130,600 units

3 hp
21,688,700 units

4 acer
17,772,400 units

5
15,340,300 units

IBM's Jeff Welser presented the quantum computer in Las Vegas, Nevada, USA, in Jan 2018. The unit is modestly sized, but requires huge cooling systems to function.

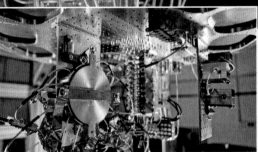

In Mar 2018, Google unveiled their 72-qubit Bristlecone quantum computing processor. As of 13 Apr 2018, however, this had not been peer-reviewed.

Most powerful quantum computer

In Nov 2017, IBM announced that they had developed a working prototype of a 50-qubit quantum computer, breaking their own record of 7 qubits. (A "qubit" is a quantum bit.) To put this into context, Google's think tank on computing power has stated that 50 qubits would be the point at which quantum computers could surpass conventional supercomputer capability. Conventional computers store and process information using either "1" or "0", but only one of them at a time. However, a quantum computer processor can use "0", "1", or both simultaneously, enabling it to store much more information, use less energy and have far greater processing power.

▲ **Floppy disk**
In 1971, a team of IBM engineers led by Alan Shugart (USA) invented the floppy disk. The 8-in (20.3-cm) plastic disk was covered with magnetic iron oxide. Its flexibility led to the nickname "floppy".

▲ **Desktop computer**
Introduced in 1972, the HP 9830 by Hewlett-Packard (USA) included a display, cassette tape drive, keyboard and processor. It used the BASIC programming language.

▲ **Clamshell laptop**
Regarded as the first "true" laptop, the GRiD Compass was designed in 1979 by William Moggridge (UK) for GRiD Systems Corporation (USA). It was introduced in 1982 with 512K of RAM.

▲ **Hypertext browser**
In Dec 1990, Tim Berners-Lee (UK) released the first web browser: WorldWideWeb. It enabled users to view and navigate between hypertext pages stored on servers anywhere in the world.

VIRTUAL REALITY

Longest marathon on a VR game system

Jack McNee (AUS) completed an epic 36-hr 2-min 16-sec session on a virtual-reality game system in Sydney, Australia, between 1 and 2 Apr 2017. For the entire duration of the marathon feat, Jack played Google's 3D paint game *Tilt Brush*.

Longest marathon watching VR video content

On 15–17 Apr 2017, Alejandro "A J" Fragoso and Alex Christison (both USA) viewed 50 hr of video content in New York City, USA, in a collaborative record with CyberLink (TPE) and supported by Diffusion PR (USA). The content included VR movies, streamed video and 360° shorts.

First virtual-reality (VR) headset

The Sword of Damocles was developed by computer graphics pioneer Ivan Sutherland and his student Bob Sproull (both USA) at the University of Utah in 1968. The headset showed wire-frame 3D environments (simple square rooms and shapes) generated by a computer. When the operator's head turned, sensors on the headset relayed the information to the computer, which redrew the model to adjust for the change of perspective and relay the images to the user. (See also below.)

First interactive 3D map

The Interactive Movie Map (aka the Aspen Movie Map) was an experimental 3D "Surrogate Travel System". It was created between Oct 1977 and Sep 1980 by a team led by Andrew Lippman and Nicholas Negroponte at the MIT Media Lab in Cambridge, Massachusetts, USA. The map comprised a 3D reconstruction of the town of Aspen in Colorado, USA, texture-mapped using thousands of photographs taken by multiple stop-motion cameras mounted on a vehicle. Users navigated around the virtual town via a touch-screen display.

First therapeutic use of VR

The earliest use of virtual-reality systems for medical treatment was outlined in an anecdotal report by Ralph Lamson – a psychotherapist with the Kaiser Permanente Medical Group in San Rafael, California, USA – in the Apr 1994 edition of the *CyberEdge Journal*. He described using VR systems to enable easily controlled, adaptable exposure therapy for people with severe acrophobia (fear of heights). Patients were placed on the walkway of a virtual bridge, which could be raised incrementally as they gained confidence.

First VR music video

WeMakeVR (NLD) pioneered the earliest virtual-reality music video, featuring hip-hop artist Brainpower (aka Gertjan Mulder, NLD, b. BEL) performing his single "Troubled Soul". Introducing editing and visual effects techniques not previously seen in VR, it was uploaded to YouTube360 on 14 Mar 2015.

First surgery live-streamed in VR

On 14 Apr 2016, medical training start-up Medical Realities live-streamed an operation by Bangladesh-born British surgeon Shafi Ahmed to remove a tumour from a patient with colon cancer. The surgery took place at The Royal London Hospital, UK.

First cross-platform VR videogame

Released on 26 Sep 2017, *EVE: Valkyrie – Warzone* is an updated version of CCP Games' multiplayer VR shooter *EVE: Valkyrie* (2016) that includes modes enabling the game to be played without VR headsets. This new feature also enables cross-platform competition between players on the existing Oculus Rift, PlayStation VR and HTC Vive versions, and PC and PS4 players – the first videogame to offer such options.

Most critically acclaimed VR videogame

As of 18 Oct 2017, rhythm shooter *Rez Infinite*, published by List and released for PS4 VR headsets in Oct 2016, had a GameRankings score of 89% based on 23 reviews. The game is a virtual-reality reimagining of the cult 2001 smash *Rez*, developed by United Game Artists. Its plaudits included Best VR Game at The Game Awards 2016.

Most expensive augmented-reality (AR) headset

The Gen III Head-Mounted Display System (HMDS) was revealed to the public in Mar 2016, with a price tag of $400,000 (£277,874) per unit. Developed as a joint venture between military contractors Rockwell Collins (USA) and Elbit Systems (ISR), this 2.17-kg (4-lb 12.5-oz) carbon-fibre helmet was designed for use by pilots of the F-35 Lightning II Joint Strike Fighter. It contains a miniaturized computer that interfaces with the fighter's systems, projecting important information as an AR overlay on the inside of the pilot's visor.

Most crowdfunded VR project

In Sep 2017, Pimax (CHN) launched a Kickstarter campaign to fund their "8K" high-field-of-view VR headset. When the campaign closed on 3 Nov 2017, they had raised $4,236,618 (£3,216,530). Their goal had been $200,000 (£151,844). The headset allows users to experience peripheral vision and counteracts sensations of motion sickness.

Most subscribers for a dedicated VR videogames channel on YouTube

As of 20 Mar 2018, Nathaniel "Nathie" de Jong (NLD) had 345,389 YouTube subscribers, who join him as he delves into the latest VR games. De Jong's channel covers games from all three of the main VR headsets currently available: the Oculus Rift, HTC Vive and Sony's PlayStation VR.

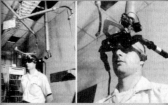

A BRIEF HISTORY OF VIRTUAL REALITY

VR has been with us for longer than you might think. In the 19th century, huge panoramic paintings enveloped viewers within a scene, while stereoscopes combined two 2D images to suggest a sense of depth. The 1950s saw a golden age for 3D movies, but attempts to enhance screenings with smells rarely succeeded. Today, advanced headsets have made gaming an increasingly immersive experience, putting the "real" into "virtual reality".

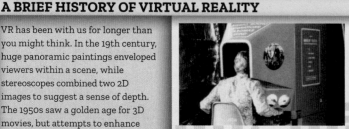

▲ **1962: Sensorama**
This box of sensory stimuli was the work of cinematographer Morton Heilig. While viewing a 3D film with stereo sound, users smelled aromas and felt breezes.

▲ **1968: Sword of Damocles**
Although slow by modern standards, this system was reportedly close enough to real time to give a convincing impression of standing inside a virtual environment.

▲ **1980s: VPL EyePhone**
Wearing goggles and a "data glove", users were able to see and manipulate objects in a virtual world. VPL Research was founded by Jaron Lanier in 1984.

Top 3 AR/VR headset brands by annual revenue*
Sony PlayStation VR (JPN): $288.4 m (£213.4 m)

Samsung Gear (KOR): $241.8 m (£178.9 m)

HTC Vive (TPE/USA): $174.1 m (£128.9 m)

according to Euromonitor, as of latest available figures (for 2016)

First VR flying roller-coaster

Galactica opened on 24 Mar 2016 at Alton Towers theme park in Staffordshire, UK. All the seats are fitted with Samsung Gear VR headsets that transport the wearers into space. Each headset is individually synced to the twists and curves of the track, so every rider experiences a seamless simulated voyage through the cosmos, regardless of their position in the car.

Prior to its public opening, *Galactica* was first tested by Canadian astronaut Chris Hadfield. His opinion? "I've been lucky enough to serve on three space flights… but this is as close as I've come to a virtual trip across the universe."

▲ 1991: Sega VR
Based on an existing Sega arcade headset, the VR was announced in 1991 and presented at a trade show in early 1993 but remained a prototype.

▲ 1995: Forte VFX1 headgear
This head-mounted display unit came with high-fidelity speakers, a hand-held "Cyberpuck" controller and the VIP Board, a graphics interface.

▲ 2013: Oculus Rift DK1
A Kickstarter campaign raised an incredible $2.4 m for the Development Kit 1, which incorporated three pairs of lenses and an adjustable focal length.

▲ 2016: HTC Vive
Features include headset tracking, 360° controllers and directional audio. A camera enables users to view the room around them and so avoid collisions.

ROBOTS & AI

First recorded robot
Born in 428 BCE, Greek philosopher Archytas is popularly credited with the invention of the first ever robot – the "Flying Pigeon". Archytas constructed his robotic bird from wood and an animal's bladder, using steam to power its movements. The bird was launched from a pivot bar, and could reportedly fly about 200 m (656 ft).

First robotic surgery
Designed to assist in orthopaedic procedures, Arthrobot was used for the first time in Vancouver, British Columbia, Canada, in 1983. The voice-controlled robot could assist with positioning patients' limbs. In 2016, US scientists developed STAR (Smart Tissue Autonomous Robot). The **first robot to perform soft-tissue surgery autonomously**, STAR uses machine vision, sensors and intelligence algorithms to track and execute precise surgical tasks.

First AI to beat a 9-dan Go player
An artificial intelligence (AI) called AlphaGo defeated Lee Sedol 4–1 in a five-game Go series on 9–15 Mar 2016. AlphaGo's developers DeepMind (UK) utilized an approach called Deep Reinforcement Learning, which trained the AI using data from past Go matches. AlphaGo's unique playing style stunned Go experts, who had not expected an AI to master Go so quickly.

The following year, artificial intelligence racked up another win against humanity. On 10 Aug 2017, an AI developed by the OpenAI Foundation (USA) defeated Sumail "Suma1L" Hassan (PAK) – the **youngest gamer to earn $1 million in eSports winnings** – in a 1-vs-1 match in the popular eSports videogame *Dota 2*, becoming the **first AI to beat a *Dota 2* world champion**.

Most skips by a robot in one minute
The aptly named Jumpen achieved 106 skips in 60 sec on 29 Apr 2017 at the ROBOCON event in Chiba, Japan. A penguin-shaped jumping robot made by the National Institute of Technology, Nara College (JPN), Jumpen is 0.8 m (2 ft 7.5 in) wide, 0.5 m (1 ft 7.6 in) tall and weighs 14.7 kg (32 lb 6.52 oz). He is made from aluminium alloy and polycarbonate.

Fastest-running quadruped robot (untethered)
On 4 Oct 2013, US company Boston Dynamics released footage of its prototype WildCat four-legged robot. Powered by a two-stroke methanol engine, WildCat employs a galloping gait like a dog or a horse. It can reach speeds of up to 25 km/h (15.5 mph) across flat terrain, leaning into turns to maintain traction and balance.

Fastest-accelerating underwater robot
The "octo-bot" can travel from 0 to 11.7 km/h (7.2 mph) in 0.95 sec, with a peak acceleration of 3.8 m/s^2 (12.4 ft/s^2). It has a 3D-printed polycarbonate skeleton and an elastic membrane, with no moving parts. It was developed by a team of international scientists and unveiled in 2015.

Smallest self-powered flying robot
Revealed in May 2017, Piccolissimo (Italian for "very small") has a 39-mm (1.5-in) diameter and is 19 mm (0.7 in) high. It was developed by Matt Piccoli and Mark Yim at the University of Pennsylvania (all USA).

The **smallest tethered flying robot capable of landing on ceilings** is the revised "RoboBee", which weighs 0.1 g (0.003 oz) – about as much as a grain of sand. In May 2016, roboticists from Harvard University (USA) announced that their tiny flying robot now included an electro-adhesive patch, allowing it to land on the underside of materials such as bricks and glass.

Atlas's hardware utilizes 3D printing to keep the robot's weight down to 75 kg (165 lb). A high strength-to-weight ratio is vital for gymnastic feats.

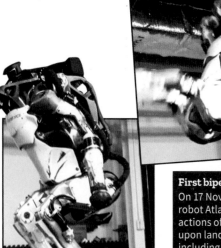

First bipedal humanoid robot backflip
On 17 Nov 2017, Boston Dynamics (USA) released a video of its robot Atlas executing a backflip. The robot performs all of the actions of a human gymnast, including using its arms to balance upon landing. Atlas can demonstrate a range of human motion including running, jumping and mid-air pirouettes. It takes a human brain many years to learn the coordination required for a backflip, so this achievement is one of the most significant robotic breakthroughs of 2017.

RAPID ROBOTS

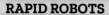

▼ **Fastest 25-m sprint by a robot**
Scuttle, built by Mike Franklin (UK), covered 25 m (82 ft) in 6.5 sec at the Royal International Air Tattoo in Fairford, Gloucestershire, UK, on 16 Jul 2005. Franklin designed several robotic combatants for the UK show *Robot Wars*.

▶ **Fastest-running humanoid robot**
On 8 Nov 2011, Honda (JPN) revealed that its robot ASIMO – which stands for "Advanced Step in Innovative Mobility" – could run at 9 km/h (5.5 mph). At this speed, both of ASIMO's feet were momentarily off the ground. Laser and infrared sensors enabled the robot to navigate autonomously.

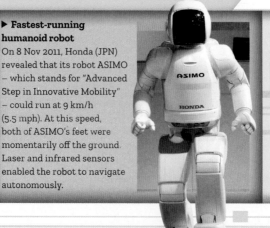

▶ **Fastest bipedal running robot**
In Aug 2011, a bipedal robot named MABEL reached a speed of 6.8 mph (10.9 km/h) – equivalent to a jog. The robot, developed by the University of Michigan (USA), spends 40% of its time with its feet off the ground – just like a human runner. It uses a complex set of computer feedback algorithms that enable it to maintain balance as it lands and propels itself forward.

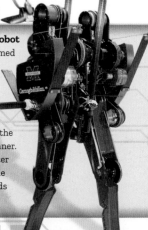

The Three Laws of Robotics, as devised by science-fiction novelist Isaac Asimov:

1 A robot may not injure a human being or, through inaction, allow a human being to come to harm.

2 A robot must obey the orders given to it by human beings except where such orders would conflict with the First Law.

3 A robot must protect its own existence as long as such protection does not conflict with the First or Second Laws.

The Alpha 1S robots were installed with hardware cards containing programmed dance steps. They were controlled from a single smartphone.

Most robots dancing simultaneously

On 1 Feb 2018, a total of 1,372 Alpha 1S robots danced in unison for 90 sec to "Another Day of Sun" by Mina in Rome, Italy. The display – part of a series of adverts by Italian telecommunications company TIM – was filmed to be broadcast during the Sanremo Music Festival. The Alpha 1S robot, made of aluminium alloy with plastic coating, measures just under 40 cm (15.7 in) tall and has 16 degrees of freedom.

GWR adjudicator Lorenzo Veltri was on hand to make the count, which had to beat the previous record of 1,069, set by WL Intelligent Technology (CHN) on 17 Aug 2017.

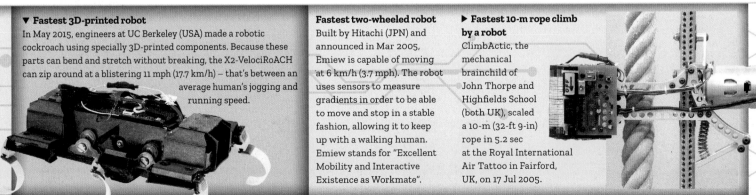

▼ Fastest 3D-printed robot
In May 2015, engineers at UC Berkeley (USA) made a robotic cockroach using specially 3D-printed components. Because these parts can bend and stretch without breaking, the X2-VelociRoACH can zip around at a blistering 11 mph (17.7 km/h) – that's between an average human's jogging and running speed.

Fastest two-wheeled robot
Built by Hitachi (JPN) and announced in Mar 2005, Emiew is capable of moving at 6 km/h (3.7 mph). The robot uses sensors to measure gradients in order to be able to move and stop in a stable fashion, allowing it to keep up with a walking human. Emiew stands for "Excellent Mobility and Interactive Existence as Workmate".

▶ Fastest 10-m rope climb by a robot
ClimbActic, the mechanical brainchild of John Thorpe and Highfields School (both UK), scaled a 10-m (32-ft 9-in) rope in 5.2 sec at the Royal International Air Tattoo in Fairford, UK, on 17 Jul 2005.

ARCHITECTURE

First royal palace
Hor-Aha, the second pharaoh of the first Egyptian dynasty, had a whitewashed mud-brick (or possibly limestone) palace built during the 31st century BCE in Memphis, Egypt. At Abydos, one of ancient Egypt's oldest cities, Hor-Aha also had the outside of his tomb decorated to resemble a palace façade.

Oldest houses
The Neolithic settlement of Çatalhöyük in present-day Turkey dates from c. 7,500 to 5,700 BCE. Approximately 5,000–8,000 residents occupied mud-brick homes here, which were entered via roof-top holes that also served for smoke ventilation. Inside, the houses were lime-plastered and had a single main living space measuring some 6 x 4 m (20 x 13 ft).

First shopping mall
In terms of a large number of separate shops grouped under a covered roof, the oldest known mall was at Trajan's Forum in ancient Rome, Italy. Designed by architect Apollodorus of Damascus and built in 100–112 CE, the forum included a market area with 150 shops and offices arranged over six gallery levels.

Largest masonry dome
Measuring some 43 m (142 ft) in diameter, the concrete dome of the Pantheon in Rome, Italy, has a greater span than any dome constructed only of masonry (that is, unreinforced stone or brick). Rising around 22 m (71 ft) above its base, it was built by the emperor Hadrian between 118 and 128 CE.

Largest airport (area)
At 780 km² (301 sq mi), King Fahd International, near Dammam in Saudi Arabia, is bigger than the nearby country of Bahrain (which has three airports).

Largest stadium roof
The transparent acrylic glass "tent" roof on the Munich Olympic Stadium in Germany has an area of 85,000 m² (915,000 sq ft). It rests on a steel net that is supported by masts.

Highest observation deck
Visitors to the Shanghai Tower (aka Shanghai Center) in China may take in the view from its 561.3-m-high (1,841-ft) observation deck. The 632-m (2,073-ft) mixed-use office and hotel building stands in the Lujiazui Finance and Trade Zone and was finished in 2015.

Tallest Hindu temple
The ornamental 13-tiered *gopura* or *gopuram* (entrance tower) at the Sri Ranganathaswamy Temple on the island of Srirangam in India reaches at least 72 m (236 ft 2 in) high. Dedicated to Ranganatha, a form of the Hindu deity Vishnu, the temple is more than a thousand years old. The *gopura*, which was only finished in 1987, is decorated with Hindu mythological carvings (inset).

Largest stadium (overall capacity)
The Indianapolis Motor Speedway in Indiana, USA, has a permanent seated capacity of 235,000 – reduced from 257,325 in 2013 – and covers 253 acres (102.3 ha). Including non-seated spectators, it can accommodate more than 350,000 fans. Built in 1909, the stadium is home to the famous "Indy 500" and "Brickyard 400" races and contains a 2.5-mi (4.09-km) oval-format race circuit.

HIGH RISERS

▼ Tallest airport control tower
Tower West at Kuala Lumpur International Airport in Malaysia measures 133.8 m (438 ft 11 in) tall and was completed on 30 Apr 2013. Shaped like an Olympic torch, the tower was built as part of the new KLIA2 terminal at the airport, and was intended to accommodate an increased amount of air traffic.

▼ Tallest pyramid
The Pyramid of Khufu at Giza, Egypt, was built c. 2560 BCE. Also known as the Great Pyramid, it was originally 146.7 m (481 ft 3 in) high, but erosion and vandalism reduced its height to 137.5 m (451 ft 1 in). It was the **tallest man-made construction** until 1311 CE, when the UK's Lincoln Cathedral was finished.

▼ Tallest cathedral spire
Ulm Minster in Germany has a tower measuring 161.53 m (529 ft 11 in) high. Designed in early Gothic style, construction on the church began in 1377. Building was halted in 1543, when the spire was 100 m (328 ft) high, and only resumed in 1817. The spire, located in the centre of the west façade, was finally completed in 1890.

▼ Tallest house
Built in 2010, Antilia is the 173-m (568-ft) home of Indian businessman Mukesh Ambani in Mumbai. Its 27, triple-height floors make the house as tall as a typical 60-storey office tower. It features helipads, swimming pools, a health spa and theatre. At an estimated cost of $2 bn (£1.29 bn), it is also the **most expensive house ever built**.

▼ Tallest hotel
The Gevora Hotel in Dubai, UAE, stands 356.33 m (1,169 ft) tall from ground level to apex, and was inaugurated on 9 Feb 2018. Known for its gold façade, it has 528 rooms set over 75 storeys and is around 1 m (3 ft 3 in) taller than the previous holder, the J W Marriott Marquis Dubai.

Tallest building: Burj Khalifa
Cost: $1.5 bn (£0.94 bn)

Weight: 100,000 elephants

Construction time: 22 million man-hours

Parking spaces: 2,957

Area equivalent: c. 2,020 tennis courts

GUINNESS WORLD RECORDS

Heaviest building

The Palace of the Parliament in the Romanian capital city of Bucharest is believed to be the heaviest building in the world. Its construction materials include 700,000 tonnes (771,617 tons) of steel and bronze – around twice the weight of the Empire State Building – plus 1 million m³ (35.3 million cu ft) of marble, 3,500 tonnes (7.7 million lb) of crystal glass and 900,000 m³ (31.7 million cu ft) of wood. Virtually all of the materials came from within Romania.

◀ The C A Rosetti Hall is dominated by a grand chandelier, one of 480 in the building. The room has 600 fixed seats and is now used for conferences, concerts and plays.

▶ The luxurious, 2,226-m² (23,960-sq-ft) Unirii ("Union") Hall boasts an abundance of marble from Transylvania. Its ceiling is 16 m (52 ft 5 in) high.

▶ **Tallest residential building**
Opened in 2015, the 425.5-m-high (1,396-ft) 432 Park Avenue in New York City, USA, is the tallest single-function residential building in the world. The concrete building consists of 85 floors; the highest occupied storey is at 392 m (1,286 ft).

▶ **Tallest twin buildings**
The 88-storey Petronas Towers in Kuala Lumpur, Malaysia, are 451.9-m (1,482-ft 7-in) high. Opened in 1996, the towers are joined at levels 41 and 42 by a double-decker "Skybridge".

▶ **Tallest office**
The 599.1-m (1,965-ft) Ping An Finance Center in the Futian District of Shenzhen in Guangdong Province, China, is the tallest all-office building. The 115-storey concrete-and-steel block opened in Mar 2017 and is occupied to a height of 562.2 m (1,844 ft). It has four basement floors.

▶ **Tallest tower**
Formerly known as New Tokyo Tower, the Tokyo Skytree rises 634 m (2,080 ft) to the top of its mast and is located in Sumida, in the Japanese capital. Completed in 2012, the building functions as a television and radio broadcasting and observation tower. It also houses a restaurant.

▶ **Tallest building**
The Burj Khalifa (Khalifa Tower) in Dubai, UAE, is 828 m (2,716 ft 6 in) tall, with 160 storeys. It was developed by Emaar Properties (UAE). Construction began on 21 Sep 2004 and the building officially opened on 4 Jan 2010. See the top of this page for more facts and figures about this iconic record-breaker.

CITIES

First city

Dating to around 3200 BCE, the world's first true city is generally thought to have been Uruk, located in southern Mesopotamia (modern-day Iraq). Home to some 50,000 inhabitants, it was the largest settlement of its time, covering 450 ha (1,112 acres) and encircled by a 9.5-km (5.9-mi) city wall. Thriving as a result of trade and agriculture, Uruk also became a great artistic centre, featuring many elaborate mosaics and monuments.

First wi-fi-enabled city

The Middle-Eastern city of Jerusalem was the first to be fully wi-fi-enabled, offering a free, public service across the entire metropolis from 1 Nov 2004. The project was initiated by the Jerusalem WiFi Project – a partnership between the Jerusalem Business Development Corporation, Intel, Compumat and the Jerusalem Municipality.

Largest gambling city (by revenue)

In 2016, the estimated annual gambling revenue for Macau, China, was $27.8 bn (£22.5 bn). Macau's gambling industry is 330% larger than that of Las Vegas, USA.

Most billionaires (city)

As of Mar 2017, New York City, USA, was home to 82 billionaires, according to Forbes. Their combined net worth amounts to a staggering $397.9 bn (£319.4 bn). By way of comparison, that's more than the nominal gross domestic product (GDP) of countries such as Austria ($386 bn; £309.9 bn), Iran ($376 bn; £301.8 bn) and the United Arab Emirates ($371 bn; £297.8 bn). The Big Apple's richest person was David Koch, with a net worth of $48.4 bn, or £38.8 bn. Koch is an American businessman and currently serves as vice president of the USA's second-largest privately held company, Koch Industries.

Longest commute for a city

After evaluating 50 million users and 167 metropolitan areas, a 2015 study by Google-owned traffic app Waze found that commuters in Manila, Philippines, faced average one-way journeys of 45.5 min. Indonesia's Jakarta (42.1 min) and Brazil's Rio de Janeiro (38.4 min) were in second and third places. Even car-clogged Los Angeles and New York City were less congested than the Filipino capital: journey times in these two large US cities were 35.9 min and 38.7 min respectively.

Least expensive city to live in

The Economist Intelligence Unit's Worldwide Cost of Living (WCOL) report 2017, published on 21 Mar, gives Kazakhstan's largest city Almaty an WCOL index rating of 38. (New York City is the base city, ranked 100.) In Almaty, a 1-kg (2-lb 3.2-oz) loaf of bread costs $0.90 (£0.72), compared with $6.81 (£5.49) in Paris, France.

Most expensive city to live in

The Economist Intelligence Unit's WCOL report (see above) ranked Singapore as the costliest city to live in. Its cost of living index is ranked 120. Owing to high excise taxes, an average-priced bottle of wine costs $23.68 (£19.11), compared to $10.35 (£8.35) in Paris, France.

City with the highest murder rate

Ruthless gang activity in the city of San Salvador in El Salvador has made the city the murder capital of the world. According to 2016 figures from the Brazilian think tank Igarapé Institute, San Salvador's murder rate has reached 137 homicides per 100,000 persons.

Safest city

The Japanese capital of Tokyo was ranked as the world's "safest city" for the third year in a row on The Economist's Safe Cities Index 2017. Out of 49 diverse indicators of safety, including digital security and personal security, Tokyo obtained a combined final score of 89.8 out of 100.

City with the worst air pollution

PM_{10} is "particulate matter" such as soot (carbon), metal or dust with a diameter of 10 microns or less. According to the World Health Organization's Ambient Air Pollution report for 2016, the most air-polluted city in the world is Onitsha, a port in southern Nigeria, which recorded levels of 594 micrograms of PM_{10} per m³ of air – around 30 times the WHO's recommended level of 20 micrograms per m³.

City with the most buildings 300 m or taller

According to The Skyscraper Center, by the end of 2017 Dubai in the United Arab Emirates had 21 buildings that were 300 m (984 ft) or taller, more than twice as many as any other city, with a further 13 under construction. These mega towers include the Burj Khalifa – currently the world's **tallest building**, at 828 m (2,716 ft) – the Princess Tower (413.4 m; 1,356 ft) and 23 Marina (392.8 m; 1,289 ft).

WISH YOU LIVED HERE?

◀ Most popular city for tourism

Bangkok in Thailand attracts more international visitors than any other city, according to the 2017 Mastercard Global Destination Cities Index. In the four years to 2016, it welcomed 19.41 million tourists, helping the Thai capital surpass tourism hubs such as London (with 19.06 million visitors) and Paris (15.45 million).

Most bicycle-friendly city

According to the Copenhagenize Index 2017, the Danish capital of Copenhagen is still the world's most bicycle-friendly city. In the past 10 years, it has spent more than $150 m (£111.16 m) on its cycling infrastructure, creating 16 bridges dedicated to cyclists and pedestrians. More people now enter the city by bike than in their cars.

▲ Most environmentally friendly city

In 2016, Arcadis (NLD) studied 100 global cities based on the "three dimensions of sustainability": people, planet and profit. Zurich was ranked top, owing to its efficient public-transit network, commitment to reducing energy usage and performance in business.

Most populated cities, as of 2016
(and projected 2030 populations)
Tokyo, Japan: 38.14 m (37.19 m)
Delhi, India: 26.45 m (36.06 m)
Shanghai, China: 24.48 m (30.75 m)
Mumbai, India: 21.35 m (27.79 m)
São Paulo, Brazil: 21.29 m (23.44 m)

Source: *The World's Cities in 2016*,
produced by the United Nations

Highest population urban agglomeration

With a population of 38,140,000 as of 2016, Tokyo is the world's most populous urban agglomeration. The Japanese capital is home to so many people that even if you combine the populations of London (10,434,000) and New York-Newark (18,604,000), Tokyo would still outnumber them by 9,102,000 residents.

Tokyo's population is expected to decline by 1 million citizens by 2030. Despite this, it will remain the world's most highly populated city.

Most densely populated city

According to 2017 figures from urban planning policy consultants Demographia (USA), the Bangladeshi capital of Dhaka is the world's most densely populated city. With a population of 16.8 million residents spread over an area of 368 km² (142 sq mi), the city has an average of 45,700 persons per km² (118,362 per sq mi).

Most elegant city

To determine the world's most elegant city, online fashion site Zalando analysed 400 cities based on three key categories: "Fashion Factors", "Urban Factors" and "Accessibility". Owing to its history of fashion and architecture, Paris was ranked first with a rating of 4.37 (out of 5). Not far behind were the cities of London (4.16), Vienna (4.13) and Venice (4.12).

◀ Most habitable city

The Economist's Global Liveability Ranking rates cities in terms of five overall categories: stability; healthcare; culture and environment; education; and infrastructure. As of Aug 2017, Melbourne in Australia was the most liveable city for the seventh year running, with 97.5 points, followed by Vienna then Vancouver.

Least habitable city

The ancient Syrian city of Damascus was once dubbed "Pearl of the East". However, since the devastating civil war in 2011, it has been torn apart, and was ranked as the least liveable city in Aug 2017 by The Economist's Global Liveability Ranking. Over the course of the last five years, the city's liveability rating has dropped by 16.1%.

AIRCRAFT

Highest altitude by an aircraft (FAI-approved)

On 31 Aug 1977, Alexandr Fedotov (USSR) flew a highly modified MiG-25 "Foxbat" to 37,650 m (123,523 ft) from Podmoskovnoe aerodrome in Russia. More than four times the height of Everest, this height was verified by the FAI (Fédération Aéronautique Internationale).

Highest flight by a hot-air balloon

Dr Vijaypat Singhania (IND) reached an altitude of 21,027 m (68,986 ft) in a Cameron Z-1600 hot-air balloon over Mumbai, India, on 26 Nov 2005.

Highest flight in a glider

On 3 Sep 2017, Jim Payne (USA) and co-pilot Morgan Sandercock (AUS) reached an altitude of 15,902 m (52,172 ft) in the Airbus *Perlan 2* glider. They flew from Comandante Armando Tola International Airport near El Calafate, Argentina.

Farthest flight by a commercial aircraft

On 9–10 Nov 2005, a Boeing 777–200LR Worldliner flew 11,664 nautical mi (21,601.7 km; 13,422.7 mi) non-stop and without refuelling from Hong Kong eastbound to London, UK, in 22 hr 42 min.

The 777–200LR is powered by two General Electric GE90–115B turbofan engines, the **most powerful jet engine**. One achieved steady-state thrust of 568,927 N (127,900 lb) during final certification testing at Peebles, Ohio, USA, in Dec 2002.

First circumnavigation in a solar-powered aeroplane (FAI-approved)

André Borschberg and Bertrand Piccard (both CHE) flew around the world in *Solar Impulse 2* between 9 Mar 2015 and 26 Jul 2016, powered entirely by energy from the Sun. Their starting and finishing point was Abu Dhabi in the UAE. The total journey time was 505 days 19 hr 53 min, but for nearly 10 months of this time the team were grounded in Hawaii, USA, owing to irreversible damage to overheated batteries in their aircraft. They resumed flying on 21 Apr 2016.

Fastest electric aircraft

On 23 Mar 2017, an Extra 330LE plane reached a speed of 342.86 km/h (213.04 mph) during a flight from the Dinslaken Schwarze Heide airfield in Germany. The aircraft, which was piloted by Walter Kampsmann (DEU), is produced by German manufacturer Extra Aircraft.

First loop-the-loop in a helicopter

On 19 May 1949, test pilot Harold E "Tommy" Thompson (USA) performed the first intentional loop-the-loop in a helicopter, a Sikorsky S-52. He went on to execute 10 perfect loops that day at the Sikorsky helicopter plant in Bridgeport, Connecticut, USA.

Longest aircraft (current)

Airlander 10 is 92 m (301 ft 10 in) long. The aircraft was built by Hybrid Air Vehicles (UK) and its first flight was completed at Cardington airfield in Bedfordshire, UK, on 17 Aug 2016. Despite appearances, it is not a traditional airship – it is a hybrid of an airship and an aeroplane. The hull is filled with helium, which generates around 60% of the aircraft's lift.

Fastest speed in a helicopter (non-FAI)

During a test on 7 Jun 2013, the Eurocopter X3 (above) reached 255 knots (472 km/h; 293 mph) over southern France. It was flown by test pilot Hervé Jammayrac (FRA).

The **fastest speed in a helicopter (FAI-approved)** is 400.87 km/h (249.09 mph), by John Trevor Egginton and Derek J Clews (both UK) over Glastonbury, Somerset, UK, on 11 Aug 1986. They flew in a Westland Lynx demonstrator.

Largest aircraft by wingspan

Rolled out on 31 May 2017 at the Mojave Air & Space Port in California, USA, the *Stratolaunch* aeroplane has a wingspan of 117.35 m (385 ft). The brainchild of Microsoft co-founder Paul Allen, the *Stratolaunch* is designed to carry space rockets to the edge of Earth's atmosphere – which is less expensive than launching them from the ground. It is scheduled to make its first flight in 2019.

GIANTS OF THE SKIES

▲ **Largest helicopter**
The Russian Mil Mi-12 had four 6,500-hp (4,847-kW) turboshaft engines and a rotor diameter of 35 m (114 ft 9 in); it was 37 m (121 ft 4.7 in) long, with a maximum take-off weight of 103.3 tonnes (227,737 lb). It first flew in 1968, but never went into production.

Largest fire-fighting aircraft

Global SuperTanker Services, founded in 2015, uses a converted Boeing 747-400 jumbo jet as an aerial firefighter. It can carry 74,200 litres (19,600 US gal) of water or fire retardant for 6,400 km (3,976 mi). The plane is designed to drop its load on to wildfires from a height of just 120–240 m (393–787 ft) at around 260 km/h (161.5 mph). It has a wingspan of 64 m (209 ft).

▲ **Largest aircraft (propeller-driven)**
The Russian Antonov An-22 (NATO code name "Cock") has a wingspan of 64.4 m (211 ft), while its maximum take-off weight is 250 tonnes (550,000 lb). Still in service with the Russian military, the An-22 has a cruising speed of 680 km/h (422 mph).

In Mar 1912, Heinrich Kubis (DEU) began working as the **first flight attendant**, on the DELAG Zeppelin LZ-10 *Schwaben*. He was later supported by an assistant steward on board the LZ-127 *Graf Zeppelin*.

The **first in-flight meal** was served up in Oct 1919 on the Handley Page Transport (UK) service from London to Paris. The pre-packed lunch of sandwiches and fruit cost three shillings (now £6.33; $8.54).

The **first in-flight movie** was First National's *The Lost World* (USA, 1925), shown in Apr 1925 during an Imperial Airways flight from London to Paris in a converted Handley Page bomber.

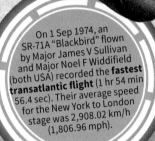
On 1 Sep 1974, an SR-71A "Blackbird" flown by Major James V Sullivan and Major Noel F Widdifield (both USA) recorded the **fastest transatlantic flight** (1 hr 54 min 56.4 sec). Their average speed for the New York to London stage was 2,908.02 km/h (1,806.96 mph).

Fastest speed for a manned aircraft (FAI-approved)

The highest recorded speed for a manned aircraft capable of taking off and landing under its own power is 3,529.56 km/h (2,193.17 mph) – some three times the speed of sound. It was achieved on 28 Jul 1976 by Captain Eldon W Joersz and Major George T Morgan Jr in a Lockheed SR-71A "Blackbird" near Beale Air Force Base in California, USA, on a 25-km (15.5-mi) course. The USA's X-15 rocket planes were faster, but are ineligible for this record as they were air-launched.

The SR-71A "Blackbird" was 107 ft 4 in (32.72 m) long and stood 18 ft 6 in (5.63 m) tall, from ground level to the tops of the rudders, with a wingspan of 55 ft 7 in (16.94 m). It was powered by two Pratt & Whitney J58 axial-flow turbojets with afterburners.

▲ **Heaviest operational bomber**
The Russian Tupolev Tu-160 "Blackjack" bomber has a maximum take-off weight of 275 tonnes (606,270 lb) and a top speed of around Mach 2.05 (2,200 km/h or 1,350 mph). Here, "maximum take-off weight" refers to its weight when fully loaded with bombs.

Heaviest production aircraft
The Airbus A380-800 is a 72.7-m-long (238-ft 6-in) double-decked behemoth of the skies, with a maximum take-off weight of 575,000 kg (1,267,658 lb). The A380 made its maiden flight on 27 Apr 2005. Airports had to modify their facilities in order to accommodate it, for example by widening runways and reinforcing tunnels.

▲ **Heaviest aircraft ever**
The Antonov An-225 "Mriya" was originally built at 600 tonnes (1.32 million lb). Its floor was strengthened in 2000–01, resulting in an increased maximum take-off weight of 640 tonnes (1.41 million lb). Only two were ever built.

Since the invention of the motor car, engineers and innovators have been seeking ways to make them go faster and faster. Here we celebrate the quickest of them all, *Thrust SSC*, and explore the history of a very contentious record.

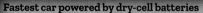

The record for the **fastest production car** is one of the most coveted and controversial around. The title has stood empty since 2015, due to the difficulties involved in verifying an outright holder. Rival manufacturers trade claims and counter-claims, with several machines purported to be the quickest (see also the **fastest car in space** on p.177). So why the confusion?

Let's be clear: to be capable of reaching speeds in excess of 400 km/h (248 mph), *all* of the cars featured here are marvels of innovation and precision engineering, to be celebrated and admired. However, in order to judge them objectively, there has to be a set of comparable criteria.

Firstly, what constitutes a production car? The holder of the **land-speed record** is *Thrust SSC* at 1,227.985 km/h (763.035 mph, see right) – but you wouldn't expect to see it at your local garage. The "production car" guidelines require "a production run of 30 or more vehicles of identical specification". But as the cars get quicker, their production numbers plummet. The McLaren F1 held the record from 1998 to 2005 at 386.46 km/h (240.14 mph), but only 64 were made. And this seems like a lot when compared with more recent contenders.

Our guidelines also meant that if a single machine had been modified too much, it couldn't qualify for the record. In 2010, the Bugatti Veyron achieved its fastest speed with the electronic limiter switched off; after consultation, however, we decided that this didn't constitute excess modification to the vehicle. In 2017, the Koenigsegg Agera RS set a two-way average of 447.19 km/h (277.87 mph), but only 11 of

Bloodhound SSC
The team behind *Thrust SSC* (see opposite) are working to break their own land-speed record. Their new vehicle, *Bloodhound SSC* (above), is set for speed trials in South Africa in 2018.

Fastest car powered by dry-cell batteries
On 4 Aug 2007, the *Oxyride Racer* reached an average speed of 105.95 km/h (65.83 mph) at JARI Shirosato Test Centre in Ibaraki, Japan, using a power pack of 194 AA batteries (left). It was the work of the Oxyride Speed Challenge Team – Matsushita Electric Industrial (now Panasonic Corporation) and Osaka Sangyo University (both JPN). The frame of the lightweight *Oxyride Racer* was made of carbon-fibre-reinforced plastic and weighed just 38 kg (83 lb).

25 cars to come off the "production line" were fitted with the optional "1 MegaWatt" engine package required to reach that speed.

There is also the question of what constitutes a car's "fastest speed". We require an average speed to be taken over a 1-km (0.6-mi) section of closed road in both directions (to take into account the effect of headwinds and tailwinds). In 2014, a Hennessey Venom GT clocked 435.31 km/h (270.49 mph) on NASA's Space Shuttle runway in Florida, USA, but was unable to take a second run. This made its incredible speed ineligible for record purposes.

With the difficulties involved in comparing these mega-quick machines, the arguments look set to continue. Perhaps the only way to settle them would be to gather all the contenders together at a track and see who crosses the finishing line first. Irrespective of who won, it would be a race worth watching…

SSC Ultimate Aero TT
Shelby SuperCars' (USA) Aero TT achieved two-way timed speeds in excess of 412 km/h (256 mph) on 13 Sep 2007.

Hennessey Venom GT
In 2014, the Venom GT recorded a speed of 435.31 km/h (270.49 mph) – but in a one-direction run. Only 12 cars (plus a prototype) were made.

McLaren F1
The McLaren F1 sports car reached 386.46 km/h (240.14 mph) at the Volkswagen proving ground in Germany on 31 Mar 1998.

Bugatti Veyron 16.4 Super Sport
The Super Sport achieved a two-way average of 431.072 km/h (267.856 mph) in 2010 – with the electronic limiter switched off.

Koenigsegg Agera RS
An advanced version of the Agera R (below), the RS was unveiled in 2015 and has a two-way average top speed of 447.19 km/h (277.87 mph) – with the right engine.

NEED FOR SPEED: FASTEST...

▼ Solar-powered vehicle
Rally driver Kenjiro Shinozuka drove Ashiya University's (both JPN) *Sky Ace TIGA* to a speed of 91.332 km/h (56.75 mph) at Shimojishima Airport in Miyakojima, Okinawa, Japan, on 20 Aug 2014. The location for the record attempt had been carefully chosen to provide the most suitable weather conditions in terms of sunlight strength, sun elevation and temperature.

▼ Compressed-air-powered car
Toyota's three-wheeled *KU:RIN* car reached a top speed of 129.2 km/h (80.3 mph) at the Japan Automobile Research Institute's Ibaraki test track on 9 Sep 2011. The car has a compressed-air "fuel tank" – as air is released, it generates thrust. Its final speed was taken from a timed average of two runs. "Ku" and "rin" are Japanese for "air" and "wheel".

▼ Steam car (FIA-approved)
On 25 Aug 2009, the British Steam Car Team's *Inspiration* reached 225.05 km/h (139.84 mph), driven by Charles Burnett III (USA) at Edwards Air Force Base in California, USA. The record was approved by the Fédération Internationale de l'Automobile (FIA). It beat the record of 205 km/h (127.7 mph) by Fred Marriott in a Stanley steam car in 1906 – an astonishing 103 years earlier.

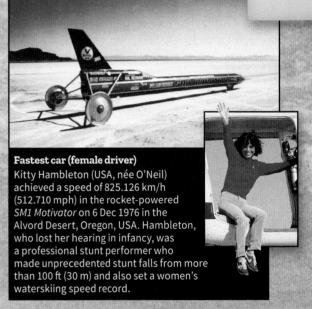

Fastest car (female driver)

Kitty Hambleton (USA, née O'Neil) achieved a speed of 825.126 km/h (512.710 mph) in the rocket-powered *SM1 Motivator* on 6 Dec 1976 in the Alvord Desert, Oregon, USA. Hambleton, who lost her hearing in infancy, was a professional stunt performer who made unprecedented stunt falls from more than 100 ft (30 m) and also set a women's waterskiing speed record.

Fastest car (land-speed record)

On 15 Oct 1997, *Thrust SSC* became the **first car to break the sound barrier** when it reached 1,227.985 km/h (763.035 mph; Mach 1.020) over 1 mi (1.6 km) in the Black Rock Desert, Nevada, USA. The resultant sonic boom caused sprinkler covers to fall off in the town of Gerlach, around 10 mi (16 km) away. *Thrust SSC* was piloted by Andy Green (UK, above left), a wing commander in the RAF. The project director was Richard Noble (UK), who in 1983 had set the previous land-speed record of 1,020.406 km/h (634.051 mph) on board *Thrust 2*.

Thrust SSC broke the sound barrier almost 50 years to the day after Captain "Chuck" Yeager (USA) made the **first supersonic flight**, on 14 Oct 1947.

▼ Electric car (FIA-approved)

The *Venturi Buckeye Bullet 3* achieved an average speed of 549.211 km/h (341.264 mph) over a two-way flying mile at the Bonneville Salt Flats in Utah, USA, on 19 Sep 2016. The electric car was designed and built by engineering students at The Ohio State University's Center for Automotive Research, in partnership with French electric car designers Venturi. It was driven by Roger Schroer (USA).

▼ Diesel-engined car

On 23 Aug 2006, Andy Green (see above) drove the *JCB Dieselmax* to a speed of 563.418 km/h (350.092 mph) at Bonneville. Green broke his own record, achieved the day before at 526.027 km/h (326.858 mph). Remarkably, he was not even in top gear. The previous mark of 379.413 km/h (235.756 mph), by Virgil Snyder in the streamliner *Thermo King-Wynns*, had stood since 1973.

▼ Rocket car

Blue Flame, a rocket-powered vehicle driven by Gary Gabelich (USA), attained a speed of 1,016.086 km/h (631.367 mph) over the first measured kilometre at Bonneville on 23 Oct 1970. The car was powered by a liquid natural-gas/hydrogen-peroxide rocket engine, which could develop thrust up to 22,000 lbf (9,979 kgf; 97,860 kN).

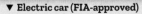

MOTORCYCLES

Most motorcycles sold (country)
According to a report by the New Atlas technology news website published on 17 Aug 2017, India overtook China in the 2016–17 financial year to sell 17.59 million motorcycles.

Greatest distance on a motorcycle in 24 hours (individual)
On 8 Oct 2014, Matthew McKelvey (ZAF) covered 3,256.5 km (2,023.5 mi) in a day at the Phakisa Freeway in Welkom, South Africa.

Longest motorcycle
Bharat Sinh Parmar (IND) created a 26.29-m-long (86-ft 3-in) motorcycle – longer than five London taxi cabs – as confirmed at Lakhota Lake in Jamnagar, Gujarat, India, on 22 Jan 2014.

Longest modified motorcycle wheelie (distance)
Yasuyuki Kudo (JPN) rode 331 km (205.7 mi) non-stop on the rear wheel of his Honda TLM220R motorcycle at the Japan Automobile Research Institute proving ground in Tsukuba, near Tsuchiura, Japan, on 5 May 1991.

On 28 Feb 2015, Robert Gull (SWE) rode the **fastest motorcycle wheelie on ice** – 206.09 km/h (128.06 mph) – on a BMW S1000RR bike in Årsunda, Sweden.

First attempted motorcycle parachute jump
In Nov 1926, aviator Fred Osborne (USA) drove a four-cylinder motorcycle off the 200-ft (61-m) Huntington Cliff, north of Los Angeles in California, USA. He pulled the ripcord on his parachute but had not allowed enough time for it to deploy fully. Osborne was seriously injured but survived – probably because telephone cables partly broke his fall. The bike was destroyed.

FASTEST...

Steam-powered motorcycle
William "Bill" Barnes (USA) reached 80.509 mph (129.566 km/h) on a steam-powered bike at the East Coast Timing Association's Ohio Mile speed trials in Wilmington, Ohio, USA, on 27 Sep 2014.

Tandem motorcycle
On 20 Sep 2011, Erin Hunter and Andy Sills (both USA) rode a BMW S1000RR to 291.98 km/h (181.426 mph) at the Bonneville Salt Flats in Utah, USA. The duo took turns as pilot and passenger over two timed runs.

Motorcycle wheelie
On 18 Apr 1999, Sweden's Patrik Fürstenhoff attained a speed of 307.86 km/h (191.3 mph) on the back wheel of a Honda Super Blackbird 1100 cc Turbo. His record run took place at Bruntingthorpe Proving Ground in Leicestershire, UK.

Fastest conventional motorcycle speed (male)
Richard Assen (NZ) reached a two-run average speed of 420.546 km/h (261.315 mph) on a modified Suzuki Hayabusa at Bonneville on 23 Sep 2011. The vehicle was partially streamlined, which meant that Assen was not fully enclosed by the fairing or bodywork.

Fastest conventional motorcycle speed (female)
Leslie Porterfield (USA) reached 374.208 km/h (232.522 mph) on a modified Suzuki Hayabusa at Bonneville on 5 Sep 2008. In accordance with standard practice, the record was the average of two timed runs over a mile (1.6 km) in opposite directions.

Motorcycle speed record (fastest motorcycle)
On 25 Sep 2010, Rocky Robinson (USA) achieved an average speed of 605.697 km/h (376.363 mph) in his *TOP 1 Ack Attack* streamliner over a measured kilometre (0.6 mi) at the Bonneville Salt Flats in Utah, USA. The speed is approximately half that of the speed of sound.

Motorcycle crash survived
Jason McVicar (CAN) was travelling at 391 km/h (243 mph) when he suddenly lost control of his Suzuki Hayabusa at Bonneville in 2008. It is believed that the accident was caused by a piece of debris that punctured the rear tyre. Paramedics were amazed to find McVicar alive. He was rushed to hospital suffering a broken kneecap and friction burns, sustained through his leathers from sliding across the salt at such speed. Remarkably, he was discharged the same day.

Most expensive motorcycle sold at auction
The "Captain America" Harley-Davidson Panhead was ridden by Peter Fonda's character Wyatt in the movie *Easy Rider* (USA, 1969). It sold for $1.35 m (£839,133) as part of an auction of Hollywood memorabilia in Los Angeles, California, USA, on 18 Oct 2014. Several bikes were made for filming, but this is thought to be the only survivor.

MOTORCYCLE STUNTS

◄ Longest motorcycle ramp jump
On 29 Mar 2008, Robbie Maddison (AUS) performed a 351-ft (106.98-m) ramp jump – around the same distance as the length of an American football field. The record-breaking leap took place at the Crusty Demons Night of World Records at Calder Park Raceway in Melbourne, Victoria, Australia.

Longest ramp-to-ramp backflip on a motorcycle
On 29 Mar 2008, Cameron "Cam" Sinclair (AUS) carried out a 39.49-m (129-ft 7-in) backflip between ramps at the Crusty Demons Night of World Records at Calder Park Raceway in Melbourne, Australia. In 2009, he had a near-fatal accident, but fought back to win the Moto X Best Trick at 2010's X Games XVI with a double backflip.

▲ Largest human motorcycle pyramid
On 5 Jul 2001, the Dare Devils Team of the Indian Army Signal Corps assembled a motorcycle pyramid of 201 men balanced on 10 motorcycles, at Gowri Shankar Parade Ground in Jabalpur, India. On 28 Dec 2013, the team also achieved the **most people on one motorcycle** – 56 – at Dumna Airport in Jabalpur.

First motorcycle: Gottlieb Daimler built a wooden-framed machine at Bad Cannstatt, Germany, in Oct–Nov 1885. It was first ridden by Wilhelm Maybach (both DEU).

First mass-production motorcycle: Germany's Hildebrand & Wolfmüller factory opened in 1894. In two years, it had issued more than 1,000 bikes with 1,488-cc (90.8-cu-in) engines.

First 3D-printed motorcycle: In 2015, TE Connectivity (CHE/USA) unveiled an orange-and-blue Harley-Davidson replica. Of its 100 parts, 76 were 3D-printed.

Smallest motorcycle

Tom Wiberg (SWE) built a motorcycle with a front-wheel diameter of 16 mm (0.62 in) and a rear-wheel diameter of 22 mm (0.86 in). He rode it for more than 10 m (32 ft 9 in) in Hökerum, Sweden, in 2003. The micro machine has an 80-mm (3.14-in) wheelbase, a seat height of 65 mm (2.55 in), weighs 1.1 kg (2 lb 6 oz) and can reach 2 km/h (1.24 mph), powered by its 0.22-kW (0.3-hp) engine.

It took six months to build the gigantic bike below. Measuring 10.03 m (32 ft 10 in) long, it is powered by a 5.7-litre V8 motor and has three forward gears, plus reverse.

Tallest rideable motorcycle

This larger-than-life chopper measures 5.10 m (16 ft 8.78 in) tall from the ground to the top of its handlebars – making it around the same height as a giraffe. It is 2.5 m (8 ft 2 in) wide, weighs some 5,000 kg (11,020 lb) and is six times larger than a standard chopper. The wheels were taken from industrial excavators. Constructed by Fabio Reggiani (ITA, pictured), it was ridden around a 100-m (328-ft) course at Montecchio Emilia, Italy, on 24 Mar 2012.

Longest motorcycle backflip (female)

On 17 Nov 2008, Jolene Van Vugt (CAN) successfully landed a backflip measuring 12.36 m (40 ft 7 in) for the MTV show *Nitro Circus* in Salt Lake City, Utah, USA. She was riding an RM125 Yamaha motorcross, but had practised using a 110-cc mini-bike and a foam pit. It was the first time a female rider had been recorded completing the stunt.

Longest motorcycle jump with a passenger

Jason Rennie (UK) jumped 96 ft (29.26 m) on his Yamaha YZ250 motorcycle, with his girlfriend Sian Phillips riding pillion, on 12 Nov 2000. Incredibly, the first time Sian rode on the back of Jason's motorcycle was at a practice session just four days before the successful jump at Rednal airfield near Oswestry in Shropshire, UK.

▶ **Most forward rolls on a motorcycle in one minute**

Balázs Balla (HUN, pictured) performed 10 forward rolls on a motorcycle in 60 sec at the "Extrém Nap Rétság" event in Nógrád, Hungary, on 27 May 2017. For the purpose of the record, a forward roll was defined as an axial roll, where the back wheel lifts up to bring the motorcycle over the rider. Balla was riding a Piaggio Zip 1996, modified with a special circular frame. He is a member of the Rétság Riders Team, and has been a licensed motorcycle competitor for a decade.

BOATS & SHIPS

Oldest shipwreck

A wreck discovered off the Greek island of Dokos in the Aegean on 23 Aug 1975 by Peter Throckmorton, of the Hellenic Institute of Marine Archaeology, dates to 2,200 BCE – making it more than 4,200 years old.

Longest time adrift at sea

The longest known time that anyone has survived adrift at sea is approximately 484 days, by Captain Oguri Jukichi and one of his sailors, Otokichi (both JPN). After their cargo ship was damaged in a storm off the Japanese coast in Oct 1813, they drifted in the Pacific before being rescued by an American ship off California, USA, on 24 Mar 1815.

Busiest port for cargo volume

The Port of Ningbo-Zhoushan (CHN) turned over 900 million tonnes (992 million US tons) of cargo in 2016. The 191-berth port rose to dominance after it merged with the neighbouring Zhoushan Port Group in 2015. Located on the East China Sea, the port was established in 738 CE, during the Tang Dynasty.

LARGEST...

Floating crane

Thialf is a 201.6-m-long (661-ft 5-in) semi-submersible barge with two cranes and a lifting capacity of 14,200 tonnes (31.3 million lb). It has accommodation for 736 people and a helicopter pad. The lower section of the hull can be flooded to increase stability and allow the barge to operate in rough seas.

Submarine

The Russian 941 Akula-class submarines are believed to have a dived displacement of 26,500 tonnes (58.422 million lb) and to measure 171.5 m (562 ft 7 in) in length. The launch of the first Akula class at the secret covered shipyard at Severodvinsk in the White Sea was announced by NATO on 23 Sep 1980.

Largest boat lift

A mechanical lift for boats and ships located at the Three Gorges Dam on China's Yangtze River can lift ships of up to 3,000 tonnes (6.6 million lb) in weight, 18 m (59 ft) in width and 120 m (394 ft) in length. It lifts or lowers them through a vertical distance of 113 m (371 ft) to the other side.

Largest rotating boat lift

Linking the Forth & Clyde and Union canals, the Falkirk Wheel in Falkirk, UK, measures 35 m (114 ft) high, 35 m wide and 30 m (98 ft) long. It can carry more than eight boats at a time, and has reduced transfer times between the two canals from almost a day to 15 min.

Largest naval hovercraft

The Russian Zubr ("Bison") class of air-cushioned landing craft (LCAC) measures 57 m (187 ft) long and 25.6 m (83 ft 11 in) wide, with a full-load displacement of 555 tonnes (1.22 million lb). Capable of speeds up to 63 knots (116 km/h; 72 mph), the huge hovercraft can deliver 360 troops or three battle tanks on to beaches.

Crew on a warship

The 10 US Navy Nimitz-class nuclear-powered aircraft carriers each transport around 5,680 personnel when battle-ready, of which 3,200 are ship's company and at least 2,280 belong to the Air Wing. The carriers are the **largest warships** afloat and each carry around 80 aircraft.

Uncrewed ship

In Apr 2016, the Defense Advanced Research Projects Agency (DARPA, USA) launched the *Sea Hunter*, an uncrewed trimaran measuring 40 m (131 ft) in length. It is a prototype for a new class of drone ship, able to head thousands of miles out to sea to monitor ocean depths for submarines. The *Sea Hunter* cost $20 million (£15.2 million) to develop.

Largest construction ship

Built in South Korea at an approximate cost of $3 bn (£2.27 bn) and launched on 26 Jan 2013, the *Pioneering Spirit* has a gross tonnage of 403,342. The ship's hull has a length of 382 m (1,253 ft) and a breadth of 124 m (407 ft). The vessel is used for super-heavy marine construction tasks, for example dismantling oil rigs.

A FLEET FLEET

▲ Fastest propeller-driven boat
At the International Hot Boat Association (IHBA) World Finals on 22 Nov 2009, Daryl Ehrlich (USA) attained a speed of 420 km/h (260.98 mph; 226.78 knots) in the propeller-driven *Problem Child* at Firebird Raceway near Phoenix, Arizona, USA. The Top Fuel Hydro boat had been built by "Fast" Eddie Knox (USA).

Fastest destroyer
Le Terrible, a 2,900-tonne (6.4-million-lb) French destroyer, reached a speed of 45.25 knots (83.8 km/h; 52 mph) in 1935. Built in Blainville, France, she was powered by four Yarrow small-tube boilers and two Rateau geared turbines giving 100,000 hp (74,570 kW). *Le Terrible* was eventually scrapped in 1962.

▲ Fastest operational class of warship
First commissioned in 1999, the six attack craft of the Royal Norwegian Navy's Skjold class can exceed 60 knots (111 km/h; 69 mph). The ships – known as *kystkorvette* (coastal corvettes) – ride upon a cushion of air and are perfectly suited for the shallow waters and rocky inlets of the Norwegian fjords.

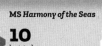

MS Harmony of the Seas

10
hot tubs

11,252
works of art

1,400
theatre seats

20
restaurants

GUINNESS WORLD RECORDS

The *Harmony of the Seas* contains a "living park" with 10,600 plants and 52 trees, which grow in automatically irrigated planter beds.

Largest passenger liner

Launched on 19 Jun 2015, the French-built MS *Harmony of the Seas* measures 1,188 ft (362.1 m) long – longer than three soccer pitches – 216 ft (66 m) wide and has a gross tonnage of 226,963. There are 18 decks, accommodating 2,100 crew and 6,780 passengers. The luxury liner is powered by six giant engines developing a total of 96,000 kW (128,738 hp) of power, giving it a top speed of 25 knots (46 km/h; 29 mph).

Water attractions on the luxury liner Harmony of the Seas *include swimming pools, a 10-storey water slide and two FlowRider surf simulators (above).*

▲ Water-speed record (fastest boat)

On 8 Oct 1978, Ken Warby (AUS) reached a speed of 275.97 knots (511.09 km/h; 317.58 mph) in the unlimited-class jet-powered hydroplane *Spirit of Australia* on Blowering Dam Lake in New South Wales, Australia. This is the official water-speed record, although Warby may have gone faster at the same location on 20 Nov 1977.

Fastest military submarine

The Russian Alfa class of hunter/killer nuclear-powered submarine had a reported maximum speed of more than 40 knots (74 km/h; 46 mph). The sub had a double-hull design constructed from lightweight titanium, and was manned by a small crew operating from a single control room. Its powerful nuclear reactor was cooled with liquid metal.

▼ Fastest ferry

Built in 2013 and owned by the Argentine ferry company Buquebus, the HSC *Francisco* is a gas-turbine-powered catamaran ferry that operates the 140-mi (225-km) route across the Río de la Plata estuary between Buenos Aires in Argentina and Montevideo in Uruguay. It has a top speed of 58.1 knots (107 km/h; 67 mph).

CUTTING-EDGE SCIENCE

Largest known prime number

On 26 Dec 2017, a free software program installed on a computer by Great Internet Mersenne Prime Search (GIMPS) subscriber Jonathan Pace (USA) discovered a new prime number with 23,249,425 digits. Known as M77232917, it was found by calculating the result of 2 to the power of 77,232,917 and then subtracting 1. At nearly 1 million digits larger than the previous record, it sits in a special class of very rare numbers known as Mersenne primes. It is the 50th Mersenne prime ever discovered.

Fastest hyperloop (vactrain) pod

A hyperloop is a proposed mass transit system that would send "pods" similar to high-speed train carriages through airless tunnels. As the pods are travelling through a near vacuum, they would not be slowed by air resistance, allowing for energy-efficient travel at speeds currently only practicably attainable by aircraft. The fastest speed reached by a hyperloop pod is 240 mph (386 km/h), by the XP-1 at the Hyperloop One (USA) test track near Las Vegas in Nevada, USA, in Dec 2017. The XP-1 is an experimental prototype measuring 28 ft 6 in (8.68 m) long and 8 ft 10.8 in (2.71 m) tall. It uses a linear electric motor for propulsion and is supported by magnetic levitation instead of wheels.

First smartphone camera to see around corners

Scientists at the Massachusetts Institute of Technology in Cambridge, Massachusetts, USA, introduced image-analysis algorithms into a smartphone camera system known as "CornerCameras" in Oct 2017. The algorithms analysed the subtle shading and colour of light scattered off floors and walls in the camera's view to anticipate what objects around a corner might be producing them. This technology could one day be incorporated into driverless vehicles, enabling them to "see" potential hazards that lie out of sight.

Smallest neutrino detector

On 4 Aug 2017, scientists from the international COHERENT project published a paper confirming that they had detected neutrinos – fundamental particles in the universe – striking the nuclei of atoms. The detector measured 103 x 325 mm (4 in x 1 ft 1 in) and weighed just 32 lb (14.5 kg). This interaction had been predicted in 1974, but never observed until this point.

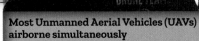

Most Unmanned Aerial Vehicles (UAVs) airborne simultaneously

Intel Corporation (USA) put 1,218 drones in the air at the same time in Pyeongchang, Republic of Korea, on 12 Dec 2017. Among other configurations, the Intel Shooting Star drones (inset) formed five interlocking rings in a display at the Jeongseon Alpine Centre in Pyeongchang, where the 2018 Winter Olympics were held.

Most wins of the World Solar Challenge

The Bridgestone World Solar Challenge is an endurance race for solar-powered cars. It was first run in 1987, and has been held biennially since 1999. The race was created to encourage research into solar-powered vehicles and takes place in Australia during the southern-hemisphere summer along a 3,022-km (1,878-mile) route from Darwin to Adelaide.

The Nuon Solar Team from the Delft University of Technology (NLD) have won the race a record seven times, in 2001 (also the first year they entered), 2003, 2005, 2007, 2013, 2015 and 2017. The Nuon team have also achieved the **fastest average speed in the World Solar Challenge**, when their *Nuna 3* completed the 2005 race in 29 hr 11 min at an average speed of 102.75 km/h (63.84 mph). The high speeds of the 2005 entrants caused major problems for the support crews trying to keep up with them in conventional cars.

This discovery has great potential for super-powerful quantum computers. Any noise makes their sensitive components vibrate, distorting information they are carrying. Chilling their parts to near absolute zero removes this "distortion", improving the computer's accuracy.

Coldest man-made object

Using uniquely configured laser beams, a team at the National Institute of Standards and Technology in Boulder, Colorado, USA, cooled a microscopic aluminium drum to 360 microkelvin (-273.14964°C; -459.66935°F). At near absolute zero (-273.15°C; 459.67°F) – the **lowest temperature possible** – this is colder than anywhere in the universe, around 10,000 times chillier than the vacuum of space.

GOING ELECTRIC

◀ Greatest distance by electric vehicle (single charge; non-solar)

On 16–17 Oct 2017, the *Phoenix* electric car covered 1,608.5 km (999.5 mi) at Auto Club Speedway in Fontana, California, USA. Recycled parts make up more than 90% of the car, which was driven and co-created by Eric Lundgren (USA, left), CEO of IT Asset Partners (ITAP).

▶ Most efficient electric vehicle

An eight-strong team from TUfast (all DEU; driver Lisa Kugler, right) created *eLi14*, which has a consumption of 81.16 Watt hours (Wh)/100 km, as verified in Neustadt, Germany, on 16 Jul 2016. It drove 25 km (15.5 mi) at an average speed of 25 km/h (15.5 mph). (1 Wh represents 1 Watt of power expended over 1 hr.)

Ig Noble prize-winners
Awarded each year since 1991, these gongs celebrate studies and experiments that combine humour with hard science. Here is a selection from the 2017 ceremony.

Can a cat be both a solid and a liquid? (Physics Prize) Marc-Antoine Fardin used this question to probe fluid dynamics.

Why do old men have big ears? (Anatomy Prize) Past the age of 30, men's ears grow 2 mm (0.07 in) each decade, James Heathcote discovered.

The didgeridoo and sleep (Peace Prize) Six scientists showed that playing one could help reduce snoring and sleep apnea.

The Aerones drone is designed for heavy-lift applications, such as search-and-rescue missions, autonomous delivery and firefighting.

First parachute jump from a drone

On 12 May 2017, BASE-jumper Ingus Augstkalns (LVA) carried out a parachute jump from a drone near the village of Māļi in Latvia. He was released from a height of 330 m (1,082 ft) by a heavy-lift multirotor built by Latvian drone-maker Aerones. The drone measures 34.4 sq ft (3.2 m²) and weighs 70 kg (154 lb). Six months' preparation had gone into this brief flight and parachute jump. During that time, the team at Aerones increased the payload, building up to 200 kg (440 lb).

The drone's 28 motors are arranged into 14 pusher-puller "nacelles" (engine housings). They give it a payload capacity of 100 kg (220 lb) – comfortably enough to lift a person.

Augstkalns climbed to the top of a radio mast, where the drone met him. He clipped himself on to it and flew a short distance before being released and parachuting to the ground.

▶ Fastest speed on an electric skateboard
On 27 Oct 2015, Mischo Erban (CAN/CZE) reached 95.83 km/h (59.55 mph) on an electric skateboard – around the same speed as a running gazelle, and nearly as fast as a cheetah, the **fastest land animal over short distances**. The record was set on a runway at Portorož Airport, near the village of Sečovlje in Slovenia.

Longest journey by electric motorcycle
Between 10 Jun and 23 Jul 2013, Nicola Colombo and Valerio Fumagalli (both ITA) rode 12,379 km (7,691.9 mi) on 44-hp (32.8-kW) Zero FX electric motorcycles. They crossed 11 countries, from Shanghai in China to Milan in Italy, as part of Meneghina Express – a project to investigate global food nutrition and sustainability.

▶ Greatest distance by electric bicycle (single charge)
Vitalii Arhipkin (UKR) covered 367.037 km (228.066 mi) on a Delfast model Prime e-bike at Kiev Velodrome in the Ukrainian capital on 12 Oct 2017. That's greater than the distance from London, UK, to Paris, France. Arhipkin completed 1,317 laps of the circuit, with two brief stops en route, taking approximately 17 hr in total.

EPIC ENGINEERING

Widest bridge
The San Francisco–Oakland Bay Bridge is a complex of bridges across San Francisco Bay in California, USA. The bridge is 78.740 m (258 ft 3 in) wide, including 10 lanes of roadway, a 4.724-m-wide (15-ft 6-in) bike path and a gap where the central pylon supports the two bridge deck sections.

Longest floating bridge
Opened in Apr 2016, the Governor Albert D Rosellini Bridge (or the Evergreen Point Floating Bridge) spans Lake Washington to connect the cities of Seattle and Bellevue in Washington, USA. It is 2,349.55 m (7,708 ft) long.

Largest highway system
The National Trunk Highway System (NTHS) in China totalled at least 131,000 km (81,399 mi) by the end of 2016.

Longest road tunnel
The tunnel between Aurland and Lærdal on the main road between Bergen and Oslo in Norway is 24.5 km (15.2 mi) long. The two-lane Lærdal Tunnel was opened by King Harald V on 27 Nov 2000, and became available for public use in 2001.

Longest rail tunnel
The Gotthard Base Tunnel is 57 km (35.42 mi) long. It runs between Göschenen and Airolo in Switzerland. The tunnel's excavation was completed on 15 Oct 2010, when engineers working 2,000 m (6,561 ft) beneath the Swiss Alps drilled through the last remaining rock. It opened on 1 Jun 2016.

Tallest electricity pylon
Completed in 2010, the Damaoshan electricity pylon carries power cables from China's Mount Damaoshan in Zhejiang Province to the Zhoushan Islands. The lattice tower stands 370 m (1,213 ft) tall and weighs 5,999 tonnes (13.2 million lb). It carries a capacity of 600,000 kW per day.

Largest offshore wind farm
The London Array wind farm occupies an offshore area of 100 km² (38.6 sq mi) in the Thames Estuary. Its 175 Siemens turbines each generate 3.6 MW, creating total capacity of 630 MW – enough power for nearly half a million UK homes. Each blade weighs 18 tonnes (39,683 lb) and has a rotor diameter of 120 m (393 ft 8 in). Each turbine tower weighs

Largest observation (Ferris) wheel
The Las Vegas High Roller, located at The LINQ in Las Vegas, Nevada, USA, has an outside diameter of 161.27 m (529 ft 1.4 in) and a total height of 167.5 m (549 ft 6.4 in). It opened to the public on 31 Mar 2014.

The Three Gorges Dam project required a total of 27.47 million m³ (970.1 million cu ft) of concrete – more than 10 times the volume of the Great Pyramid of Giza.

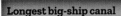

Longest big-ship canal
The Suez Canal, which links the Red and Mediterranean seas, opened on 17 Nov 1869. It took 10 years to build, utilizing a workforce of 1.5 million people, of whom 120,000 perished during the construction. The canal is 193.3 km (120.11 mi) long, running from Port Said harbour to the Gulf of Suez. It is 205 m (673 ft) at its narrowest and 365 m (1,198 ft) at its widest.

415 tonnes (457.4 tons) and reaches 147 m (482 ft 3 in) in height, 12 m (39 ft 4 in) more than the London Eye observation wheel.

Highest dam
The Jinping-I Dam in Sichuan, China, sits across the Yalong River. Featuring a double curvature thin arch, it peaks at 1,000 ft (305 m), making it almost as tall as the Eiffel Tower in Paris, France. The wall has a crest length of 568.5 m (1,865 ft). Designed by HydroChina Chengdu Engineering Corporation (CHIDI), the dam is owned by the Ertan Hydropower Development Company (both CHN).

Largest concrete dam
Construction of the Three Gorges Dam on the Yangtze River in China officially began on 14 Dec 1994 and it became operational in 2005. The dam was built using 14.86 million m³ (525 million cu ft) of concrete and is 2,335 m (7,661 ft) long. Its top reaches 185 m (607 ft) above sea level – higher than the Great Pyramid of Giza, London's St Paul's Cathedral or Seattle's Space Needle.

MONSTER MACHINES

◄ Largest land vehicle
The Bagger 293 bucket wheel weighs 14,196 tonnes (31.3 million lb). This mammoth earth-mover is manufactured by TAKRAF of Leipzig in Germany. It is 220 m (722 ft) long, 94.5 m (310 ft) tall at its highest point and is capable of moving 240,000 m³ (8.475 million cu ft) of earth in one day. To see it in full LEGO® glory go to pp.148-49.

► Largest tunnel-boring machine
Made by Japanese firm Hitachi Zosen, "Bertha" is 300 ft (91 m) long and weighs 6,900 tons (6,259 tonnes). Her colossal 17.5-m-diameter (57-ft 6-in) cutting head – mounted with 600 small grinding discs – began drilling out the State Route 99 tunnel below Seattle, USA, in 2013. It finished in 2017, having cut through 2 mi (3.2 km).

GUINNESS WORLD RECORDS

Deepest holes

- **1.2 km** – **deepest open pit mine** (Bingham Canyon mine in Utah, USA)
- **3.9 km** (as of 2012) – **deepest mine** (Mponeng gold mine near Johannesburg in South Africa)
- **12.2 km** – **deepest research borehole** (Zapolyarny on Kola Peninsula in Russia)
- **12.3 km** – **deepest oil well** (Z-44 Chayvo Well on the Sakhalin Shelf in Russia)

Longest bridge

The Danyang-Kunshan Grand Bridge, on the Jinghu High-Speed Railway (aka the Beijing–Shanghai High-Speed Railway) is 164 km (102 mi) in length. The line, which opened in Jun 2011, crosses the 114-km-long (70.8-mi) Langfang–Qingxian viaduct – itself the second-longest bridge in the world. It took 10,000 workers four years to complete the bridge, which stands at an average height of 100 ft (30.48 m) above ground level.

One 9-km (5.6-mi) part of the bridge running across Yangcheng Lake has been reinforced to withstand natural disasters, including earthquakes with a magnitude of 8 on the Richter scale, and impact from naval vessels.

Longest cable suspension bridge

Linking Honshu and Awaji Island in Japan, the Akashi-Kaikyō road bridge has a main span of 1,990.8 m (6,532 ft, or 1.24 mi) between its 297-m-tall (974-ft) towers. The length of a suspension bridge is typically taken to be its main span, as opposed to its total length.

Longest Tibet-style footbridge

The 494-m (1,621-ft) Charles Kuonen Suspension Bridge stretches 85 m (278 ft 10 in) above the Grabengufer ravine near Randa in Switzerland. It is just 65 cm (2 ft 1.5 in) wide. Built by Swissrope and Lauber Seilbahnen AG (both CHE), the bridge opened on 29 Jul 2017.

Tallest bridge

The 2,460-m-long (8,070-ft) Millau Viaduct over the Tarn Valley in France stands on seven concrete piers, the loftiest being 244.96 m (804 ft) above the ground. The piers also support seven 87-m-tall (285-ft) masts; the distance from the top of the masts to the deepest point in the valley is 343 m (1,125 ft). It was designed by Foster + Partners (UK).

Largest tower crane

In standard configuration, the Danish-made Kroll K-10000 is capable of lifting 120 tonnes (264,555 lb) at an 82-m (269-ft) radius (i.e., the distance from the central supporting column). It stands 120 m (393 ft) high on a rotating cylinder just 12 m (39 ft 4 in) in diameter, but has 223 tonnes (491,631 lb) of counterweights to offset its 84-m (275-ft) load-carrying boom.

Largest dumper truck (two-axle)

The BelAZ 75710 has a rated payload capacity of 450 tonnes (992,080 lb). Made by BelAZ (BLR), it was first tested at their premises in Zhodino, Belarus, on 22 Jan 2014. The truck was built as part of the trend in the mining industry for increasing unit sizes of machinery so that they can move greater loads per haul cycle.

▶ Largest grab dredger

The gigantic scooping machines "Gosho" and "Tosho" each have a capacity of 200 m³ (7,062.9 cu ft), as verified in Tuas, Singapore, on 26 Jan 2017. Both are manufactured by Kojimagumi Co. in association with Sumitomo Heavy Industries, Kawasaki Heavy Industries (all JPN) and Germany's Walter Hunger GmbH and Co. KG.

ROUND-UP

Largest fatberg
A fatberg is a lump of congealed fat, cooking oil, nappies, wet wipes and other personal hygiene products flushed down the toilet that causes a blockage in sewage systems. The largest one ever documented and reported by a water authority measured 250 m (820 ft) long and weighed an estimated 130 tonnes (286,601 lb), according to inspectors from Thames Water (UK). They encountered the blockage in a sewage pipe in London's Whitechapel area in Sep 2017.

Smallest greetings card
In Dec 2017, the National Physical Laboratory in Teddington, UK, used a beam of ions (positively charged atomic particles) to etch a Christmas card only 15 x 20 micrometres (0.00059 x 0.00078 in) in size. The card is made from a substrate of platinum-coated silicon nitride, and Christmas greetings are etched on its inner side. The greetings card is so small that when an electron microscope was used to "photograph" it, it moved off its stand and was lost somewhere in the microscope itself.

Longest time survived on Mars by a rover
On 25 Jan 2004, NASA's *Opportunity* rover touched down on the surface of Mars, within a plain named Meridiani Planum. Two weeks earlier, its twin, *Spirit*, had landed on the other side of the planet. The two solar-powered rovers were intended to remain active for around 90 Earth days, but proved to be surprisingly resilient. As of 29 Jan 2018, *Opportunity* was still functioning a total of 14 years 4 days later. *Spirit* remained operational until it became stuck in soft soil in May 2009; its solar panels became obscured by dust and it finally lost power on 22 Mar 2010.

Farthest distance driven on Mars
Paolo Bellutta (ITA/USA) is a rover planner at NASA's Jet Propulsion Laboratory (JPL). As of 10 Jan 2018, JPL's Mars rovers had travelled slightly more than 16.881 km (10.489 mi) under his control. This total combines the driving distance of the twin rovers *Spirit* and *Opportunity* (12,982 m; 42,591 ft) with that of the *Curiosity* rover (3,898 m; 12,788 ft).

First 3D-printed ship propeller (prototype)
The WAAMpeller was a collaboration between Rotterdam Additive Manufacturing LAB (RAMLAB), Promarin, Autodesk, Damen and Bureau Veritas. Created for tug boats, it has 298 layers of nickel-aluminium-bronze alloy. Promarin provided the design in Apr 2017; RAMLAB used Wire+Arc Additive Manufacturing (WAAM) methods to create the propeller itself; and Bureau Veritas verified the process, approving the propeller in Nov 2017.

Longest orbital survey of an outer planet
At 11:55 Coordinated Universal Time (UTC) on 15 Sep 2017, the *Cassini* spacecraft completed the "Grand Finale" phase of its near-20-year-long mission to study the planet Saturn and its moons. It then burned up on its final dive into the planet's upper atmosphere. *Cassini* had begun its orbital survey 13 years 76 days earlier.

Longest orbital flight by a reusable spacecraft
Manufactured by Boeing (USA), the X-37B autonomous spaceplane spent 1 year 352 days in orbit from 2015 to 2017. Its mission began on 20 May 2015, when it launched on an Atlas V booster from Cape Canaveral Air Force Station in Florida, USA. It returned on 7 May 2017, descending through the atmosphere with a sonic boom before touching down on the old Space Shuttle landing runway at the Kennedy Space Center.

Oldest ice core
On 15 Aug 2017, scientists drilling in the Antarctic announced that they had extracted a core of ice containing gas bubbles from 2.7 million years ago. This beats the previous record holder by almost 2 million years and is only possible because of the particular nature of the "blue ice" area drilled, which enables it to preserve ancient frozen layers. Air bubbles in the core were analysed and did not exceed 300 parts per million (PPM) of carbon dioxide. Compared with the levels of carbon dioxide in the air today, which have exceeded 410 PPM, this shows how much less greenhouse gas was present in the earlier atmosphere.

Loudest room
The Reverberant Acoustic Test Facility (RATF) is a concrete-walled room 57 ft (17.37 m) high, 47 ft 6 in (14.47 m) long and 37 ft 6 in

Longest duration spinning a fidget spinner (one finger)
Takayuki Ishikawa (JPN) kept a fidget spinner spinning on one finger for 24 min 46.34 sec in Minato, Tokyo, Japan, on 11 Dec 2017. The spinner was made by MinebeaMitsumi Inc. and Mitsubishi Precision Co., Ltd (both JPN).
MinebeaMitsumi also made the **smallest fidget spinner** (inset), which measures just 5.09 mm (0.20 in) wide. It weighs 0.027 g (0.00095 oz) – lighter than a grain of rice.

(11.43 m) wide. The facility was completed in 2011. Part of NASA's Glenn Research Center, it is located in the Plum Brook Station, a 6,400-acre (2,590-ha) campus near Sandusky, Ohio, USA. It has 36 huge loudspeaker horns (or "noise sources") covering one wall. Driven by pressurized nitrogen gas, these speakers can saturate the room with 163 dB of continuous noise for 10 min. The RATF's purpose is to test rocket parts, satellites and other space-related hardware to ensure that they can cope with the punishing noise of a rocket launch.

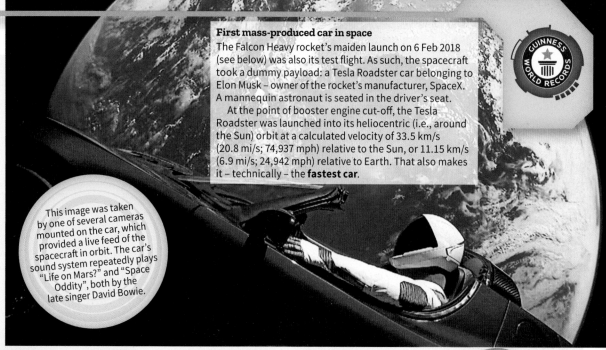

First mass-produced car in space

The Falcon Heavy rocket's maiden launch on 6 Feb 2018 (see below) was also its test flight. As such, the spacecraft took a dummy payload: a Tesla Roadster car belonging to Elon Musk – owner of the rocket's manufacturer, SpaceX. A mannequin astronaut is seated in the driver's seat.

At the point of booster engine cut-off, the Tesla Roadster was launched into its heliocentric (i.e., around the Sun) orbit at a calculated velocity of 33.5 km/s (20.8 mi/s; 74,937 mph) relative to the Sun, or 11.15 km/s (6.9 mi/s; 24,942 mph) relative to Earth. That also makes it – technically – the **fastest car**.

This image was taken by one of several cameras mounted on the car, which provided a live feed of the spacecraft in orbit. The car's sound system repeatedly plays "Life on Mars?" and "Space Oddity", both by the late singer David Bowie.

Tightest knotted structure

Knots can occur on a molecular level – even DNA has them. On 12 Jan 2017, a team from the University of Manchester, UK, announced that by braiding together three strands of molecules they had created a microscopic knot 192 atoms long that crosses itself eight times – approximately once every 2.5 nanometres (24 atoms). Known as the 8_{19} knot, it is represented as a model in the photograph above.

Newest chemical element

The most recent chemical element to be synthesized is Tennessine (Ts), created in 2010 by Russian and American scientists at the Joint Institute for Nuclear Research (JINR) in Dubna, Russia. Six atoms were produced by shooting a beam of calcium ions into a target of berkelium. Tennessine has an atomic number of 117 and was formally recognized as a new element in Dec 2015.

Most powerful rocket (current)

On 6 Feb 2018, the Falcon Heavy rocket made its maiden flight, with lift-off at 3:45 p.m. Eastern Standard Time (EST) from Cape Canaveral Air Force Station in Florida, USA. Built by US company SpaceX, Falcon Heavy has 27 engines and three booster cores, creating 22,819 kN

(5.12 million lbf) of thrust at sea level and 24,681 kN (5.54 million lbf) in the vacuum of space. The rocket is 70 m (229 ft 7 in) tall and weighs 1,420.788 tonnes (3.13 million lb).

Able to carry payloads of 63,800 kg (140,655 lb) into low-Earth orbit, Falcon Heavy is also the **most powerful rocket by lift capacity**, with around twice the payload-lifting capability of other operational heavy-lift rockets. Its second stage is embarked on an orbit around the Sun that may last for billions of years, carrying an unorthodox payload on its long trip (for more, see above).

First living organism with artificial DNA base pairs

In Nov 2017, a new form of the bacterium *E. coli* was created at the Scripps Research Institute in California, USA. It contained two synthetic DNA base pairs that can create previously unknown proteins. The two new synthetic "X" and "Y" bases integrate into the natural DNA of *E. coli*. Scientists hope that this will lead to longer-lasting, more effective drugs for treating illnesses. The ability to make hardier proteins that the human body cannot easily break down could greatly improve the effectiveness of some drugs.

Largest Klein bottle

First described in 1882 by Felix Klein, his eponymous vessel is closed, with no border, and only one "side" (i.e., no discrete "inside" and "outside"). Clifford Stoll (USA, above) designed one 41.75 in (106 cm) high and 24.5 in (62.2 cm) wide, with a circumference of 64.37 in (163.5 cm). It was built by the Killdee Scientific Glass Company (USA) between 2001 and 2003. The bottle is on display at the Kingbridge Centre in Toronto, Canada – owned by John Abele (USA), who commissioned the vessel.

First 3D robotic billboard

On 8 Aug 2017, The Coca-Cola Company (USA) erected a 210.22-m² (2,262.78-sq-ft) three-dimensional billboard in Times Square, New York City, USA. It comprises 1,960 robotic LED cubes; of these, 1,715 move and 245 are static. The billboard is able to detect inclement weather and account for any changes in temperature.

08/04/2016

30/03/2017

First reuse of an orbital-class rocket stage

At 22:27 UTC on 30 Mar 2017, a SpaceX Falcon 9 rocket carrying communications satellite SES-10 took off from Launch Complex 39A at the Kennedy Space Center in Florida, USA. It was deployed into orbit at 22:59 UTC, some 32 min after launch. This rocket had previously flown (and landed) on 8 Apr 2016, having carried NASA commercial resupply mission CRS-8 to the *International Space Station*. This is the first time that a stage from an orbital-class rocket has been reused successfully.

CONTAINER SHIP

At nearly 400 m (1,312 ft) from bow to stern, the largest container ships carry thousands of tonnes of cargo around the globe every day. In 2014, to celebrate the world's largest ship at the time – the Maersk Line *Triple E* – LEGO® released a 1,518-piece reproduction. The real thing may be more than 600 times larger, but even at this reduced scale, the model reveals just how staggeringly enormous these container ships are.

Sea-faring vessels such as the *Triple E*, and the current record holder – the *OOCL Hong Kong* (right) – are among the largest structures built by humans. Technically, they are known as Ultra-Large Container Vessels (ULCVs), meaning that they can accommodate a minimum of 18,000 containers. Container-ship capacity is measured in "twenty-foot equivalent units", or TEUs, in reference to the number of 20-ft-long (6-m) containers it can carry. More than 90% of cargo is transported by ship – including this very book! – so most of the world relies on these giants of the seas.

FOR THE RECORD

A number of vessels are around the 400-m (1,312-ft) mark – equivalent in length to eight Olympic-size swimming pools – but the **largest container ship by capacity** is currently the *OOCL Hong Kong* (above), built by the Orient Overseas Container Line (HKG) and christened on 12 May 2017. It has a registered capacity of 21,413 TEU and measures 399.87 m (1,311 ft 10 in) long. It has a beam (width) of 58.80 m (192 ft 10 in), a depth of 32.50 m (106 ft 7 in) from deck edge to keel, and a displacement – i.e., fully loaded weight – of 253,104.7 long tons (257,166 tonnes; 283,477 US tons).

Foremast

Reusable freight containers, typically 20 or 40 ft (6 or 12 m) long; stored in the hull and lashed to the deck

MAERSK LINE

A P Møller-Mærsk (DEN) is the world's **largest container shipping line by TEU capacity**, with a total of 4,158,171 owned and chartered containers as of Nov 2017. It is also the largest by **market share**, operating 19.4% of the global cargo fleet, and by **number of vessels**, with 779 owned and chartered ships. The firm was founded in 1904 and is headquartered in Copenhagen, Denmark.

Steel hull

Bulbous bow, designed to reduce wave resistance and lower fuel costs

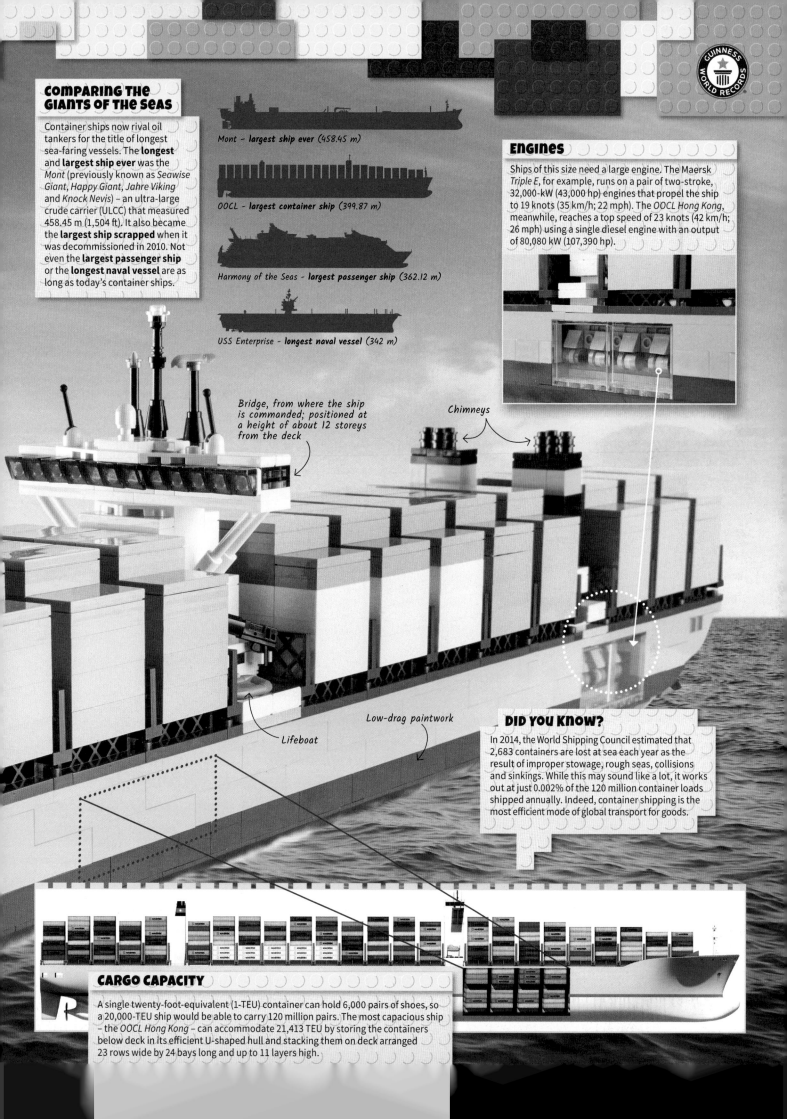

COMPARING THE GIANTS OF THE SEAS

Container ships now rival oil tankers for the title of longest sea-faring vessels. The **longest** and **largest ship ever** was the *Mont* (previously known as *Seawise Giant*, *Happy Giant*, *Jahre Viking* and *Knock Nevis*) – an ultra-large crude carrier (ULCC) that measured 458.45 m (1,504 ft). It also became the **largest ship scrapped** when it was decommissioned in 2010. Not even the **largest passenger ship** or the **longest naval vessel** are as long as today's container ships.

Mont - **largest ship ever** (458.45 m)

OOCL - **largest container ship** (399.87 m)

Harmony of the Seas - **largest passenger ship** (362.12 m)

USS Enterprise - **longest naval vessel** (342 m)

ENGINES

Ships of this size need a large engine. The Maersk *Triple E*, for example, runs on a pair of two-stroke, 32,000-kW (43,000 hp) engines that propel the ship to 19 knots (35 km/h; 22 mph). The *OOCL Hong Kong*, meanwhile, reaches a top speed of 23 knots (42 km/h; 26 mph) using a single diesel engine with an output of 80,080 kW (107,390 hp).

Bridge, from where the ship is commanded; positioned at a height of about 12 storeys from the deck

Chimneys

Lifeboat

Low-drag paintwork

DID YOU KNOW?

In 2014, the World Shipping Council estimated that 2,683 containers are lost at sea each year as the result of improper stowage, rough seas, collisions and sinkings. While this may sound like a lot, it works out at just 0.002% of the 120 million container loads shipped annually. Indeed, container shipping is the most efficient mode of global transport for goods.

CARGO CAPACITY

A single twenty-foot-equivalent (1-TEU) container can hold 6,000 pairs of shoes, so a 20,000-TEU ship would be able to carry 120 million pairs. The most capacious ship – the *OOCL Hong Kong* – can accommodate 21,413 TEU by storing the containers below deck in its efficient U-shaped hull and stacking them on deck arranged 23 rows wide by 24 bays long and up to 11 layers high.

ARTS & MEDIA

Highest-grossing opening weekend at the global box office

On 27–29 Apr 2018, Marvel's cross-franchise blockbuster *Avengers: Infinity War* (USA) took $640,398,183 (£464.5 m) worldwide, according to The-Numbers. com. With US-only takings of $257,698,183 (£186.9 m) for this period, it is also the **highest-grossing opening weekend at the domestic box office.**

CONTENTS

MARVEL STUDIOS

AVENGERS
INFINITY WAR

Avengers: Infinity War carried on breaking records beyond its opening weekend. It became the **fastest movie to gross $1 billion** just 11 days after its release, beating the 12 days taken by *Star Wars VII: The Force Awakens* (USA, 2015)

BLOCKBUSTERS

HIGHEST GLOBAL BOX-OFFICE GROSSERS

Comedy
Riotous comedy sequel *The Hangover Part II* (USA, 2011) – in which a group of friends live to regret their pre-wedding feast – has grossed $586,464,305 (£433,653,000).

The **highest-grossing black comedy** is *The Wolf of Wall Street* (USA, 2013), starring Leonardo DiCaprio and directed by Martin Scorsese (both USA), which has earned $389,870,414 (£288,284,000).

Romantic comedy
Released worldwide in Feb 2016, Stephen Chow's fantasy adventure film *Mei Ren Yu* (aka *The Mermaid*; CHN) has earned $552,198,479 (£398,638,000) worldwide. Although only the 160th highest-grossing film of all time, it is the most financially successful romantic comedy ever.

Drama
The Twilight Saga: Breaking Dawn – Part 2 (USA, 2012) accumulated $829,724,737 (£585,958,000) worldwide. It was the fifth and final instalment of the teen vampire drama series based on the books by Stephenie Meyer.

Documentary
Michael Jackson's This Is It, documenting concert rehearsals by the US pop legend, was released on 28 Oct 2009. The film took $200 m (£119,673,000) in its first two weeks and went on to gross $252,091,016 (£186,405,000) worldwide.

Justin Bieber: Never Say Never (2011), a rare inside look at the rise of the Canadian singer from street performer to superstar, is the **highest-grossing concert film** ever. It has posted a box-office gross of $99,034,125 (£73,229,400).

Live-action musical
Disney's live-action remake of its classic 1991 animation *Beauty and the Beast* (USA), which premiered at Spencer House in London, UK, on 23 Feb 2017, has taken $1,263,109,573 (£845,738,000) at the global box office. The blockbuster musical, starring Emma Watson as Belle and Dan Stevens (both UK) as Beast, beat out the previous record holder, *Mamma Mia!* (USA/UK/DEU, 2008), which now ranks second with a lifetime gross of $615,748,877 (£455,307,000).

* all figures as of 11 Apr 2018

First fully oil-painted feature film

Loving Vincent (POL/UK/USA, 2017) tells the story of the last days of the artist Vincent van Gogh. In a complex, 10-year production process, actors were filmed in live-action footage, each frame of which was then meticulously over-painted by a team of 125 animators. They used oil paints to mimic van Gogh's characteristic swirling brushstrokes.

Highest-grossing superhero "origin" movie
Black Panther (USA, 2018) had grossed $1,300,716,032 (£918,576,000) as of 11 Apr 2018. The Marvel film, starring Chadwick Boseman (USA, above) as hero T'Challa, passed the $1-billion (£706-m) mark in just 26 days.

Horror
Adapted from Stephen King's 1986 novel about a group of children terrorized by an evil clown named Pennywise, *It* (USA, 2017) has taken $697,459,228 (£492,551,000) at the box office.

Western
Django Unchained (USA, 2012), written and directed by Quentin Tarantino and starring Jamie Foxx, Christoph Waltz, Leonardo DiCaprio, Kerry Washington and Samuel L Jackson, has grossed $449,948,323 (£318,238,000) since its release on 25 Dec 2012. In 2013, the western became the director's highest-grossing film and won Oscars for both Waltz and Tarantino.

Highest-grossing film
Avatar (US/UK, 2009) had taken $2,783,918,982 (£2,058,530,000) worldwide as of 11 Jan 2018. Its director, James Cameron (CAN), also masterminded the **first movie to gross $1 billion at the worldwide box office**: *Titanic* (USA, 1997). *Avatar* became the fifth movie to do so, in 2009.

The blue skins of certain Hindu deities were an influence on the look of the Na'vi species. The word "avatar" derives from Sanskrit and refers to the incarnation of a god on Earth.

THE NUMBERS
The Numbers is the web's biggest database of movie financial information, with figures on more than 31,000 movies and 144,000 people in the film industry. It was founded in 1997 by Bruce Nash, and is visited by more than 8 million people every year. As well as movie fans, the major studios, independent production companies and investors use the site and its services to decide which movies to make and when to release them. The site gathers data from the movie studios, retailers, news reports and other sources to compile its database, known as OpusData. The database contains in excess of 8 million facts about the movie business.

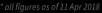
THE NUMBERS

CEL MATES – ANIMATED CLASSICS

▲ **Highest-grossing animation (domestic, inflation-adjusted)**
Walt Disney's first full-length feature film, *Snow White and the Seven Dwarfs* (USA, 1937), took $184.9 m (then £37.4 m) at the US box office – equivalent to $1.2 bn (£890 m) as of 10 May 2018. It was also the **first movie with an official soundtrack**.

Highest-grossing animation (global, non-adjusted) ▶
Disney's *Frozen* (USA, 2013; re-released as a singalong version in 2014) has enjoyed box-office takings of $1.27 bn (£829 m). Based on Hans Christian Andersen's story *The Snow Queen*, it ranked 10th in the highest-grossing movies ever at the global box office until overtaken by *Black Panther* (see above).

Highest-grossing stop-motion animation
Chicken Run, created by Aardman Animations (UK) in partnership with DreamWorks (USA), earned $227 m (£152.5 m) upon its release in 2000. Stop-motion animation involves making a tiny change to a model, taking a snapshot, then making another tiny change. After months, even years, of this, you end up with a movie!

Most searched-for movies of 2017
Film fans love superheroes, classic fairy tales and – most of all – scaring themselves silly. That's what 2017's Google searches suggest, anyway…

1: *It*. A horror smash hit: seven children take on an evil entity in the form of creepy clown Pennywise.

2: *Beauty and the Beast*. Disney's live-action take on the fairy tale was a monster hit at the box office.

3: *Wonder Woman*. Starring Gal Gadot, this superhero smash was the 10th highest-grossing movie of the year.

Highest-grossing film series

As of 5 Apr 2018, the 10 Star Wars movies had collectively grossed $8,926,704,817 (£6,342,370,000) worldwide, overtaking the Harry Potter series. This figure includes re-issues, special editions and *Episode VIII: The Last Jedi* (USA), which was released on 15 Dec 2017. It also covers the 2008 animation *The Clone Wars* (USA) and *Rogue One: A Star Wars Story* (USA, 2016), the first "Anthology" film. The second – the upcoming *Solo: A Star Wars Story* – will see the sci-fi series' gross rise.

Highest-grossing adventure film
Star Wars VII: The Force Awakens (USA, 2015) had grossed $2,058,662,225 (£1,522,250,000) at the worldwide box office by 11 Apr 2018. On its release, the long-awaited seventh instalment in the legendary sci-fi franchise smashed several box office records, including **fastest movie to gross $100 million** (in 24 hr), **$200 million** (in three days) and **$500 million** (in 10 days).

▶ Highest-grossing animation (opening day)
Disney-Pixar's *Finding Dory* (USA, 2016) – the long-awaited sequel to *Finding Nemo* (USA, 2003) – grossed $54.7 m (£39.6 m) from 4,305 US cinemas when it opened to the public on 17 Jun 2016. The 30th highest-grossing film of all time as of Apr 2018, *Finding Dory* is also the **highest-grossing film without a villain**.

Highest-grossing Japanese animated film
Released in 2016, *Your Name* ("*Kimi no na wa*", JPN) grossed $342.8 m (£245.6 m) internationally. A romantic fantasy written and directed by Makoto Shinkai (JPN), the plot revolves around two teenagers who magically swap bodies. In Sep 2017, director JJ Abrams announced plans to make a live-action version of the film.

▶ Most Oscar wins for Best Animated Feature
Since this category was added to the Academy Awards in 2001, Pixar have won nine of the 17 Oscars thus far presented. The winning animations (all USA) were: *Finding Nemo* (2003), *The Incredibles* (2004), *Ratatouille* (2007), *WALL-E* (2008), *Up* (2009), *Toy Story 3* (2010), *Brave* (2012), *Inside Out* (2015) and *Coco* (2017, right).

MOVIE MAKERS

Highest annual earnings for a film actor (ever)

Will Smith (USA) earned $80 m (£40.3 m) in the year to 1 Jun 2008 according to Forbes, with hits such as *I Am Legend* (USA, 2007) and *Hancock* (USA, 2008). Iron Man star Robert Downey Jr (USA) matched the feat in the 12 months to 1 Jun 2015, earning $80 m (£50.8 m) after the release of *Avengers: Age of Ultron* (USA, 2015).

Most Academy Awards for Best Actress

Katharine Hepburn (USA, 1907–2003) won a total of four Academy Awards, for lead roles in *Morning Glory* (USA, 1933) in 1934, *Guess Who's Coming to Dinner* (USA, 1967) in 1968, *The Lion in Winter* (UK, 1968) in 1969 and *On Golden Pond* (USA, 1981) in 1982.

On 24 Feb 2013, Daniel Day-Lewis (UK) won his third Academy Award for a lead role, the **most Academy Awards for Best Actor.** He picked up a statue for his portrayal of Abraham Lincoln in 2012's *Lincoln* (USA/IND), to add to his wins for *There Will Be Blood* (USA, 2007) and *My Left Foot* (IRL/UK, 1989). Day-Lewis was the first actor to win three Oscars for a lead part.

First woman to be nominated for an Oscar for Best Cinematography

On 23 Jan 2018, Rachel Morrison (USA) received an Oscar nomination for her work on the film *Mudbound* (USA, 2017), making her the first woman to be so honoured in the 89-year history of the Academy Awards. On the night, she was pipped to the prize by Roger Deakins for his work on *Blade Runner 2049* (USA/UK/HUN/CAN, 2017).

HIGHEST-GROSSING...

Actor in cameo roles

As of 15 Jan 2018, movies in which Marvel Comics creator Stan Lee (USA) made only a fleeting appearance had grossed $21,413,689,417 (£15,589,300,000). This figure combines the total global revenue (not adjusted for inflation) from the 37 movies that he had appeared in to that date. Lee made his cinematic debut in *Mallrats* (USA, 1995).

Film producer (male)

Movies produced by Kevin Feige (USA) had generated $13,508,528,266 (£9,806,310,000) globally as of 16 Jan 2018. His credits include Marvel blockbusters such as the three Iron Man movies (all USA, 2008–13), *Thor* (USA, 2011), *Avengers: Age of Ultron* and *Captain America: Civil War* (USA, 2016).

Kathleen Kennedy (USA) is the **highest-grossing film producer (female)**, her movies having taken more than $11,346,882,599 (£8,237,100,000) worldwide as of 16 Jan 2018. Kennedy's 32 films include such box-office smashes as *E.T. the Extra-Terrestrial* (USA, 1982), *Jurassic Park* (USA, 1993) and the three instalments of the Star Wars franchise up to *Star Wars Episode VIII: The Last Jedi* (USA, 2017).

Highest annual earnings for a film actress (current year)

Emma Stone (USA) earned around $26 m (£20.2 m) pre-tax in the year to 1 Jun 2017, according to Forbes, largely because of the success of multiple-Oscar-winner *La La Land* (USA, 2016; above).

Highest annual earnings for a film actor (current year)

From 1 Jun 2016 to 1 Jun 2017, US actor Mark Wahlberg enjoyed estimated pre-tax earnings of $68 m (£52.9 m), as revealed by Forbes. He is shown above playing Cade Yeager in 2017's *Transformers: The Last Knight* (USA/CHN/CAN).

Most profitable actor for a Hollywood studio

According to Forbes, Jeremy Renner (USA) returned $93.80 (£73.04) for every $1 (£0.77) he was paid in the year to 1 Jun 2017. During that time, he appeared in franchises such as Mission: Impossible and Marvel's Captain America, as well as sci-fi movie *Arrival* (USA, 2016), which had grossed more than $203 m (£158 m) globally as of the same date. He is seen above as Hawkeye filming *The Avengers* (USA, 2012).

Highest-grossing film directors

• **Male:** The 32 theatrically released films by Steven Spielberg (USA, top inset), from *The Sugarland Express* (USA, 1974) to *The Post* (USA, 2017), had grossed $9,834,087,200 (£7,138,910,000) as of 16 Jan 2018. Above is a scene from his *Ready Player One* (USA, 2018), released as we went to press.
• **Female:** As of 16 Jan 2018, the six films by Nancy Meyers (USA, bottom inset), from *The Parent Trap* (USA, 1998) to *The Intern* (USA, 2015), had taken $1,351,805,585 (£981,323,000).

HIGHEST-GROSSING LEADING MOVIE STARS FOR...*

◀ Superhero films
The seven superhero movies starring Robert Downey Jr have cumulatively grossed $7,382,381,753 (£4,943,010,000) at the worldwide box office. His role as Marvel's Iron Man made Downey Jr the world's best-paid actor between 2012 and 2015.

▲ Comedies
The 22 comedy movies starring Adam Sandler (USA) have grossed $2,613,261,211 (£1,902,480,000). They include *Grown Ups* (USA, 2010), *I Now Pronounce You Chuck and Larry* (USA, 2007), *Click* (USA, 2006) and *The Longest Yard* (USA, 2005).

▼ Dramas
The 21 drama films in which Tom Hanks (USA) played a leading role have grossed $4,323,924,637 (£3,147,850,000) at the worldwide box office. Hanks is shown below playing newspaper editor Ben Bradlee in *The Post* (USA, 2017).

*source: The-Numbers.com. All figures accurate as of 15 Jan 2018

Highest-grossing*...

Cinematographer:
Andrew Lesnie
(AUS, 1956–2015) –
$7.96 bn (£5.76 bn)
from 13 movies

Film editor:
Michael Kahn (USA) –
$11.32 bn (£8.20 bn)
from 53 movies

Screenwriter:
Steve Kloves (USA) –
$7.57 bn (£5.48 bn)
from nine movies

Film composer:
Hans Zimmer (DEU) –
$27.71 bn (£20.07 bn)
from 98 movies

*figures correct as of 5 Mar 2018

Jackson's most famous roles include Marvel's Nick Fury (pictured) and Jules Winnfield in *Pulp Fiction* (USA, 1994).

Highest-grossing actor (all roles)

Movies featuring Samuel L Jackson (USA) had taken a total global box-office gross of $17,831,510,183 (£12,981,500,000) as of 15 Jan 2018. He had acting credits in 127 films, including 53 starring or co-star parts and 49 supporting appearances in such box-office hits as *Avengers: Age of Ultron*.

Highest-grossing actress (all roles)

Based on all her movie appearances – including three roles as narrator and minor parts – Cate Blanchett (AUS) had grossed $10,884,289,810 (£7,923,850,000) in her 52 films as of 15 Jan 2018. She is shown above playing Hela, the goddess of death, in *Thor: Ragnarok* (USA, 2017).

Highest-grossing actor (leading roles)

Globally, the 46 movies starring or co-starring Johnny Depp (USA) had grossed $9,561,438,698 (£6,960,810,000) by 15 Jan 2018.

Highest-grossing actress (leading roles)

Emma Watson (UK) has appeared in 14 movies (including all eight Harry Potter films), grossing $9,092,218,924 (£6,619,210,000).

Highest-grossing actor (supporting roles)

As of 15 Jan 2018, films featuring Warwick Davis (UK) in a supporting part had taken $14,548,112,029 (£10,591,100,000) worldwide.

Highest-grossing actress (supporting roles)

The 17 movies featuring the voice of actress Mickie McGowan (USA) in a supporting role have grossed $8,286,733,896 (£6,032,810,000).

◄ Musicals

The global cumulative gross of movies *Moulin Rouge!* (AUS/USA, 2001) and *Beauty and the Beast* (USA, 2017), both starring Ewan McGregor (UK), is $1,442,923,008 (£1,050,460,000). He is shown here in *Moulin Rouge!*, playing the part of the love-struck poet Christian.

▲ Romantic comedies

US actress Julia Roberts, whose breakthrough came in *Pretty Woman* (USA, 1990), has appeared in eight romantic comedy movies to date. Also including *Notting Hill* (UK/USA, 1999) and *Runaway Bride* (USA, 1999), they have taken $1,651,919,358 (£1,202,610,000).

► Action films

Vin Diesel (USA, b. Mark Sinclair) has starred in 13 actions films since 2001, grossing a total of $5,855,350,823 (£3,920,560,000). Notable action roles include xXx's stuntman-turned-spy Xander Cage and street racer Dominic Toretto from the *Fast and the Furious* series (right).

THE YEAR IN POP

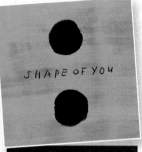

SHAPE OF YOU

Biggest-selling album worldwide (current year)
Ed Sheeran's (UK) ÷ ("Divide") sold 6.1 million albums in 2017 – the latest year for which full figures are available – according to the International Federation of the Phonographic Industry (IFPI).

Most streamed track worldwide
"Despacito" ("Slowly") had been streamed more than 4.6 billion times as of 19 Jul 2017. Originally performed by Luis Fonsi (b. Luis Alfonso López-Cepero) with Daddy Yankee (b. Ramón Rodríguez; both PRI), its popularity was boosted by a remix featuring Justin Bieber (CAN), which took it into the record books just 188 days after its release on 12 Jan 2017 (see right).

On 3 Aug 2017, exactly 203 days after it was uploaded, the original "Despacito" video became the **most watched video online ever**, with 3 billion views (see p.198).

DESPACITO REMIX
LUIS FONSI & DADDY YANKEE

FEAT.
JUSTIN BIEBER

Best-selling digital single worldwide (current year)
Ed Sheeran's "Shape of You" sold 26.6 million units (single-track downloads and track-equivalent audio streams) in 2017, according to the IFPI. The track spent 33 consecutive weeks in the Top 10 of *Billboard*'s Hot 100, including 12 weeks at No.1 – the **most weeks in the Top 10 of the US Hot 100**. "Shape of You" is also the **most streamed track on Spotify**, with 1,655,258,694 streams as of 6 Mar 2018.

Most streamed track in one week in the USA (female)
Taylor Swift's (USA) "Look What You Made Me Do" attracted 84.4 million US streams for the week ending 31 Aug 2017, according to Nielsen Music. The track was streamed more than 8 million times on Spotify on 24–25 Aug 2017, making it the **most streamed track on Spotify in the first 24 hours**.

With 43.2 million YouTube viewers on 27–28 Aug 2017, "Look What You Made Me Do" is also the **most watched video online in 24 hours** and the **mostwatched video on VEVO in 24 hours**.

Most consecutive years with a Japanese No.1 single
KinKi Kids' (JPN) single "Topaz Love"/"DESTINY" extended their run of consecutive years with a No.1 hit on the Oricon Singles Chart to 22 (1997–2018). Find another KinKi Kids record on p.187.

Highest percentage of internet users listening to licensed audio-streaming services (single year)
In Sep 2017, a report by the IFPI revealed that 45% of consumers listened to recorded music via a licensed audio-streaming service such as Apple Music or Spotify, a 21.6% rise from 2016.

Most Latin Grammy Award wins
At the 18th Annual Latin Grammy Awards on 16 Nov 2017, Residente, aka René Pérez, won his 23rd ("Best Urban Music Album") and 24th ("Best Urban Song" for "Somos Anormales") awards. This equalled the Latin Grammys won by his Calle 13 band-mate Eduardo "Visitante" Cabra (both PRI), who was named "Producer of the Year".

At the same ceremony, Shakira (COL, b. Shakira Isabel Mebarak Ripoll) won her 11th award, taking home the "Best Contemporary Pop Vocal Album" prize for her 2017 album *El Dorado*. This represents the **most Latin Grammy Award wins by a female**.

The **longest stay at No.1 on the US Hot Latin Songs chart by a single artist** is 22 weeks, by J Balvin (COL) with "Ginza", from the chart weeks dated 11 Oct 2015 to 12 Mar 2016.

The **most Top 10 hits on the *Billboard* Tropical Airplay chart (female)** is 27, by Olga Tañón (PRI),

Most weeks at No.1 in the USA (single)
On the *Billboard* Hot 100 dated 9 Sep 2017, "Despacito" by Luis Fonsi, Daddy Yankee and Justin Bieber spent a record-tying 16th straight week at No.1, matching the achievement of the ballad "One Sweet Day", by Mariah Carey and Boyz II Men (both USA), in 1995–96.

with the first on 5 Nov 1994 and the latest on 29 Apr 2017. She also has the **most Premio Lo Nuestro Awards by an individual**: 30, between 1990 and 2015.

Farthest recorded music from Earth
The Voyager Golden Record was 21.15 billion km (13.14 billion mi) from Earth, as of 9 Mar 2018. The 12-inch, gold-plated disc, a time capsule for any alien life out there, is on NASA's *Voyager 1* probe – the **most remote man-made object**, which launched on 5 Sep 1977. It includes "Melancholy Blues" by Louis Armstrong and his Hot Seven, "Johnny B Goode" by Chuck Berry and "Dark was the Night, Cold was the Ground" by Blind Willie Johnson.

Most consecutive weeks on the US singles chart (multiple singles)
Between the debut of "Best I Ever Had" on 23 May 2009 and the final chart weeks of "Passionfruit" and "Signs" on 19 Aug 2017, Drake (CAN) spent 431 consecutive weeks – eight years 88 days – on the *Billboard* Hot 100. The Toronto-born rapper charted with 157 tracks, including 105 as lead artist.

IN THE GLOBAL GROOVE

◀ **Most viewed music video online in 24 hours by a K-pop group**
With 21 million YouTube viewers on 18–19 Sep 2017, "DNA" by BTS (KOR) is the most watched video by a K-pop group in a 24-hr period. On 19 Nov 2017, BTS became the first K-pop act to perform at the American Music Awards, singing "DNA". "K-pop" stands for "Korean pop".

◀ **Oldest winner at the Latin Grammy Awards**
Magín Díaz (COL, b. 30 Dec 1922) picked up a Latin Grammy for "Best Recording Package" for the album *El Orisha de la Rosa* at the age of 94 years 321 days. Diaz was honoured at the 18th Annual Latin Grammy Awards, which was staged at the MGM Grand Garden Arena in Las Vegas, Nevada, USA, on 16 Nov 2017.

US music industry*
On average, Americans listen to music for more than 4 hr every day. AM/FM radio attracts the majority (52%) of all listeners.

Vinyl sales have risen by 4% to $430 m (£349.4 m). In all, however, physical music products fell to just 22% of the market.

Digital sales account for 78% of all music industry revenue. This has risen 23% from 2015 to $5.8 bn (£4.7 bn).

Streaming makes up 51% of revenue – some $3.9 bn (£3.1 bn). Around 432 billion songs were streamed on demand in 2016.

*Source: Recording Industry Association of America (RIAA). Figures for 2016

Most million-selling weeks on the US albums chart

Taylor Swift is the only act to have notched up four million-selling weeks on the *Billboard* 200 albums chart since Nielsen started tracking sales in 1991. The country-music star turned pop icon achieved the feat with first-week sales of her four most recent albums, which all debuted at No.1: *Speak Now* (1.047 million copies; 13 Nov 2010); *Red* (1.208 million; 10 Nov 2012); *1989* (1.287 million; 15 Nov 2014) and *Reputation* (1.216 million; 2 Dec 2017). Swift had previously shared the record of three weeks with Adele (UK).

Most Grammy Award nominations for a female artist
As announced on 28 Nov 2017, Beyoncé (USA) received her 63rd Grammy nomination for "Family Feud" (above), on which she features alongside husband Jay-Z. The track was a contender for "Best Rap/Sung Collaboration".

Swift is shown in a still from the video for "Look What You Made Me Do" – the first release from 2017's *Reputation*, an international No.1 (see opposite).

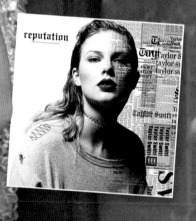

First Middle-Eastern musician to crowdfund a debut single

Faia Younan (SYR) used the Arabian crowdfunding platform Zoomaal to launch her professional career with the single "Ohebbou Yadayka" ("I Love Your Hands"). Backed by 119 contributors, the project reached its funding target of $25,000 (£16,696; SYP5,361,250) on 19 Apr 2015.

◀ Most consecutive Japanese No.1 singles from debut

KinKi Kids, aka the (unrelated) duo Koichi Domoto and Tsuyoshi Domoto, have had 39 consecutive No.1 hits since debuting on the Oricon Singles Chart with "Garasu no Shōnen" on 28 Jul 1997. Their 39th chart-topper was "Topaz Love"/"DESTINY", which debuted at No.1 on 5 Feb 2018.

Most points scored at the Eurovision Song Contest

On 13 May 2017, Salvador Sobral (PRT) secured Portugal's first-ever Eurovision win, with "Amar Pelos Dois". The ballad received 758 points from the combined jury (382 points) and public (376) votes, including 30 top scores of 12 points. Sobral smashed the record set in 2016 by Jamala (UKR), whose "1944" won 534 points.

TOP OF THE POPS

First million-selling record
The earliest record to sell more than a million copies was "Vesti la giubba" from Leoncavallo's opera *Pagliacci*, sung by Italian opera singer Enrico Caruso (1873–1921). It was recorded in Nov 1902 and released by Victor Talking Machine Company.

Best-selling single
Bing Crosby's "White Christmas" has sold an estimated 50 million copies worldwide. The festive favourite was written by Irving Berlin in 1940 and recorded in just 18 min on 29 May 1942. It was introduced in Berlin's musical movie *Holiday Inn* (USA, 1942), which starred Crosby and Fred Astaire.

The **best-selling single since charts began** – in the 1950s – is Elton John's "Something About the Way You Look Tonight"/ "Candle in the Wind 1997", with worldwide sales of 33 million.

Best-selling album
First released in Nov 1982, *Thriller* by Michael Jackson has racked up estimated sales of more than 66 million copies worldwide. On 16 Feb 2017, it received its 33rd platinum certificate from the Recording Industry Association of America (RIAA). This marked sales of 33 million units in Jackson's homeland, making *Thriller* the biggest-selling album in the USA.

Fastest-selling album (one country)
Adele's (UK) *25* sold 3,378,000 first-week copies in the USA to debut at No.1 on the *Billboard* 200 albums chart on 26 Nov 2015, according to Nielsen Music. No other album in history has sold as many copies in a single country during its first week of release.

The **fastest-selling album** is *1* by The Beatles (UK), which shifted 3.6 million copies on its first day of release – 13 Nov 2000 – and went on to sell 13.5 million copies around the world in its first month.

Highest-grossing music tour
The "360° Tour" by Irish band U2 grossed $736,137,344 (£465,350,113) from 110 shows staged between 30 Jun 2009 and 30 Jul 2011. More than 7 million fans witnessed the spectacle.

Largest simultaneous rock-concert attendance
On 2 Jul 2005, an estimated 1 million people attended concert venues in 10 cities around the world, including London, Philadelphia, Johannesburg and Moscow, for Live 8.

The **largest simultaneous rock-concert TV audience** is 1.9 billion people in 150 countries, who watched the dual-venue Live Aid charity concerts on 13 Jul 1985.

Most UK chart singles by a songwriter
Sir Paul McCartney (UK) has written or co-written 192 songs that have charted on the UK's Official Singles Chart since its launch. This total includes 32 hits with The Beatles (see right), 21 with Wings and 36 as a soloist or as part of a duo or group.

Highest annual earnings for a celebrity (ever)
Michael Jackson (USA, 1958–2009) earned $825 m (£636 m) in the year up to 1 Oct 2016, according to Forbes. The bulk of the "King of Pop"'s earnings came from the sale of Jackson's half of the Sony/ATV music publishing catalogue for $750 m (£521 m) in Mar 2016.

Highest annual earnings for a band (current year)
Rock group Coldplay (UK) earned an estimated $88 m (£68.5 m) in the 12 months to 1 Jun 2017, according to the Forbes "Celebrity 100" list. Their "A Head Full of Dreams Tour" visited five continents and earned the band in excess of $5 m (£3.8 m) for every city in which they played.

Longest-running group with no line-up changes (active)
Dusty Hill (vocals/bass, left), Billy Gibbons (vocals/guitar, above centre) and Frank Beard (drums, right) have been members of ZZ Top (USA) since 1969 – a total of 48 years, as of Jan 2018. Only Gibbons featured in the band's first line-up, which lasted less than a year. Famous for hits such as "Gimme All Your Lovin'", the hirsute rockers were inducted into the Rock & Roll Hall of Fame in 2004.

Most hits on the US Hot Country Songs chart by a female artist
In 2016, Dolly Parton (USA) scored her 107th entry on *Billboard*'s Hot Country Songs chart with a version of her 1974 hit "Jolene" with *a cappella* quintet Pentatonix. A living legend of country music, Dolly has also achieved the **most decades with a Top 20 hit on the US Hot Country Songs chart** – six consecutively (1960s–2010s).

SOUNDS FAMILIAR?

◄ Most remixed act
There are 324 remixes of songs by Madonna (USA). "Give It 2 Me" (2008), featuring Pharrell Williams, from her album *Hard Candy*, has received the remix treatment 17 times alone. House music DJ Eddie Amador's four versions ("Dub", "House Lovers Mix", "House Lovers Edit" and "Club") lead the way.

Most covered act
The songs of The Beatles (see opposite top) have been covered 4,136 times. "Yesterday" (1965) is the most popular choice for those looking to pay homage to the world-renowned quartet. The plaintive Lennon & McCartney ballad has been recorded by artists including Eva Cassidy, Marvin Gaye, Elvis Presley, Frank Sinatra... and Bugs Bunny & Daffy Duck!

◄ Most covered track
Jazz standard "Summertime", composed by George Gershwin (left) with lyrics by DuBose Heyward, was recorded by soprano Helen Jepson (all USA) for Gershwin's 1935 opera *Porgy and Bess*. This version has since been covered 214 times, by artists including Billie Holiday (1936), Miles Davis (1958), Paul McCartney (1988), Leona Lewis (2006) and Willie Nelson (2016).

ABBA
GOLD

Most weeks on the...
Official Albums Chart (UK):
Gold – Greatest Hits (1992) by ABBA (SWE) – 828 weeks, as of 22 Mar 2018

Official Singles Chart (UK):
"Mr Brightside" (2004) by The Killers (USA) – 200 weeks, as of 22 Mar 2018

Billboard Hot 100 – singles (USA):
"Radioactive" (2013) by Imagine Dragons (USA) – 87 weeks, up to 10 May 2014

Billboard 200 – albums (USA):
The Dark Side of the Moon (1973) by Pink Floyd (UK) – 937 weeks, as of 13 Jan 2018

GUINNESS WORLD RECORDS

ARTS & MEDIA

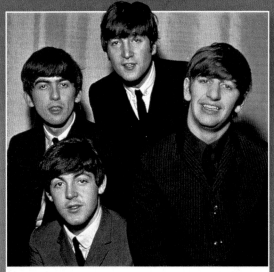

Best-selling group

All-time sales of records by The Beatles (UK) have been estimated by their record company EMI at more than 1 billion discs and tapes to date. On 8 Jun 2017, their classic album *Sgt. Pepper's Lonely Hearts Club Band* returned to No.1 a total of 49 years 125 days after it had previously topped the UK chart – the **longest time for an album to return to No.1 in the UK**.

In 2001, Elvis became the **first musical artist to be inducted into three different Halls of Fame:** Rock & Roll, Country Music and Gospel Music.

Best-selling female solo artist

Madonna (USA, b. Madonna Ciccone) has sold an estimated 335 million albums and singles (including digital tracks) since 1983. Her biggest-selling album is *The Immaculate Collection* (1990; c. 28.2 million copies sold), while five of her singles have sales in excess of 5 million. Only The Beatles, Elvis Presley and Michael Jackson are thought to have sold more records.

Best-selling solo artist

Elvis Presley (USA, 1935–77) has amassed 1 billion sales worldwide, according to his record label RCA. Known as "The King", Presley brought the sounds of rock and roll to the masses and remains a huge influence on popular music. As of 21 Mar 2018, he had earned 171 gold, 94 platinum and 34 multi-platinum discs from the Recording Industry Association of America – the **most RIAA certificates ever**.

◄ Most sampled act
The songs of James Brown (USA) have been sampled 7,094 times. "Funky Drummer" (1969), which first appeared on an album – *In the Jungle Groove* – some 17 years after it was written, is the most sampled. It has appeared on 1,440 tracks, from Public Enemy's "Fight the Power" to Ed Sheeran's "Shirtsleeves".

Most remixed track
"Dominator", a 1991 single by Human Resource (NLD), has been remixed a total of 41 times. C J Bolland, Vincent De Moor, Klubbheads and Armin Van Buuren have all worked their magic on the hardcore track. The band themselves produced three remixes of "Dominator" – "'96" and "Happy to the Core" in 1996, and "Human Resource Mix" in 2005.

► Most sampled track
Halfway through The Winstons' (USA) 1969 track "Amen, Brother" occurs a 6-sec drum solo performed by Gregory "G C" Coleman (far right in pic), dubbed the "Amen break". It has been sampled 2,835 times in a variety of music genres, and used by artists ranging from NWA to Lupe Fiasco, Oasis, Björk and Nine Inch Nails.

TV

Highest annual earnings for a television actor in a current series

Jim Parsons (USA), star of CBS sitcom *The Big Bang Theory* (in which he plays Sheldon Cooper), earned an estimated $27.5 m (£21.4 m) from 1 Jun 2016 to 1 Jun 2017, according to Forbes. He is the top-earning male TV actor for the third year running.

Highest annual earnings for a television actress in a current series

For the second year in a row, Sofía Vergara (COL), star of ABC's mockumentary sitcom *Modern Family*, was paid more than any other TV actress or actor. She earned $41.5 m (£32.3 m) in the 12 months to 1 Jun 2017, according to Forbes.

Most popular TV show worldwide (current)

According to Parrot Analytics, HBO's *Game of Thrones* (USA) drew 16.31 million average "demand expressions" in 2017. This evaluation takes into account various ways of interacting with TV shows, including blogging, social-media chatter and illegal pirating. The ratings are weighted: for example, a download is seen as a stronger indication of demand than a Facebook "like".

For the sixth year in a row, *Game of Thrones* was declared the **most pirated TV show** by download monitoring website TorrentFreak. One episode (the finale of season 7, aired on 27 Aug 2017) was shared on more than 400,000 torrents simultaneously.

Highest-rated TV series (current)

First aired on 16 Apr 2017, the third season of the HBO drama *The Leftovers* (USA) enjoyed a Metacritic rating of 98/100, and a user rating of 9.1/10, as of 19 Feb 2018. The Metacritic rating draws on the critiques of 17 professional reviewers, including those from *The Hollywood Reporter*, *The New York Times*, *Variety*, *Salon* and *New York* magazine.

Most Primetime Emmy Awards for a TV series

NBC's *Saturday Night Live* won a further nine Primetime Emmy Awards in 2017, taking its overall total to 59. Created by Lorne Michaels and developed by Dick Ebersol, the late-night comedy sketch show first aired in 1975.

Most subscriptions for a TV streaming service

TV- and film-streaming service Netflix (USA) has 117 million subscribers in 190 countries. It reputedly earmarked $8 bn (£5.6 bn, as of 29 Mar 2018) for productions in 2018.

Highest-paid TV host

According to Forbes, Dr Phil (aka Phil McGraw, USA) earned $79 m (£61.5 m) in the 12 months to 1 Jun 2017.

Based on the same period, Ellen DeGeneres (USA) is the **highest-paid female TV host**, with annual earnings of $77 m (£59.9 m), also based on estimates from Forbes.

Oldest TV continuity announcers

The UK's Channel Four (C4) employed three centenarian women as continuity announcers on 3 Feb 2018. Millie, Beattie and Margaret (all UK) were born in 1918, the year when most women over 30 were given the right to vote.

Longest TV career by an entertainer

Betty Marion White Ludden (aka Betty White, USA, b. 17 Jan 1922) debuted on TV in 1939 and still appears in hit shows 79 years later, aged 96 years 24 days as of 10 Feb 2018. Her most famous role is Rose Nylund in *The Golden Girls* (NBC, 1985–92).

The **longest TV career by an entertainer (male)** is 76 years, by the late Sir Bruce Forsyth (UK, 1928–2017) from 1939 to 2015.

Most successful cookery television format

MasterChef, produced by Endemol Shine (NLD), has been sold to 52 countries since its relaunch on 21 Feb 2005. The British version of the show is hosted by John Torode and Gregg Wallace (above, left and right), while Christina Tosi and Gordon Ramsay (left) present the US edition. The programme first ran in the UK from 1990 to 2001, hosted by Loyd Grossman, while *MasterChef USA* debuted in 2000, helmed by Gary Rhodes. Its variants include *Celebrity MasterChef* and *Junior MasterChef*.

First woman to play the Doctor in *Doctor Who*

Jodie Whittaker (UK) is the first female incarnation of Doctor Who in the hugely popular and long-running BBC sci-fi series of the same name. She became the 13th person to play the role on TV, debuting at the end of the 2017 Christmas Day special.

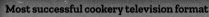

The original run of *Doctor Who* aired for 694 episodes consecutively across 26 seasons between 23 Nov 1963 and 6 Dec 1989 – the **most consecutive sci-fi TV episodes ever**.

LONGEST-RUNNING TV...

▲ **Chat show**
NBC's *The Tonight Show* first aired on 27 Sep 1954, hosted by Steve Allen (USA), and is still on air 64 years later, as of 2018. *The Tonight Show Starring Jimmy Fallon* has been helmed by the eponymous host since 2014. Fallon (USA) is shown above with then presidential candidate Donald Trump in Sep 2016.

Music talent show
Created by Japan's NHK (Nippon Hōsō Kyōkai), the first televised episode of *Nodo Jiman* ("Proud of My Voice") was broadcast on 15 Mar 1953. As of 8 Apr 2018 – 65 years later – the karaoke-based show was still running. Amateur singers perform for a minute and are then rated and given advice by industry experts. The winner is announced at the end of each programme.

◄ **Children's magazine programme**
Blue Peter (BBC, UK) – first transmitted from London's Lime Grove Studios on 16 Oct 1958 – marks 60 years on air in Oct 2018. Its longest-serving presenter was John Noakes (UK), who co-hosted the show from 1965 to 1978. Current presenters Lindsey Russell and Radzi Chinyanganya are seen here with GWR's Craig Glenday.

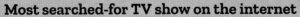

TV on Twitter
Based on data from US Twitter users, these shows attracted more tweets than any other streamed series in 2017.

1. Stranger Things 2 The search for Will is over, but the Upside Down still exerts a malevolent influence.

2. 13 Reasons Why A box of cassette tapes holds the secret to the 13 motivations that lie behind a teenager's death.

3. Orange is the New Black A riot, mock trial and talent show all feature in the fifth season of this comedy drama set in a women's prison.

Most searched-for TV show on the internet

For the second year running, the sci-fi horror series *Stranger Things* (Netflix) was searched for more frequently than any other television show. Created, written and directed by brothers Matt and Ross Duffer, it is set in the 1980s and regularly references pop culture of that period, notably the movies of Steven Spielberg and the creepy novels of Stephen King. Shown below, from left to right, are four of the young stars of the show: Noah Schnapp (USA), Finn Wolfhard (CAN), Gaten Matarazzo and Caleb McLaughlin (both USA).

An estimated 8.8 million people – similar to the size of the population of New York City, USA – saw *Stranger Things 2* within the first three days of its 27 Oct 2017 release on Netflix.

▼ Sketch show (current)

Sábados Felices, produced by Caracol Televisión (COL), premiered on 5 Feb 1972 and had run for 46 years 58 days as of 2 Apr 2018. It is also Colombia's longest-running TV show and has launched the careers of many of the country's comedians.

▲ Show with the same presenter

Astronomy programme *The Sky at Night* (BBC) was hosted by Patrick Moore (both UK) for 55 years, from its debut in 1957 until his death on 9 Dec 2012. The show's long list of guests included Buzz Aldrin and Neil Armstrong, the **first men on the Moon** (see p.23).

▶ Sports programme with the same host

Lo Mejor del Boxeo, hosted by Juan Carlos Tapia Rodríguez (PAN), premiered on 9 Jan 1975 and had run for 43 years 83 days as of 2 Apr 2018. The show has aired fights featuring many notable boxers, including Muhammad Ali and Floyd Mayweather Jr.

VIDEOGAMES

From the platform-hopping antics of Mario to the gritty underworld of *Grand Theft Auto*, videogames are big business. And as the number of platforms grows, determining the best-selling titles has become an increasingly complicated affair.

82.64 MILLION

WII SPORTS

As of 8 Jan 2018, Nintendo's five-game compendium had sold 82.64 million copies according to VGChartz, making it the game with the highest *recorded* sales and the **best-selling sports videogame**. It made its debut in 2006.

How do you define the most successful videogame? Is it the game with the highest recorded lifetime sales? In that case, the gong would fall to *Wii Sports* (see left), the Nintendo Wii pack-in game that had both young and old alike playing virtual tennis in living rooms across the planet. It has sold a massive 82.64 million copies according to VGChartz. However, this is small change in comparison to the ultimate pack-in game: *Tetris*.

The famous puzzler – perhaps best known for being the game that came bundled with the original Nintendo Game Boy way back in 1989 – is estimated to have sold a truly remarkable 170 million copies. But owing to the wide range of platforms that it's available for (which includes everything from arcade cabinets to smartphones), this figure can't be proven.

Of course, not every game is so fortunate as to be bundled with a popular console, so perhaps we should reserve our praise for games that can stand on their own two feet. The biggest seller that fits this criteria is *Pokémon Red and Blue* (1996). For those who've never ventured to "catch 'em all", these games are two nigh-on-identical (but separately sold) halves of Game Freak's original Pokémon game. According to VGChartz, they've sold a combined 31.37 million copies across the globe, making *Pokémon Red* and *Blue* the **best-selling game never bundled with a console**.

By now, *Minecraft* fans will be scratching their heads as to why the hugely popular building game has yet to be

GRAND THEFT AUTO V

Released on 17 Sep 2013, within three days this Rockstar game had become the **fastest entertainment property to gross $1 billion**. With 63.06 million copies sold as of 4 May 2018 according to VGChartz, it is also the **best-selling action-adventure videogame**.

SUPER MARIO BROS.

Having racked up sales of 40.24 million copies since 1985, this legendary Nintendo title is the **best-selling platform videogame**. Its enormous popularity helped seal the success of the NES console and saw Mario become an iconic character.

mentioned. The title has been released on every gaming platform under the Sun, selling 144 million copies along the way according to its creator, Mojang. But the lack of official PC-based sales figures means that we can't be certain exactly how many copies have been sold. Let's just agree that it's a lot.

Then there are gaming's highest-selling series. *Super Mario*, *The Legend of Zelda*, *Grand Theft Auto*, *Call of Duty* and *The Sims* are all household names, but which franchise boasts the most sales? Well, a big clue is that the owner of this particular record is jumping for joy on this very page. The *Super Mario* franchise has amassed a staggering 577 million sales since Mario first appeared in the classic 1981 platformer *Donkey Kong*.

One final way of measuring videogaming's success is to compare it to the rest of the entertainment industry. On 27–29 Apr 2018, *Avengers: Infinity War* (USA; see pp.180–81) achieved the **highest-grossing worldwide opening weekend for a film** – $640.3 m (£464.5 m). But even this figure is eclipsed by the $815.7 m (£511.8 m) taken by *Grand Theft Auto V* (2013) in just 24 hours – the **highest revenue generated by an entertainment product in one day**.

CALL OF DUTY: MODERN WARFARE 3

Unleashed in 2011, *Call of Duty: Modern Warfare 3* (Activision) had amassed global sales of 30.98 million as of 13 Nov 2017, making it the **best-selling first-person shooter (FPS) videogame**. The *Call of Duty* series dominates the FPS genre, boasting six of the all-time Top 10 best-sellers.

◀ Largest arcade machine
Built by Jason Camberis (USA), Arcade Deluxe measures 14 ft 5 in tall, 6 ft 4 in wide and 3 ft 5 in deep (4.39 x 1.93 x 1.04 m), as verified in Bensenville, Illinois, USA, on 23 Mar 2015. The machine plays more than 250 classic arcade games such as *PAC-Man*. The illuminated 40-cm (15.7-in) glass trackball had to be cut out by a bowling-ball company.

Largest Game Boy
Ilhan Ünal (BEL) built a Game Boy console measuring 3 ft 3.7 in tall, 2 ft 0.4 in wide and 7.8 in deep (1.01 x 0.62 x 0.2 m), as verified on 13 Nov 2016. The machine runs off a Raspberry Pi hidden in the external connector socket. It's more than six times the size of a regular Game Boy, but is fully capable of playing classic Nintendo titles, including *Pokémon Red/Blue* and *Tetris*.

Smallest Game Boy
A Game Boy hand-held console measuring just 54 mm (2.12 in) long was created by Jeroen Domburg (NLD) and measured in Shanghai, China, on 15 Dec 2016. The tiny device fits on a key chain and boasts an impressive selection of the original Game Boy games. Jeroen designed and built the console himself from minuscule components.

Largest official *Tetris* cabinet
Debuting in Japanese arcades in Dec 2009, *Tetris Giant* is the largest officially licensed version of the game. The cabinet measures 7 ft 2 in tall, 5 ft 2 in wide and 5 ft 6 in deep (2.2 x 1.6 x 1.7 m). *Tetris Giant* also boasts a pair of super-sized controller sticks and a 177-cm (5-ft 9-in) display. *Tetris* is the **most ported videogame**, available on at least 65 platforms.

144 MILLION COPIES SOLD

BEST-SELLING PC VIDEOGAME?

Guinness World Records sources its videogaming sales records from VGChartz, but PC digital downloads are not included in this data. In Jan 2018, *Minecraft* maker Mojang claimed total sales of 144 million for its blockbusting block-builder. While not independently verifiable, a significant proportion of these sales will have been PC-based. *Minecraft* achieved one million of its sales in its first five days, making it the **fastest-selling Xbox Live Arcade game**.

11,888,347,943 VIEWS

MOST VIEWS FOR A DEDICATED *MINECRAFT* CHANNEL

Launched on 14 Jul 2012, the "DanTDM" channel by Daniel Middleton (UK) had accrued a total of 11,888,347,943 views – and 17,526,286 subscribers – as of 19 Jan 2018. This also makes it the record holder for the **most viewed channel dedicated to a single videogame** and the overall holder for the **most viewed gaming channel on YouTube**.

3,280,569

LONGEST JOURNEY IN *MINECRAFT*

Since Mar 2011, Kurt J Mac (USA) has been travelling through the *Minecraft* realm towards the fabled Far Lands in aid of charity. As of 6 Mar 2018 – exactly seven years into his quest – he had walked 3,280,569 blocks (3,280.56 km; 2,038.44 mi).

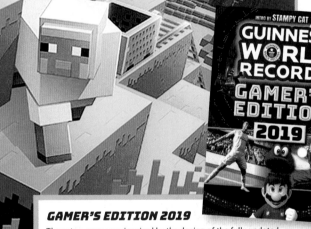

GAMER'S EDITION 2019

These two pages are inspired by the design of the fully updated *Guinness World Records Gamer's Edition 2019*, which is out now. It's packed with high scores, speed-runs, best-sellers and technical achievements from the world of videogaming. Also, look out for the special feature chapter dedicated to make-your-own games. For more, visit **www.guinnessworldrecords.com/gamers**.

◄ Largest joypad
A fully functional NES pad measuring 366 x 159 x 51 cm (12 ft x 5 ft 2.59 in x 1 ft 8 in) – 30 times the size of a standard controller – was verified in Aug 2011. It was created by engineering student Ben Allen, aided by Stephen van't Hof and Michel Verhulst, all of whom were students at the Delft University of Technology in the Netherlands.

► Smallest arcade machine
In 2009, computer engineer Mark Slevinsky (CAN) built a fully playable arcade machine measuring 124 x 52 x 60 mm (4.88 x 2.05 x 2.36 in). He wrote his own operating system, FunkOS, for his micro-"Markade" in order to program its *Tetris*, *Space Invaders* and *Breakout* clones. Mark's wife, Esther, painted the unit.

INSTAGRAM

First photograph uploaded

On 16 Jul 2010, Instagram's co-founder and CEO Kevin Systrom (USA) uploaded a picture of a golden retriever to the app, which was known as "Codename" at the time. The names of the dog and its owner are not known, but the foot in the picture belongs to Systrom's girlfriend. The photograph was taken at a taco stand named Tacos Chilakos in Todos Santos, on the Baja California peninsula in Mexico. The app was made available to the public in October that year, by which time it had been retitled "Instagram".

On 27 Jan 2011 – the day that Instagram introduced hashtags – Jennifer Lee (USA) added the tag #selfie to a photograph of herself that she had uploaded 11 days earlier, creating the **first hashtagged selfie**. To date, #selfie has been used some 329.4 million times.

First person with 100 million followers

On 25 Sep 2016, actress and singer Selena Gomez (USA) passed 100 million followers on Instagram. When her fans became aware that she was so close to the magical 100-million mark, they made a concerted effort to get the hashtag #SelenaBreakTheInternet trending.

Among her other Instagram achievements, Gomez has acquired the **most followers for a musician** and **most followers for an actress** (see right for more). Canadian singer Justin Bieber has attracted the **most followers for a musician (male)** – 98,336,586 to date.

Fastest time to gain 1 million followers

Under the handle @franciscus, Pope Francis (b. Jorge Mario Bergoglio, ARG) surpassed the 1-million-follower milestone just 12 hr after he joined Instagram on 19 Mar 2016. This halved the time taken by the previous record holder – retired footballer David Beckham (UK), who achieved 1 million followers in 24 hr on 2 May 2015. The Pope has attracted 5.3 million followers and made 536 posts.

Most popular hashtag (current)

As of Dec 2017, the most widely used hashtag on Instagram was #love (a perennially popular hashtag that has topped Instagram's end-of-year lists several times). The second-most popular was #fashion, followed by #photooftheday. The hashtag that had seen the greatest rise in popularity during the previous year was #photography, followed by #travelphotography and #memes respectively.

Biggest emoji user (country)

A study carried out in 2015 by researchers working for Instagram found that the country with the most prolific emoji users is Finland. The study analysed the content of text comments on the photo-sharing app and discovered that 63% of comments made by Finnish users contained one emoji or more. In second place was France, where the figure is 50%, followed by the UK on 48%, Germany on 47% and then Italy and Russia tied on 45%. Bottom of the table was Tanzania, on 10%.

Most Instagrammed location

Disneyland in Anaheim, California, USA, was the most popular location overall on photo-sharing app Instagram in 2017. In second and third place respectively were two sites in New York City, USA – Times Square and Central Park – with four other US locations in the top 10.

Most Instagrammed city

As of Dec 2017, New York City, USA, was the most popular metropolis on Instagram. The Russian capital, Moscow, was second on the list, with London, UK, taking third place. Overall, US and Russian cities represented almost half of all the conurbations that were geo-tagged on Instagram in 2017.

All figures as of 3 Apr 2018, unless otherwise stated

Most followers

The most popular person on Instagram is Selena Gomez, who has amassed 135,458,041 followers on the social network to date. The only account that surpasses hers is that of Instagram itself, which has built up 233,898,533 followers.

Real Madrid footballer Cristiano Ronaldo (PRT) has the **most followers (male)**, with 123,328,883. His closest rival is "The Rock" (see below).

First Instagram from space

On 7 Apr 2014, NASA astronaut Steve Swanson (USA) posted on Instagram from orbit around Earth. Swanson sent the message "Back on ISS, life is good" from the *International Space Station*, while posing in a T-shirt that referenced the cult US TV sci-fi show *Firefly*.

MOST INSTAGRAM FOLLOWERS FOR...

◀ An athlete (female)
No female sportsperson has more fans on the image-sharing network than World Wrestling Entertainment (WWE) superstar Ronda Rousey (@rondarousey, USA), with 10,135,847 followers. This put her considerably ahead of her nearest rival female athlete, US tennis star Serena Williams (@serenawilliams), with 7,893,232 followers.

An actor
"The Rock" (aka Dwayne Johnson; @therock, USA) has amassed a total of 102,677,668 followers on Instagram. A semi-retired pro wrestler, he has appeared in movies such as *Snitch* (USA/UAE, 2013), *Hercules* (USA, 2014), *Moana* (USA, 2016; a voice-only role) and *Rampage* (USA, 2018) along with several entries in the lucrative franchise Fast & Furious.

◀ A pig
Miniature pig Priscilla (@prissy_pig) has 690,516 followers on Instagram, making her page the most popular for a pig. Priscilla shares the profile with fellow pigs Poppleton (aka Pop), Primrose and Pinkerton. The porcine quartet live in Ponte Vedra Beach, Florida, USA, with their owner, Melissa Nicholson.

A snapshot of Instagram

Every day, around 500 million active users take to Instagram, sharing 300 million stories and uploading approximately 95 million photos.*

Number of monthly active users: **800 million**

Number of photos shared to date: **40 billion**

Number of daily likes: **4.2 billion**

* as of Dec 2017

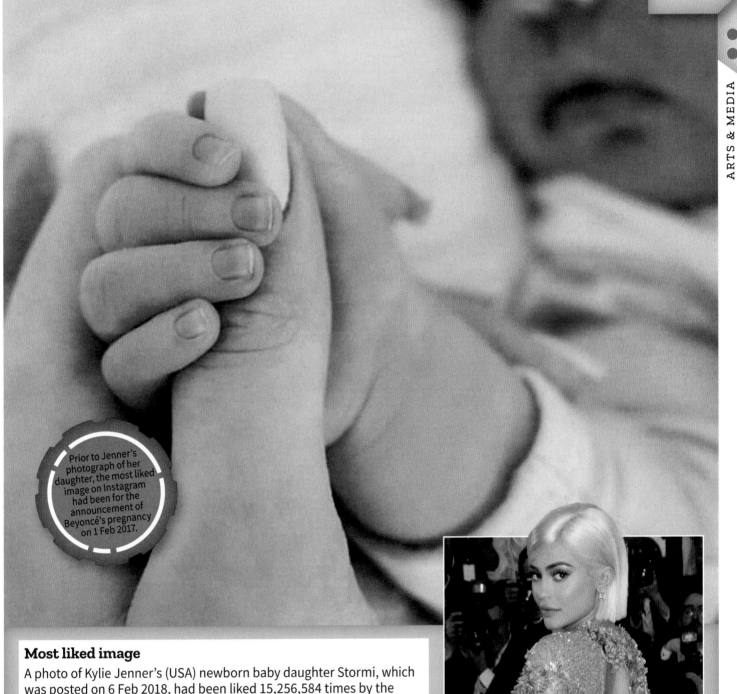

Prior to Jenner's photograph of her daughter, the most liked image on Instagram had been for the announcement of Beyoncé's pregnancy on 1 Feb 2017.

Most liked image

A photo of Kylie Jenner's (USA) newborn baby daughter Stormi, which was posted on 6 Feb 2018, had been liked 15,256,584 times by the following day. The picture shows the infant girl, who was born on 1 Feb 2018, holding on to her mother's thumb. To date, the three most liked Instagram images are connected with Stormi.

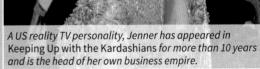

A US reality TV personality, Jenner has appeared in Keeping Up with the Kardashians *for more than 10 years and is the head of her own business empire.*

▲ A music group

Despite being on a career break, One Direction (@onedirection, UK/IRL) have 17,229,071 followers on Instagram, more than any other band. Former member Zayn Malik (@zayn) has 27,712,098 followers on his own account.

▼ A sports team

In the off-pitch battle for Instagram fans, Spain's Real Madrid (@realmadrid) comes top of the league with 56,661,661 followers. Real Madrid's closest competitors are arch rivals FC Barcelona (@fcbarcelona), with 55,793,211 followers.

▶ A videogame cosplayer

Cosplayer and gamer Jessica Nigri (@jessicanigri, USA) has 2,895,679 Instagram followers. Jessica has cosplayed a range of gaming characters, as well as providing the voice for the manga and game character Super Sonico.

TWITTER

First tweet
Twitter was invented by Jack Dorsey (USA) in 2006 as a microblogging and social-networking tool. The first tweet was posted by Dorsey at 9:50 p.m. Pacific Standard Time on 21 Mar 2006, and read "just setting up my twttr". On 23 Jan 2013, Twitter CEO Dick Costolo (USA) posted the **first video tweet**. It showed him making steak tartare.

First live tweet from space
On 22 Jan 2010, NASA astronaut Timothy J Creamer (USA) tweeted directly from space for the first time. He posted the following message: "Hello Twitterverse! We r now LIVE tweeting from the International Space Station -- the 1st live tweet from Space! :) More soon, send your ?s".

First Pope with an account
Pope Benedict XVI (aka Joseph Aloisius Ratzinger, DEU) became the first Holy Father to sign up to Twitter. Using the handle @Pontifex (Latin for "bridge builder"), he tweeted his first message on 12 Dec 2012. It read: "Dear friends, I am pleased to get in touch with you through Twitter. Thank you for your generous response. I bless all of you from my heart."

Most liked message
A tweet by former US President Barack Obama has received 4,586,103 likes. In the wake of racially charged unrest in Charlottesville, Virginia, USA, Obama quoted the former South African president Nelson Mandela: "No one is born hating another person because of the color of his skin or his background or his religion..."
Obama is the third most popular person on Twitter, and has the **most followers for a politician** – 101,971,379.

Most discussed sporting event
The 2014 FIFA World Cup prompted 672 million tweets. The semi-final match between hosts Brazil and Germany (which Germany won 7–1) attracted 35.6 million tweets, more than any other game. Although the final between Germany and Argentina resulted in fewer tweets, its peak rate of 618,725 per minute is the **most tweets per minute**.

Most engagements (average retweets)
South Korean boy band BTS (@BTS_twt) have registered 330,624 engagements on Twitter. The septet's alternative Twitter accounts – @bts_bighit and @bts_love_myself – had amassed 93,522 and 88,281 engagements, respectively. They overtook One Direction's Harry Styles (@Harry_Styles), who had 147,653 engagements as of the same date.

Oldest user (ever)
Born on 8 Sep 1905, Ivy Bean (UK) was 104 years 323 days old when she died on 28 Jul 2010. She had signed up to Twitter in May 2009 and went on to post more than 1,000 tweets to some 56,000 followers before she passed away.

Most followed dedicated videogame character
The "personal" Twitter account belonging to the robot Claptrap (@ECHOcasts) from 2K's *Borderlands* series has 123,390 followers – the most for a specific videogame character. Despite his name, Claptrap has kept fairly quiet – he's tweeted only once since 2 Apr 2015.

Most followed videogame
The official account for EA's soccer sim series *FIFA* (@EASPORTSFIFA) has 6,408,784 followers – making it the sixth most followed videogaming account overall, and the most for a specific game. It was top of the table above *League of Legends* (4,480,928), *Assassin's Creed* (4,265,063) and *Call of Duty* (3,555,586).

All figures as of 23 Apr 2018, unless otherwise stated

Most retweeted message
In the hope of securing a year's supply of Wendy's chicken nuggets, 16-year-old Carter Wilkerson (USA) attempted to get 18 million retweets in 2017. With the help of some famous names, he managed 3,651,498, overtaking Ellen DeGeneres's famous Oscar selfie for the most retweets of a message and earning Carter his "nuggs".

Fastest time to reach 1 million followers
On 1 Jun 2015, reality TV star Caitlyn Jenner (USA) reached 1 million Twitter followers in the space of just 4 hr 3 min. The first tweet on Caitlyn's page, picturing her appearance on the cover of *Vanity Fair* (above), was posted at 12:17 p.m. Eastern Standard Time (EST). Her account passed the million-follower mark at 4:20 p.m. EST.

MOST FOLLOWERS FOR...

◄ An entrepreneur
Microsoft co-founder Bill Gates (@BillGates, USA) has 45,846,749 followers, making his account the 21st most popular on Twitter. Although President Donald Trump has more than 51 million followers, he gained the majority of these after embarking upon his political career.

▲ An actor (male)
Best known for his roles in movies such as *Ride Along* (USA, 2014) and *Jumanji: Welcome to the Jungle* (USA, 2017), US actor and comedian Kevin Hart (@KevinHart4real) has 35,188,999 followers.

► An actress
The most followers for a female with a substantial history of acting roles is 56,516,652, for Selena Gomez (@selenagomez, USA). Gomez is a hugely popular figure on social media, also boasting the **most followers on Instagram** (see p.194).

Tweet all about it...
Twitter can handle 18 quintillion accounts. A total of 83% of UN member countries have an official presence on the site.

Monthly active users: 330 million

Tweets sent per day: 500 million

80%

Percentage of Twitter users on mobile phone: 80%

Figures from OmnicoreAgency.com

GUINNESS WORLD RECORDS

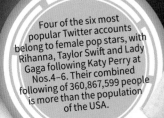

Four of the six most popular Twitter accounts belong to female pop stars, with Rihanna, Taylor Swift and Lady Gaga following Katy Perry at Nos.4–6. Their combined following of 360,867,599 people is more than the population of the USA.

Most followers

Pop star and actor Katy Perry (b. Katheryn Hudson, USA) has 109,330,720 followers on Twitter. On 16 Jun 2017, the site announced that she had become the **first user to reach 100 million followers**. Perry has been active on the site since Feb 2009, and has posted more than 9,000 tweets. She follows just 212 accounts, giving her a staggering follower-to-following ratio of 515,710.

Most followers (male)
Pop phenomenon Justin Bieber (CAN) has 106,280,929 followers, the second-highest overall on the site behind Katy Perry. He joined in Mar 2009, and has posted more than 30,000 tweets. Bieber follows 315,022 accounts, giving him a follower-to-following ratio of 337.37.

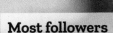

◀ **A fashion personality**
Model and reality TV star Kim Kardashian West (@KimKardashian, USA) has 59,721,292 Twitter followers, making her the 12th most followed person on the platform. Kardashian West joined in Mar 2009, and has posted in excess of 26,000 tweets.

▲ **A DJ**
Known as the "Grandfather of EDM" (electronic dance music), David Guetta (@davidguetta, FRA) has 22,205,936 followers – ahead of Calvin Harris (@CalvinHarris), who has 13,329,541.

▶ **An athlete (female)**
Tennis player and 23-time Grand Slam winner Serena Williams (@serenawilliams, USA) has 10,895,119 followers. She has posted more than 14,000 tweets. Williams is also the second most followed female athlete on Instagram (see p.194).

YOUTUBE

Most liked videogame video on YouTube
When EA published its "Official Reveal Trailer" for the World War I-set *Battlefield 1* on 6 May 2016, it sparked unprecedented celebrations for a gaming video. In just four days, the trailer had received 1.9 million likes. Those likes now total 2,194,348.

Most watched movie trailer (official)
The movie trailer for Marvel Studios' *Avengers: Infinity War* (USA, 2018 – see pp.180-81) was published on YouTube on 29 Nov 2017. It has now been watched 170,206,979 times. The next-highest total is 101,387,836, for *Star Wars VII: The Force Awakens* (USA, 2015).

All figures as of 24 Apr 2018, unless otherwise stated

First video uploaded
On 23 Apr 2005, an 18-sec clip entitled "Me at the zoo" by YouTube co-founder Jawed Karim (USA, b. DEU) became the video-sharing website's first upload. As of 27 Mar 2018, it had been viewed 47,228,525 times.

Most searched-for keyword
The keyword "music" had attracted some 789 million searches on YouTube as of Sep 2017. "Songs" was in second place, with 453 million searches, followed by "Minecraft", with 83.4 million.

Most subscribers
"PewDiePie" – aka Felix Arvid Ulf Kjellberg (SWE) – has 62,295,689 subscribers. He is a games reviewer who posts over-the-top commentaries as he plays, as well as occasionally controversial comedy sketches. His videos have received 17,631,722,806 views, with the most popular, "A Funny Montage", earning more than 80 million on its own.

On 8 Dec 2016, "PewDiePie" became the **first YouTuber to reach 50 million subscribers**.

Fastest time for a video to reach 1 billion views
Uploaded to YouTube on 22 Oct 2015, the music video for "Hello" by Adele (UK) reached 1 billion views on 17 Jan 2016 – a period of just 87 days. She beat the mark of 158 days set by PSY's international smash "Gangnam Style" in 2012.

MOST VIEWED...

Animal video
Uploaded on 1 May 2011, "Ultimate Dog Tease" – starring a German shepherd called Clarke and Andrew Grantham (CAN), the creator of the "Talking Animals" YouTube channel – has been viewed 192,347,992 times.

Cartoon/animated movie video
"Masha and the Bear: Recipe for Disaster (Episode 17)" has logged 2,995,219,745 views. Produced by Animaccord Animation Studio, the cartoon was uploaded by Get Movies (both RUS) on 31 Jan 2012. *Masha and the Bear* is a children's TV series starring a mischievous child and a retired circus bear called Mishka ("Bear" in Russian).

Gaming video
Uploaded by Denmark's KilooGames in 2012, "Subway Surfers – Official Google Play Trailer" has amassed 358,761,216 views. The video for the mobile game is also the **most viewed trailer**, eclipsing its movie rivals (see left).

Channel for a music group
The YouTube channel for Maroon 5 (USA), "Maroon5VEVO", has registered 9,035,970,802 video views. The group's most popular video is for their single "Sugar", with more than 2.5 billion views.

Most viewed video online
On 4 Apr 2018, the video for the original Spanish-language version of the track "Despacito" – starring Luis Fonsi (b. Luis Alfonso López-Cepero, above right), Daddy Yankee (b. Ramón Rodríguez, above left) and Miss Universe 2006, Zuleyka Rivera (all PRI) – became the **first YouTube video to receive 5 billion views**. It had become the most watched clip in YouTube's history on 3 Aug 2017, the same day it passed the 3-billion-view mark.

Channel for a "post-post-millennial"
"Ryan ToysReview" has been viewed 21,120,857,370 times since launching on 16 Mar 2015, making it the most watched YouTube channel for someone born in 2010 or later (a "post-post-millennial", aka "Generation Alpha"). Seven-year-old Ryan (USA, b. 6 Oct 2010) uploads videos of himself playing with and reviewing toys and games. As of the same date, the channel had amassed 13,499,980 subscribers.

First YouTuber to gain 1 million subscribers
Lucas Cruikshank's (USA) "Fred" channel reached 1 million subscribers in Apr 2009. It centred on the comic exploits of character Fred Figglehorn, a six-year-old boy with a high-pitched voice. The first episode, "Fred on Halloween", was uploaded on 30 Oct 2006. As of 28 Mar 2018, the episode "Fred Goes Grocery Shopping feat. Annoying Orange" (inset) had amassed 85,132,180 views.

MOST SUBSCRIBERS FOR A...

▲ **Musician (male)**
34,594,144, for the VEVO channel of Justin Bieber (CAN)

▲ **Musician (female)**
28,506,973, for the VEVO channel of Taylor Swift (USA)

▲ **Gaming channel**
27,659,478, for "Fernanfloo" (aka Luis Fernando Flores Alvarado, SLV)

▲ **TV show**
24,793,504, for "TheEllenShow", hosted by Ellen DeGeneres (USA)

YouTube by the numbers
In Jun 2017, YouTube announced that it had 1.5 billion monthly active users, making it the **largest video-sharing website**.

Daily active users:
More than 30 million, as of 24 Jan 2018

Videos shared to date:
More than 5 billion, as of 24 Jan 2018

Videos uploaded per minute:
300 hr worth, as of 24 Jan 2018

GUINNESS WORLD RECORDS

Highest-earning YouTube contributor

As of Dec 2017, Forbes estimated that "DanTDM" (aka Daniel Middleton, UK) had earned something in the range of $16.5 m (£12.2 m) in a year from his YouTube videos. Formerly known as "TheDiamondMinecart", he launched his *Minecraft*-based YouTube channel on 14 Jul 2012, since when it has attracted more than 11 billion views. Dan has gone on to tour the world, selling out shows at the Sydney Opera House in Australia.

"MOM STEALS MY COMPUTER!! | YouTuber's Life #2" (see inset above) by "DanTDM" is the **most viewed *YouTubers Life* video on YouTube**. As of 12 Mar 2018, Dan's attempts to recreate his online fame in the life sim had gained 7,380,703 views.

▲ **Fail video channel**
13,640,876, for "FailArmy", produced by Jukin Media (USA)

▲ **Science channel**
13,191,372, for "Vsauce", hosted by Michael Stevens (USA)

▲ **Animal**
1,390,272, for Maymo the lemon Beagle, based in the USA

▲ **Cat**
743,442, for Nylah the silver savannah cat, based in the USA

ROUND-UP

Largest snow painting
Tonghua Wine Industry Development and Promotion Center (CHN) produced a 2,221.74-m² (23,914.61-sq-ft) snow painting in Tonghua, Jilin, China, on 20 Jan 2018. The artwork measured 59.95 x 37.06 m (196 ft 8 in x 121 ft 7 in). It took 23 workers three days and nights to finish the piece on the frozen surface of the Hunjiang River.

Longest music composition
"Longplayer" is a 1,000-year-long piece of music written by banjo player Jem Finer (UK), a member of punk-folk band The Pogues. Finer uses a bank of computers at Trinity Buoy Wharf Lighthouse in London, UK, to sequence simultaneous combinations of parts from six short pieces that he composed, played on Tibetan singing bowls. The composition was started as the clocks moved in to the new millennium on 1 Jan 2000, and will not repeat the same combination of music until the last second of 31 Dec 2999, when the piece can start its second rendition.

As of 27 Feb 2018, "Longplayer" had been playing for 18 years 57 days of its 1,000-year projected run, which also makes it the **longest music recital**.

Most ship horns in a piece of music
On 22 Jun 2013, a total of 55 ships gathered in the North Sea to perform a musical score entitled the "Foghorn Requiem". It was written by artists Lise Autogena (DNK) and Joshua Portway in conjunction with composer Orlando Gough (both UK) to mark the end of the use of foghorns in the UK. The "Foghorn Requiem" was played by three brass bands, the 55 ships at sea and the Souter Lighthouse foghorn – the last one in the UK to sound off before being decommissioned. The piece was "conducted" by computers connected to each ship's GPS.

Largest bust sculpture
Isha Foundation (IND) erected a 34.24-m-tall (112-ft 4-in), 24.99-m-wide (81-ft 11.8-in), 44.9-m-long (147-ft 3.7-in) sculpture in Tamil Nadu, India, as verified on 11 Mar 2017. The bust depicts Adiyogi Shiva – the name refers to the fact that, in yoga practice, the Hindu god Shiva is known as the first yogi.

Largest animal sound archive
As of Sep 2017, the Macaulay Library at the Cornell Lab of Ornithology in New York, USA, had 279,106 recordings of more than 9,000 species in an online searchable database. The sound archive takes up 10 terabytes of storage, with a running time of 7,513 hr. Begun in 1929, it holds recordings of approximately three-quarters of all bird species. The archive also stores audio of whales, insects, bears, elephants, primates and nearly every other animal on Earth.

Most Laurence Olivier Award nominations for a show
On 6 Mar 2018, *Hamilton* – with music, lyrics and book by Lin-Manuel Miranda (USA) – was nominated for an unprecedented 13 Laurence Olivier Awards. The show's nominations included one for Best New Musical, one for Best Director and six in the musical acting categories. It went on to win seven awards, only two fewer than *Harry Potter and the Cursed Child* in 2017 – the **most Laurence Olivier award wins**.

Most Tony Awards won by a musical
The Producers picked up 12 Tony Awards from 15 nominations, including Best Musical, on 3 Jun 2001. Directed by Susan Stroman (USA), and starring Matthew Broderick and Nathan Lane (both USA), it broke the record of 10 wins, held by *Hello, Dolly!* since 1964.

The **most Tony Award nominations for a musical** is 16, achieved by *Hamilton* – playing at the Richard Rodgers Theatre in New York City, USA – on 3 May 2016.

Largest flute
On 25 Dec 2014, Bharat Sinh Parmar, Charunsudan Atri Jay Bhayani and Shri 5 Navtanpuri Dham temple (all IND) presented a 3.63-m-long (11-ft 11-in), fully playable flute in Jamnagar, India. The instrument was then played in a public performance of the Indian national anthem.

Oldest videogame music composer
Japan's Koichi Sugiyama (b. 11 Apr 1931) was aged 86 years 109 days as of 29 Jul 2017, when the videogame *Dragon Quest XI* (Square Enix) was released for the Nintendo 3DS and PlayStation 4.

Most followers on Weibo
One of the largest of China's social media and micro-blogging sites, Weibo boasts 340 million active monthly users, making it larger than Twitter. The most popular contributor is the Chinese TV host, singer and actress Xie Na, with 100,396,561 followers as of 9 Apr 2018. She is also the **first person to accumulate 100 million users on Weibo**.

While Xie Na is the **most followed female on Weibo**, the **most followed male on Weibo** is He Jiong (CHN), with 92,686,353 fans as of the same date.

Most popular Snapchat name (music)

Snoop Dogg (USA; @snoopdogg213) was the most popular musician on social-media platform Snapchat as of 1 Mar 2018. Born Calvin Cordozar Broadus Jr, the rapper/singer/record producer/actor was followed by Thirty Seconds to Mars frontman and actor Jared Leto and DJ Khaled. Music station MTV and hip-hop artist Schoolboy Q completed the Top 5.

105,000 glasses filled with coloured water in Guatemala City, Guatemala, on 10 Sep 2017. It depicted the pyramid of Tikal and two Guatemalan national symbols: the quetzal bird and the orchid *Lycaste skinneri alba*.

Day of the Dead altar

On 28 Oct 2017, the government of the state of Hidalgo in Mexico presented an 846.48-m² (9,111.43-sq-ft) altar for the Day of the Dead holiday in the city of Pachuca. It took four weeks and more than 1,000 volunteers to create the altar, which is decorated with 9,200 cempasúchil flowers and filled with an array of sugar skulls, candles, flags and skeletons dressed in traditional Mexican clothing.

LED cinema screen

Produced by Samsung Electronics (KOR), the Lotte Cinema Super S Screen in the Lotte World Tower in Seoul, South Korea, measures 55.296 m² (595.2 sq ft).

Highest-grossing year on Broadway

According to The Broadway League, the most lucrative year for theatres on Broadway in New York City, USA, was 2017, with $1.637 bn (£1.213 bn) earned in ticket sales from 13.736 million attendees. The **highest-grossing week on Broadway** was the final week of the year ($50.3 m; £37.2 m), and the **highest single-week box-office gross** came courtesy of *Hamilton* (centre), which took $3.85 m (£2.85 m) that same week. Other successful shows in 2017 included *Waitress* (left) and *Springsteen on Broadway* (right).

Light-and-sound show on a single building

On 1 Jan 2018, Emaar Properties PJSC (UAE) staged a 109,252-m² (1,175,978-sq-ft) mixed-media show at the Burj Khalifa – the **tallest building**, at 828 m (2,716 ft 6 in) – in Dubai, UAE. It was part of a New Year's Eve show combining lighting, projections, lasers, an LED screen, sound and fountains.

Papier-mâché sculpture

The National Chamber of Commerce of Guadalajara (MEX) created a papier-mâché model of a mariachi musician that measured 3.82 m (12 ft 6.39 in) tall, 3.46 m (11 ft 4.22 in) long and 1.15 m (3 ft 9.27 in) wide. The sculpture was presented at the XXIV International Mariachi and Charrería Festival in Guadalajara, Jalisco, Mexico, on 25 Aug 2017.

Most short films produced

Epiphany Morgan and Carl Mason (both AUS) made 365 short movies in 70 cities, as verified on 7 Jun 2016. As part of their project entitled "365 docobites", the pair travelled across five continents in a year. Their goal was to introduce the world to a "stranger a day" via bite-sized documentaries.

LARGEST...

Coloured-water mosaic

YUS de Toki (GTM) unveiled a 603.47-m² (6,495.69-sq-ft) mosaic made from around

Most expensive painting sold at auction

Salvator Mundi by Leonardo da Vinci sold for $450,312,500 (£343,033,000; €383,867,000), including buyer's premium, at an auction held by Christie's in New York City, USA, on 15 Nov 2017. More than 1,000 art collectors, advisors, dealers and journalists were present at the auction, with thousands more tuned in via a live stream. There's still speculation over the painting's origins, with some specialists arguing that the work should be attributed to one of da Vinci's apprentices.

It is possible that da Vinci originally painted *Salvator Mundi* for the French royal family, but it was to be owned by a range of collectors over the centuries. The work went missing altogether from 1763 until 1900, when it was bought by a British collector.

MILLENNIUM FALCON

Initially christened a "piece of junk" by Luke Skywalker, the modified YT-1300 Corellian light freighter from *Star Wars Episode IV: A New Hope* (USA, 1977) – better known as the *Millennium Falcon* – went on to become one of the most beloved vehicles in cinema history. In 2017, LEGO® celebrated Han Solo's smuggling ship with its largest set to date, boasting more than 7,500 pieces.

SECRET SHIP

Only one full-scale version of the *Millennium Falcon* was ever constructed for the Star Wars films. It was built over three months in 1979 for *The Empire Strikes Back* in a hangar in Pembroke Dock, UK. The secret project was codenamed "The Magic Roundabout".

The *Millennium Falcon* is a cargo-transportation ship made by the Corellian Engineering Corporation and helmed by smuggler Han Solo and his Wookiee first mate, Chewbacca. It has appeared in six Star Wars films in total, including a brief cameo in *Revenge of the Sith*, playing a key role in the Rebels' fight against the Empire. The *Falcon* owes its design to effects artist Joe Johnston, who created it in just four weeks after the original model was deemed too close to the *Eagle Transporter* in the TV show *Space: 1999*. (A modified version of this craft would go on to be used as *Tantive IV*, Princess Leia's ship.) With its offset cockpit and cargo mandibles, the *Millennium Falcon* is an iconic landmark in movie-effects design.

FALCON'S BLUEPRINT

In 2017, a set of recently discovered blueprints from the Star Wars and Star Trek films went up for auction. They included a detailed schematic of the *Millennium Falcon* for *The Empire Strikes Back* (USA, 1980), detailing the interior and exterior of the smuggling ship. Other original designs from the series include Darth Vader's meditation pod and Chewbacca and Princess Leia's handcuffs.

"LET THE WOOKIEE WIN"

The LEGO *Millennium Falcon*'s main hold contains an engineering station and seating area. Fans will recognize the iconic circular Dejarik board (above, left), where Chewbacca and R2-D2 do battle with 6-in (15-cm) holographic fighters in *A New Hope*. The kit contains Minifigures both from the classic original trilogy (above, right) and more recent characters such as Rey and Finn.

The ship's cockpit is offset to provide the pilot with a clear view when cargo is being transported in the front mandibles

DID YOU KNOW?

In May 2013, LEGO unveiled a 1:1 scale model of a Star Wars X-wing starfighter in Times Square in New York City, USA. It comprised a total of 5,335,200 bricks, making it the **largest LEGO Star Wars sculpture (number of bricks) with internal support structure**. It had a wingspan of 44 ft (13.4 m) and weighed 45,979.61 lb (20,856 kg), including the supporting steel structure.

The LEGO set contains interchangeable sensor dishes, allowing builders to recreate the original Falcon or the slight variation that appeared in Episodes VII and VIII

FOR THE RECORD

The **largest commercially available LEGO set** is the 7,541-piece *Millennium Falcon* (set number 75192), which was launched by the Danish toy manufacturer at one minute to midnight on 13 Sep 2017. When completed, the Star Wars spacecraft model measures more than 8 in (20 cm) high, 2 ft 9 in (84 cm) long and 1 ft 10 in (56 cm) wide.

LEGO has released various versions of the *Falcon*. Its previous set – part of the Star Wars "Ultimate Collector's Series" – contained 5,195 pieces and was itself the largest set upon its release in 2007, until it was beaten by the 5,922-piece Taj Mahal in 2008.

The front mandibles were designed to grip cargo for transportation

SPORTS

Youngest snowboarding gold medallist at a Winter Olympics (female)

Chloe Kim (USA, b. 23 Apr 2000) won the Winter Olympic women's halfpipe on 13 Feb 2018 aged 17 years 296 days. On her final run at Phoenix Park in Pyeongchang, South Korea, she landed back-to-back 1080s to record her highest score of 98.25 – 8.5 points ahead of the rest of the field. Kim, who was unable to compete at Sochi 2014 owing to age restrictions, is also the **youngest X Games triple gold medallist** – achieved aged 15 years 309 days in 2016.

CONTENTS

GUINNESS WORLD RECORDS

SPORTS

PyeongChang 2018

1

Chloe Kim first landed back-to-back 1080s in competition during her final run at the US Grand Prix on 6 Feb 2016. They helped her earn the **first score of 100 in women's halfpipe**.

AMERICAN FOOTBALL

Most Grey Cup wins in the Canadian Football League (CFL)

The Toronto Argonauts claimed their 17th Grey Cup in 2017, defeating the Calgary Stampeders (both CAN) 27–24 in the CFL championship game on 26 Nov. It was a fourth win for quarterback Ricky Ray – the **most Grey Cup victories by a starting quarterback**.

All teams and players USA, unless otherwise indicated.

Most 500-yard passing games in the National Football League (NFL)

Quarterback Ben Roethlisberger of the Pittsburgh Steelers has thrown three 500-yard passing games: against the Green Bay Packers on 20 Dec 2009, the Indianapolis Colts on 26 Oct 2014 and the Baltimore Ravens on 10 Dec 2017.

Highest pass completion percentage in an NFL season

In 2017, New Orleans Saints quarterback Drew Brees completed 386 of 536 attempted passes – 72%. He beat Sam Bradford's 2016 mark of 71.6%.

First player to throw and catch a touchdown in a Super Bowl

Quarterback Nick Foles turned receiver during the Philadelphia Eagles' 41–33 Super Bowl win on 4 Feb 2018, catching a pass from tight end Trey Burton to score. He also completed three passing touchdowns, and was named Super Bowl MVP.

Most consecutive NFL 50-yard field goals

Stephen Hauschka converted 13 consecutive field goals of 50 yards or more for the Seattle Seahawks and Buffalo Bills between 2014 and 2017. Hauschka connected on a 50-yard attempt against the Los Angeles Chargers on 19 Nov 2017, breaking the previous record of 12 in a row from that distance that he had shared with Blair Walsh, Robbie Gould, Justin Tucker and Matt Prater.

Longest field goal in NFL postseason

On 7 Jan 2018, Graham Gano (UK) kicked a 58-yard field goal for the Carolina Panthers during a 31–26 defeat against the New Orleans Saints in an NFL wild-card playoff game. He matched the feat of Pete Stoyanovich, who kicked a 58-yard field goal for the Miami Dolphins against the Kansas City Chiefs on 5 Jan 1991.

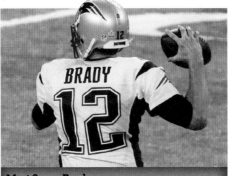

Most Super Bowl appearances by a quarterback

Tom Brady appeared in eight Super Bowls for the New England Patriots from 2001 to 2018. His 37 postseason starts constitute the **most career NFL postseason appearances**.

On 4 Feb 2018, Brady achieved the **most yards gained passing in a Super Bowl** – 505 – in a losing cause (see below). He also increased his record for the **most Super Bowl touchdown passes** to 18.

Most consecutive seasons for an NFL player to make 100 receptions

The Pittsburgh Steelers' Antonio Brown completed his fifth straight season making at least 100 receptions in 2017. Brown, the highest-paid wide receiver in the NFL, surpassed the previous best of four, by Marvin Harrison for the Indianapolis Colts in 1999–2002.

Most NFL career touchdowns by a tight end

Antonio Gates scored 114 touchdowns for the San Diego/Los Angeles Chargers from 2003 to 2017. The 37-year-old moved one clear of Tony Gonzalez with his score in the third quarter of the Chargers' 19–17 loss to the Miami Dolphins on 17 Sep 2017.

Most yards from scrimmage in a player's first NFL game

On 7 Sep 2017, rookie running back Kareem Hunt compiled 246 yards playing for the Kansas City Chiefs in their 42–27 win over the New England Patriots. He went for 148 yards rushing and 98 receiving.

Most team losses in an NFL season

The Cleveland Browns equalled an unwanted record in 2017, finishing the season with 16 defeats and no victories. The only other team to end up with a 0–16 season record in the NFL was the Detroit Lions, in 2008.

Most Super Bowl appearances by a team

In 2018, the New England Patriots appeared in their 10th Super Bowl since 1986. They have won five and lost five – the **most Super Bowl defeats**, shared with the Denver Broncos.

The **most Super Bowl victories** is six, achieved by the Pittsburgh Steelers in 1975–76, 1979–80, 2006 and 2009.

Most all-purpose yards in a CFL game

Diontae Spencer recorded 496 all-purpose yards for the Ottawa Redblacks during a 41–36 victory over the Hamilton Tiger-Cats (both CAN) on 28 Oct 2017. Spencer amassed 133 receiving yards, 165 yards on kickoff returns, 169 yards on punt returns and 29 yards on a missed field goal return.

Most combined total yards in an NFL game (both teams)

Super Bowl LII on 4 Feb 2018 saw the Philadelphia Eagles and the New England Patriots achieve a total combined yardage of 1,151 – the most in any NFL game in history. In a spectacle of offensive intent, the Eagles ran out 41–33 winners. The combined total of 74 points was only one point lower than the **highest aggregate score in a Super Bowl** – set in 1995, when the San Francisco 49ers beat the San Diego Chargers 49–26.

BASEBALL

All teams and players USA, unless otherwise indicated.

Most strikeouts by a pitching staff in a Major League Baseball (MLB) season

Cleveland Indians pitchers struck out a total of 1,614 batters during the 2017 season. They averaged 10.1 strikeouts per nine innings, the highest ever recorded in the MLB.

Fewest pitched innings to reach 1,500 strikeouts

Chris Sale struck out 1,500 batters in 1,290 innings for the Chicago White Sox and the Boston Red Sox from 2010 to 2017. The previous fewest was 1,303 innings, by Kerry Wood.

Most games for a pitcher in a World Series

Only two pitchers have faced a batter in all seven games of a World Series: Darold Knowles of the Oakland Athletics in 1973, and Brandon Morrow for the Los Angeles Dodgers in 2017.

Most positions played by an individual in an MLB match

On 30 Sep 2017, Andrew Romine played all nine positions for the Detroit Tigers during their 3–2 defeat of the Minnesota Twins. Romine started the game in left field, played catcher in the seventh innings and pitched in the eighth. Only four MLB players have done the same: Bert Campaneris (CUB), César Tovar (VEN), Scott Sheldon and Shane Halter.

Longest MLB uninterrupted winning streak

Between 24 Aug and 14 Sep 2017, the Cleveland Indians were victorious in 22 consecutive games. They were finally defeated on 15 Sep by the Kansas City Royals – a team the Indians had defeated four times in the course of their streak. The 1916 New York Giants are credited with winning 26 games during a 27-game span on 7–30 Sep 1916, but this includes a nine-innings tie with the Pittsburgh Pirates on 18 Sep.

Most home runs in a baseball match

Eighteen players have hit four home runs in a single MLB game since Bobby Lowe in 1894. In 2017, the feat was achieved twice – by Scooter Gennett (left) for the Cincinnati Reds on 6 Jun, and by the Arizona Diamondbacks' J D Martinez on 4 Sep.

Most home runs in a World Series (teams)

The Houston Astros and the Los Angeles Dodgers combined to hit 25 home runs in seven games during the 2017 World Series. This is four more than the previous highest total, set in 2002.

During Game 2 on 25 Oct 2017, the teams hit the **most combined home runs in a World Series game** – eight (four per side).

Most extra-base hits in an MLB game

On 3 Sep 2017, José Ramírez (DOM) recorded five extra-base hits (i.e., either a double, triple or home run) for the Cleveland Indians in an 11–1 win over the Detroit Tigers. He hit two home runs and three doubles. Ramírez became only the 13th player in MLB history to notch five extra-base hits since George Strief first did so on 25 Jun 1885.

The **most extra-base hits in an MLB career** is 1,477, by Hank Aaron from 1954 to 1976.

Most times reaching first base on catcher's interference in an MLB career

On 11 Sep 2017, the New York Yankees' Jacoby Ellsbury celebrated his birthday by reaching base due to catcher's interference for the 30th time. He beat Pete Rose's mark of 29, achieved from 1963 to 1986. Catcher's interference occurs when the batter's bat touches the catcher's mitt mid-swing.

Most times hit by a pitch in an MLB game

Jarrod Dyson was hit by a pitch three times while batting for the Seattle Mariners against the Oakland Athletics on 16 May 2017. This equalled the MLB record, achieved on 24 previous occasions stretching back to Wally Schang on 15 May 1923.

> Aaron Judge also recorded the **most base on balls in an MLB season by a rookie** – 127. He beat a record that had stood since 1890.

Most home runs in an MLB season by a rookie

Aaron Judge hit 52 home runs for the New York Yankees in 2017. In a season notable for big hitting, 6-ft 7-in (2.01-m) Judge made the headlines by becoming the first rookie to hit 50 in a season. He surpassed the previous best of 49 – set by Mark McGwire while playing for the Oakland Athletics in 1987 – with a pair of home runs against the Kansas City Royals on 25 Sep 2017.

Most home runs in a World Series by a player

The Houston Astros' George Springer was named 2017 World Series MVP after hitting five home runs in seven games against the Los Angeles Dodgers. He equalled the mark of Reggie Jackson in 1977 and Chase Utley in 2009.

Springer also achieved two further World Series records: **most total bases** (29) and **most extra-base hits** (eight).

BASKETBALL

Greatest second-half comeback by a team in a playoff game

The Cleveland Cavaliers erased a 25-point half-time deficit to beat the Indiana Pacers 119–114 in Game 3 of their first-round Eastern Conference playoff series on 20 Apr 2017. The previous largest deficit was 21 points, overturned by the Baltimore Bullets against the Philadelphia Warriors on 13 Apr 1948.

Greatest half-time lead in a playoff game

On 19 May 2017, the Cleveland Cavaliers raced to a 41-point half-time lead against the Boston Celtics during Game 2 of the Eastern Conference Finals in Boston, Massachusetts, USA.

Cleveland ended the game 130–86 winners, some way off the **highest margin of victory in a playoff game** – 58, by the Minneapolis Lakers in 1956 and the Denver Nuggets in 2009.

Most triple-doubles in a season

Russell Westbrook recorded 42 triple-doubles for the Oklahoma City Thunder in 2016–17. He broke Oscar Robertson's record of 41, which had stood since 1961–62. On 28 Oct 2017, Westbrook became the **first player to triple-double against every NBA team**.

Most points scored in a WNBA career

By the close of the 2017 WNBA season, guard Diana Taurasi had amassed 7,867 points for the Phoenix Mercury since 2004. She had played in 398 games, giving her an average of 19.76 points per match.

Taurasi, who is nicknamed the "White Mamba", had also scored the **most three-point field goals in a WNBA career** – 996.

All records are National Basketball Association (NBA) and all teams and players USA, unless otherwise indicated.

Youngest player to achieve a triple-double

Guard Markelle Fultz (b. 29 May 1998) registered 13 points, 10 rebounds and 10 assists for the Philadelphia 76ers against the Milwaukee Bucks aged 19 years 317 days on 11 Apr 2018. Fultz beat Lonzo Ball's record of 20 years 15 days to become the **first teenager to record a triple-double in the NBA**.

On 23 Jan 2018, LeBron James (b. 30 Dec 1984) became the **youngest player to score 30,000 career points**, aged 33 years 24 days.

Most three-point field goals in a season

The Houston Rockets made 1,181 three-pointers during the 2016–17 season. This was due in part to the fact that they attempted 3,306 – the **most three-point field goals attempted in a season**.

The **most three-point field goals in a Finals game** is 24, by the Cleveland Cavaliers against the Golden State Warriors on 9 Jun 2017.

Fewest games for a coach to win 200 matches

Steve Kerr (USA, b. LBN) earned 200 career victories in just 238 games. He reached the milestone with the Golden State Warriors' 113–106 win over the Houston Rockets on 28 Mar 2017.

Most assists in a WNBA career

As of 18 Dec 2017, Sue Bird had provided a total of 2,610 assists playing for the Seattle Storm in the Women's National Basketball Association (WNBA).

Bird also set the record for **most assists in a WNBA All-Star Game**, making 11 during the West's 130–121 win over the East on 22 Jul 2017.

Most points scored in a postseason career

As of the end of the 2017 NBA season, LeBron James had recorded 6,163 points in 217 postseason games for the Cleveland Cavaliers and Miami Heat. He surpassed Michael Jordan (5,987) on 25 May 2017. During the Finals against the Golden State Warriors in 2017, James became the first player to average a triple-double with 33.6 points, 12 rebounds and 10 assists.

Longest postseason winning streak by a team
Between 16 Apr and 7 Jun 2017, the Golden State Warriors won 15 consecutive playoff games en route to the NBA championship. They came back from a 25-point deficit to beat the San Antonio Spurs on 14 May, and lost just one game – against the Cleveland Cavaliers on 9 Jun – to finish with a 16–1 postseason record.

Largest margin of victory in a WNBA regular-season game

On 18 Aug 2017, the Minnesota Lynx beat the Indiana Fever 111–52, finishing with a 59-point margin of victory. This was 13 points more than the previous highest, by the Seattle Storm in 2010. The Lynx also hit the **most consecutive points by a WNBA team** – 37 – during the game.

On 4 Oct 2017, Minnesota equalled the **most WNBA championship titles** – four – tied with the Houston Comets from 1997 to 2000.

ICE HOCKEY

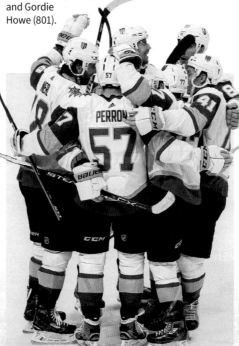

Most goals scored by an individual in a regular-season period

On 23 Jan 2017, the San Jose Sharks' Patrick Marleau (CAN) scored four times in the third period against the Colorado Avalanche. This feat had previously been achieved by 11 other NHL players.

The **most goals scored by a team in a regular-season period** is nine, by the Buffalo Sabres versus the Toronto Maple Leafs (CAN) on 19 Mar 1981.

Most career game-winning goals

Jaromír Jágr (CZE) netted 135 game-winners for nine teams between 1990 and 2017. He had scored 765 goals in total, the third-highest in NHL history behind Wayne Gretzky (894) and Gordie Howe (801).

Most overtime goals in a regular-season career

Alex Ovechkin (RUS) scored his 20th regular-season game-winning goal during overtime while playing for the Washington Capitals in a 4–3 win over the Detroit Red Wings on 20 Oct 2017. He had previously been tied for the record with Jaromír Jágr (see right).

All records relate to the National Hockey League (NHL) contested in the USA and Canada. All teams and players are USA, unless otherwise indicated.

Most overtime goals in a season

Three players have scored five overtime goals in an NHL season: Steven Stamkos (CAN) for the Tampa Bay Lightning in 2011–12, the Chicago Blackhawks' Jonathan Toews (CAN) in 2015–16 and the Montreal Canadiens' (CAN) Alex Galchenyuk in 2016–17.

Most overtime goals in a single postseason

Corey Perry (CAN) scored three overtime goals for the Anaheim Ducks during the 2017 Stanley Cup playoffs. He equalled the mark set by the Boston Bruins' Mel Hill (CAN) in 1939 and Maurice Richard of the Montreal Canadiens (both CAN) in 1951.

Fastest overtime goal

Two players scored just 6 sec into overtime in Jan 2018: Andreas Athanasiou (CAN) for the Detroit Red Wings on 3 Jan, and the Toronto Maple Leafs' William Nylander (SWE, b. CAN) on 24 Jan. They matched the NHL record set by Mats Sundin (SWE) in 1995 and equalled by David Legwand and Alex Ovechkin in 2006. Since 2015, overtime has been contested by teams with just three skaters per side.

Most wins in a season by an expansion team

On 1 Feb 2018, the Vegas Golden Knights defeated the Winnipeg Jets (CAN) 3–2 for their 34th victory of the season. This was more than any other expansion team in their debut season, exceeding the 33 wins of the Anaheim Ducks and Florida Panthers in 1993–94. As of 22 Mar 2018, the Knights' record was up to 47.

Most postseason points scored by a rookie

Jake Guentzel scored 21 points in his first postseason for the Pittsburgh Penguins, racking up 13 goals and eight assists. He matched the feat of Dino Ciccarelli (CAN, 14 goals and seven assists) in 1981 and Ville Leino (FIN, seven goals and 14 assists) in 2010.

Most consecutive seasons winning 20 matches by a goaltender

Two goaltenders have achieved 12 consecutive NHL seasons with 20 or more victories: Martin Brodeur (CAN), playing for the New Jersey Devils from 1995 to 2008, and the New York Rangers' Henrik Lundqvist (SWE) from 2005 to 2017. Lundqvist became the first player to win 20 or more games in each of his first 12 seasons in the NHL.

On 11 Feb 2017, Lundqvist achieved his 400th career win in his 727th game, during the New York Rangers' 4–2 victory over the Colorado Avalanche. This is the **fastest 400 wins by a goaltender**. He beat the previous record – also set by Martin Brodeur – by eight matches.

Most consecutive defeats to start a season

On 28 Oct 2017, the Arizona Coyotes lost 4–3 against the New Jersey Devils to find themselves 0–11 for the season (with one defeat occurring in overtime). Their 11 straight losses equalled the worst start in NHL history, joining the 1943–44 New York Rangers.

The **most consecutive wins to start a season** is 10, by the Buffalo Sabres from 4–26 Oct 2006 and the Toronto Maple Leafs from 7–28 Oct 1993.

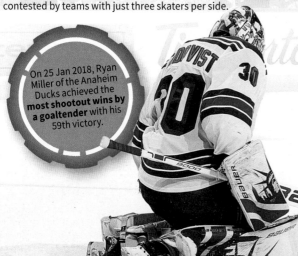

On 25 Jan 2018, Ryan Miller of the Anaheim Ducks achieved the **most shootout wins by a goaltender** with his 59th victory.

Most career shootout goals

On 29 Dec 2017, Frans Nielsen (DNK) scored his 47th shootout goal, past goaltender Henrik Lundqvist, to lift the Detroit Red Wings to a 3–2 victory over the New York Rangers. It was Nielsen's 21st game-winning strike – the **most career shootout winning goals**. His 47 goals had come from 94 attempts, giving him an NHL-high average of 50% since 2006–07.

SOCCER

Most wins of the FIFA Beach Soccer World Cup
Brazil has won the FIFA Beach Soccer World Cup five times: in 2006–09 and 2017. Following an eight-year drought, they secured their fifth title at the 2017 tournament in The Bahamas with a 6–0 win over Tahiti on 7 May.

Most wins of the UEFA European Cup/Champions League
Real Madrid (ESP) won their 12th European top-flight title when they defeated Juventus (ITA) 4–1 in the Champions League final on 3 Jun 2017. The victory ensured Real became the **first team to win the Champions League in consecutive years**. Before the competition changed format in 1992, they were also responsible for the **most consecutive wins of the European Cup** – five, in 1956–60.

As of 23 Apr 2018, Real Madrid had also achieved the **most UEFA Champions League victories** – 149, from 248 games over 22 campaigns.

Most wins of the UEFA Women's Champions League
On 1 Jun 2017, Olympique Lyonnais Féminin (FRA) secured their fourth UEFA Women's Champions League title, defeating Paris Saint-Germain 7–6 on penalties at the Cardiff City Stadium, UK. They matched 1. FFC Frankfurt, who won in 2002, 2006, 2008 and 2015.

Manchester City won the 2017/18 EPL title in record-breaking style, amassing the **most points** (100), **most wins** (32) and **most goals** (106) in a single season.

Most clubs played for in the UEFA Champions League
Zlatan Ibrahimović (SWE) has played for seven clubs in Europe's top-flight competition since 17 Sep 2002. They are: Ajax (NLD), Juventus, Inter Milan (both ITA), Barcelona (ESP), AC Milan (ITA), Paris Saint-Germain (FRA) and Manchester United (UK).

Most team goals in a UEFA Champions League group stage
Paris Saint-Germain scored 25 goals in six games during the group stages of the UEFA Champions League 2017/18 – an average of over four goals a game. They finished top of Group B with a goal difference of +21.

During the 2016/17 Champions League, Borussia Dortmund (DEU) set a record for the **most goalscorers in a UEFA Champions League season (team)**, with 15 different players finding the net.

Most consecutive UEFA Champions League matches won at home
Bayern Munich (DEU) won 16 Champions League home ties at the Allianz Arena from 17 Sep 2014 to 15 Feb 2017. Now-retired captain Philipp Lahm (left) and Thomas Müller (right) are pictured above with their GWR certificate.

Most consecutive wins in the top division of English football by a team
Manchester City (UK) won 18 English Premier League games in a row between 26 Aug and 27 Dec 2017 – the most ever in the history of England's top division. On 13 Dec 2017, they surpassed Arsenal's previous mark of 14 from 2002 in style, defeating Swansea 4–0. City's run finally came to an end on 31 Dec 2017, when they were held to a goalless draw by Crystal Palace.

Most goals in a 38-game English Premier League (EPL) season
Liverpool's Mo Salah (EGY) scored 32 league goals during the 2017/18 EPL season. The prolific forward also achieved the **most games scored in during a 38-game EPL season** – 24.

Salah's goal tally was only two short of the 34 hit by Andy Cole in 1993/94 and Alan Shearer (both UK) in 1994/95 – the **most goals in a 42-game EPL season**.

Most consecutive matches unbeaten in La Liga
FC Barcelona went unbeaten for 43 Spanish league games between 15 Apr 2017 and 9 May 2018, recording 34 wins and nine draws. Closing in on an unbeaten La Liga season, Barcelona were finally defeated 5–4 by Levante on 13 May 2018.

Most La Liga goals scored by a player
Lionel Messi (ARG) had scored 383 goals for FC Barcelona in Spain's top division since 1 May 2005, as of 13 May 2018. He amassed this total in 417 matches, giving him a strike rate of 0.91 goals per La Liga game.

Messi scored his 20th goal of the 2017/18 season against Alavés in a 2–1 victory on 28 Jan 2018, completing the **most consecutive La Liga seasons to score 20 goals** – 10.

Most Serie A seasons scored in by a player
Francesco Totti (ITA) retired at the end of the 2016/17 season having scored at least once in 23 seasons of Italy's Serie A. He made his debut for AS Roma on 28 Mar 1993, and scored his first league goal for the club in the top flight against Foggia on 4 Sep 1994.

Over the course of his career, Totti scored the **most Serie A penalties** – 71, ahead of Roberto Baggio's 68.

Most wins of the Italian top division by a player
On 13 May 2018, goalkeeper Gianluigi Buffon (ITA) became the first player to win nine Serie A titles. His league triumphs all occurred at the same club, Juventus, in 2002–03 and 2012–18.

Most English Premier League goals scored for one club

On 14 May 2017, Wayne Rooney (UK) scored his 183rd goal for Manchester United, against Tottenham Hotspur at White Hart Lane in London. It proved to be his final strike for the club, as he returned to boyhood team Everton in the subsequent close season.

As of 13 May 2018, Rooney had scored 208 career EPL goals in all – second behind Alan Shearer (UK), the **highest EPL goalscorer** with 260.

Most English Premier League appearances

As of 13 May 2018, Gareth Barry (UK) had played 653 matches in the English top flight since 2 May 1998. He surpassed the previous record of 632 by Ryan Giggs on 25 Sep 2017. Barry has lined up for four clubs during his career: Aston Villa, Manchester City, Everton and West Bromwich Albion.

Youngest goalscorer at the CONCACAF Gold Cup

Alphonso Davies (b. 2 Nov 2000) scored twice for Canada aged 16 years 247 days in a 4–2 victory against French Guiana on 7 Jul 2017. He went on to finish as the Gold Cup's joint-top scorer, and was named as the tournament's Best Young Player.

Most UEFA Champions League goals

As of 8 May 2018, Cristiano Ronaldo (PRT) had scored 120 goals in the UEFA Champions League. On 12 Apr, he converted a late penalty against Juventus to send Real Madrid into the semi-finals and extend his record for the **most consecutive UEFA Champions League matches scored in** – 11.

Most wins of the CONIFA European Football Cup

Padania has won the CONIFA European Football Cup both times it has been held, in 2015 and 2017. The unofficial northern Italian state retained its title on 10 Jun 2017 by defeating hosts Northern Cyprus 4–2 on penalties at the Nicosia Atatürk Stadium. CONIFA is a world football federation for stateless peoples and internationally unrecognized nations and territories.

Most games won by a coach with the same international soccer team

On 25 Jun 2017, Joachim Löw (DEU) celebrated his 100th victory in charge of the German national team when they defeated Cameroon 3–1 at the FIFA Confederations Cup. By 13 May 2018, Löw's tally had increased to 106.

Most English Premier League goals scored in a calendar year

From 1 Jan to 26 Dec 2017, Tottenham Hotspur striker Harry Kane (UK) scored 39 goals in the EPL. He claimed the record with a Boxing Day hat-trick against Southampton. It was Kane's sixth league treble of 2017 – the **most EPL hat-tricks in a calendar year**.

Most career regular-season NWSL goals

As of 13 May 2018, Samantha Kerr (AUS) had scored 45 goals in the National Women's Soccer League. In 2017, she hit the **most goals in an NWSL season** – 17, for Sky Blue FC (above) – and the **most goals in an NWSL game** (four), against Seattle Reign on 19 Aug.

Oldest professional player to score a competitive league goal

Kazuyoshi Miura (JPN, b. 26 Feb 1967) scored the only goal in Yokohama FC's 1–0 win over Thespakusatsu Gunma aged 50 years 14 days, at the Nippatsu Mitsuzawa Stadium in Yokohama, Japan, on 12 Mar 2017.

Most games won at the CONCACAF Gold Cup by a team

The USA have won 56 games in 14 tournaments of the CONCACAF Gold Cup since 1991. They won their sixth title on 26 Jul 2017, beating Jamaica 2–1 in the final. It took their competition record to 73 games, 56 wins, nine draws and eight defeats.

The USA may have won the most games, but rivals Mexico have recorded the **most wins of the CONCACAF Gold Cup** – seven, from 1993 to 2015.

Highest margin of victory in a UEFA Women's European Championship Finals match

On 19 Jul 2017, England beat old rivals Scotland 6–0 in their Women's Euro 2017 Group D match at the Stadion Galgenwaard in Utrecht, Netherlands. Jodie Taylor hit the first hat-trick by an English woman at a major tournament.

Most expensive player transfer

On 3 Aug 2017, Brazilian forward Neymar Jr transferred from FC Barcelona to Paris Saint-Germain upon the activation of his release clause of €222 m (£198.7 m; $262.8 m). This also made Neymar the **most expensive player (combined transfer fees)**, having cost a total of €308.2 m (£275.9 m; $364.8 m) in his career.

MOST DOMESTIC LEAGUE TITLES (2017 WINNERS ONLY)

TEAM	DOMESTIC LEAGUE	FIRST TITLE	NO. OF TITLES
Olympiacos	Greece	1931	44
Al Ahly	Egypt	1949	39
S L Benfica	Portugal	1936	36
RSC Anderlecht	Belgium	1947	34
Juventus	Italy	1905	33
Real Madrid	Spain	1932	33
Bayern Munich	Germany	1932	27
ASEC Mimosas	Côte d'Ivoire	1963	25
Rosenborg	Norway	1967	25
Malmö FF	Sweden	1944	20

Figures as of the end of the 2016/17 season

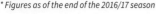

RUGBY

Most wins of the Women's Rugby World Cup

New Zealand secured their fifth Rugby World Cup title by defeating England Women 41–32 on 26 Aug 2017. The Black Ferns had trailed the final 17–5, only to come roaring back with 31 second-half points. The aggregate score of 73 points was the **highest combined score in a Women's Rugby World Cup final**.

Most Super Rugby titles

The Crusaders (NZ) secured their eighth title in Super Rugby – the Southern Hemisphere and Japan-based club competition – on 5 Aug 2017, defeating the Lions (ZAF) 25–17 in the final.

Most tries scored by a team in a Super Rugby regular season

Wellington-based Hurricanes (NZ) scored 89 tries during the 2017 Super Rugby regular season. They got off to a whirlwind start, scoring 13 in their opening match against the Sunwolves. Ngani Laumape (NZ) scored 15 tries for the Hurricanes in 2017 – the **most individual tries scored in a single Super Rugby season**. He equalled the mark set by Joe Roff (AUS, 1997) and Rico Gear (NZ, 2005).

Most tries scored in an English Premiership regular season

Wasps winger Christian Wade (UK) scored 17 tries during the 2016–17 English Premiership season, equalling the record of Dominic Chapman (UK), who scored 17 for Richmond in 1997–98.

On 16 Apr 2016, Wade scored the **most tries in an English Premiership match** with a six-try haul against Worcester. He equalled Ryan Constable (AUS, b. ZAF), who scored six for Saracens on 16 Apr 2000.

Saracens' Champions Cup victory over Clermont Auvergne on 13 May 2017 earned them not only the trophy but also the record for the **most consecutive Champions Cup games without defeat**. They played 20 games on the spin without defeat from 14 Nov 2015 to 21 Oct 2017, before finally losing... to Clermont Auvergne.

Most tries scored at a Rugby League World Cup

Valentine Holmes (Australia) scored 12 tries in six games during Australia's triumphant campaign in the 2017 Rugby League World Cup. On 24 Nov, Holmes achieved the **most tries in a Rugby League World Cup game**, scoring six against Fiji.

Holmes's team-mate Billy Slater claimed the **most overall tries at the Rugby League World Cup**, with 16 between 2008 and 2017.

Most points in an international rugby league career

Johnathan Thurston (AUS) scored 382 international points from 5 May 2006 to 5 May 2017. The half-back, who announced his international retirement following injury sustained during the State of Origin series, scored 13 tries and kicked 165 goals.

Fastest Super League hat-trick

On 29 May 2017, Castleford's Greg Eden (UK) scored three tries in 4 min 59 sec against Leigh Centurions. He went over for his first score on 32 min 43 sec and completed his hat-trick after 37 min 42 sec. Incredibly, it was the fourth consecutive Super League game in which Eden had scored a hat-trick.

Most National Rugby League appearances

Cameron Smith (AUS) made 358 appearances in the NRL for Melbourne Storm between 2002 and 1 Oct 2017. In 15 years of playing, Smith missed just 11 games owing to injury. The two-time Premiership winner also recorded the **most wins in the NRL by an individual** – 254.

First transatlantic professional rugby league team

On 25 Feb 2017, Canada's Toronto Wolfpack made its UK professional rugby league debut against Siddal in the Challenge Cup third round.

Most British and Irish Lions tours as captain

Wales's Sam Warburton led the British and Irish Lions on their 2017 tour of New Zealand, his second tour as captain. He equalled the feat of England's Martin Johnson, Lions captain in 1997 and 2001.

Most Super Rugby appearances

Wyatt Crockett (NZ) had played 189 Super Rugby games for the Crusaders as of 3 Mar 2018. The prop, who also achieved the **most consecutive international wins by a player** (32 with New Zealand from 2014 to 2017), beat Keven Mealamu's mark of 175 on 14 Apr 2017.

Most tries scored in the European Rugby Champions Cup by an individual

On 20 Jan 2018, Chris Ashton (UK) scored his 38th try in European rugby's top-tier competition for French side Toulon. He had previously scored 29 tries for Saracens (UK), including one in the 2017 final (see pic) that took him past Vincent Clerc's record of 36. Ashton had also notched eight for Northampton Saints (UK) in 2009–12, when the tournament was known as the Heineken Cup.

RUGBY WORLD CUP

Largest margin of victory
Australia beat Namibia 142–0 in Adelaide, Australia, on 25 Oct 2003. They scored 22 tries in total, with Chris Latham scoring five and Mat Rogers successfully kicking 16 conversions.

Highest aggregate match score
On 4 Jun 1995, New Zealand ran rampant against Japan, defeating them 145–17 in Bloemfontein, South Africa. Winger Marc Ellis helped himself to six tries, the **most individual tries scored in a match**.

Most appearances
Two players have made 22 appearances at the Rugby World Cup: England's Jason Leonard (1991–2003) and New Zealand's Richie McCaw (2003–15). Leonard, a 2003 cup winner, won 16 games and lost six. McCaw – who made the **most international rugby union appearances** (148) – won 20 of his finals matches, the **most wins by an individual**.

Most clean breaks made
According to World Rugby statistics, Australian winger David Campese made 37 clean breaks through the opposition's defensive line between 1987 and 1995. Campese scored 10 tries in 15 matches, earning a winner's medal in 1991. He was renowned for the "goose-step" hitch-kick motion he used to elude defenders.

Longest time between wins
On 19 Sep 2015, Japan caused one of the great rugby union upsets by defeating South Africa 34–32 in Brighton, East Sussex, UK. The Brave Blossoms had not won a World Cup match since beating Zimbabwe on 14 Oct 1991 – a gap of 23 years 340 days.

Most wins
New Zealand have claimed the William Webb Ellis winner's trophy on three occasions: in 1987, 2011 and 2015. They defeated Australia 34–17 on 31 Oct 2015 to become the first side to defend the title. On the other two occasions, France finished as runners-up – having also lost to Australia in 1999, Les Bleus have suffered the **most final losses**, with three.

Youngest player
Vasil Lobzhanidze lined up for Georgia against Tonga aged 18 years 340 days at Kingsholm in Gloucester, UK, on 19 Sep 2015.

The **youngest try scorer** is Welsh winger George North, who went over against Namibia aged 19 years 166 days on 26 Sep 2011.

The **oldest player** is Diego Ormaechea (URY), who was aged 40 years 26 days when he took to the field for Uruguay against South Africa at Hampden Park in Glasgow, UK, on 15 Oct 1999.

Fastest try
Australia's Elton Flatley scored after 18 sec during the Wallabies' 90–8 victory over Romania on 18 Oct 2003.

All records relate to the International Rugby Board/ World Rugby men's Rugby World Cup

Most points scored in a single tournament
Grant Fox scored 126 points for New Zealand at the inaugural 1987 World Cup. He kicked 30 conversions – the **most conversions in a tournament** – 21 penalties and a drop goal in six matches, helping the All Blacks to the title.

Most penalty goals
Gonzalo Quesada (ARG) successfully kicked 31 penalties at the 1999 World Cup. The Pumas' fly-half finished the competition as its highest scorer with 102 points.

Most conversions
Daniel Carter (NZ) kicked 58 conversions in 16 World Cup matches between 2003 and 2015. The player with the **most international rugby union conversions**, 293, Carter kicked his final-ever conversion in the dying moments of the 2015 final right-footed – the first and only time he did this.

Jonny Wilkinson is the only player to have scored points in more than one Rugby World Cup final. He added two penalties in 2007 to his 15-point haul from 2003.

Most tries scored in a single tournament
Three players have scored eight tries at a single World Cup tournament: Jonah Lomu (NZ, above) in 1999, Bryan Habana (ZAF) in 2007 and Julian Savea (NZ) in 2015. Lomu, who sadly died in 2015, scored a total of 15 World Cup tries in 1995 and 1999; a number matched by Habana in 2007, 2011 and 2015 – meaning that they also share the record for **most tries scored**.

Most points
England's Jonny Wilkinson scored 277 points in 19 matches from 1999 to 2011. The prolific fly-half holds the record for the **most penalty goals** – 58 – and **most drop goals** – 14, including the winning score in the 2003 final. He also successfully kicked 28 conversions and scored a single try, against Italy in 1999.

COMBAT SPORTS

St-Pierre became only the fourth UFC two-weight world champion. His record stood at 20 wins from 22 fights, with only two defeats.

St-Pierre's victory was also his 13th in UFC title bouts – the **most UFC title-bout wins**. As of 15 Mar 2018, he was one ahead of Demetrious Johnson.

Michael Bisping returned to the octagon on 25 Nov 2017 for his 29th bout – the **most UFC fights**. He lost again, to Kelvin Gastelum.

Most ONE Championship title defences (female)

Inaugural ONE Championship women's atomweight champion Angela Lee (SGP, b CAN 8 Jul 1996) had made two title defences as of 22 Nov 2017. She became the **youngest Mixed Martial Arts world champion** on 6 May 2016 aged 19 years 303 days, beating Mei Yamaguchi in Kallang, Singapore. Lee's second successful title defence occurred at ONE Championship 55: Dynasty of Heroes on 26 May 2017, where she defeated Istela Nunes via an anaconda choke.

Youngest boxing super-middleweight world champion

David Benavidez (USA, b. 17 Dec 1996) became WBC super-middleweight world champion aged 20 years 265 days, defeating Ronald Gavril on a split decision at the Hard Rock Hotel & Casino in Las Vegas, Nevada, USA, on 8 Sep 2017.

Most light-heavyweight gold medals won at the AIBA World Boxing Championships

Julio César La Cruz (CUB) has won four consecutive light-heavyweight gold medals at the biennial amateur boxing competition organized by the International Boxing Association (formerly known as the Association Internationale de Boxe Amateur). He triumphed in 2011, 2013, 2015 and 2017, overcoming the same fighter – Joe Ward of Ireland – in the last two finals.

The **most gold medals won at the AIBA World Boxing Championships** is six, by the Cuban heavyweight Félix Savón between 1986 and 1997.

Most consecutive UFC title defences
Flyweight Demetrious Johnson (USA) made 11 consecutive defences of his Ultimate Fighting Championship (UFC) title between 26 Jan 2013 and 7 Oct 2017. He surpassed Anderson Silva's mark of 10 with victory over Ray Borg at UFC 216, achieved via a dramatic suplex-to-armbar submission in the fifth round.

Most consecutive UFC heavyweight title defences
Stipe Miocic (USA) made three successful defences of his UFC heavyweight title between 25 May 2016 and 20 Jan 2018. He recorded his third at UFC 220, defeating Francis Ngannou by unanimous decision in Boston, Massachusetts, USA.

Most UFC wins
Three fighters have won 20 bouts in the UFC: Donald Cerrone (USA), Georges St-Pierre (CAN) and Michael Bisping (UK). The latter two came together at UFC 217 on 4 Nov 2017, with St-Pierre returning after a four-year absence from the octagon to win the middleweight title via a rear naked choke in the third round. A former welterweight,

Most significant strikes landed during a UFC title match
On 13 May 2017, Joanna Jędrzejczyk (POL) landed 225 significant strikes over five rounds during her Women's Strawweight Championship bout against Jéssica Andrade at UFC 211, held at the American Airlines Center in Dallas, Texas, USA. She went on to win the fight by unanimous decision.

During the same bout, Jędrzejczyk landed the **most leg kicks during a UFC match** – 75, beating her own record of 70. As of 22 Jan 2018, she had recorded the **most UFC wins (female)** – eight – together with Amanda Nunes (BRA).

The **most significant strikes landed during a UFC match** is 238, by Nate Diaz (USA) over three rounds against Donald "Cowboy" Cerrone (see left) at UFC 141 on 30 Dec 2011.

Most world heavyweight boxing title bouts
Wladimir Klitschko (UKR, right) fought in his 29th heavyweight title bout on 29 Apr 2017, when he faced off against the UK's Olympic gold medallist Anthony Joshua at Wembley Stadium in London, UK. A two-time heavyweight champion, Klitschko was first crowned WBO champion on 14 Oct 2000. He lost a thrilling contest with Joshua to an 11th-round TKO, and subsequently announced his retirement.

Longest reign as a four-belt undisputed world boxing champion
As of 15 Mar 2018, Cecilia Bræmus (NOR) had held the WBO, WBC, WBA and IBF women's welterweight titles for 3 years 183 days. The "First Lady" of boxing, with 32 wins from 32 fights, Bræmus became undisputed champion on 13 Sep 2014 and made her sixth successful defence of her belts (which also include the IBO title) on 21 Oct 2017.

Klitschko's two reigns as heavyweight champion totalled 4,382 days – the **most days as heavyweight boxing champion**.

Most World Taekwondo Grand Prix victories in a calendar year

Bianca Walkden (UK) won the women's +67 kg category at all four Grand Prix events on the World Taekwondo calendar in 2017. She triumphed in Moscow, Rabat and London before taking gold at the Grand Prix Final in Abidjan, Côte d'Ivoire, on 2 Dec 2017. No other fighter had ever completed a clean sweep of Grand Prix events in a calendar year. Walkden also defended her +73 kg title at the 2017 World Taekwondo Championships.

Most medals won at the World Taekwondo Championships by a country

South Korea won 232 taekwondo World Championship medals from 25 May 1973 to 30 Jun 2017. They topped the medal table at the 2017 tournament in Muju, South Korea, with a total of 10, including five gold.

Most Muay Thai gold medals won at the World Games by a country

Ukraine won three gold medals at the inaugural Muay Thai competition at the 2017 World Games in Wrocław, Poland. In the 11 finals that took place on 30 Jul 2017, Ukraine won titles at men's 91 kg (Oleh Pryimachov), men's 67 kg (Serhii Kuliaba) and men's 63.5 kg (Igor Liubchenko). With a silver medal to boot, Ukraine earned the award for "Muaythai team of TWG2017".

Most career wins by a sumo wrestler

Hakuhō Shō (MNG) finished the 2017 Kyushu Grand Sumo Tournament on 26 Nov having achieved 1,064 career sumo victories. His tournament record of 14–1 was enough to secure Hakuhō his 40th championship – the **most top-division sumo championship wins**. He had sealed the title on 25 Nov, overcoming Endō Shōta at the Fukuoka Kokusai Center. As of 15 Mar 2018, Hakuhō had increased his tally of wins to 1,066.

On 28 May 2017, Hakuhō secured his 13th *zenshō-yūshō* – a tournament victory without a single loss – winning the Summer Grand Slam in Tokyo, Japan, with a 15–0 record. This is the **most top-division undefeated sumo championship wins**.

Most individual gold medals won at the IBJJF World Championships

Marcus Almeida (BRA, above in blue) has won 10 individual gold medals at the International Brazilian Jiu-Jitsu Federation (IBJJF) World Championships. He triumphed in the +100 kg and open categories at the 2017 Mundials on 1–4 Jun to match the feat of Roger Gracie (BRA), who won 10 golds in the 100 kg, +100 kg and open categories between 2004 and 2010.

Fastest knockout victory in a boxing world title fight

Zolani Tete (ZAF) won his WBO bantamweight title bout with Siboniso Gonya after 11 sec on 18 Nov 2017 at the SSE Arena in Belfast, Northern Ireland, UK. He knocked out his opponent with his first punch, a right hook after just 6 sec.

Most gold medals won by a country at the World Taekwondo Beach Championships

Thailand won seven gold medals at the inaugural World Taekwondo Federation (WTF) World Taekwondo Beach Championships, staged on the Greek island of Rhodes on 5–6 May 2017. The championships featured 26 non-sparring categories such as kyukpa artistic solo events and poomsae, where individuals or teams perform "a sequence of movements arranged in a meaningful order in response to attacks from multiple imaginary assailants".

Most World Judo Championship gold medals won by an individual (male)

On 11 Nov 2017, Teddy Riner (FRA, b. GLP, above in white) won his 10th judo world title at the Openweight World Championships in Marrakesh, Morocco. His final victory, against Toma Nikiforov, was his 144th consecutive official bout without defeat. It was Riner's second Openweight title, adding to the eight golds he had won in the +100 kg division at the World Judo Championships from 2007 to 2017.

Youngest winner of an International Judo Federation (IJF) Grand Prix

On 24 Feb 2017, Uta Abe (JPN, b. 14 Jul 2000) won the women's -52 kg category at the IJF Düsseldorf Grand Prix in Düsseldorf, Germany, aged 16 years 225 days. Abe sealed the title by defeating France's Amandine Buchard with a low *uchi-mata* – a type of judo throw – securing the decisive score. Her older brother Hifumi, also a *judoka*, took gold in the men's 66 kg at the 2017 World Championships at the age of just 20.

Floyd Mayweather Jr fought 16 pay-per-view (PPV) bouts between 25 Jun 2005 and 26 Aug 2017, generating an estimated $1.7 bn (£1,323,660,000) in PPV revenue from 23,980,000 buys – the **highest career PPV sales for a boxer**.

Most bouts undefeated by a world champion boxer in a career

Quintuple weight champion Floyd Mayweather Jr (USA, right) retired from boxing with a record of 50 wins and no defeats, achieved between 11 Oct 1996 and 26 Aug 2017. At the age of 40, Mayweather came out of retirement to defeat two-division UFC champion Conor McGregor via a 10th-round stoppage at the T-Mobile Arena in Las Vegas, Nevada, USA.

CRICKET

Most runs scored in a Twenty20 (T20) career

Chris Gayle (JAM) had hit 11,068 runs in 323 T20 matches as of 4 Mar 2018. The hard-hitting left-hander has scored runs for domestic T20 sides such as the St Kitts & Nevis Patriots (above), plus 1,589 runs for the West Indies.

On 12 Dec 2017, Gayle hit 146 not out for the Rangpur Riders in the final of the Bangladesh Premier League. His match-winning innings included the **most sixes by a player in a T20 innings (male)** – 18.

Highest score carrying bat through a completed innings

On 27–28 Dec 2017, England opener Alastair Cook scored 244 not out against Australia in the Fourth Ashes Test at the MCG in Melbourne, Australia. It was the highest-ever Test score by an unbeaten opening batsman following the dismissal of all 10 team-mates in an innings.

Most Test matches hosted

The Third Test between England and the West Indies on 7–9 Sep 2017 was the 135th Test match staged at Lord's Cricket Ground in London, UK. The iconic venue hosted its first Test match, England vs Australia, on 21–23 Jul 1884.

Most expensive player in the Indian Premier League

India's cross-format master Virat Kohli was bought by Royal Challengers Bangalore for 17 crore ($2.67 m; £1.97 m) on 5 Jan 2018.

Highest score by a batsman "retired hurt"

Evin Lewis (TTO) made 176 runs for the West Indies before inside-edging a ball into his foot and retiring hurt from a One-Day International against England at The Oval in London, UK, on 27 Sep 2017. He beat the 140-year-old all-format record of Charles Bannerman (AUS), who made 165 runs before retiring hurt on 15–16 Mar 1877, during the **first Test match**.

Most wickets taken by a player in an U19s World Cup match

Australian leg spinner Lloyd Pope took eight wickets for 35 runs against England in the quarter-finals of the ICC Under-19s World Cup in Queenstown, New Zealand, on 23 Jan 2018.

On the same day, Sri Lankan opener Hasitha Boyagoda scored the **most runs by a player in an U19s World Cup match** – 191, against Kenya.

Fastest ambidextrous bowler

Pace bowler Yasir Jan (PAK) has been clocked bowling at 145 km/h (90 mph) with his right hand and 135 km/h (83.8 mph) with his left. A bowler may change hands during an over or a spell, but must inform the umpire beforehand.

Most wickets taken in an ICC World Cup final

On 23 Jul 2017, England's Anya Shrubsole took six wickets for 46 runs against India in the final of the ICC Women's World Cup at Lord's, UK – more than any player (male or female) in a World Cup final. Her figures included five wickets in 19 balls.

Highest successful run chase in a T20 match

On 16 Feb 2018, Australia replied to New Zealand's score of 243 for 6 by hitting 245 for 5 in a T20 Tri-Series match at Eden Park in Auckland, New Zealand. The triumphant run chase was built on an opening stand of 121 in 8.3 overs by D'Arcy Short and David Warner.

Most international hat-tricks

On 6 Apr 2017, Lasith Malinga (LKA) bowled his fourth international hat-trick (i.e, taking three wickets in three balls) during a T20 International against Bangladesh. He matched Wasim Akram (PAK), who took four hat-tricks from 1989 to 1999.

Best One-Day International (ODI) bowling figures by a player from an associate nation (male)

On 9 Jun 2017, leg spinner Rashid Khan took seven wickets for 18 runs – the fourth-best figures in ODI history – for Afghanistan against the West Indies at Gros Islet, Saint Lucia. Afghanistan were granted full membership of the International Cricket Council 13 days later, ending their status as an associate nation.

Most runs scored in ODIs (female)

As of 4 Mar 2018, India captain Mithali Raj had scored 6,259 ODI runs in 189 matches (170 innings) since her debut in the format in 1999.

Between 7 Feb and 24 Jun 2017, Raj hit the **most consecutive fifties in One-Day Internationals (female)** – seven. Together with England's Charlotte Edwards, she has the **most fifties scored in an ODI career (female)** – 55.

Fastest Twenty20 International hundred (male)

On 22 Dec 2017, Rohit Sharma (IND) made a century off just 35 balls – including eight sixes and 11 fours – against Sri Lanka in Indore, India. Sharma matched the feat of David Miller (ZAF), who made his own 35-ball century two months earlier, on 29 Oct, against Bangladesh in Potchefstroom, South Africa.

TENNIS

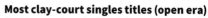

Most Grand Slam singles titles won (male)

On 28 Jan 2018, Roger Federer (CHE) secured his 20th Grand Slam title with victory at the Australian Open. Incredibly, the 36-year-old has won 10% of the 200 men's Grand Slams – comprising Wimbledon (see below) and the US, French and Australian Opens – staged since tennis turned professional in 1968.

The **most Grand Slam singles tennis titles won** by any player is 24, by Margaret Court (née Smith, AUS) between 1960 and 1973.

Most matches played on the ATP World Tour without retiring

As of 4 Mar 2018, Roger Federer had completed 1,394 consecutive matches on the ATP World Tour. His run stretched all the way back to his tour debut in Jul 1998, when the 16-year-old Federer lost to Lucas Arnold Ker in Gstaad, Switzerland.

Lowest-ranked player to win the US Open

Sloane Stephens (USA) had a world ranking of 83 when she lifted the US Open winner's trophy on 9 Sep 2017. Her maiden Grand Slam title was even more remarkable for the fact that it came just 69 days after she had returned from an 11-month injury layoff, which had seen her ranking plummet as low as 957.

First player to win 10 singles titles at the same Grand Slam (open era)

Clay-court king Rafael Nadal (ESP) collected his 10th French Open title on 11 Jun 2017, defeating Stan Wawrinka in straight sets. His previous triumphs occurred in 2005–08 and 2010–14. As of the 2017 final, Nadal's record at Roland Garros stood at an unbelievable 79 wins and just two defeats – to Robin Söderling in 2009 and Novak Djokovic in 2015.

Highest career earnings (female)

Serena Williams (USA) had earned $84,463,131 (£61,181,700) in career prize money as of 4 Mar 2018. Incredibly, the 23-time Grand Slam singles champion won her seventh Australian Open title on 28 Jan 2017 while eight weeks pregnant with daughter Alexis.

Most clay-court singles titles (open era)

On 23 Apr 2017, Rafael Nadal won his 50th title on clay at the Monte-Carlo Masters. He surpassed the feat of Guillermo Vilas (ARG), who won 49 clay-court titles between 1973 and 1983.

It was the 10th time Nadal had triumphed in Monte Carlo, making him the **first player to win 10 singles titles at the same ATP World Tour event (open era)** – see also above.

Most Grand Slam quad wheelchair doubles titles won (male)

David Wagner (USA) won his 16th Grand Slam quad doubles title at the 2017 US Open on 9 Sep, partnering Great Britain's Andrew Lapthorne to a 7–5, 6–2 win against Dylan Alcott and Bryan Barten.

Wagner has also claimed the **most Grand Slam quad singles titles won (male)** – six, tied with Peter Norfolk (UK).

Longest women's match at the US Open

Shelby Rogers (USA) defeated Daria Gavrilova (AUS) in a marathon second-round tie lasting 3 hr 33 min on 31 Aug 2017. Rogers squandered four match points before prevailing 7–6 (8–6), 4–6, 7–6 (7–5).

Most Wimbledon singles titles won (male)

On 16 Jul 2017, Roger Federer (CHE, see above) defeated Marin Čilić 6–3, 6–1, 6–4 for his eighth Wimbledon title. This took him one clear of Pete Sampras (USA) and William Renshaw (UK), who both won the event seven times.

The **most Wimbledon singles title won** by any player is nine, by Martina Navratilova (USA, b. CZE). She triumphed in 1978–79, 1982–87 and 1990.

First winner of the Next Gen ATP Finals

On 11 Nov 2017, Chung Hyeon (KOR) beat Andrey Rublev 3–4, 4–3, 4–2, 4–2 to win the first edition of the Next Gen ATP Finals, staged in Milan, Italy.

Tallest Grand Slam quarter-final match

On 5 Sep 2017, the US Open quarter-finals saw 6-ft 8-in (2.03-m) Kevin Anderson (ZAF, below left) take on 6-ft 6-in (1.98-m) Sam Querrey (USA). The battle of the giants – a combined height 13 ft 2 in (4.01 m) – was won by Anderson, who came through 7–6, 6–7, 6–3, 7–6.

AUTO SPORTS

Most views of a live testing session featuring a professional racing driver

On 3 May 2017, a live stream of Spanish Formula 1 driver Fernando Alonso's first IndyCar testing session for Andretti Autosport was watched by an unprecedented 2.149 million viewers on Facebook and YouTube. Alonso aims to complete the unofficial "Triple Crown of Motorsport" by winning the Monaco F1 Grand Prix, the Indianapolis 500 and the 24 Hours of Le Mans.

The **first winner of the Triple Crown of Motorsport** was Graham Hill (UK), who completed the set with victory at Le Mans in 1972. No other driver has matched his feat.

First female to win an individual world championship motorcycle race

On 17 Sep 2017, Ana Carrasco (ESP) won the seventh round of the FIM Supersport 300 World Championship at the Autódromo Internacional do Algarve in Portugal. Riding a Kawasaki Ninja 300, 20-year-old Carrasco took the lead in the final straight of the 11-lap race to win by 0.053 sec.

Most consecutive wins of the Superbike World Championship

Jonathan Rea (UK) secured his third straight Superbike World Championship with his 50th race victory, at Magny-Cours in France on 30 Sep 2017. He finished the season on 3–4 Nov with two wins in Qatar for a grand total of 556 points – the **most points earned in a Superbike World Championship season**.

Most World Motorcycle Championship career race wins in Moto GP/500cc

Valentino Rossi (ITA) won 89 championship races riding for Honda, Ducati and Yamaha from 9 Jul 2000 to 25 Jun 2017.

Fastest sidecar lap at the Isle of Man TT races

On 5 Jun 2017, brothers Ben and Tom Birchall (both UK) completed an Isle of Man TT lap in an LCR Honda 600cc sidecar in 19 min 19.746 sec. It was the first time a sidecar had recorded an average lap speed of more than 117 mph: 117.119 mph (188.485 km/h).

Most career wins in NHRA drag racing

John Force (USA) registered his 148th victory in NHRA drag racing on 19 Mar 2017, beating Jonnie Lindberg in the Funny Car final at the Amalie Motor Oil NHRA Gatornationals at Gainesville Raceway in Florida, USA. Force (b. 4 May 1949) was aged 67 years 319 days.

Fastest speed in a National Hot Rod Association (NHRA) Funny Car race (1,000 ft)

Two-time Funny Car champion Robert Hight (USA) clocked 339.87 mph (546.96 km/h) on 29 Jul 2017 at Sonoma Raceway in California, USA. This is the fastest speed in the history of NHRA professional drag racing.

On 18 Aug 2017, Hight followed up with the **lowest elapsed time in an NHRA Funny Car race (1,000 ft)** – winning in just 3.793 sec.

Most Formula 1 pole positions

As of 26 Mar 2018, Lewis Hamilton (UK) had secured 73 pole positions in Formula 1. He surpassed Michael Schumacher's record of 68 at the Italian Grand Prix on 2 Sep 2017.

On 7 Oct 2017, Hamilton qualified fastest at his 26th different circuit, the Suzuka International Racing Course in Japan – the **most Formula 1 circuits for a driver to secure pole position**.

Youngest rookie driver to achieve a podium finish in Formula 1

Lance Stroll (CAN, b. 29 Oct 1998) finished third in the Azerbaijan Grand Prix on 25 Jun 2017 in Baku, aged 18 years 239 days. The second-youngest F1 driver in history behind Max Verstappen, Stroll had been hired by the Williams team for his debut season.

Fastest completion of the Mount Washington Hillclimb Auto Race

On 9 Jul 2017, Subaru Rally Team USA's Travis Pastrana (USA) reached the summit of Mount Washington in New Hampshire, USA, in 5 min 44.72 sec. He beat the previous record for the 7.6-mi-long (12.2-km) course by 24.37 sec.

Fewest laps to lead the Daytona 500 by a winner

On 18 Feb 2018, Austin Dillon (USA) took the checkered flag at NASCAR's Daytona 500 having only taken the lead on the final lap in overtime. He matched the feat of 2017 winner Kurt Busch (USA), who also hit the front with one lap to go.

Highest average speed during a lap at the 24 Hours of Le Mans

On 16 Jun 2017, Kamui Kobayashi (JPN) secured pole for the 24 Hours of Le Mans in a Toyota TS050 Hybrid thanks to a qualifying lap with an average speed of 251.882 km/h (156.512 mph). His lap time of 3 min 14.791 sec was the quickest since chicanes were introduced to the Mulsanne Straight on the Circuit de la Sarthe in 1989.

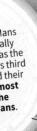
The 24 Hours of Le Mans of 2017 was eventually won by Porsche. It was the German constructor's third consecutive win and their 19th overall – the **most team wins at the 24 Hours of Le Mans**.

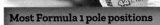

EXTREME SPORTS

Most appearances at the Summer X Games

Skateboarding legend Bob Burnquist (BRA) announced that the 2017 X Games would be his last as a competitor, having participated in all 26 Games since the inaugural event in 1995.

Burnquist won the **most medals at the Summer X Games** – 14 gold, eight silver and eight bronze between 1997 and 2015, for a total of 30.

Most medals won at the X Games (female)

Jamie Anderson (USA) won her 15th Winter X Games medal in the Women's Snowboard Big Air event on 27 Jan 2018. She has amassed five golds, seven silvers and three bronze, making every Snowboard Slopestyle podium between 2006 and 2018.

Most Summer X Games gold medals won in BMX Street (male)

Garrett Reynolds (USA) won his ninth BMX Street gold medal at the 2017 Summer X Games. He has only ever missed out on the title once, finishing second at X Games Los Angeles 2013.

Most event wins at a Nitro World Games

On 24 Jun 2017, Ryan Williams (AUS) became the first multi-event winner at a Nitro World Games. "R-Willy" won BMX Best Tricks and Scooter Best Tricks in Salt Lake City, Utah, USA.

Youngest X Games double gold medallist

On 29 Jan 2017, Kelly Sildaru (EST, b. 17 Feb 2002) won her second X Games gold in the Women's Ski Slopestyle, aged 14 years 347 days.

Even younger is Brighton Zeuner (USA, b. 14 Jul 2004), who became the **youngest Summer X Games gold medallist (female)**, aged 13 years 1 day, in the Women's Skateboard Park on 15 Jul 2017.

First winner of the FAI Swoop Freestyle World Championships

David "Junior" Ludvik (USA) was crowned world champion at the inaugural Fédération Aéronautique Internationale (FAI) Swoop Freestyle World Championships, held on 25–26 Aug 2017 in Copenhagen, Denmark. Swoop freestyle pilots parachute from a height of 1,500 m (4,921 ft), reaching speeds of 150 km/h (93 mph) before performing a series of acrobatic manoeuvres upon the water. Points are awarded for execution and style.

Farthest distance flown in a wingsuit (FAI-approved)

On 27 May 2017, Anastasis Polykarpou (CYP) flew 5.192 km (3.226 mi) in a wingsuit during Round 1 of the UK Wingsuit Performance Nationals 2017 at Netheravon in Wiltshire.

On the same day, Jackie Harper (UK) covered the **farthest distance flown in a wingsuit (female, FAI-approved)**: 4.359 km (2.708 mi). She achieved a speed of 254.2 km/h (157.9 mph) during her run.

Farthest distance canopy piloting (FAI-approved)

Skydiving instructor Cédric Veiga Rios (FRA) piloted his canopy parachute for 196.52 m (644 ft) at the World Games in Wrocław, Poland, on 22 Jul 2017.

The next day, Cornelia Mihai (UAE, b. ROM) achieved the **farthest distance canopy piloting (female, FAI-approved)** – 175.77 m (576 ft), also at the World Games.

Joe Parsons took his medal tally to 17 with bronze in the 2017 Snowmobile Best Trick final. He is one behind Shaun White (USA), who has the **most Winter X Games medals** (18).

Most wins of the Red Bull Cliff Diving World Series (female)

Rhiannan Iffland (AUS) won four out of six Red Bull Cliff Diving World Series events in 2017 to retain the King Kahekili Trophy. Iffland, who comes from a trampolining background, triumphed in her debut series in 2016 as a wildcard. She matched the feat of Rachelle Simpson (USA), also a two-time champion.

Most consecutive wins of the Winter X Games Snowmobile Freestyle event

On 28 Jan 2017, Joe Parsons (USA) became the first repeat champion in the Snowmobile Freestyle competition at Winter X Games XXI in Aspen, Colorado, USA. He landed a rare volt – spinning around 360° in his seat in the middle of a jump – to earn him a score of 93.00 for his second consecutive Freestyle title and third overall.

TARGET SPORTS

Most points scored in 70 m 72-arrow outdoor recurve archery (female)
Choi Mi-sun (KOR) scored 687 out of a possible 720 points during the women's recurve ranking round at the 2017 Universiade student games in Taipei, Chinese Taipei, on 20 Aug 2017.

Most points scored in 50 m 72-arrow outdoor recurve para-archery (W1, female)
Jessica Stretton (UK) scored 657 out of a possible 720 points during the ranking round for the 50-m W1 final at the 2017 World Archery Para Championships on 14 Sep 2017 in Beijing, China. It was her 10th world-record score of the year, having twice set four records in one day.

Highest score in ISSF 10 m Air Rifle (women)
On 24 Feb 2017, China's Shi Mengyao won gold at an ISSF World Cup event in New Delhi, India, with a score of 252.1. It also counted as an ISSF Junior World Record, as she was aged 19 at the time.

Highest score in ISSF 10 m Air Pistol (men)
On his ISSF World Cup debut in Guadalajara, Mexico, Shahzar Rizvi (IND) won the 10 m Air Pistol with a record score of 242.3 points on 3 Mar 2018.
The **highest score in ISSF 10 m Air Pistol (women)** is 246.9 points, by Zorana Arunović (SRB) at the European 10 m Shooting Championship in Maribor, Slovenia, on 11 Mar 2017.

First Pétanque World Championships mixed doubles gold medallists
Nadia ben Abdessalem and Khaled Lakhal (TUN) defeated the Cambodian pair of Sreang Sorakhim and Nhem Bora 13–7 in the final of the *doublettes mix* at the Pétanque World Championships on 16 Apr 2017 in Ghent, Belgium. Pétanque is usually played head-to-head or in *triplettes* – teams of three.

Youngest player at the Mosconi Cup
On 4 Dec 2017, Joshua Filler (DEU, b. 2 Oct 1997) made his debut for Europe against the USA in pool's Mosconi Cup, aged 20 years 63 days. He enjoyed a dream tournament, winning the Most Valuable Player award and sinking the pot that sealed Europe's 11–4 triumph.
Europe's victory over the USA was its 12th in total – the **most wins of the Mosconi Cup**. The USA has won 11 times, with one tie in 2006.

Most points scored in 18 m 60-arrow indoor recurve archery (male)
On 20 Jan 2017, Brady Ellison (USA) scored 599 out of 600 points at the Indoor Archery World Cup event in Nîmes, France. Ellison broke his own record of 598, set just two months earlier.
The **most points scored in 18 m 60-arrow indoor compound archery (male)** is 600 out of 600, by Mike Schloesser (NLD) on 24 Jan 2015.

Most men's doubles raffa gold medals at the World Games by a country
Italy have won all three finals of the raffa men's doubles at the World Games: in 2009, 2013 and 2017, when they defeated San Marino 12–7 on 24 Jul in Wrocław, Poland. Similar to pétanque, raffa is played with plastic balls, usually on carpet or clay.

Youngest snooker player to record a competitive 147 break
On 9 Jul 2017, Sean Maddocks (UK, b. 10 Apr 2002) hit a maximum break aged 15 years 90 days during the LiteTask Pro-Am series in Leeds, West Yorkshire, UK. He beat the record of snooker legend Ronnie O'Sullivan by eight days.
The **oldest snooker player to record a 147 break in professional competition** is Mark Davis (UK, b. 12 Aug 1972), who hit his second-ever maximum during a Championship League match on 2 Mar 2017 aged 44 years 202 days. He had recorded his first just two months earlier, on 10 Jan.

Phil Taylor is one of only two players, along with Michael van Gerwen, to have hit two nine-dart finishes – i.e., winning a leg using the fewest possible darts – in the same match.

PHIL TAYLOR
Phil "The Power" Taylor (UK) retired from darts following the final of the Professional Darts Corporation (PDC) World Championship on 1 Jan 2018, in which he was defeated 7–2 by Rob Cross. Taylor's legacy of darting domination includes the **most World Championship wins** (16 – two with the British Darts Organisation and 14 with the PDC), the **most Premier League Darts titles** (six) and the **most World Matchplay titles** (16). "The Power" won his 16th World Matchplay crown on 30 Jul 2017, defeating Peter Wright 18–8 in the final.

GOLF

Youngest golfer to win an event on the Ladies European Tour

Atthaya Thitikul (THA, b. 20 Feb 2003) won the Ladies European Thailand Championship on 6–9 Jul 2017 aged 14 years 139 days. She finished the event on a 5-under-par score of 283, but was unable to claim the €45,000 ($51,322; £39,838) prize owing to her amateur status.

Lowest round to par at the US Open

On 17 Jun 2017, Justin Thomas (USA) shot a 9-under-par round of 63 during the third round of the US Open at Erin Hills in Wisconsin, USA. He bettered the mark of -8 (also a score of 63), shot by Johnny Miller (USA) at the 1973 US Open.

Both Thomas and Miller share the record for the **lowest score in a US Open round** – their respective scores of 63 were equalled by Jack Nicklaus and Tom Weiskopf (both USA) on the same day, 12 Jun 1980, and by Vijay Singh (FJI) in 2003.

Lowest score to par at the US Open

Brooks Koepka (USA) won the 2017 US Open with a score of -16 on 15–18 Jun. He matched the winning score of Rory McIlroy (UK) at the 2011 US Open.

Lowest final round by a winner at a World Golf Championship event

Hideki Matsuyama (JPN) holed seven birdies and an eagle in a final-round 61 en route to victory at the Bridgestone Invitational on 6 Aug 2017, in Akron, Ohio, USA. The four annual World Golf Championship tournaments are counted among the most prestigious events outside the majors.

Most career holes-in-one on the PGA Tour

According to official PGA Tour statistics, Hal Sutton (USA) and Robert Allenby (AUS) had hit 10 holes-in-one on the tour, as of 28 Nov 2017.

The **most career holes-in-one on the European Tour** is also 10, by Miguel Ángel Jiménez (ESP).

Youngest winner of The Players Championship

On 14 May 2017, Kim Si-woo (KOR, b. 28 Jun 1995) won The Players Championship in Florida, USA, aged 21 years 320 days. Si-woo became only the fourth golfer to win two PGA Tour events before the age of 22, joining Jordan Spieth, Sergio García and Tiger Woods.

Fastest time for a golfer to earn $1 million on the LPGA Tour

Park Sung-hyun (KOR) earned $1 m (£763,068) on the LPGA Tour in 136 days from 2 Mar to 16 Jul 2017 – just 14 events, culminating in her victory at the US Women's Open. In Nov 2017, Sung-hyun became the first LPGA golfer to reach world No.1 in their rookie season. She and Ryu So-yeon (KOR) became the first co-winners of the LPGA Rolex Player of the Year since it was first awarded in 1966.

First winners of the GolfSixes tournament

Denmark (Lucas Bjerregaard and Thorbjørn Olesen) were the victors at the inaugural GolfSixes European Tour event at Centurion Club in St Albans, Hertfordshire, UK, on 6–7 May 2017. Two-man teams from 16 nations competed over a six-hole course, with a shot clock penalizing slow play.

Most birdies recorded in a single round on the PGA Tour

Adam Hadwin (CAN) shot 13 birdies in 18 holes at the CareerBuilder Challenge on 21 Jan 2017. He equalled Chip Beck (USA), who also made 13 birdies at the 1991 Las Vegas International.

On 15 Jun 2017, Hadwin shot the **most consecutive birdies at the US Open** – six, matching the feat of George Burns in 1982 and Andy Dillard (both USA) in 1992.

Most PGA Tour Champions major tournament victories

As of 14 Aug 2017, Bernhard Langer (DEU) had won 10 majors on the PGA Tour Champions circuit, which is open to players aged 50 and above. His ninth victory, at the 2017 Senior PGA Championship, meant that he had triumphed at all five Tour Champions majors.

The **most PGA Tour Champions tournament victories** is 45, achieved by Hale Irwin (USA) between 1995 and 2007.

Most major tournaments played before winning

Sergio García (ESP) recorded his maiden major victory at the 2017 Masters Tournament in his 74th major. This is two more than Tom Kite, who won the 1992 US Open in his 72nd major attempt. García defeated England's Justin Rose in a sudden-death play-off on 9 Apr at Augusta National Golf Club in Georgia, USA.

As of 16 Mar 2018, the **most major tournaments played without winning (current)** is 79, by Lee Westwood (UK).

The **most major tournaments played without winning ever** is 87, by Jay Haas (USA) between 1974 and 2008.

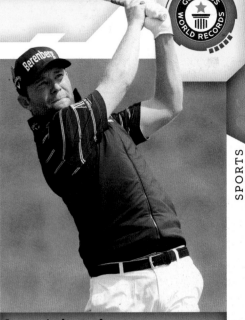

Lowest single-round score at a major championship (male)

On 22 Jul 2017, Branden Grace (ZAF) shot an 8-under-par round of 62 during the third round of The Open Championship at Royal Birkdale Golf Club in Southport, Merseyside, UK. Grace carded eight birdies and no bogeys. The previous lowest major round of 63 had been achieved 31 times, by 29 different golfers.

TRACK & FIELD

First sub-four-minute mile

On 6 May 1954, medical student Roger Bannister (UK) ran a mile in 3 min 59.4 sec before a 3,000-strong crowd at the Iffley Road track in Oxford, UK. He became the first person to break the four-minute barrier for the distance, and although his time was beaten just 46 days later it remains a landmark in the history of sport. (See p.232 for the current record). Track announcer Norris McWhirter would go on to compile the first edition of *The Guinness Book of Records* with his twin Ross. Roger Bannister died on 3 Mar 2018, aged 88.

Most medals won at an IAAF Athletics World Championships by a country

The USA won an unprecedented 30 medals at the 2017 IAAF World Championships in London, UK: 10 gold, 11 silver and nine bronze.

Since the first World Championships in Athletics in 1983, Team USA have won the **most World Championship gold medals**: 155 in total.

Largest margin of victory in an IAAF World Championship 4 x 400 m relay

On 13 Aug 2017, the USA – Quanera Hayes, Allyson Felix, Shakima Wimbley and anchor Phyllis Francis – claimed gold in the women's 4 x 400 m relay in a time of 3 min 19.02 sec, a total of 5.98 sec ahead of second-place Great Britain.

Farthest discus throw (F52, male)

On 18 Jul 2017, Andre Rocha (BRA) won the F52 men's discus at the World Para Athletics Championships with a throw of 23.80 m (78 ft 1 in) at the Olympic Stadium in London, UK. A former military police officer, Rocha suffered a spinal cord injury in a fall suffered in the line of duty.

Rocha set more than six world records in the same season, rounding off with the **farthest shot put (F52, male)** – 11.74 m (38 ft 6 in) in São Paulo, Brazil, on 28 Oct 2017.

Fastest 400 m (T63, female)

Gitte Haenen (BEL) won a para 400 m in a time of 1 min 28.76 sec on 5 Jun 2017 at a Grand Prix event in Nottwil, Switzerland. A former kick-boxer, Haenen had her left leg amputated above the knee following damage sustained in training. Incredibly, it was her first-ever competitive 400 m race.

Fastest 400 m (T37, female)

On 20 Jul 2017, Georgina Hermitage (UK) won World Championship gold in the T37 women's 400 m in 1 min 0.29 sec in London, UK.

Hermitage is also responsible for the **fastest 100 m (T37, female)** – 13.13 sec, on 9 Sep 2016.

Fastest 200 m (T38, female)

Sophie Hahn (UK) won the T38 women's 200 m at the World Para Athletics Championships in 26.11 sec on 15 Jul 2017, in London, UK.

On 22 Jul 2017, Hahn improved her own record for **fastest 100 m (T38, female)**, taking gold in 12.44 sec.

Most medals won at the IAAF Athletics World Championships (male)
Usain Bolt (JAM) retired in 2017 having won 14 World Championship medals since 2009. He won bronze in the 100 m in London to add to his collection of 11 gold (see below) and two silver medals. Bolt's 100 m victory at the 2009 World Championships came in 9.58 sec – still the **fastest 100 m (male)**.

Most medals won at the IAAF Athletics World Championships
Allyson Felix (USA) won 16 World Championship medals between 2005 and 2017 – more than any other athlete, male or female. Her tally includes the **most World Championship gold medals**: 11, shared with Usain Bolt (see above). In 2017, Felix added relay golds in the 4 x 100 m and 4 x 400 m, and individual bronze in the 400 m.

Fastest wheelchair 1,500 m (T54, male)

Canada's Brent Lakatos won the men's 1,500 m T53–54 race in 2 min 51.84 sec in Nottwil, Switzerland, on 3 Jun 2017. It was the culmination of a remarkable 10-day period in which he set five world records.

On 27 May, Lakatos broke the **fastest wheelchair 100 m (T53, male)** record for the second time in three days, crossing the line in 14.10 sec at the Swiss Nationals in Arbon, Switzerland. The next day, he added the **fastest wheelchair 200 m (T53, male)** – 25.04 sec – and the **fastest wheelchair 800 m (T53, male)** – 1 min 31.91 sec.

Cockroft began racing at the age of 13 – her father, a welder, built her first racing wheelchair. She broke her first world record in 2010, and in June that year set seven fastest-ever times in just eight days!

Fastest wheelchair 100 m (T34, female)

On 14 Jul 2017, Hannah Cockroft (UK) won gold at the World Para Athletics Championships in London, UK, in a time of 17.18 sec. It was the first of three gold medals for the multiple record holder, who followed up with wins in the 400 m and 800 m T34 events.

On 3 Jun 2017, Cockroft achieved the **fastest wheelchair 1,500 m (T34, female)**: 3 min 50.22 sec, in Nottwil, Switzerland. She took 11 sec off the previous record time, set three years earlier.

Most IAAF Diamond Race titles won (female)

Sandra Perković (HRV) won six consecutive Diamond League titles in the discus from 2012 to 2017. She won four out of five events in 2017, recording victories in Shanghai, Oslo, Birmingham and the series climax in Brussels. As of 1 Sep 2017, Perković had won 38 individual discus events – the **most Diamond League event victories**.

The **most IAAF Diamond Race titles won (male)** is seven, by pole vaulter Renaud Lavillenie (FRA) from 2010 to 2016 (see p.235).

Most wins of the IAAF Hammer Throw Challenge

Anita Włodarczyk (POL) won the women's IAAF Hammer Throw Challenge five consecutive times between 2013 and 2017. She remained undefeated in competition throughout the 2017 season, the third year in a row that this had occurred.

The **most wins of the IAAF Hammer Throw Challenge (male)** is four, by Paweł Fajdek, also from Poland, who won in 2013, 2015, 2016 and 2017. In his most recent triumph, Fajdek recorded the competition's **highest-ever overall score** of 248.48. He won gold at the IAAF World Championships.

Farthest shot put (F43, male)
Akeem Stewart (TTO) took shot-put gold with a throw of 19.08 m (62 ft 7 in) at the IPC World Para Athletics Championships in London, UK, on 23 Jul 2017. Stewart, who has a congenital leg discrepancy, also won javelin gold with the **farthest javelin throw (F43, male)** – 57.61 m (189 ft), on 18 Jul.

Largest winning margin at an IAAF World Athletics Championships

On 13 Aug 2017, Yohann Diniz (FRA, b. 1 Jan 1978) won the men's 50 km road walk by a margin of 8 min 5 sec, the largest in the championship's history. Diniz's time of 3 hr 33 min 12 sec was the second-fastest ever recorded in the event, while at 39 years 224 days he became the **oldest IAAF World Championship gold medallist (male)**.

Fastest 300 m (male)
On 28 Jun 2017, Wayde van Niekerk (ZAF) ran a world-best time of 30.81 sec for the 300 m at an IAAF World Challenge meeting in Ostrava, Czech Republic. He took the record for the rarely run distance from Michael Johnson (USA), having previously relieved him of the **fastest 400 m (male)** by running 43.03 sec in 2016.

Most team wins at the IAAF World Cross Country Championships (women)

Kenya won their 12th senior women's title at the 2017 IAAF World Cross Country Championships on 26 Mar. Led by overall winner Irene Chepet Cheptai, Kenyan athletes finished in the first six places, ensuring an unprecedented lowest-possible team score of 10. Kenya had previously triumped in 1991–93, 1995–96, 1998, 2001 and 2009–13.

The **most team wins at the IAAF World Cross Country Championships (men)** was also recorded by Kenya, with 24 titles between 1986 and 2011.

Fastest one-mile race walk

Tom Bosworth (UK) won the Anniversary Games one-mile race walk in 5 min 31.08 sec on 9 Jul 2017 at the Olympic Stadium in London, UK. He beat the previous world-best time, set 27 years earlier by Algis Grigaliūnas, by almost 6 sec.

Most IAAF World Athletics Championship gold medals won in an individual event (female)

Brittney Reese (USA) won her fourth World Championship long jump title on 11 Aug 2017 with a third-round jump of 7.02 m (23 ft). She had previously triumphed in 2009, 2011 and 2013, only to fail to make the 2015 final. Reese equalled shot-putter Valerie Adams (née Vili, NZ), who achieved the **most consecutive World Championship individual gold medals (female)** – four, between 2007 and 2013.

Although Reese and Adams won the most World Championship golds in an individual women's event, Allyson Felix (above left) also won four in the 4 x 400 m relay. Her compatriot Natasha Hastings has five golds in the same event, although she ran in the preliminary heats only in 2007–11.

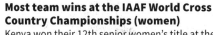

MARATHONS

Most wins of the London Marathon (male)

On 22 Apr 2018, Eliud Kipchoge (KEN) won his third London Marathon, finishing in 2 hr 4 min 17 sec. He joined three-time winners António Pinto (PRT), Dionicio Cerón (MEX) and Martin Lel (KEN). Kipchoge ran the **fastest London Marathon** – 2 hr 3 min 5 sec – on 24 Apr 2016.

The **most wins of the London Marathon (female)** is four, by Ingrid Kristiansen (NOR) in 1984–85 and 1987–88.

Fastest completion of the Sri Chinmoy Self-Transcendence 3100 Mile Race (female)

An ultra-marathon staged around an extended block in Jamaica, New York City, USA, the Sri Chinmoy Self-Transcendence 3100 Mile Race is the **longest running race held annually**. On 6 Aug 2017, Kaneenika Janakova (SVK) completed the course in 48 days 14 hr 24 min 10 sec. She averaged more than 63 mi (101 km) a day for almost two months, beating the previous women's record by more than 17 hr.

The **fastest completion of the Sri Chinmoy Self-Transcendence 3100 Mile Race** is 40 days 9 hr 6 min 21 sec, achieved by Ashprihanal Aalto (FIN) on 24 Jul 2015. He averaged more than 76 mi (122 km) a day, recording his eighth victory in the event.

Most wins of the Ultra-Trail du Mont-Blanc (male)

On 2 Sep 2017, François D'Haene (FRA) won his third Ultra-Trail du Mont-Blanc, following victories in 2012 and 2014. He matched the feat of Kílian Jornet (ESP), who won in 2008–09 and 2011. First staged in 2003, the race is a c. 167-km (103-mi) mountain ultra-marathon held annually in the Alps across France, Switzerland and Italy.

The **most wins of the Ultra-Trail du Mont-Blanc** is five, achieved by Lizzy Hawker (UK) in 2005, 2008 and 2010–12.

Fastest time to win the Ironman World Championship (male)

Patrick Lange (DEU) won the 2017 Ironman World Championship on Big Island in Hawaii, USA, in a time of 8 hr 1 min 40 sec on 14 Oct. He completed a 2.4-mi (3.8-km) swim in 48:45, a 112-mi (180-km) bike ride in 4:28:53 and a 26.2-mi (42.1-km) marathon run in 2:39:59.

Farthest run in 24 hours (female)

Patrycja Bereznowska (POL) ran 259.99 km (161.55 mi) in 24 hr at the 12th IAU 24 Hour World Championships in Belfast, UK, on 1–2 Jul 2017. It was the second time she had broken the 24-hr record that year, surpassing her distance of 256.27 km (159.24 mi) at the 24 Hour Polish Championships in Łódź, Poland, on 8–9 Apr.

The **farthest run in 24 hours** is 303.50 km (188.58 mi), achieved by the legendary ultra-marathon runner Yiannis Kouros (GRC) in Adelaide, Australia, on 4–5 Oct 1997.

Farthest run in 6 hours (female)

Nele Alder-Baerens (DEU) covered 85.49 km (53.12 mi) in 6 hr at the 6-Stunden-Lauf Münster ultra-distance race in Münster, Germany, on 11 Mar 2017. Alder-Baerens has impaired vision and has been completely deaf since the age of 13.

Farthest run in 12 hours (female)

On 9–10 Dec 2017, Camille Herron (USA) covered 149.13 km (92.66 mi) in 12 hr at the Desert Solstice track meeting in Phoenix, Arizona, USA. She beat Ann Trason's 1991 mark of 147.60 km (91.71 mi).

Virgin LONDON MARATHON money 2018

On 22 Apr 2018, around 40,000 runners lined up for the 38th annual London Marathon in the UK. GWR partnered with the event for the 11th year, and saw a host of records fall to fleet-footed fancy-dress runners. Check them out below:

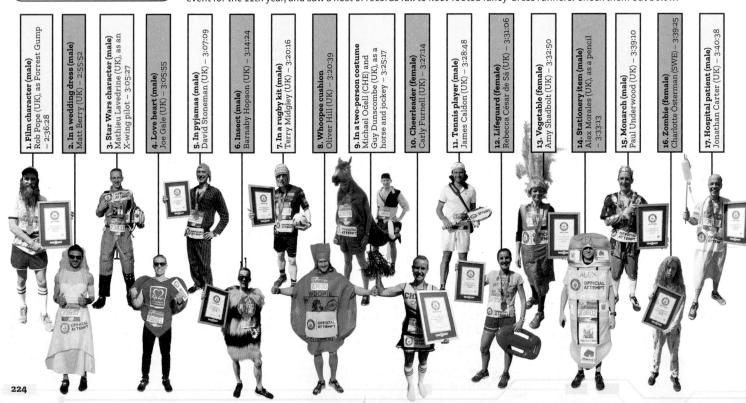

1. **Film character (male)** Rob Pope (UK), as Forrest Gump – 2:36:28
2. **In a wedding dress (male)** Matt Berry (UK) – 2:55:52
3. **Star Wars character (male)** Mathieu Lavedrine (UK), as an X-wing pilot – 3:05:27
4. **Love heart (male)** Joe Gale (UK) – 3:05:55
5. **In pyjamas (male)** David Stoneman (UK) – 3:07:09
6. **Insect (male)** Barnaby Hopson (UK) – 3:14:24
7. **In a rugby kit (male)** Terry Midgley (UK) – 3:20:16
8. **Whoopee cushion** Oliver Hill (UK) – 3:20:39
9. **In a two-person costume** Michael Odell (CHE) and Guy Dunscombe (UK), as a horse and jockey – 3:25:17
10. **Cheerleader (female)** Carly Furnell (UK) – 3:27:14
11. **Tennis player (male)** James Caldon (UK) – 3:28:48
12. **Lifeguard (female)** Rebecca César de Sá (UK) – 3:31:06
13. **Vegetable (female)** Amy Shadbolt (UK) – 3:32:50
14. **Stationery item (male)** Alex Morales (UK), as a pencil – 3:33:13
15. **Monarch (male)** Paul Underwood (UK) – 3:39:10
16. **Zombie (female)** Charlotte Österman (SWE) – 3:39:25
17. **Hospital patient (male)** Jonathan Carter (UK) – 3:40:38

Fastest time to win the Chicago Wheelchair Marathon (female)

On 8 Oct 2017, Tatyana McFadden (USA, b. RUS) won the Chicago Wheelchair Marathon in Illinois, USA, in 1 hr 39 min 15 sec. She edged out compatriot Amanda McGrory in a tight finish that saw them both given the same time. It was McFadden's seventh consecutive win in Chicago, and her eighth overall.

Fastest time to complete the Boston Push-Rim Wheelchairs

Marcel Hug (CHE) won the World Marathon Majors wheelchair event in Massachusetts, USA, in 1 hr 18 min 4 sec on 17 Apr 2017. It was the third consecutive victory in the race for the "Silver Bullet".

On the same date, Hug's compatriot Manuela Schär achieved the **fastest time to complete the Boston Push-Rim Wheelchairs (female)** – 1 hr 28 min 17 sec.

Most wins of the Wheelchair London Marathon

David Weir (UK) claimed his eighth men's title at the London Marathon, UK, on 22 Apr 2018. This is the most wins by any wheelchair athlete at the event.

Largest women's marathon

Held on 11 Mar 2018, the Nagoya Women's Marathon attracted a field of 21,915 runners in Aichi Prefecture, Japan. The race has improved upon its own record every year since 2012. The 38th edition of the IAAF Gold Label road race was won by Ethiopia's Meskerem Assefa in 2 hr 21 min 45 sec.

Most wins of the Great North Run

On 10 Sep 2017, Mo Farah (UK, b. SOM) claimed his fourth consecutive title at the Great North Run half-marathon in Newcastle-upon-Tyne, UK. He equalled the feat of Benson Masya (KEN), who triumphed in 1991–92, 1994 and 1996.

The **most wins of the Great North Run (female)** is three, achieved by Lisa Martin (AUS) in 1986–87 and 1989, Liz McColgan (UK) in 1992 and 1995–96 and Mary Keitany (KEN) in 2014–15 and 2017.

Fastest time to run the Paris Marathon (female)

On 9 Apr 2017, Purity Rionoripo (KEN) won the Paris Marathon in France in 2 hr 20 min 55 sec. She beat the course record, set by Ethiopia's Feyse Tadese in 2013, by 11 sec, and her lifetime best by nearly 4 min. Rionoripo's husband Paul Lonyangata won the men's race on the same day – turn to p.90 to see the record they broke together.

The **fastest time to run the Paris Marathon** is 2 hr 5 min 4 sec, by Kenenisa Bekele (ETH) on 6 Apr 2014. It was Bekele's marathon debut.

Fastest-run marathon on debut
On 24 Sep 2017, Guye Adola (ETH, above) finished second at the Berlin Marathon in Germany in a time of 2 hr 3 min 46 sec. This was the 11th-fastest marathon ever run. Adola averaged a mile every 4 min 43.3 sec.

In 2011, Kenyan runner Moses Mosop ran the then second-fastest marathon in history on his debut, completing the Boston Marathon in 2 hr 3 min 6 sec. However, the IAAF does not classify Boston as a record-eligible course, owing to the fact that its start and finish points are too far apart and it exceeds the maximum permitted decrease in elevation.

Fastest-run Dubai Marathon
Mosinet Geremew (ETH) won the Dubai Marathon in the UAE in 2 hr 4 min on 26 Jan 2018. He won an extraordinary sprint finish that saw the first six athletes cross the finish line within 15 sec of one another. A total of seven runners clocked times under 2 hr 5 min – a first in marathon history.

Fastest time to run the Dubai Marathon (female)

Roza Bekele (ETH) triumphed at the 2018 Dubai Marathon on 26 Jan in 2 hr 19 min 17 sec – the 12th-fastest time ever run over the distance by a woman at that point. The first four finishers at Dubai recorded times under 2 hr 20 min, the most ever in a women's marathon.

Fastest time to run the Marathon des Sables (female)

On 9–15 Apr 2017, Elisabet Barnes (SWE) recorded her second win in three years at the gruelling 250-km (155.3-mi) ultra-marathon across the Sahara desert, in 23 hr 16 min 12 sec. Barnes beat the previous women's record, set by Laurence Fricotteaux-Klein in 2007, by almost 15 min.

The **fastest time to run the Marathon des Sables** is 16 hr 22 min 29 sec, by Mohamad Ahansal (MAR) in 1998.

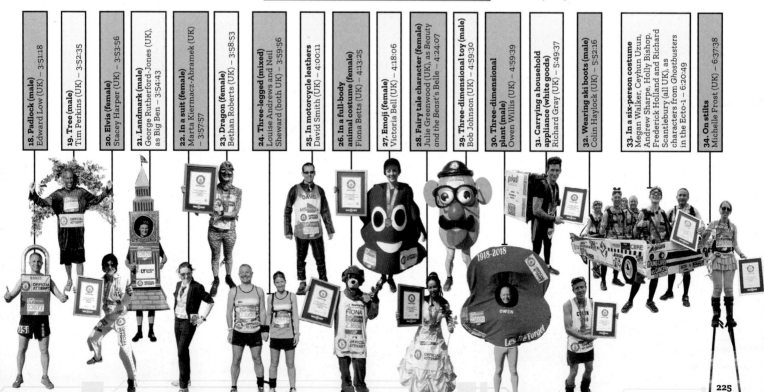

18. Padlock (male)
Edward Low (UK) – 3:51:18

19. Tree (male)
Tim Perkins (UK) – 3:52:35

20. Elvis (female)
Stacey Harper (UK) – 3:53:56

21. Landmark (male)
George Rutherford-Jones (UK), as Big Ben – 3:54:43

22. In a suit (female)
Marta Kiermacz-Abramek (UK) – 3:57:57

23. Dragon (female)
Bethan Roberts (UK) – 3:58:53

24. Three-legged (mixed)
Louise Andrews and Neil Sheward (both UK) – 3:59:56

25. In motorcycle leathers
David Smith (UK) – 4:00:11

26. In a full-body animal costume (female)
Fiona Betts (UK) – 4:13:25

27. Emoji (female)
Victoria Bell (UK) – 4:18:06

28. Fairy tale character (female)
Julie Greenwood (UK), as Beauty and the Beast's Belle – 4:24:07

29. Three-dimensional toy (male)
Bob Johnson (UK) – 4:59:30

30. Three-dimensional plant (male)
Owen Willis (UK) – 4:59:39

31. Carrying a household appliance (white goods)
Richard Gray (UK) – 5:49:37

32. Wearing ski boots (male)
Colin Haylock (UK) – 5:52:16

33. In a six-person costume
Megan Walker, Ceyhun Uzun, Andrew Sharpe, Holly Bishop, Frederick Holland and Richard Scantlebury (all UK), as characters from Ghostbusters in the Ecto-1 – 6:20:49

34. On stilts
Michelle Frost (UK) – 6:37:38

SWIMMING

Most gold medals won at a single FINA World Championships

Caeleb Dressel (USA) won seven gold medals at the 2017 FINA World Championships, equalling the record set by compatriot Michael Phelps in 2007. Dressel won the 50 m and 100 m freestyle, 100 m butterfly, 4 x 100 m freestyle and mixed freestyle, and 4 x 100 m medley and mixed medley, setting two world-record times (see below).

Fastest long course relay 4 x 100 m freestyle (mixed)

On 29 Jul 2017, a US team featuring Caeleb Dressel, Nathan Adrian, Simone Manuel and Mallory Comerford won the World Championships 4 x 100 m freestyle mixed relay in a time of 3 min 19.60 sec.

The **fastest long course relay 4 x 100 m medley (mixed)** is 3 min 38.56 sec, also achieved by the USA at the 2017 World Championships on 26 Jul 2017. The team comprised Matt Grevers, Lilly King, Caeleb Dressel and Simone Manuel.

The **fastest long course relay 4 x 100 m medley (female)** is 3 min 51.55 sec, achieved by the USA – Kathleen Baker (backstroke), Lilly King (breaststroke), Kelsi Worrell (butterfly) and Simone Manuel (freestyle) – on 30 Jul 2017.

Most gold medals won at the FINA Swimming World Championships (female)

Katie Ledecky (USA) won 14 World Championship gold medals between 2013 and 2017. She added five to her tally in Budapest in 2017, winning the 400 m, 800 m, 1,500 m, 4 x 100 m and 4 x 200 m freestyle.

The **most gold medals won at the FINA Swimming World Championships (overall)** is 26, by Michael Phelps (USA) in 2001–11.

Fastest finswimming 100 m bi-fins (female)

At the World Games 2017 in Wrocław, Poland, Petra Senánszky (HUN) won the 100 m bi-fins in 45.16 sec on 22 Jul. It was her second world record of the games, having swum the **fastest finswimming 50 m bi-fins (female)** in 20.52 sec the previous day. Bi-fin competitors race on the surface of the water using a mask, snorkel and a pair of fins.

Fastest short course 200 m freestyle (female)

Sarah Sjöström (SWE) won the short course 200 m freestyle in 1 min 50.43 sec at the FINA World Cup in Eindhoven, Netherlands, on 12 Aug 2017. It was one of five world records she set in 2017 (see p.238).

However, Sjöström went on to lose the **fastest short course 100 m freestyle (female)** record when Cate Campbell (AUS) swam 50.25 sec at the Australian Short Course Championships on 26 Oct 2017.

Fastest 100 m butterfly – S13 (female)

On 4 Dec 2017, Carlotta Gilli (ITA) won gold at the World Para Swimming Championships in 1 min 2.64 sec. In her debut season, the 16-year-old also set the **fastest 50 m butterfly – S13 (female)** (27.98 sec) and **fastest 200 m individual medley – SM13 (female)** (2 min 23.62 sec), both on 9 Jul.

Fastest swim 50 m backstroke –S4 (male)

Arnošt Petráček (CZE) swam the 50 m backstroke in 41.63 sec in Berlin, Germany, on 7 Jul 2017. It was the second time in three months that Petráček – who has no humerus bones in his arms owing to phocomelia syndrome – had set a fastest time for the event.

Fastest long course 50 m breaststroke (male)

At the FINA (Fédération Internationale de Natation) World Swimming Championships in Budapest, Hungary, on 25 Jul 2017, Adam Peaty (UK) won his 50 m breaststroke semi-final in 25.95 sec. It was the first time any swimmer had broken the 26-sec barrier in this event. Peaty broke his own record twice in the same day, having recorded a time of 26.10 sec in an earlier heat.

Fastest long course 100 m backstroke (female)

Kylie Masse (CAN) became the first Canadian female FINA world swimming champion by winning the women's 100 m backstroke final in 58.10 sec on 25 Jul 2017. She beat Gemma Spofforth's fastest time of 58.12 sec from 2009, which had been the longest-standing existing record in women's swimming until that point.

Fastest International Life Saving Federation (ILSF) 100 m manikin tow with fins (male)

On 22 Jul 2017, Jacopo Musso (ITA) won gold in the men's 100 m manikin tow with fins life-saving event in 49.02 sec at the 2017 World Games. Competitors are required to swim 50 m freestyle with fins and rescue tube before fixing the tube around a manikin floating at the surface by the turning edge. They then tow the manikin back to the finish.

On the same day, Justine Weyders (FRA) achieved the **fastest ILSF 100 m manikin tow with fins (female)** in 57.18 sec, also at the World Games in Wrocław, Poland.

Adam Peaty not only holds the record for the **fastest long course 100 m breaststroke (male)** – 57.13 sec – but is also responsible for all 10 fastest times ever swum in the event!

WATER SPORTS

VINCENT-LAPOINTE L

Fastest flatwater C1 women's 200 m

On 27 Aug 2017, Laurence Vincent-Lapointe (CAN) won the C1 (canoe singles) women's 200 m final in 45.478 sec at the ICF Canoe Sprint World Championships in Račice, Czech Republic. The previous day, she and Katie Vincent (CAN) had set the **fastest flatwater C2 (canoe doubles) women's 500 m** – 1 min 56.752 sec.

Fastest flatwater K1 men's 200 m

On 16 Jul 2017, Liam Heath (UK) won the men's K1 (kayak singles) 200 m title in a time of 33.38 sec at the European Canoe Association (ECA) Canoe Sprint European Championships in Plovdiv, Bulgaria.

The **fastest flatwater K2 (kayak doubles) men's 1,000 m** is 3 min 5.624 sec, achieved by Francisco Cubelos and Iñigo Peña (both ESP) in Szeged, Hungary, on 27 May 2017.

Fastest speed windsurfing (female)

On 22 Nov 2017, Zara Davis (UK) windsurfed along a 500-m (1,640-ft) course at an average speed of 46.49 knots (53.49 mph; 86.09 km/h) in Lüderitz, Namibia. This record was approved by the World Sailing Speed Record Council (WSSRC).

Most wins of the Water Polo World Championships by a team (female)

Since the competition's introduction in 1986, the USA women's water polo team has won gold at the FINA World Aquatics Championships five times: in 2003, 2007, 2009, 2015 and 2017. The pre-tournament favourites sealed their fifth title with a 13–6 victory over Spain on 28 Jul 2017 at the Alfréd Hajós National Swimming Stadium in Budapest, Hungary. Attacker Kiley Neushul scored four times.

Fastest University Boat Race (women's)

On 2 Apr 2017, Cambridge secured the Women's Boat Race Trophy by beating Oxford in a time of 18 min 33 sec. This was not only the fastest time recorded since the women's race was moved to the River Thames in London, UK, in 2015, but also quicker than the winning time set by the men over the same course in both 2014 and 2016.

Fastest para-row, women's single sculls

On 16 Jun 2017, Birgit Skarstein (NOR) won a para-rowing women's single sculls exhibition race in 10 min 49.940 sec in Poznań, Poland. Skarstein also represented Norway in cross-country skiing at the 2014 Paralympic Games.

The **fastest para-row, men's single sculls** is 9 min 39.480 sec – by Erik Horrie (AUS) at the 2017 World Rowing Championships, on 1 Oct.

Fastest rowing, men's single sculls

Robert Manson (NZ) won the final of the men's single sculls in 6 min 30.740 sec at the Rowing World Cup in Poznań, Poland, on 18 Jun 2017. He knocked almost 3 sec off the previous best time over 2,000 m, set by Mahé Drysdale in 2009.

Youngest APB drop-knee bodyboarding world champion

Sammy Morretino (USA, b. 29 Nov 1996) became the Association of Professional Bodyboarders' (APB) drop-knee bodyboarding world champion aged 20 years 292 days on 17 Sep 2017. He overcame seven-time champion Dave Hubbard in the final of the Sintra Pro event to take the title.

Longest freediving, dynamic apnea without fins (female)

Magdalena Solich-Talanda (POL) swam 191 m (626 ft 7 in) underwater on a single breath at the Polish Freediving Pool Championships in Opole, Poland, on 1 Jul 2017.

Longest gap between diving gold medals at the FINA World Aquatics Championships (male)

On 22 Jul 2017, Tom Daley (UK) won gold in the men's 10 m platform at the FINA World Aquatics Championships a total of 8 years 1 day after he had triumphed in the same event, aged 15, at the 2009 championships.

Also at the 2009 championships, Yuliya Pakhalina (RUS) won gold in the women's 1 m springboard 11 years 182 days after she had topped the podium in the 3 m synchronized springboard on 18 Jan 1998 – the **longest gap between diving gold medals at the FINA World Aquatics Championships**.

Deepest freedive – constant weight (female)

On 10 May 2017, Alessia Zecchini (ITA) dived to a depth of 104 m (341 ft 2 in) at the Vertical Blue competition at Dean's Blue Hole in The Bahamas. It was the second time in four days she had set a constant weight record – on 6 May she dived to 102 m (334 ft 7 in), only for Hanako Hirose to reach 103 m (337 ft 11 in) just minutes before Zecchini reclaimed her title.

WINTER OLYMPICS

Oldest Winter Olympic gold medallist in Alpine skiing

Aksel Lund Svindal (NOR, b. 26 Dec 1982) won the men's downhill aged 35 years 51 days on 15 Feb 2018. He finished 0.12 sec ahead of compatriot Kjetil Jansrud at the Jeongseon Alpine Centre to secure Norway's first-ever gold medal in the event.

The **oldest female Winter Olympic medallist in Alpine skiing** is Lindsey Vonn (USA, b. 18 Oct 1984), who earned a bronze in the women's downhill competition on 21 Feb 2018 aged 33 years 126 days.

Most Winter Paralympic Games snowboarding gold medals

On 16 Mar 2018, Bibian Mentel-Spee (NLD) won her third Paralympic snowboarding gold in the SB-LL2 banked slalom, having successfully defended her snowboard cross title on 12 Mar. This came less than a year after she was diagnosed with cancer for the ninth time. Mentel-Spee had her right leg amputated below the knee owing to a bone-cancer tumour while trying to qualify for the 2002 Winter Olympics.

Most medals won at a Winter Olympics (country)

Norway won 39 medals at the XXIII Winter Games in Pyeongchang, South Korea, on 9–25 Feb 2018. They won 14 gold, 14 silver and 11 bronze medals in total.

Norway's 14 titles are the **most gold medals won at a Winter Olympics (country)**, a record shared with Germany (also 2018) and Canada (on home soil at Vancouver 2010).

Most medal-winning countries at a Winter Paralympic Games

A total of 26 nations medalled at the XII Winter Paralympics in Pyeongchang, South Korea, on 9–18 Mar 2018. An unprecedented 21 countries won events, with four – China, Croatia, Kazakhstan and hosts South Korea – claiming their first-ever gold.

Most Winter Olympic speed skating medals

Ireen Wüst (NLD, below) won 11 medals between 2006 and 2018: five golds, five silvers and a bronze. In Pyeongchang, she won silver in the 3,000 m and team pursuit and gold in the 1,500 m, becoming the most decorated speed skater in Olympic history. Four years earlier, Wüst had won a total of five medals at Sochi – more than any other athlete at that Games.

Wüst's compatriot Sven Kramer won his ninth medal in Pyeongchang – the **most Winter Olympic speed skating medals (male)**.

Most Olympic figure skating medals

Tessa Virtue and Scott Moir (both CAN) won five Olympic medals between 2010 and 2018. Their ice dance victory in Pyeongchang saw Virtue equal Sonja Henie (NOR) for **most women's Olympic figure skating gold medals** (three), while Moir matched Gillis Grafström's (SWE) record for **most men's Olympic figure skating gold medals** (also three).

Youngest snowboarding gold medallist at a Winter Olympics (male)

Redmond "Red" Gerard (USA, b. 29 Jun 2000) won the men's slopestyle on 11 Feb 2018 aged 17 years 227 days. Lying 11th out of 12 before his third and final run, Gerard posted the day's highest score of 87.16 to claim gold.

On 16 Feb 2018, Julia Pereira de Sousa Mabileau (FRA, b. 20 Sep 2001) won silver in the women's snowboard cross aged 16 years 149 days to become the **youngest snowboarding medallist at a Winter Olympics (female)**.

Most snowboarding gold medals won at the Winter Olympics

Shaun White (USA) won the men's halfpipe in 2006, 2010 and 2018. In Pyeongchang, White landed his first competitive back-to-back 1440s for a winning score of 97.75. He shares the title for **most snowboarding Winter Olympic medals** (three) with Kelly Clark (USA), who won a gold and two bronze in 2002–14.

The **most snowboard slopestyle gold medals at the Winter Olympics** is two, by Jamie Anderson (USA) in 2014–18. (For Anderson's record-breaking X Games exploits, turn to p.219.)

Most Winter Olympic medals

Cross-country skier Marit Bjørgen (NOR) brought Pyeongchang 2018 to a fitting end with victory in the women's 30 km mass start on 25 Feb. It was her 15th Winter Olympic medal, the most by any athlete. Bjørgen medalled at five consecutive Games, amassing three bronze, four silvers and eight golds – the **most Winter Olympic gold medals**, tied with fellow Norwegian cross-country skier Bjørn Dæhlie.

Most para ice hockey goals at a Winter Paralympic Games (male)

Declan Farmer scored 11 goals for the USA at the 2018 Winter Paralympics, including the overtime winner in the final against Canada. He matched the tally of Sylvester Flis (USA, b. POL) from 2002.

Farmer won his second Winter Paralympic gold aged just 20. His team-mates Steve Cash, Adam Page, Josh Pauls and Nikko Landeros have all won three – the **most Winter Paralympic Games para ice hockey gold medals**.

Greatest margin of victory in a Winter Olympic skeleton event

On 16 Feb 2018, Yun Sung-bin (KOR) claimed the men's skeleton title by 1.63 sec at the Alpensia Sliding Centre near Pyeongchang, South Korea. The home favourite posted the fastest time on all four runs, setting a track record of 50.02 sec on his final attempt.

Fastest two goals at a Winter Olympic ice hockey match

Jocelyne Lamoureux-Davidson (USA) scored twice in 6 sec against the Olympic Athletes from Russia (OAR) on 13 Feb 2018. She beat the record of 8 sec, set by Carl-Göran Öberg (SWE) at Squaw Valley in California, USA, on 21 Feb 1960.

Most luge gold medals won at the Winter Olympics

Natalie Geisenberger (DEU) won the women's singles and the mixed team relay at both Sochi 2014 and Pyeongchang to take her tally to four – more than any other luger.

Most Winter Olympic gold medals won in biathlon (female)

On 22 Feb 2018, Dárya Dómracheva anchored the Belarus team to victory in the women's 4 x 6 km relay in Pyeongchang, bringing her total gold medal tally to four. She won three events at Sochi 2014.

Dómracheva is married to retired biathlete Ole Einar Bjørndalen (NOR), who has won the **most Winter Olympic biathlon gold medals (male)** – eight.

PyeongChang 2018

Youngest Olympic freestyle skiing medallist (male)

Nico Porteous (NZ, b. 23 Nov 2001) won bronze in the halfpipe event aged 16 years 91 days on 22 Feb 2018. Porteous became the third-youngest male to medal in an individual Winter Olympic event, after snowboarder Ayumu Hirano in 2014 and Scott Allen (USA, b. 8 Feb 1949), who won bronze in the men's singles figure skating on 6 Feb 1964 aged 14 years 363 days – the **youngest individual medallist at the Winter Olympics (male)**.

Most Winter Olympic appearances

Ski-jumper Noriaki Kasai (JPN) competed in eight consecutive Winter Games from Albertville 1992 to Pyeongchang 2018. He intends to keep competing into his fifties, with the lure of a home Olympics in Sapporo, Japan, in 2026. Kasai is pictured receiving his GWR certificates, including **most individual starts in FIS Ski Jumping World Cup competitions** – 543, from 17 Dec 1988 to 25 Mar 2018.

Most Winter Paralympic Games cross-country skiing gold medals (male)

Brian McKeever (CAN) won 13 Paralympic golds at five different Games between 2002 and 2018. He claimed three more titles in Pyeongchang, in the 20 km freestyle, 1.5 km sprint and 10 km classic visually impaired categories.

The **most Winter Paralympic biathlon gold medals** is six, achieved by Vitaliy Lukyanenko (UKR) from 2006 to 2018.

Fastest short track speed skating 3,000 m relay (women)

On 20 Feb 2018, the Netherlands – represented by Suzanne Schulting, Jorien ter Mors, Lara van Ruijven and Yara van Kerkhof – won the B Final of the women's 3,000 m relay in 4 min 3.471 sec. The Dutch team were eventually promoted to a bronze medal after both China and Canada were disqualified in the A Final.

Wu Dajing won the 500 m Winter Olympic title having led from start to finish in every race of the competition.

Fastest short track speed skating 500 m

In the final of the Winter Olympic men's 500 m event on 22 Feb 2018, short track speed skater Wu Dajing (CHN) took gold in 39.584 sec at the Gangneung Ice Arena in South Korea. Wu broke J R Celski's six-year-old record of 39.937 sec twice over the course of the competition.

First woman to win individual gold medals in different sports at a Winter Olympics

Ester Ledecká (CZE) made history at the 2018 Winter Olympics by winning gold in the Alpine skiing Super-G on 17 Feb and the snowboarding parallel giant slalom on 24 Feb. A snowboarding world champion, Ledecká caused the upset of the Games by winning the Super-G on a pair of borrowed skis, beating defending champion Anna Veith by 0.01 sec. It was the first time she had even made the podium at an international-level ski race.

ROUND-UP

Fastest 15 m speed climb (female)

Iuliia Kaplina (RUS) won gold in the women's speed climbing in a time of 7.32 sec at the World Games in Wrocław, Poland, on 22 Jul 2017. It was the third time she had broken the record that year, having set new fastest times at International Federation of Sport Climbing (IFSC) events in the Chinese cities of Chongqing and Nanjing.

Fastest winning time for the Oaks

On 2 Jun 2017, Enable won the Oaks Stakes in a time of 2 min 34.13 sec at Epsom Downs Racecourse in Surrey, UK. With Frankie Dettori on board (see below), she battled driving rain to win by five lengths.

Most goals scored in a Super Netball regular season (individual)

Caitlin Thwaites scored 594 goals from 647 attempts for Collingwood Magpies Netball (both AUS) during the 2017 Super Netball regular season (see right).

First winners of the Super Netball title

On 17 Jun 2017, Sunshine Coast Lightning beat GIANTS Netball (both AUS) 65–48 in the inaugural Super Netball Grand Final, held in Brisbane, Australia. Captain and goalkeeper Geva Mentor (UK, above right) was named Player of the Year. She achieved the **most deflections in a Super Netball regular season** – 90.

Heaviest para powerlift (-49 kg, male)

Lê Văn Công (VNM) successfully lifted 183.5 kg (404 lb 8.7 oz) at the 2017 World Para Powerlifting Championships in Mexico City, Mexico, on 4 Dec.

At the same tournament, Lingling Guo (CHN) achieved the **heaviest para powerlift (-45 kg, female)** – 110 kg (242 lb 8.1 oz), also on 4 Dec. It was her first major powerlifting competition.

On 19 Feb 2018, Paul Kehinde (NGA) broke his own record for **heaviest para powerlift (-65 kg, male)** with a 221-kg (487-lb 3.5-oz) lift in Dubai, United Arab Emirates.

Most Group 1/Grade 1 flat races won by a trainer in a calendar year

Trainer Aidan O'Brien (IRE) won 28 Group 1/Grade 1 flat races in 2017. He surpassed the record of 25 – set by Bobby Frankel in 2003 – when his horse Saxon Warrior won the Racing Post Trophy in Doncaster, South Yorkshire, UK, on 28 Oct 2017. O'Brien's most prolific horse was Winter, which won four Group 1 races, while Roly Poly and Highland Reel won three each. He won an unprecedented eight out of 10 British and Irish Classics.

Most wins of the Prix de l'Arc de Triomphe by a jockey

Frankie Dettori (ITA) has ridden the winner of the Prix de l'Arc de Triomphe, Europe's richest horse race, five times: on board Lammtarra (1995), Sakhee (2001), Marienbard (2002), Golden Horn (2015) and Enable (2017). His fifth victory took place in his 29th Arc, held on 1 Oct 2017 at the Chantilly Racecourse in Oise, France.

Fastest 15 m speed climb

On 30 Apr 2017, Reza Alipourshenazandifar (IRN) won his semi-final of the men's speed climb in 5.48 sec at an IFSC World Cup event in Nanjing, China. The previous record of 5.60 sec by Danyil Boldyrev had stood since 2014.

Most points needed to win a set of international team volleyball

The third set of the Fédération Internationale de Volleyball World League Group 3 intercontinental round match between Qatar and Venezuela on 11 Jun 2017 ended 45–43 in favour of Qatar. The marathon set lasted 49 min at Kalev Sports Hall in Tallinn, Estonia. Qatar won the match 3–1 (27–29, 25–16, 45–43, 25–13).

Most wins of the IWRF European Championship

Great Britain's wheelchair rugby team secured their sixth International Wheelchair Rugby Federation European Championship title by beating Sweden 49–41 in the final in Koblenz, Germany, on 1 Jul 2017. Also known as "murderball", wheelchair rugby is played on a basketball-court-sized indoor space, with four-player teams trying to score points by carrying a ball over a line.

Most consecutive UCI Mountain Bike Downhill World Cup race wins

On 30 Apr 2017, Rachel Atherton (UK) won her 14th consecutive race at the UCI Mountain Bike Downhill World Cup in Lourdes, France. She completed an unprecedented perfect season in 2016, winning all seven races. Atherton's winning run was halted by injury, when she dislocated her shoulder during a practice run.

Most UCI Mountain Bike Downhill World Cup wins (male)

On 26 Aug 2017, Aaron Gwin (USA) won the final race of the season in Val di Sole, Italy, to secure his fifth Downhill World Cup title. He had previously triumphed in 2011–12 and 2015–16. Gwin matched the feat of five-time champion Nicolas Vouilloz (FRA), who won in 1995–96 and 1998–2000.

Fastest average speed recorded at the Paris-Roubaix cycling race

Greg van Avermaet (BEL) won the 2017 Paris-Roubaix on 9 Apr with an average speed of 45.2 km/h (28.08 mph). He completed the 257-km (159.69-mi) course in 5 hr 41 min 7 sec. The previous record of 45.1 km/h (28.02 mph), by Peter Post, had stood since 1964. Known as the "Hell of the North", the Paris-Roubaix is famed for its cobbled streets and testing weather conditions.

Most wins of the Women's Lacrosse World Cup

The USA have won the Federation of International Lacrosse (FIL) World Cup eight times: in 1982, 1989, 1993, 1997,

2001, 2009, 2013 and 2017. On 22 Jul 2017, they defeated Canada 10–5 to secure their eighth title in Guildford, Surrey, UK.

Most World Polo Championship wins

On 29 Oct 2017, Argentina claimed their fifth Federation of International Polo (FIP) World Championship with an 8–7 overtime victory over Chile in Richmond, New South Wales, Australia. Lucio Fernandez Ocampo equalled the scores in the

Most broken tackles in an Australian rules football (AFL) regular season

Dustin Martin (AUS, above left) broke 68 tackles playing for Richmond during the 2017 AFL regular season. He has become famous for his stiff arm fend-off, known as the "don't argue". Martin capped a stellar 2017 by winning the Brownlow Medal, Norm Smith Medal and a premiership winners' medallion – all in the space of a week.

*Robinson's mile record attempt was held in conjunction with the annual Antarctic Ice Marathon – the **most southerly marathon**.*

Fastest Antarctic mile

Irish runner Paul Robinson ran a mile in Antarctica in 4 min 17.9 sec on 25 Nov 2017. The straight point-to-point course across the remote Union Glacier was measured four times by a GPS satellite before the race to ensure the distance was accurate. Accounting for wind chill, the temperature was -25°C (-13°F).

last second of regular time before hitting the winning golden goal.

Youngest helmsman to win the America's Cup

On 26 Jun 2017, helmsman Peter Burling (NZ, b. 1 Jan 1991) guided the Emirates Team New Zealand to a 7–1 victory over Oracle Team USA aged 26 years 176 days. First staged in 1851 at Cowes, Isle of Wight, UK, the America's Cup is the **oldest international yacht race**.

Most wins of the Gordon Bennett Cup (individual)

First held in 1906, the Gordon Bennett Cup is the **oldest aviation race**. Winners are the pilots who can guide their 1,000-m³ (35,314-cu-ft) gas balloons the farthest from the launch site. In 2017, Vincent Leys and Christophe Houver (both FRA) piloted their balloon 1,834.72 km (1,140.04 miles) – from Fribourg in Switzerland to Estonia – to take first place. It was Leys' ninth overall victory in the race.

Most elements named after a gymnast in the FIG Code of Points (male)

Kenzō Shirai (JPN) has six elements (original skills) named after him in the Fédération Internationale de Gymnastique's Code of Points: three on the floor and three on the vault. His sixth element is the Shirai 3 vault, a variation on a vault performed by Vitaly Scherbo and first demonstrated in competition by Shirai on 25 Feb 2017.

*Kenzō Shirai debuted three original skills at the 2013 World Artistic Gymnastics Championships, where he also became the **first person to perform a quadruple twist in a major gymnastics final**. He was aged just 17 at the time.*

SHIRAI
Kenzo

ATHLETICS

ATHLETICS – OUTDOOR TRACK EVENTS

MEN

	Time/Distance	Name & Nationality	Location	Date
100 m	9.58	Usain Bolt (JAM)	Berlin, Germany	16 Aug 2009
200 m	19.19	Usain Bolt (JAM)	Berlin, Germany	20 Aug 2009
400 m	43.03	Wayde van Niekerk (ZAF)	Rio de Janeiro, Brazil	14 Aug 2016
800 m	1:40.91	David Rudisha (KEN)	London, UK	9 Aug 2012
1,000 m	2:11.96	Noah Ngeny (KEN)	Rieti, Italy	5 Sep 1999
1,500 m	3:26.00	Hicham El Guerrouj (MAR)	Rome, Italy	14 Jul 1998
1 mile	3:43.13	Hicham El Guerrouj (MAR)	Rome, Italy	7 Jul 1999
2,000 m	4:44.79	Hicham El Guerrouj (MAR)	Berlin, Germany	7 Sep 1999
3,000 m	7:20.67	Daniel Komen (KEN)	Rieti, Italy	1 Sep 1996
5,000 m	12:37.35	Kenenisa Bekele (ETH)	Hengelo, Netherlands	31 May 2004
10,000 m	26:17.53	Kenenisa Bekele (ETH)	Brussels, Belgium	26 Aug 2005
20,000 m	56:26.00	Haile Gebrselassie (ETH)	Ostrava, Czech Republic	27 Jun 2007
1 hour	21,285 m	Haile Gebrselassie (ETH)	Ostrava, Czech Republic	27 Jun 2007
25,000 m	1:12:25.40	Moses Cheruiyot Mosop (KEN)	Eugene, USA	3 Jun 2011
30,000 m	1:26:47.40	Moses Cheruiyot Mosop (KEN)	Eugene, USA	3 Jun 2011
3,000 m steeplechase	7:53.63	Saif Saaeed Shaheen (QAT)	Brussels, Belgium	3 Sep 2004
110 m hurdles	12.80	Aries Merritt (USA)	Brussels, Belgium	7 Sep 2012
400 m hurdles	46.78	Kevin Young (USA)	Barcelona, Spain	6 Aug 1992
4 x 100 m relay	36.84	Jamaica (Yohan Blake, Usain Bolt, Michael Frater, Nesta Carter)	London, UK	11 Aug 2012
4 x 200 m relay	1:18.63	Jamaica (Yohan Blake, Nickel Ashmeade, Warren Weir, Jermaine Brown)	Nassau, The Bahamas	24 May 2014
4 x 400 m relay	2:54.29	USA (Andrew Valmon, Quincy Watts, Harry Reynolds, Michael Johnson)	Stuttgart, Germany	22 Aug 1993
4 x 800 m relay	7:02.43	Kenya (Joseph Mutua, William Yiampoy, Ismael Kombich, Wilfred Bungei)	Brussels, Belgium	25 Aug 2006
4 x 1,500 m relay	14:22.22	Kenya (Collins Cheboi, Silas Kiplagat, James Kiplagat Magut, Asbel Kiprop)	Nassau, The Bahamas	25 May 2014

WOMEN

	Time/Distance	Name & Nationality	Location	Date
100 m	10.49	Florence Griffith-Joyner (USA)	Indianapolis, USA	16 Jul 1988
200 m	21.34	Florence Griffith-Joyner (USA)	Seoul, South Korea	29 Sep 1988
400 m	47.60	Marita Koch (GDR)	Canberra, Australia	6 Oct 1985
800 m	1:53.28	Jarmila Kratochvílová (CZE)	Munich, Germany	26 Jul 1983
1,000 m	2:28.98	Svetlana Masterkova (RUS)	Brussels, Belgium	23 Aug 1996
1,500 m	3:50.07	Genzebe Dibaba (ETH)	Fontvieille, Monaco	17 Jul 2015
1 mile	4:12.56	Svetlana Masterkova (RUS)	Zurich, Switzerland	14 Aug 1996
2,000 m	*5:23.75	Genzebe Dibaba (ETH)	Sabadell, Spain	7 Feb 2017
3,000 m	8:06.11	Wang Junxia (CHN)	Beijing, China	13 Sep 1993
5,000 m	14:11.15	Tirunesh Dibaba (ETH)	Oslo, Norway	6 Jun 2008
10,000 m	29:17.45	Almaz Ayana (ETH)	Rio de Janeiro, Brazil	12 Aug 2016
20,000 m	1:05:26.60	Tegla Loroupe (KEN)	Borgholzhausen, Germany	3 Sep 2000
1 hour	18,517 m	Dire Tune (ETH)	Ostrava, Czech Republic	12 Jun 2008
25,000 m	1:27:05.90	Tegla Loroupe (KEN)	Mengerskirchen, Germany	21 Sep 2002
30,000 m	1:45:50.00	Tegla Loroupe (KEN)	Warstein, Germany	6 Jun 2003
3,000 m steeplechase	8:52.78	Ruth Jebet (BHR)	Paris, France	27 Aug 2016
100 m hurdles	12.20	Kendra Harrison (USA)	London, UK	22 Jul 2016
400 m hurdles	52.34	Yuliya Pechonkina (RUS)	Tula, Russia	8 Aug 2003
4 x 100 m relay	40.82	USA (Tianna Madison, Allyson Felix, Bianca Knight, Carmelita Jeter)	London, UK	10 Aug 2012
4 x 200 m relay	1:27.46	USA "Blue" (LaTasha Jenkins, LaTasha Colander- Richardson, Nanceen Perry, Marion Jones)	Philadelphia, USA	29 Apr 2000
4 x 400 m relay	3:15.17	USSR (Tatyana Ledovskaya, Olga Nazarova, Maria Pinigina, Olga Bryzgina)	Seoul, South Korea	1 Oct 1988
4 x 800 m relay	7:50.17	USSR (Nadezhda Olizarenko, Lyubov Gurina, Lyudmila Borisova, Irina Podyalovskaya)	Moscow, Russia	5 Aug 1984
4 x 1,500 m relay	16:33.58	Kenya (Mercy Cherono, Irene Jelagat, Faith Kipyegon, Hellen Obiri)	Nassau, The Bahamas	24 May 2014

indoor performance (see p.234)

All information correct, as of 4 Apr 2018

Fastest mile (male)
Hicham El Guerrouj (MAR) won a mile race in 3 min 43.13 sec in Rome, Italy, on 7 Jul 1999. Runner-up Noah Ngeny also beat the previous world record. El Guerrouj had earmarked the Stadio Olimpico for a record attempt having run the **fastest 1,500 m (male)** – 3 min 26 sec – there the previous year.

Fastest 2,000 m (female)
On 7 Feb 2017, Genzebe Dibaba (ETH) won a 2,000 m indoor race in 5 min 23.75 sec in Sabadell, Spain. Although the indoor 2,000 m is not an official IAAF world record event, Dibaba's time was faster than the previous outdoor record and can be classed as the outright record (see p.234).

ATHLETICS – INDOOR TRACK EVENTS

MEN	Time	Name & Nationality	Location	Date
50 m	5.56	Donovan Bailey (CAN)	Reno, USA	9 Feb 1996
60 m	6.34	Christian Coleman (USA)	Albuquerque, USA	18 Feb 2018
200 m	19.92	Frankie Fredericks (NAM)	Liévin, France	18 Feb 1996
400 m	**44.52	Michael Norman Jr (USA)	College Station, USA	10 Mar 2018
800 m	1:42.67	Wilson Kipketer (DNK)	Paris, France	9 Mar 1997
1,000 m	2:14.20	Ayanleh Souleiman (DJI)	Stockholm, Sweden	17 Feb 2016
1,500 m	3:31.18	Hicham El Guerrouj (MAR)	Stuttgart, Germany	2 Feb 1997
1 mile	3:48.45	Hicham El Guerrouj (MAR)	Ghent, Belgium	12 Feb 1997
3,000 m	7:24.90	Daniel Komen (KEN)	Budapest, Hungary	6 Feb 1998
5,000 m	12:49.60	Kenenisa Bekele (ETH)	Birmingham, UK	20 Feb 2004
50 m hurdles	6.25	Mark McKoy (CAN)	Kobe, Japan	5 Mar 1986
60 m hurdles	7.30	Colin Jackson (GBR†)	Sindelfingen, Germany	6 Mar 1994
4 x 200 m relay	1:22.11	Great Britain & Northern Ireland (Linford Christie, Darren Braithwaite, Ade Mafe, John Regis)	Glasgow, UK	3 Mar 1991
4 x 400 m relay	**3:01.77	Poland (Karol Zalewski, Rafał Omelko, Łukasz Krawczuk, Jakub Krzewina)	Birmingham, UK	4 Mar 2018
4 x 800 m relay	7:13.11	USA All Stars (Richard Jones, David Torrence, Duane Solomon, Erik Sowinski)	Boston, USA	8 Feb 2014
5,000 m walk	18:07.08	Mikhail Shchennikov (RUS)	Moscow, Russia	14 Feb 1995

WOMEN	Time	Name & Nationality	Location	Date
50 m	5.96	Irina Privalova (RUS)	Madrid, Spain	9 Feb 1995
60 m	6.92	Irina Privalova (RUS)	Madrid, Spain	11 Feb 1993 / 9 Feb 1995
200 m	21.87	Merlene Ottey (JAM)	Liévin, France	13 Feb 1993
400 m	49.59	Jarmila Kratochvílová (CZE)	Milan, Italy	7 Mar 1982
800 m	1:55.82	Jolanda Batagelj (SVN)	Vienna, Austria	3 Mar 2002
1,000 m	2:30.94	Maria de Lurdes Mutola (MOZ)	Stockholm, Sweden	25 Feb 1999
1,500 m	3:55.17	Genzebe Dibaba (ETH)	Karlsruhe, Germany	1 Feb 2014
1 mile	4:13.31	Genzebe Dibaba (ETH)	Stockholm, Sweden	17 Feb 2016
3,000 m	8:16.60	Genzebe Dibaba (ETH)	Stockholm, Sweden	6 Feb 2014
5,000 m	14:18.86	Genzebe Dibaba (ETH)	Stockholm, Sweden	19 Feb 2015
50 m hurdles	6.58	Cornelia Oschkenat (GDR)	Berlin, Germany	20 Feb 1988
60 m hurdles	7.68	Susanna Kallur (SWE)	Karlsruhe, Germany	10 Feb 2008
4 x 200 m relay	1:32.41	Russia (Yekaterina Kondratyeva, Irina Khabarova, Yuliya Pechonkina, Yulia Gushchina)	Glasgow, UK	29 Jan 2005
4 x 400 m relay	3:23.37	Russia (Yulia Gushchina, Olga Kotlyarova, Olga Zaytseva, Olesya Krasnomovets)	Glasgow, UK	28 Jan 2006
4 x 800 m relay	8:06.24	Team Moscow (Aleksandra Bulanova, Yekaterina Martynova, Elena Kofanova, Anna Balakshina)	Moscow, Russia	18 Feb 2011
3,000 m walk	11:40.33	Claudia Ştef (ROM)	Bucharest, Romania	30 Jan 1999

Fastest indoor 60 m (male)
On 18 Feb 2018, Christian Coleman (USA) won the men's 60 m in 6.34 sec at the USA Indoor Track and Field Championships in Albuquerque, New Mexico, USA. The 21-year-old sprinter, a 100 m silver medallist at the 2017 IAAF World Championships, broke Maurice Greene's record of 6.39 sec that had stood for almost 20 years.

† GBR = Great Britain, as per IAAF listings   ** pending ratification

ATHLETICS – ULTRA LONG DISTANCE

MEN	Time/Distance	Name & Nationality	Location	Date
50 km	2:43:38	Thompson Magawana (ZAF)	Cape Town, South Africa	12 Apr 1988
100 km	6:10:20	Donald Ritchie (GBR)	London, UK	28 Oct 1978
100 miles	11:28:03	Oleg Kharitonov (RUS)	London, UK	20 Oct 2002
1,000 km	5 days 16:17:00	Yiannis Kouros (GRC)	Colac, Australia	26 Nov–1 Dec 1984
1,000 miles	10 days 10:30:36	Yiannis Kouros (GRC)	New York City, USA	20–30 May 1988
6 hours	97.2 km (60.39 mi)	Donald Ritchie (GBR)	London, UK	28 Oct 1978
12 hours	163.785 km (101.77 mi)	Zach Bitter (USA)	Phoenix, USA	14 Dec 2013
24 hours	303.506 km (188.59 mi)	Yiannis Kouros (GRC)	Adelaide, Australia	4–5 Oct 1997
48 hours	473.495 km (294.21 mi)	Yiannis Kouros (GRC)	Surgères, France	3–5 May 1996
6 days	1,036.8 km (644.2 mi)	Yiannis Kouros (GRC)	Colac, Australia	20–26 Nov 2005

WOMEN	Time/Distance	Name & Nationality	Location	Date
50 km	3:08:39	Frith van der Merwe (ZAF)	Cape Town, South Africa	25 Mar 1989
100 km	6:33:11	Tomoe Abe (JPN)	Tokoro, Japan	25 Jun 2000
100 miles	13:45:49	Gina Slaby (USA)	Phoenix, USA	10–11 Dec 2016
1,000 km	7 days 1:28:29	Eleanor Robinson (GBR)	Nanango, Australia	11–18 Mar 1998
1,000 miles	12 days 14:38:40	Sandra Barwick (NZ)	New York City, USA	16–28 Oct 1991
6 hours	85.492 km (53.12 mi)	Nele Alder-Baerens (DEU)	Münster, Germany	11 Mar 2017
12 hours	149.130 km (92.66 mi)	Camille Herron (USA)	Phoenix, USA	9–10 Dec 2017
24 hours	259.990 km (161.55 mi)	Patrycja Bereznowska (POL)	Belfast, UK	1–2 Jul 2017
48 hours	397.103 km (246.75 mi)	Sumie Inagaki (JPN)	Surgères, France	21–23 May 2010
6 days	883.631 km (549.06 mi)	Sandra Barwick (NZ)	Campbelltown, Australia	18–24 Nov 1990

Fastest 100 miles ultra distance (women)
On 10–11 Dec 2016, Gina Slaby (USA) ran 100 mi in 13 hr 45 min 49 sec at an ultra-distance race in Phoenix, Arizona, USA. She registered for the 24-hr event, only to switch focus mid-race when she realized that Ann Trason's 1991 record for 100 mi was within reach. Slaby averaged 8.15 min per mile around a 400–m high-school track.

ATHLETICS & CYCLING

Fastest road run 10 km (female)
On 9 Sep 2017, Joyciline Jepkosgei (KEN) won the Prague Grand Prix 10 km race in the Czech Republic in 29 min 43 sec. It was the first time that any female athlete had gone under the 30-min mark over this distance, and the fifth world-record time that Jepkosgei had run in Prague in the same calendar year.

ATHLETICS – ROAD RACE

MEN	Time	Name & Nationality	Location	Date
10 km	26:44	Leonard Patrick Komon (KEN)	Utrecht, Netherlands	26 Sep 2010
15 km	41:13	Leonard Patrick Komon (KEN)	Nijmegen, Netherlands	21 Nov 2010
20 km	55:21	Zersenay Tadese (ERI)	Lisbon, Portugal	21 Mar 2010
Half marathon	58:23	Zersenay Tadese (ERI)	Lisbon, Portugal	21 Mar 2010
25 km	1:11:18	Dennis Kipruto Kimetto (KEN)	Berlin, Germany	6 May 2012
30 km	1:27:13	Eliud Kipchoge (KEN) Stanley Kipleting Biwott (KEN)	London, UK	24 Apr 2016
Marathon	2:02:57	Dennis Kipruto Kimetto (KEN)	Berlin, Germany	28 Sep 2014
100 km	6:13:33	Takahiro Sunada (JPN)	Tokoro, Japan	21 Jun 1998
Road relay	1:57:06	Kenya (Josephat Ndambiri, Martin Mathathi, Daniel Mwangi, Mekubo Mogusu, Onesmus Nyerere, John Kariuki)	Chiba, Japan	23 Nov 2005

WOMEN	Time	Name & Nationality	Location	Date
10 km	29:43	Joyciline Jepkosgei (KEN)	Prague, Czech Republic	9 Sep 2017
15 km	45:37	Joyciline Jepkosgei (KEN)	Prague, Czech Republic	1 Apr 2017
20 km	1:01:25	Joyciline Jepkosgei (KEN)	Prague, Czech Republic	1 Apr 2017
Half marathon	1:04:51	Joyciline Jepkosgei (KEN)	Valencia, Spain	22 Oct 2017
25 km	1:19:53	Mary Jepkosgei Keitany (KEN)	Berlin, Germany	9 May 2010
30 km	1:36:05	Mary Jepkosgei Keitany (KEN)	London, UK	23 Apr 2017
Marathon	2:15:25	Paula Radcliffe (GBR)	London, UK	13 Apr 2003
100 km	6:33:11	Tomoe Abe (JPN)	Tokoro, Japan	25 Jun 2000
Road relay	2:11:41	China (Jiang Bo, Dong Yanmei, Zhao Fengting, Ma Zaijie, Lan Lixin, Lin Na)	Beijing, China	28 Feb 1998

Since 1998, the International Association of Athletics Federations (IAAF) has ruled that world records can be set in a facility "with or without a roof" – meaning that times, heights and distances achieved indoors can also stand as outdoor records, providing they meet certain conditions e.g. no banked running track. This applies to Renaud Lavillenie's pole vault (see right) and Genzebe Dibaba's 2,000 m world record on p.232.

ATHLETICS – OUTDOOR FIELD EVENTS

MEN	Distance/Points	Name & Nationality	Location	Date
High jump	2.45 m (8 ft 0.45 in)	Javier Sotomayor (CUB)	Salamanca, Spain	27 Jul 1993
Pole vault	6.16 m (20 ft 2.51 in)*	Renaud Lavillenie (FRA)	Donetsk, Ukraine	15 Feb 2014
Long jump	8.95 m (29 ft 4.36 in)	Mike Powell (USA)	Tokyo, Japan	30 Aug 1991
Triple jump	18.29 m (60 ft 0.07 in)	Jonathan Edwards (GBR)	Gothenburg, Sweden	7 Aug 1995
Shot	23.12 m (75 ft 10.23 in)	Randy Barnes (USA)	Los Angeles, USA	20 May 1990
Discus	74.08 m (243 ft 0.52 in)	Jürgen Schult (GDR)	Neubrandenburg, Germany	6 Jun 1986
Hammer	86.74 m (284 ft 6.95 in)	Yuriy Sedykh (USSR)	Stuttgart, Germany	30 Aug 1986
Javelin	98.48 m (323 ft 1.15 in)	Jan Železný (CZE)	Jena, Germany	25 May 1996
Decathlon†	9,045 points	Ashton Eaton (USA)	Beijing, China	28–29 Aug 2015

† 100 m, 10.23 sec; long jump, 7.88 m; shot, 14.52 m; high jump, 2.01 m; 400 m, 45.00 sec; 110 m hurdles, 13.69 sec; discus, 43.34 m; pole vault, 5.20 m; javelin, 63.63 m; 1,500 m, 4 min 17.52 sec

WOMEN	Distance/Points	Name & Nationality	Location	Date
High jump	2.09 m (6 ft 10.28 in)	Stefka Kostadinova (BGR)	Rome, Italy	30 Aug 1987
Pole vault	5.06 m (16 ft 7.21 in)	Yelena Isinbayeva (RUS)	Zurich, Switzerland	28 Aug 2009
Long jump	7.52 m (24 ft 8.06 in)	Galina Chistyakova (USSR)	Leningrad, USSR	11 Jun 1988
Triple jump	15.50 m (50 ft 10.23 in)	Inessa Kravets (UKR)	Gothenburg, Sweden	10 Aug 1995
Shot	22.63 m (74 ft 2.94 in)	Natalya Lisovskaya (USSR)	Moscow, Russia	7 Jun 1987
Discus	76.80 m (251 ft 11.61 in)	Gabriele Reinsch (GDR)	Neubrandenburg, Germany	9 Jul 1988
Hammer	82.98 m (272 ft 2.92 in)	Anita Włodarczyk (POL)	Warsaw, Poland	28 Aug 2016
Javelin	72.28 m (237 ft 1.66 in)	Barbora Špotáková (CZE)	Stuttgart, Germany	13 Sep 2008
Heptathlon††	7,291 points	Jacqueline Joyner-Kersee (USA)	Seoul, South Korea	23–24 Sep 1988

†† 100 m hurdles, 12.69 sec; high jump, 1.86 m; shot, 15.80 m; 200 m, 22.56 sec; long jump, 7.27 m; javelin, 45.66 m; 800 m, 2 min 8.51 sec

Decathlon†††	8,358 points	Austra Skujytė (LTU)	Columbia, Missouri, USA	14–15 Apr 2005

††† 100 m, 12.49 sec; long jump, 6.12 m; shot, 16.42 m; high jump, 1.78 m; 400 m, 57.19 sec; 100 m hurdles, 14.22 sec; discus, 46.19 m; pole vault, 3.10 m; javelin, 48.78 m; 1,500 m, 5 min 15.86 sec

* indoor performance

Farthest long jump (male)
Mike Powell (USA) won long-jump gold at the 1991 World Championships in Athletics with a leap of 8.95 m (29 ft 4.36 in). He emerged triumphant after a thrilling battle with rival Carl Lewis, beating one of the most enduring records in sport: Bob Beamon's mark of 8.90 m (29 ft 2.3 in), set in 1968.

ATHLETICS – INDOOR FIELD EVENTS

MEN	Distance/Points	Name & Nationality	Location	Date
High jump	2.43 m (7 ft 11.66 in)	Javier Sotomayor (CUB)	Budapest, Hungary	4 Mar 1989
Pole vault	6.16 m (20 ft 2.51 in)	Renaud Lavillenie (FRA)	Donetsk, Ukraine	15 Feb 2014
Long jump	8.79 m (28 ft 10.06 in)	Carl Lewis (USA)	New York City, USA	27 Jan 1984
Triple jump	17.92 m (58 ft 9.51 in)	Teddy Tamgho (FRA)	Paris, France	6 Mar 2011
Shot	22.66 m (74 ft 4.12 in)	Randy Barnes (USA)	Los Angeles, USA	20 Jan 1989
Heptathlon†	6,645 points	Ashton Eaton (USA)	Istanbul, Turkey	9–10 Mar 2012

† 60 m, 6.79 sec; long jump, 8.16 m; shot, 14.56 m; high jump, 2.03 m; 60 m hurdles, 7.68 sec;
pole vault, 5.20 m; 1,000 m, 2 min 32.77 sec

WOMEN	Distance/Points	Name & Nationality	Location	Date
High jump	2.08 m (6 ft 9.88 in)	Kajsa Bergqvist (SWE)	Arnstadt, Germany	4 Feb 2006
Pole vault	5.02 m (16 ft 5.63 in)	Jennifer Suhr (USA)	Albuquerque, USA	2 Mar 2013
Long jump	7.37 m (24 ft 2.15 in)	Heike Drechsler (GDR)	Vienna, Austria	13 Feb 1988
Triple jump	15.36 m (50 ft 4.72 in)	Tatyana Lebedeva (RUS)	Budapest, Hungary	6 Mar 2004
Shot	22.50 m (73 ft 9.82 in)	Helena Fibingerová (CZE)	Jablonec, Czechoslovakia	19 Feb 1977
Pentathlon††	5,013 points	Natallia Dobrynska (UKR)	Istanbul, Turkey	9 Mar 2012

†† 60 m hurdles, 8.38 sec; high jump, 1.84 m; shot, 16.51 m; long jump, 6.57 m; 800 m, 2 min 11.15 sec

Highest pole vault (male, indoors)
Renaud Lavillenie (FRA) successfully cleared a height of 6.16 m (20 ft 2.51 in) at the Pole Vault Stars meeting in Donetsk, Ukraine, on 15 Feb 2014. As the highest-ever pole vault, it is acknowledged by the IAAF as both the indoor and the outdoor record, eclipsing the mark of 6.14 m (20 ft 1.73 in) set by Sergei Bubka in 1994.

Fastest road walk 50 km (female)
On 13 Aug 2017, Inês Henriques (PRT) took gold in the women's 50 km walk at the IAAF World Championships in 4 hr 5 min 56 sec in London, UK. It was the first time the race had been staged at the championships – only four athletes finished, from seven starters. Henriques improved her own world-record time by more than 2 min.

ATHLETICS – RACE WALKING

MEN	Time	Name & Nationality	Location	Date
20,000 m	1:17:25.6	Bernardo Segura (MEX)	Bergen, Norway	7 May 1994
20 km (road)	1:16:36	Yusuke Suzuki (JPN)	Nomi, Japan	15 Mar 2015
30,000 m	2:01:44.1	Maurizio Damilano (ITA)	Cuneo, Italy	3 Oct 1992
50,000 m	3:35:27.2	Yohann Diniz (FRA)	Reims, France	12 Mar 2011
50 km (road)	3:32:33	Yohann Diniz (FRA)	Zurich, Switzerland	15 Aug 2014

WOMEN	Time	Name & Nationality	Location	Date
10,000 m	41:56.23	Nadezhda Ryashkina (USSR)	Seattle, USA	24 Jul 1990
20,000 m	1:26:52.3	Olimpiada Ivanova (RUS)	Brisbane, Australia	6 Sep 2001
20 km (road)	1:24:38	Liu Hong (CHN)	La Coruña, Spain	6 Jun 2015
50 km (road)	4:05:56	Inês Henriques (PRT)	London, UK	13 Aug 2017

CYCLING – ABSOLUTE TRACK

MEN	Time/Distance	Name & Nationality	Location	Date
200 m (flying start)	9.347	François Pervis (FRA)	Aguascalientes, Mexico	6 Dec 2013
500 m (flying start)	24.758	Chris Hoy (GBR)	La Paz, Bolivia	13 May 2007
Team 750 m (standing start)	41.871	Germany (Joachim Eilers, René Enders, Robert Förstemann)	Aguascalientes, Mexico	5 Dec 2013
1 km (standing start)	56.303	François Pervis (FRA)	Aguascalientes, Mexico	7 Dec 2013
4 km (standing start)	4:10.534	Jack Bobridge (AUS)	Sydney, Australia	2 Feb 2011
Team 4 km (standing start)	3:50.265	Great Britain (Edward Clancy, Owain Doull, Bradley Wiggins, Steven Burke)	Rio de Janeiro, Brazil	12 Aug 2016
1 hour	54.526 km	Bradley Wiggins (GBR)	London, UK	7 Jun 2015

WOMEN	Time/Distance	Name & Nationality	Location	Date
200 m (flying start)	10.384	Kristina Vogel (DEU)	Aguascalientes, Mexico	7 Dec 2013
500 m (flying start)	28.970	Kristina Vogel (DEU)	Frankfurt, Germany	17 Dec 2016
500 m (standing start)	32.268	Jessica Salazar Valles (MEX)	Aguascalientes, Mexico	7 Oct 2016
Team 500 m (standing start)	32.034	China (Jinjie Gong, Tianshi Zhong)	Saint-Quentin-en-Yvelines, France	18 Feb 2015
3 km (standing start)	3:20.060	Chloé Dygert Owen (USA)	Apeldoorn, Netherlands	3 Mar 2018
Team 4 km (standing start)	4:10.236	Great Britain (Katie Archibald, Laura Trott, Elinor Barker, Joanna Rowsell Shand)	Rio de Janeiro, Brazil	13 Aug 2016
1 hour	47.980 km	Evelyn Stevens (USA)	Colorado Springs, USA	27 Feb 2016

Fastest cycle 500 m unpaced (flying start, female)
On 17 Dec 2016, Kristina Vogel (DEU) cycled 500 m from a flying start in 28.970 sec in Frankfurt, Germany. It was the first time a female rider had broken the 29-sec barrier. Vogel's time of 10.384 sec is also the **fastest cycle 200 m unpaced flying start (female)**.

DIVING, ROWING & SKATING

FREEDIVING

MEN'S DEPTH DISCIPLINES	Depth	Name & Nationality	Location	Date
Constant weight with fins	129 m (423 ft 2 in)	Alexey Molchanov (RUS)	Isla Espíritu Santo, Mexico	28 Oct 2016
Constant weight without fins	102 m (334 ft 7 in)	William Trubridge (NZ)	Long Island, The Bahamas	20 Jul 2016
Variable weight	146 m (479 ft)	Stavros Kastrinakis (GRC)	Kalamata, Greece	1 Nov 2015
No limit	214 m (702 ft 1 in)	Herbert Nitsch (AUT)	Spetses, Greece	14 Jun 2007
Free immersion	124 m (406 ft 9 in)	William Trubridge (NZ)	Long Island, The Bahamas	2 May 2016

MEN'S DYNAMIC APNEA	Distance	Name & Nationality	Location	Date
With fins	300 m (984 ft 3 in)	Mateusz Malina (POL)	Turku, Finland	3 Jul 2016
		Giorgos Panagiotakis (GRC)		
Without fins	244 m (800 ft 6 in)	Mateusz Malina (POL)	Turku, Finland	2 Jul 2016

MEN'S STATIC APNEA	Time	Name & Nationality	Location	Date
Duration	11 min 54 sec	Branko Petrovic (SRB)	Dubai, UAE	7 Oct 2014

WOMEN'S DEPTH DISCIPLINES	Depth	Name & Nationality	Location	Date
Constant weight with fins	104 m (341 ft 2 in)	Alessia Zecchini (ITA)	Long Island, The Bahamas	10 May 2017
Constant weight without fins	72 m (236 ft 2 in)	Sayuri Kinoshita (JPN)	Long Island, The Bahamas	26 Apr 2016
Variable weight	130 m (426 ft 6 in)	Nanja van den Broek (NLD)	Sharm el-Sheikh, Egypt	18 Oct 2015
No limit	160 m (524 ft 11 in)	Tanya Streeter (USA)	Turks and Caicos Islands	17 Aug 2002
Free immersion	92 m (301 ft 10 in)	Jeanine Grasmeijer (NLD)	Bonaire, Caribbean Netherlands	6 Sep 2016

WOMEN'S DYNAMIC APNEA	Distance	Name & Nationality	Location	Date
With fins	237 m (777 ft 6 in)	Natalia Molchanova (RUS)	Cagliari, Italy	26 Sep 2014
Without fins	191 m (626 ft 7 in)	Magdalena Solich-Talanda (POL)	Opole, Poland	1 Jul 2017

WOMEN'S STATIC APNEA	Time	Name & Nationality	Location	Date
Duration	9 min 2 sec	Natalia Molchanova (RUS)	Belgrade, Serbia	29 Jun 2013

Deepest freedive – free immersion (male)
William Trubridge (NZ) dived to a depth of 124 m (406 ft 9 in) on 2 May 2016 at Dean's Blue Hole in The Bahamas. He overcame problems retrieving his target tag at the bottom of his dive to break his own record of 121 m (396 ft 11 in) from 2011. In total, Trubridge's dive lasted 4 min 24 sec.

ROWING (All events take place over a 2,000-m course)

MEN	Time	Name & Nationality	Location	Date
Single sculls	6:30.74	Robert Manson (NZ)	Poznań, Poland	18 Jun 2017
Double sculls	5:59.72	Croatia (Valent Sinković, Martin Sinković)	Amsterdam, Netherlands	29 Aug 2014
Quadruple sculls	5:32.26	Ukraine (Morozov, Dovgodko, Nadtoka, Mikhay)	Amsterdam, Netherlands	30 Aug 2014
Coxless pairs	6:08.50	New Zealand (Eric Murray, Hamish Bond)	London, UK	28 Jul 2012
Coxless fours	5:37.86	Great Britain (Reed, James, Triggs Hodge, Gregory)	Lucerne, Switzerland	25 May 2012
Coxed pairs**	6:33.26	New Zealand (Caleb Shepherd, Eric Murray, Hamish Bond)	Amsterdam, Netherlands	29 Aug 2014
Coxed fours**	5:58.96	Germany (Ungemach, Eichholz, Weyrauch, Rabe, Dederding)	Vienna, Austria	24 Aug 1991
Eights	5:18.68	Germany (Jakschik, Sauer, Schmidt, Weissenfeld, Johannesen, Schneider, Planer, Ocik, Wimberger)	Poznań, Poland	18 Jun 2017

LIGHTWEIGHT	Time	Name & Nationality	Location	Date
Single sculls**	6:43.37	Marcello Miani (ITA)	Amsterdam, Netherlands	29 Aug 2014
Double sculls	6:05.36	South Africa (John Smith, James Thompson)	Amsterdam, Netherlands	30 Aug 2014
Quadruple sculls**	5:42.75	Greece (Magdanis, Giannaros, E Konsolas, G Konsolas)	Amsterdam, Netherlands	29 Aug 2014
Coxless pairs**	6:22.91	Switzerland (Simon Niepmann, Lucas Tramèr)	Amsterdam, Netherlands	29 Aug 2014
Coxless fours	5:43.16	Denmark (Barsøe, Jørgensen, Larsen, Winther)	Amsterdam, Netherlands	29 Aug 2014
Eights**	5:30.24	Germany (Altena, Dahlke, Kobor, Stomporowski, Melges, März, Buchheit, Von Warburg, Kaska)	Montreal, Canada	13 Aug 1992

WOMEN	Time	Name & Nationality	Location	Date
Single sculls	7:07.71	Rumyana Neykova (BGR)	Seville, Spain	21 Sep 2002
Double sculls	6:37.31	Australia (Sally Kehoe, Olympia Aldersey)	Amsterdam, Netherlands	29 Aug 2014
Quadruple sculls	6:06.84	Germany (Annekatrin Thiele, Carina Bär, Julia Lier, Lisa Schmidla)	Amsterdam, Netherlands	30 Aug 2014
Coxless pairs	6:49.08	New Zealand (Grace Prendergast, Kerri Gowler)	Poznań, Poland	18 Jun 2017
Coxless fours**	6:14.36	New Zealand (Prendergast, Pratt, Gowler, Bevan)	Amsterdam, Netherlands	29 Aug 2014
Eights	5:54.16	USA (Regan, Polk, Snyder, Simmonds, Luczak, Robbins, Schmetterling, Opitz, Lind)	Lucerne, Switzerland	14 Jul 2013

LIGHTWEIGHT	Time	Name & Nationality	Location	Date
Single sculls**	7:24.46	Zoe McBride (NZ)	Varese, Italy	20 Jun 2015
Double sculls	6:47.69	Netherlands (Maaike Head, Ilse Paulis)	Poznań, Poland	19 Jun 2016
Quadruple sculls**	6:15.95	Netherlands (Woerner, Paulis, Kraaijkamp, Head)	Amsterdam, Netherlands	29 Aug 2014
Coxless pairs**	7:18.32	Australia (Eliza Blair, Justine Joyce)	Aiguebelette-le-Lac, France	6 Sep 1997

** Denotes non-Olympic boat classes

Fastest row, men's coxless pairs
At the London 2012 Olympics, Eric Murray and Hamish Bond (NZ) smashed a decade-old record by winning the men's coxless pairs in 6 min 8.50 sec. They recorded 69 consecutive wins in the event before Murray retired in May 2017.

Fastest row, women's coxless pairs
On 18 Jun 2017, Kerri Gowler and Grace Prendergast (NZ) won the final of the women's pair in a time of 6 min 49.08 sec at a Rowing World Cup regatta. It was one of three world-best times set on the same day in Poznań, Poland.

SPEED SKATING – LONG TRACK

MEN	Time/Points	Name & Nationality	Location	Date
500 m	33.98	Pavel Kulizhnikov (RUS)	Salt Lake City, USA	20 Nov 2015
2 x 500 m	1:08.31	Jeremy Wotherspoon (CAN)	Calgary, Canada	15 Mar 2008
1,000 m	1:06.42	Shani Davis (USA)	Salt Lake City, USA	7 Mar 2009
1,500 m	1:41.02	Denis Yuskov (RUS)	Salt Lake City, USA	9 Dec 2017
3,000 m	3:37.28	Eskil Ervik (NOR)	Calgary, Canada	5 Nov 2005
5,000 m	6:01.86	Ted-Jan Bloemen (CAN, b. NLD)	Salt Lake City, USA	10 Dec 2017
10,000 m	12:36.30	Ted-Jan Bloemen (CAN, b. NLD)	Salt Lake City, USA	21 Nov 2015
Sprint combination	136.065 points	Kai Verbij (NLD)	Calgary, Canada	25–26 Feb 2017
Small combination	146.365 points	Erben Wennemars (NLD)	Calgary, Canada	12–13 Aug 2005
Big combination	145.742 points	Shani Davis (USA)	Calgary, Canada	18–19 Mar 2006
Team pursuit (eight laps)	3:35.60	Netherlands (Blokhuijsen, Kramer, Verweij)	Salt Lake City, USA	16 Nov 2013

WOMEN	Time/Points	Name & Nationality	Location	Date
500 m	36.36	Lee Sang-hwa (KOR)	Salt Lake City, USA	16 Nov 2013
2 x 500 m	1:14.19	Heather Richardson (USA)	Salt Lake City, USA	28 Dec 2013
1,000 m	1:12.09	Nao Kodaira (JPN)	Salt Lake City, USA	10 Dec 2017
1,500 m	1:50.85	Heather Richardson-Bergsma (USA)	Salt Lake City, USA	21 Nov 2015
3,000 m	3:53.34	Cindy Klassen (CAN)	Calgary, Canada	18 Mar 2006
5,000 m	6:42.66	Martina Sáblíková (CZE)	Salt Lake City, USA	18 Feb 2011
Sprint combination	146.390 points	Nao Kodaira (JPN)	Calgary, Canada	25–26 Feb 2017
Mini combination	155.576 points	Cindy Klassen (CAN)	Calgary, Canada	15–17 Mar 2001
Small combination	154.580 points	Cindy Klassen (CAN)	Calgary, Canada	18–19 Mar 2006
Team pursuit (six laps)	2:50.87	Japan (Miho Takagi, Nana Takagi, Ayano Sato)	Salt Lake City, USA	8 Dec 2017

Fewest points for long-track speed skating sprint combination (male)

On 25–26 Feb 2017, Kai Verbij (NLD) won the men's sprint combination at the 2017 ISU World Sprint Speed Skating Championships in Calgary, Canada, with 136.065 points. The event comprises two 500-m and two 1,000-m races.

Fastest short-track speed skating 5,000 m relay (male)

On 12 Nov 2017, a US team comprising Thomas Hong, John-Henry Krueger, Keith Carroll and J R Celski (right, in picture) won the 5,000 m relay at the ISU Short Track World Cup in 6 min 29.052 sec in Shanghai, China. They edged out their South Korean rivals by just 0.024 sec, improving upon a record time set by a Canadian relay team that had stood since 2012.

SPEED SKATING – SHORT TRACK

MEN	Time	Name & Nationality	Location	Date
500 m	*39.584	Wu Dajing (CHN)	Gangneung, South Korea	22 Feb 2018
1,000 m	1:20.875	Hwang Dae-heon (KOR)	Salt Lake City, USA	12 Nov 2016
1,500 m	2:07.943	Sjinkie Knegt (NLD)	Salt Lake City, USA	13 Nov 2016
3,000 m	4:31.891	Noh Jin-kyu (KOR)	Warsaw, Poland	19 Mar 2011
5,000 m relay	6:29.052	USA (John "J R" Celski, John-Henry Krueger, Keith Carroll, Thomas Hong)	Shanghai, China	12 Nov 2017

WOMEN	Time	Name & Nationality	Location	Date
500 m	42.335	Elise Christie (GBR)	Salt Lake City, USA	13 Nov 2016
1,000 m	1:26.661	Shim Suk-hee (KOR)	Calgary, Canada	21 Oct 2012
1,500 m	2:14.354	Choi Min-jeong (KOR)	Salt Lake City, USA	12 Nov 2016
3,000 m	4:46.983	Jung Eun-ju (KOR)	Harbin, China	15 Mar 2008
3,000 m relay	*4:03.471	Netherlands (Suzanne Schulting, Yara van Kerkhof, Lara van Ruijven, Jorien Ter Mors)	Gangneung, South Korea	20 Feb 2018

* pending ratification

FIGURE SKATING

MEN	Points	Name & Nationality	Location	Date
Combined total	330.43	Yuzuru Hanyu (JPN)	Barcelona, Spain	12 Dec 2015
Short programme	112.72	Yuzuru Hanyu (JPN)	Montreal, Canada	22 Sep 2017
Free skating	223.20	Yuzuru Hanyu (JPN)	Helsinki, Finland	1 Apr 2017

WOMEN	Points	Name & Nationality	Location	Date
Combined total	241.31	Evgenia Medvedeva (RUS)	Tokyo, Japan	20 Apr 2017
Short programme	82.92	Alina Zagitova (RUS)	Gangneung, South Korea	21 Feb 2018
Free skating/ Long programme	160.46	Evgenia Medvedeva (RUS)	Tokyo, Japan	20 Apr 2017

PAIRS	Points	Name & Nationality	Location	Date
Combined total	245.84	Aljona Savchenko & Bruno Massot (DEU)	Milan, Italy	22 Mar 2018
Short programme	84.17	Tatiana Volosozhar & Maxim Trankov (RUS)	Sochi, Russia	11 Feb 2014
Free skating	162.86	Aljona Savchenko & Bruno Massot (DEU)	Milan, Italy	22 Mar 2018

ICE DANCE	Points	Name & Nationality	Location	Date
Combined total	207.20	Gabriella Papadakis & Guillaume Cizeron (FRA)	Milan, Italy	24 Mar 2018
Short dance	83.73	Gabriella Papadakis & Guillaume Cizeron (FRA)	Milan, Italy	23 Mar 2018
Free dance	123.47	Gabriella Papadakis & Guillaume Cizeron (FRA)	Milan, Italy	24 Mar 2018

Highest score in figure skating's short programme (women)

On 21 Feb 2018, Alina Zagitova (RUS) scored 82.92 points during the Winter Olympics ladies' singles at the Gangneung Ice Arena in South Korea. Skating to "Black Swan", the 15-year-old broke the record just minutes after compatriot Evgenia Medvedeva had set a new world-best score of 81.61. Zagitova went on to win the gold medal.

STOP PRESS

The following entries were approved and added to our database after the official closing date for this year's submissions.

Largest prize-linked bank account payout
Gulf Bank (KWT) made a payout of KWD1,000,000 ($3,269,680; £2,634,033) in a prize draw at the Grand Avenue Mall in Kuwait City, Kuwait, on 5 Jan 2017.

Longest baking marathon (individual)
On 26–27 Jan 2017, Sarah Corley, Hayley Christine Finkelman, Katherine Hinrichs, Cherise Nicole Ragland, Soyoung Shin and Eric Casper Wang (all USA) each baked for 25 hr. The marathon was part of Nestlé Toll House's Bake Some Good campaign in Chicago, Illinois, USA.

Largest smoothie
Cabot Creamery Cooperative (USA) served up a 1,000-US-gal (3,785-litre) smoothie at the Florida Strawberry Festival in Plant City, Florida, USA, on 3 Mar 2017.

Largest carpet of flowers and plants
Yanbu Flower Festival (SAU) presented a 16,134.07-m² (173,665.68-sq-ft) display featuring 1.8 million flowers of 14 different varieties in Yanbu, Saudi Arabia, on 14 Mar 2017.

Largest kaikottikali dance
On 1 May 2017, a group of 6,582 kaikottikali dancers performed together in Kizhakkambalam, Kerala, India. The event was organized jointly by Twenty20 Kizhakkambalam Association charitable organization, textile manufacturers Kitex, the Parvanendu School of Thiruvathira and Chavara Cultural Centre (all IND).

Greatest light output in a projected image
An image with a light output of 4.66 million lumens was projected skywards by WestJet (CAN) in Hildale, Utah, USA, on 3 May 2017. WestJet attempted the record as part of the launch of a new daily non-stop flight from Toronto, Canada, to Las Vegas, Nevada, USA. Passengers flying overhead were able to watch the rotating circular projection that displayed the number of a seat, the owner of which won a trip back to Las Vegas.

Most bird species in an aviary
Created by Sri Ganapathy Sachchidananda Swamiji (IND), the Shuka Vana aviary houses 468 bird species, as verified on 6 May 2017. It is located at the SGS Avadhoota Datta Peetham in Mysuru, Karnataka, India.

Most people performing a jumping high five simultaneously
Grupo Bolívar S.A. (COL) brought together 2,209 pairs of people to do a jumping high five at the same time in Bogotá, Distrito Capital, Colombia, on 18 May 2017.

Most consecutive wins of the real tennis Ladies World Championship
On 20 May 2017, Claire Fahey (UK, née Vigrass) sealed her fourth consecutive world title with a 6–0, 6–0 win over her sister Sarah Vigrass (UK) at The Tuxedo Club in New York, USA.

Highest average speed in an open-road race
The Nevada Open Road Challenge is held every May on Route 318 in Nevada, USA. On 21 May 2017, Robert Allyn (driver) and David Bauer (navigator, both USA) set the highest-ever average speed for this race – 353.4811 km/h (219.6429 mph) – in a 2001 Chevrolet Monte Carlo. This authorized event is staged under the aegis of the Silver State Classic Challenge (USA) and can see cars hit peak speeds in excess of 394 km/h (244 mph) along the 145-km (90-mi) course.

Largest doormat
On 23 May 2017, a 39.82-m² (428.62-sq-ft) doormat was laid out at the Guinness World Records attraction in Gatlinburg, Tennessee, USA, by Woods Hippensteal (USA). This is equivalent to the wing surface of a Boeing 747 aeroplane.

Largest gathering of people wearing traditional Yakut clothing
The mayor of Yakutsk, Aysen Nikolayev (RUS), organized a gathering of 16,620 people wearing national costume in the capital of the Republic of Sakha, Russian Federation, on 24 Jun 2017.

Most consecutive wins in professional shogi matches
On 26 Jun 2017, Sōta Fujii (JPN) recorded his 29th consecutive victory in the game known as "Japanese chess" – breaking a 30-year-old record at the age of just 14. This was also the **most consecutive wins in professional shogi matches from debut**.

Largest basketball lesson (multiple venues)
NBA Properties Inc. (USA) and Reliance Foundation (IND) set up a basketball lesson for 3,459 players at five locations across India on 28 Jul 2017.

Fastest ground speed by a battery-powered remote-controlled quadcopter
A DRL drone piloted by Ryan Gury of the Drone Racing League (both USA) reached a ground speed of 265.87 km/h (165.20 mph) at Cunningham Park in Queens, New York City, USA, on 13 Jul 2017.

Longest line of water inflatables
On 30 Jul 2017, Welland Floatfest (CAN) put together a 165.74-m-long (543-ft 9-in) line of buoyant inflatables in Ontario, Canada.

Largest parade of Indian motorcycles
On 19 Aug 2017, a parade of 274 Indian motorbikes rode through St Paul, Minnesota, USA, in an event planned by Indian Motorcycle of the Twin Cities Minnesota and Welch Charities (both USA).

Deepest underground half marathon distance run
Millán Ludeña (ECU) completed a half marathon 3,559.08 m (11,676 ft 9 in) below ground at the Mponeng mine in Gauteng, South Africa, on 20 Aug 2017. Ludeña clocked a time of 2 hr 31 min 17.43 sec.

Largest parade of alpacas
Municipalidad Provincial de Carabaya (PER) assembled a line of 460 alpacas in the town of Macusani in Puno, Peru, on 21 Aug 2017.

Tallest sandcastle
On 1 Sep 2017, Schauinsland-Reisen GmbH (DEU) erected a 16.68-m-tall (54-ft 8-in) sandcastle in a disused coal plant in Duisburg, Germany.

Largest foam finger/hand
Dell Technologies (USA) created a 6.12-m-tall, 2.86-m-long and 0.47-m-wide (20-ft 0.9-in x 9-ft 4-in x 1-ft 6-in) sports-style foam hand, as confirmed in Grand Prairie, Texas, USA, on 5 Sep 2017.

Fastest return journey from Land's End to John O'Groats by bicycle (male)
Starting and finishing at John O'Groats in Caithness, James MacDonald (UK) cycled to Land's End in Cornwall and back in 5 days 18 hr 3 min. His journey between these geographical extremities of the UK took place on 4–10 Sep 2017.

Largest display of tomato varieties
On 17 Sep 2017, the World Tomato Society Foundation (USA) presented 241 varieties of tomato at the Heirloom Tomato Harvest Celebration in Los Gatos, California, USA.

Greatest distance skied on an indoor ski slope in 8 hours
On 8 Oct 2017, instructors from the Ski Dubai (UAE) school covered a combined distance of 302.3 km (187.84 mi) on an indoor slope in 8 hr in Dubai, UAE.

Largest human image of a forklift truck
On 10 Oct 2017, a total of 694 participants came together to create the likeness of a forklift truck in Dormagen, Germany. The attempt was arranged by Covestro Deutschland AG (DEU) to celebrate its rebranding.

Largest shipping container image
PSA Corporation Limited (SGP) assembled 359 multi-coloured shipping containers to form a giant lion's head at Tanjong Pagar in Singapore on 15 Oct 2017.

Longest nail bar
On 21 Oct 2017, OPI Products (USA) unveiled a 47.42-m-long (155-ft 6-in) nail bar in Santa Monica, California, USA. Fifty nail technicians provided 501 manicures, with guests including actress Peyton List.

Most netball goals scored in one hour (individual)
Lydia Redman (UK) scored 756 goals in a 60-min netball "shoot-a-thon" on 23 Oct 2017. Redman, who was just 13 years old, achieved her feat on the outside courts of The Kibworth School in Leicestershire, UK.

Largest race series on sand
On 5 Nov 2017, the Surfing Madonna Oceans Project (USA) brought together 4,288 runners in Encinitas, California, USA. There were races over various distances for adults, and a shorter course for children.

Largest wave surfed (unlimited)
On 8 Nov 2017, Rodrigo Koxa (BRA) surfed a monster 80-ft (24.38-m) wave off the coast of Praia do Norte in Nazaré, Portugal. The record was authenticated by the Quiksilver XXL Biggest Wave Awards judging committee.

Largest serving of green-bean casserole
On 16 Nov 2017, a 288.93-kg (636-lb 15.7-oz) green-bean casserole was prepared by Green Giant (USA) at Stella 34 Trattoria in Macy's Herald Square, New York City, USA. The meal was donated to Citymeals on Wheels.

Largest wheelchair race
Dubai Police (UAE) arranged a race involving 289 wheelchair users in Dubai, UAE, on 18 Nov 2017.

The following month, on 3 Dec, Dubai Police HQ and Meydan (UAE) organized the **longest line of horses**, which boasted a total of 116 animals.

Most couples kissing under the mistletoe (single venue)

Gaylord Palms Resort & Convention Center (USA) brought together 448 couples to kiss under the mistletoe in Kissimmee, Florida, USA, on 7 Dec 2017.

Greatest distance vehicle drift in 8 hours

Skilled drivers can produce a controlled "drift" of a car, spinning or skidding the rear wheels while driving through a corner. BMW of North America (USA) achieved a vehicle drift of 374.17 km (232.5 mi) in 8 hr in a vehicle driven by Johan Schwartz (DNK) in Greer, South Carolina, USA, on 11 Dec 2017.

The attempt took place concurrently with the longest twin vehicle drift (water assisted), also achieved by BMW of North America. Drivers Matt Mullins (USA) and Johan Schwartz covered 79.26 km (49.25 mi).

Largest roulette wheel

Casino du Liban (LBN) produced a roulette wheel with an 8.75-m (28-ft 8.48-in) diameter in Jounieh, Lebanon, on 16 Dec 2017.

Safest year for air travel

According to Dutch consultancy To70 and the Aviation Safety Network (ASN), the year 2017 was the safest yet for air travel, with no passenger jet crashes anywhere in the world. The ASN reported 10 accidents involving cargo carriers and small commercial aircraft, leading to 79 fatalities. This is a decrease from 2016, when 16 accidents caused 303 fatalities. The rate of lives lost has been reduced to "one fatal accident for every 16 million flights", according to To70.

Largest aerial firework shell

Al Marjan Island (UAE) and Fireworks by Grucci (USA) produced an aerial firework shell weighing 2,397 lb (1,087.26 kg). It was launched on Al Marjan Island in Ras al-Khaimah, UAE, on 1 Jan 2018.

Most people dunking cookies

On 6 Jan 2018, the Girl Scouts of Greater Chicago and Northwest Indiana (USA) brought together 3,236 participants to dunk cookies at Allstate Arena in Rosemont, Illinois, USA.

Farthest wheelie on a quad bike (ATV)

Abdulla Al Hattawi (UAE) sustained a quad-bike wheelie for 60 km (37.28 mi) in Dubai, UAE, on 12 Jan 2018.

Greatest distance on a motorcycle in 24 hours (individual)

Carl Reese (USA) drove 3,406.17 km (2,116.5 mi) in 24 hr at the Uvalde Proving Grounds in Texas, USA, on 25–26 Feb 2017. He stopped with 1 hr 18 min still on the clock, as his team had run out of fresh tyres.

Fastest unpaced 3 km in track cycling (standing start, female)

On 3 Mar 2018, American cyclist Chloé Dygert Owen took gold in the women's individual pursuit at the UCI Track World Championships in Apeldoorn, Netherlands, with a time of 3 min 20.060 sec. She broke her compatriot Sarah Hammer's 2010 record of 3 min 22.269 sec twice in one day.

Most awards won by a short film

Luminaris (2011), directed by Juan Pablo Zaramella (both ARG), received a total of 324 awards, as confirmed on 6 Mar 2018. The film has a running time of 6 min and uses stop-motion animation to create scenes with real actors and animated objects.

First centibillionaire

According to the annual Billionaires list, published by Forbes on 6 Mar 2018, eCommerce entrepreneur and Amazon CEO Jeff Bezos (USA) is the first person to surpass $100 bn in personal wealth. He has an estimated net worth of $112 bn (£81 bn).

According to Forbes, the richest person (female) is Alice Walton (USA), co-owner of supermarket chain Wal-Mart. Her estimated net worth was $46 bn (£33.2 bn) as of 6 Mar 2018.

Most expensive camera sold at auction

On 10 Mar 2018, a prototype Leica 35-mm-film camera was sold to a private collector from Asia for €2.40 m (£2.13 m; $2.95 m) at the WestLicht Photographica Auction in Vienna, Austria. The early model, known as the Leica 0-series No.122, was one of just 25 produced for testing in 1923 – two years before the first Leica camera went on sale to the public.

Most crowdfunded project (overall)

The appeal for public support from publisher Cloud Imperium Games for its *Star Citizen* videogame project began in Sep 2012, and has continued to make headlines and generate funds. As of 19 Mar 2018, the as-yet-unreleased space-faring sim had raised a remarkable $180,386,613 (£129,326,000) from 1,997,150 backers (referred to as Star Citizens).

Fastest time to cycle the length of South America (Ushuaia to Cartagena)

Dean Stott (UK) cycled from Ushuaia police station in Tierra del Fuego, Argentina, to the Casa Cochera del Gobernador hotel in the Colombian city of Cartagena in 48 days 54 min from 1 Feb to 21 Mar 2018. He raised money for the mental-health charity Heads Together.

Tallest lantern

Wuhan East Lake Tingtao Tourism Development (CHN) produced a 26.28-m-tall (86-ft 2.6-in) lantern, as verified in Wuhan, Hubei Province, China, on 21 Mar 2018. It has a diameter of 28.26 m (92 ft 8.5 in) and covers an area of 400.59 m² (4,311 sq ft).

Most consecutive NBA regular-season games scoring at least 10 points

LeBron James (USA) played 867 regular-season games in which he scored 10 points or more for the Cleveland Cavaliers and the Miami Heat between 6 Jan 2007 and 30 Mar 2018. James broke Michael Jordan's record of 866 games during the Cavaliers' 107–102 win against the New Orleans Pelicans.

Least expensive city

According to The Economist Intelligence Unit in Mar 2018, the Syrian capital of Damascus has replaced Almaty (see p.162) as the world's least expensive city. It fell 14 places to finish with an index score of 26, where New York City, USA, is 100.

Tallest hat

Milliner Odilon Ozare (USA) sported a hat measuring 4.8 m (15 ft 9 in) in Tampa, Florida, USA, on 2 Apr 2018. He had to walk more than 10 m (32 ft 10 in) while wearing it to qualify for the record.

Most competitive 147 breaks in snooker

On 3 Apr 2018, Ronnie O'Sullivan (UK) recorded his 14th competitive maximum break, at the China Open.

Largest chess piece

A 20-ft-tall (6.09-m) king piece measuring 2.79 m (9 ft 2 in) in diameter at its base was created by the World Chess Museum (USA) and presented in St Louis, Missouri, USA, on 6 Apr 2018. It was 53 times the size of a standard king piece.

Largest passenger liner

The MS *Symphony of the Seas* departed for her maiden voyage on 7 Apr 2018. She measures 362.12 m (1,188 ft) long and 65.6 m (215 ft) wide, and has a gross tonnage of 228,081 across 18 decks. She supersedes *Harmony of the Seas* (see p.171) as the largest liner on the ocean.

Most full-body revolutions maintaining a chest stand in one minute

Nine-year-old Tanushree Udupi (IND) completed 42 rotations of her legs around her body in 60 sec while supporting herself on her chest in Udupi, Karnataka, India, on 7 Apr 2018.

Most turbans tied in 8 hours

On 7 Apr 2018, Sikhs of NY (USA) celebrated World Turban Day by tying 3,010 of them in New York City, USA.

Most followed Twitch channel

As of 8 Apr 2018, American gamer and broadcaster "ninja" (aka Richard Tyler Blevins) had 5,144,968 followers on Twitch. His statistics surged by around 2 million following an all-star Twitch stream on 14 Mar 2018 featuring musicians Drake and Travis Scott and gridiron icon JuJu Smith-Schuster.

Largest cinnamon roll

Wolferman's (USA) produced a 521.5-kg (1,149-lb 11-oz) cinnamon roll, as confirmed in Medford, Oregon, USA, on 10 Apr 2018.

Most basketball three-pointers scored by a rookie in an NBA season

Donovan Mitchell (USA) threw his 187th successful three-pointer for the Utah Jazz on 11 Apr 2018. He beat Damian Lillard's rookie tally of 185 from the 2012/13 season.

Most simultaneous US Hot 100 hits (female)

On 16 Apr 2018, rapper Cardi B (USA, b. Belcalis Almanzar) had 13 hits on the *Billboard* Hot 100 at the same time.

Fastest time to solve a Rubik's Cube

Feliks Zemdegs (AUS) solved a standard 3 x 3 x 3 Rubik's Cube in 4.22 sec at the Cube for Cambodia competition in Melbourne, Australia, on 6 May 2018.

Longest soccer drop-kick

On 10 May 2018, goalkeeper Ederson de Moraes (BRA) celebrated Manchester City's league title by drop-kicking a football 75.35 m (247 ft 2.53 in) at the Etihad Campus in Manchester, UK.

Fastest swim long course 1,500 m freestyle (female)

On 16 May 2018, Katie Ledecky (USA) won a 1,500 m freestyle race in 15 min 20.48 sec in Indianapolis, Indiana, USA. She smashed her own record by 5 sec.

Most ascents of Everest

Nepalese Sherpa Kami Rita successfully climbed Everest for the 22nd time on 16 May 2018. On the same day, Lakpa Sherpa (NPL) also broke her own record for most ascents of Everest (female), reaching the summit for the ninth time.